Plants, Health and Healing

Series: Epistemologies of Healing

General Editors: David Parkin and Elisabeth Hsu,
Institute of Social and Cultural Anthropology, University of Oxford

This series in medical anthropology will publish monographs and collected essays on indigenous (so-called traditional) medical knowledge and practice, alternative and complementary medicine, and ethnobiological studies that relate to health and illness. The emphasis of the series is on the way indigenous epistemologies inform healing, against a background of comparison with other practices, and in recognition of the fluidity between them.

Plants, Health and Healing

On the Interface of Ethnobotany and Medical Anthropology

Edited by
Elisabeth Hsu and Stephen Harris

Berghahn Books
New York • Oxford

Published in 2010 by
Berghahn Books

www.berghahnbooks.com

©2010, 2012 Elisabeth Hsu and Stephen Harris

First paperback edition published in 2012.

Library of Congress Cataloging-in-Publication Data

Plants, health and healing : on the interface of ethnobotany and
medical anthropology / Edited by Elisabeth Hsu and Stephen Harris.
p. cm. -- (Epistemologies of healing ; v.6)
Includes bibliographical references and index.
ISBN 978-1-84545-060-1 (hbk.) -- ISBN 978-0-85745-633-5 (pbk.)
1. Ethnobotany. 2. Medicinal plants. 3. Botany, Medical. 4.
Medical anthropology. I. Hsu, Elisabeth. II. Harris, Stephen, 1966-
GN476.73.P6 2010
581.6'34--dc22

2010006692

British Library Cataloguing in Publication Data
A catalogue record for this book is available from the British Library

Printed in the United States on acid-free paper.

ISBN: 978-0-85745-633-5 (paperback)
ISBN: 978-0-85745-634-2 (ebook)

*This book is dedicated to Gilbert Lewis
for his seventieth birthday.*

He taught us to keep our feet on the ground.

Contents

List of Illustrations

List of Tables

Introduction.
Plants in Medical Practice and Common Sense: On the Interface of Ethnobotany and Medical Anthropology
Elisabeth Hsu

There is a dearth of scholarship on the interface of ethnobotany and medical anthropology, which is surprising considering that plants are frequently used in 'traditional' medicines and ritual treatments. Roy Ellen (2006: S10) comments: 'Medical anthropology has seemed hitherto to lack in full engagement with phytomedical reality, and the acceptance that the health care practices of most people on this planet depend on plants and animals. At the same time, many accounts of folk medicinal uses still lack serious consideration of local ethnographic context. Here, it seems to us, is an enormous opportunity and challenge for research.'

This volume takes up the challenge,[1] not least by formulating questions that may encourage future research at the interface between medical anthropology and medicinal ethnobotany. To be sure, there is a vast literature on medicinal plants that provides long lists of local names, equated to Linnaean species names, and their usage; often given in a colloquial language (rather than in specialist local or biomedical terminology). Despite the value that these books undoubtedly have for a first approximation, they are not very interesting to the botanist nor to the anthropologist, and they can even be misleading. Many present knowledge out of context (e.g., divorced from details on technical preparation, the social context of application, and the means by which they were collected) and some lack rigour of inquiry (e.g., repeating hearsay information, often unacknowledged, from multiple sources).

This volume is about plants in medical practice. It emphasizes that knowledge about plants is not merely decontextualized paradigmatic knowledge. Rather, knowledge about plants is generated in dynamic social fields and is often highly situational, as it constitutes an intrinsic aspect of social relationships and their negotiation. The research presented in this book explores when, under which circumstances, and within which social relationships plants are collected, prepared, exchanged and consumed, tested and cherished, evaluated and remembered. In doing things with plants people give them cultural form. Given this thematic focus on practice, botanical species identification according to the 'Linnaean grid', which structures so much of ethnobiology (Ellen 2006: S4), sometimes plays a secondary role in this volume. For example, in some situations the locally perceived ethnobotanical 'life form' (of being an herb rather than a tree) may matter more than the modern scientific name of the species.

The contributors to the volume work within a wide range of fields: medical anthropology, ethnobotany, history of botany, and clinical medicine. The themes they discuss cover a similarly wide spectrum, as do the angles whence they discuss them. Even if their convictions about the significance of plants in medicine may differ, they do share certain concerns. Their articles have all been written with the ordinary person in mind, who, through interaction with plants, intends to remain healthy and awake, enhance personal growth or recover from a sickness episode. This person may be an aged pensioner in the U.K. who suffers from memory loss and cannot afford overpriced CAM (complementary and alternative medicines) products, a stressed employee who needs a cup of coffee to wake up in the morning, a Kenyan Luo girl who gets a less than daily wash, or a patient in ancient China or in early modern England who is feverish, delirious or anaemic and requests medical treatment. Contributions generally focus on practices that are taken for granted, regardless of whether the article provides a portrait of a plant, the biology of specific plants, an ethnographic description of their application or a history of plant exchanges. The contributors explore practices of using plants for maintaining health, enhancing growth, stimulating the brain, and treating sickness; some deal with the way in which bodies affected by them have been sensitized to feel in culturally specific ways; others are interested in how these practices could be improved. All discuss practices involving plants.

The volume explores the interface of biological and cultural, physiological and psychological, material and social worlds. It emphasizes the social aspects of how plants are applied in medical practice without, however, explaining them in terms of bioculturalist arguments that ultimately account for social action in a Darwinian framework (by attending to questions of 'adaptation' and 'survival of the fittest'). The authors are certainly acutely aware of the groundbreaking bioculturalist research on human-environment interactions, among which the work of Nina Etkin and colleagues (Etkin and Ross 1991, Etkin 1996, Etkin 2006) particularly stands out, for the nuance with which it researches what the Hausa in Nigeria do to prevent and treat sickness with plants. Rather, the contributions to this volume are often more social constructivist in orientation, in that they highlight how plants and their parts become cultural artefacts pregnant with situational and social significance as they are applied in medical practice. Nevertheless, although all contributors emphasize the cultural specificities of the practices involving plants, none of them endorse the strong cultural constructivist programme. All consider the bodily processes that plant use triggers as being 'real'[2], and not merely the result of self-deception achieved through technologies of persuasion, metaphor and meaning. They all engage with the materiality of plants, even if for some the materiality of the plant is not primarily assessed in terms of chemistry, but is best described in terms of its phenomenal appearances through touch and smell. However, here the commonalities end.

Some contributors discuss the plant's surface structures and morphology, chemistry and physiological effects in terms of biomedicine and biology, while others explain its materiality in local terms of relatedness. Some present clinical, chemical and other empirical data; others voice doubts as to whether the cultural practices, which involve humans and plants in daily life, are meant to produce the sort of empirical knowledge that scientists call 'objective'. People often make use of plants in ways that emphasize an unmediated, direct relatedness of humans to their environment. Moreover, medical practices that involve plants are often best interpreted in the light of the material significance they have for maintaining social relations. Hence, the contributions in this volume are perhaps best characterized as medical anthropological rather than ethnomedical in orientation.[3]

3

Outline of the Book

The volume begins with two contributions that concern the history of plants in medical practice. Stephen Harris opens with a beautiful blend of the historical, the practical and the taxonomical in his discussion of the long and ongoing history of plants in cultural exchanges. He thereby debunks the stereotype that each ethnic group has its own medicinal plants. By highlighting that the *materia medica* of any society incorporates plants from varied provenance, he counters the naïve idea of one culture, one medicine, one pharmacopeia. Since time immemorial, the movement of plants between societies was often prompted by practical knowledge of their usefulness, which sometimes led to new medical routines, and sometimes to entirely new applications of the plant. As the technology of transport proliferated, plant exchanges increased around the globe. In this light, the current practices of bioprospecting are merely the latest chapter in a long history of borrowing and stealing, trading and exchanging plants and plant materials.

Harris notes that culturally known applications may change over time and in different contexts. People may transport plants or their seed from one place to the other, but not always the cultural knowledge that motivated the transfer in the first place. For example, ginkgo fruit was recommended in China, but leaf extracts are now used in the West. *Artemisia annua* L. is nowadays known as an anti-malarial but its earliest recordings document its use for treating so-called 'female haemorrhoids'.[4] Although one may be inclined to argue that 'empirical knowledge' appears to be key to the cross-cultural exchanges Harris describes, his observations actually question this assumption. The ways in which plants are put to medical use, and affect human bodies with their culture-specific sensitivities, and the knowledge that arises from those interactions, are highly complex.

The second article focuses on one age-old Chinese herbal remedy, *qing hao* (Herba *Artemisiae annuae*, sweet wormwood), which has been found to contain the anti-malarial artemisinin that is currently recommended by the World Health Organisation in combination with other anti-malarials. Elisabeth Hsu provides a longitudinal study of this herbal preparation's name, usages and effects in the Chinese *materia medica*. Although the materials analysed in this article are textual, she is concerned with practice. She demonstrates

4

how the history of the cultural practices of preparing the plant for medical use is paralleled by a history of changes in purported medical efficacy. In particular, she shows that an ingenious invention of plant preparation, namely wringing out the fresh plant after soaking it in water, led to the recommendation of using it in the treatment of acute fever episodes.

Hsu critiques the concept of 'natural herbs' as remedy. She emphasizes that every plant-based preparation was developed through a series of cultural practices, and therefore speaks of *qing hao* as a 'drug' rather than a 'natural herb'. Herbal remedies, just like pharmaceutical drugs, are subject to culture-specific processing. Their therapeutic efficacy depends on the timing of collection of the plants; the techniques of persuading plants to be effective, sometimes through spells and charms, sometimes by cunning action; and their mode of preparation. Modes of preparation may involve culturally specific forms of cutting, drying, frying, cooking, fermenting, often mixed with other cultural-specific products, such as the ashes of particular cloths, chalk or lime, honey, and the like. They may furthermore involve combination with other plant, animal and mineral ingredients from the *materia medica*. Modes of application (oral, parenteral, external) also play a role, as do their dosage and timing (at which stage in the course of the illness, at which frequency, when in the day). These procedures, which require what Ingold (2000a and b) calls 'enskilment', also encompass aesthetic considerations, cultural dispositions and local history, which shape the medical practice of using plants alongside observations of how they impinge on bodily processes.

The two historical accounts are complemented by two anthropological contributions that foreground social practice in specific localities. Françoise Barbira Freedman, who worked for over twenty years among the Lamista Quechua in northwest Amazonia, addresses a blatantly obvious topic that to date has barely been explored. In line with many other authors, she notes that female shamans are exceptional in Amazonia, although she is careful to nuance the different ways in which they are subordinate to their male relatives (after all, every female shaman is linked through ties of kinship or affinity, or both, to male shamans). Barbira Freedman argues that the material plant world, with which shamans engage, and their access to the spirit world, are gendered. This finding leads her to a critical engagement with the notion of gender in Amazonia.

Barbira Freedman highlights the fact that most plants are paired, where each pair comprises a male and female counterpart. She provides concrete examples of such pairs of water plants, which belong in a cosmological female domain, and plants of the upland forests, which cosmologically are a male domain. She details the parts used and their colours, the mother spirits they have, the different shades of shamanic knowledge required to access them, the known pharmaco-active substances and the local conditions they treat. She then argues that the gendering of plants and spirits and the ensuing shamanic gender dynamics are best understood in the light of how action is conceptualized in Amazonian contexts. There is the well-known predation, which generally is seen in opposition to seduction, to which must be added an additional action, that of taming. Male shamans make themselves attractive to spirits in the same way as women do to men: they relate to plant spirits in terms of seduction and taming.

Wenzel Geissler and Ruth Prince, by contrast, engage in a research project that aims to overcome thinking in terms of homologies and attends to the materiality of the people and plants involved in medical practice. They stress that social relatedness is constituted through practices that involve plants. Since plants grow in certain places to which people are related, their materiality can modulate social relations and rectify transgressions. Geissler and Prince stress that the practice-derived knowledge of plants is not positive, objective knowledge in the indicative mood, nor is it a sort of belief. Rather, the Luo know their plants in the subjunctive mode. Their knowledge of plants is intrinsic to social situations within which an attitude of 'trying out' prevails. This disposition of 'trying out' differs fundamentally from that of acquiring objective 'empirical knowledge'. The authors emphasize the playfulness of these situations. They describe how a grandmother identifies and selects the relevant plants, digs them out, throws them into a bucket of hot water and applies them externally to her grandchildren: she cherishes and strokes, rubs and gently touches the skin of toddlers who delight in the washing and obviously are the centre of everyone's attention. This, the Luo say, enhances growth. Perhaps many so-called ethnomedicinal practices fall into the realm of preventive care and stand out primarily for the life-affirmative sociality they generate?

The volume ends with two portrayals of specific plants, which are both shrouded in legend. One concerns the portrayal of one of the oldest and most robust plant species on this planet, *Ginkgo biloba* L., the second is an account of a group of plants – the caffeine-containing plants, which humans all over the globe have recognized for their stimulating and mood-modulating effects. The fruits of *Ginkgo biloba* are described in the traditional Chinese *materia medica*, but its leaf extracts are currently marketed to combat memory loss and for treating Alzheimer's disease. Broadly speaking, the article concerns knowledge production and the question of how to test effectiveness. Where Luo mothers have an attitude of 'trying them out' in ways that do not lead to positive, clearly bounded, objective knowledge, the double-blinded randomized control trials (RCTs) aim precisely to produce such factual knowledge. Sir John Grimley Evans demonstrates that RCTs of the leaf extract *Ginkgo biloba* do not meet rigorous scientific criteria and, accordingly, he voices doubts about the clinical efficacy of this herbal remedy. However, this is not the end of the story.

Grimley Evans furthermore points out that the measurement of clinical reality through RCTs is historically contingent and was culturally warranted by health services particular to the U.K. Their beginnings can be traced to the slaughter of the First World War, which, in turn, led to social movements within British society against the aristocratic social strata that were held responsible for it; this brought about a revolutionizing of health care and, after the Second World War, resulted in the institutionalization of the National Health Service. He suggests that RCTs were developed and refined within this socialist institution of a patronizing state. Without invoking any verbose social theory, he demonstrates that the current gold standard for evaluating CAM (complementary and alternative medicines) in the U.K. – and ethnobotanical and ethnomedical knowledge more generally – is 'history turned into nature'. His article ends with a recommendation on how to refine the trials in order to determine the clinical effects and physiological mechanisms of the leaf extract *Gingko biloba*.

The volume concludes with an ethnobotanist's viewpoint which, like the opening article by a botanist, provides a global perspective.

Caroline Weckerle, Philip Blumenshine and Verena Timbul begin with the chemistry of plants. They note that every plant species that produces caffeine has become a culturally known plant in geographically disparate regions and in completely different societies. This is all the more remarkable as caffeine is produced by only six genera in the entire plant world, in entirely unrelated families (more recently, it has been found also in a seventh genus, *Citrus*). Regardless of which part of the plant (leaves, fruit or seeds), in which part of the world and in which ecological niche the caffeine-containing plants grew, human beings have ritualized their use.

Weckerle and colleagues insist on the importance of the chemical compound of caffeine within the plants, and its ubiquitously observed chemical effects on the human body, and explain its cultural history in this light. These findings are easily worked into a bioculturalist argument, but the authors go beyond that to expand on the cultural diversity of the way in which caffeine-containing plant use affected, and was affected by, different forms of sociality. The article ends with a juxtaposition of different legends on how these plants were discovered, which have as a recurrent theme that humans observed how caffeine-containing plants affected animals. This highlights the fact that the direct interrelatedness between humans and the environment may often involve humans, plants and animals.

Common Sense

The focus of the book is on practices that involve plants. While it stresses their cultural, social and situational specificity, it aims to discuss them with regard to a cross-culturally relevant dimension of doing, namely that which people consider as common sense. In English common parlance, common sense is positively valued: 'You don't have to think about it' and 'it feels right'; you take it for granted; it is a desirable attribute of both academics and the peoples they study. Initially, these peoples may appear to engage in strange practices that upon closer inspection turn out to be 'common sensical'.

However, among politicians, common sense seems to be invoked particularly by the conservative ones and, for this reason, the revolutionary thinker Gramsci (1891–1937) developed ambivalence towards common sense. As Crehan (2002: 114) comments: 'for those who are interested in radical social change, common sense, apart from its nucleus of good sense, is something to be opposed'.[5] In scholarly circles, common sense has variously made its entry into the literature, most recently in the cognitive sciences, where it is often equated with 'intuitive knowledge' and opposed to 'counter-intuitive knowledge', where the latter is considered to have cognitive effects that are particularly advantageous for cultural transmission (Boyer 1996). In the cognitive sciences, common sense is often equated to cross-culturally found, basic, empirical knowledge that is considered pan-human (e.g. Atran 1990). However, as argued in what follows, common sense has yet another facet of meaning.

The notion of common sense that is relevant for us here elaborates on meanings evoked by an Enlightenment philosopher in order to argue that human beings perceive the ongoing processes of their social and natural environment in an unmediated and direct way. In a sustained argument against the early modern empiricist understanding of perception,[6] this philosopher, Thomas Reid (1710–1796), raised examples of hypothetical situations where what he called common sense would trigger humans into action. His later commentators, such as Madden, Wolterstorff and Van Cleve (see below), remarked that Reid's discussion of common sense was perhaps the least developed aspect of his philosophy and philosophically not well founded. However, what presents an unresolved problem to philosophers may well be a fruitful theme of exploration for anthropologists, particularly those who consider humans to interact with the material and living environment in unmediated and direct ways.

If common sense is freed from its appropriation in the cognitive sciences as basic factual knowledge about the world, and if, as argued below, the attitude of 'taking for granted' is not mistaken as a proposition about belief, but rather as a form of enskilled practice, common sense can be understood as a sort of social action at the interface of knowledge and practice that is crucial for all human beings in daily life. Rather than reducing scientific knowledge, religious belief and common sense to a kind of basic factual knowledge, one could let oneself be inspired by Gramsci (1971: 330), who highlighted continuities between 'science, religion and common sense'. One could argue that there are three different modalities of the way in which humans interact with the natural environment: in scientific frameworks, religious contexts, or those practice-based day-to-day involvements with the environment that the notion of common sense invokes.

With this in mind, namely, that humans interact with plants in a practice-based modality, this introductory essay discusses recent research relevant to ethnobotany and medical anthropology. First, it summarizes major issues in medical anthropology in response to an article that outlined a study programme of the interface between ethnomedicine and ethnobotany (Waldstein and Adams 2006). This is followed by a critical appraisal of 'common sense' in the ethnobotanical literature that associates itself with the cognitive sciences. It thereby highlights the limitations of the empiricist approach in assessing how plants are used in medical practice. After a brief excursion into the anthropology of material culture and Science and Technology Studies (STS), which put materials and materiality centre stage, the essay presents James Gibson's *Ecological approach to visual perception* ([1979] 1986) as relevant for anthropological research because it provides a basis for radically rethinking the empiricist understanding of the perceptual processes currently labelled as sensation, perception and cognition, which are key to our current understanding at how humans relate to their environments. The article ends by pointing out that Ingold's notion of enskilment and the 'taking for granted' that Thomas Reid's common sense implies can open up a field for anthropological research on the unmediated, direct connectedness between humans and their material environment. It is hoped that the study of plants in medical practice, undertaken in this conceptual framework that takes the organism-in-the-environment as a single analytic entity, may feed constructively into innovative medical anthropological research on the materiality of the body and cause fertile discussion within the ethnobotanical research programme, so that the current chasm may ultimately be reduced.

Disease, Illness, Sickness, and Local Biologies

From its inception, medical anthropology engaged with local knowledge, wherever possible, in ways that took seriously local epistemologies and ontologies.[7] While ethnobiological research concerned with mapping local classifications of plant knowledge onto modern botanical taxa has proven fertile (e.g. Berlin 1992, Atran 1990, Ellen 1993), ethnoscientific attempts (e.g. Frake 1961) to account for nosological taxonomies were attacked even in early medical anthropological publications (e.g. Good 1977). The taxonomic approach to disease quickly became outdated in medical anthropology, as had the classificatory medicine centuries earlier (Foucault [1963] 1976: 4), even if it persists, in modified form, in some of the contemporary anatomo-clinical fields.

Ethnobotany and medical anthropology both engage with the interface of the biological and cultural, but apparently the biological presents itself in different ways in those two fields. It would appear that human beings show more cross-cultural continuities in the handling and conceiving of flowering plant taxa and vertebrates than in dealing with and conceptualizing sickness events. For the realist who relies on findings produced through natural scientific empiricist research, the explanation for this may well lie in the complex biology of the diseased human being in its interaction with the environment and other people. With the exception of germ theory, which classifies disease in respect of the taxonomy of the aetiological pathogens, many conditions that people perceive as sickness generally have aetiologies and pathologies which are much less distinctive (Pelling 1993).

Despite its exceptional status, germ theory and its emphasis on aetiological agents as classificatory factors continues to provide the prototype for understanding biomedical processes, particularly in ethnomedicine and applied medical anthropology. While Green (1999) rightly calls for a research agenda away from witchcraft towards investigating local conceptions of infectious diseases, which are a daily concern in Africa, and while there certainly is a place for the ethnomedical research that Waldstein and Adams (2006) advocate,[8] their research continues to endorse an outdated and ethnocentric toolkit. They continue to adhere to Foster and Anderson (1978), for example, who, according to aetiological considerations, classed the world's medical systems into two types: personalistic and naturalistic. Medical anthropologists have long criticized this typology. Not only does it overemphasize aetiological considerations, it also projects onto other medical systems the epistemological distinction the Western sciences make between 'empirical' knowledge (naturalistic aspects) and unexplained, so-called 'supernatural' forces (personalistic aspects). If researchers really have an urge to divide the world's medical systems into two types, Young (1976) has long sketched out an alternative framework that highlights contrasting and overlapping features between 'externalizing' and 'internalizing' medical systems. Young's typology, which does justice to local conceptualizations, can be used productively in cross-cultural comparison. More radically, the medical systems approach has long been shown to be problematic, not least because it overemphasizes doctrinal knowledge contained in systematizing written medical corpuses (Last 1981) and grossly overestimates people's interest in illness causation (Pool 1994).

In medical anthropology, an early attempt to account for biological continuities and culture-specific conceptualizations consisted of differentiating between 'disease' and 'illness'. Kleinman (1980: 72) defined disease as 'the malfunctioning of biological and/or psychological processes' and illness as 'the psychosocial experience and meaning of perceived disease'. He developed this definition on the basis of fieldwork in Taiwan, where he attended to patients suffering from psychiatric problems, including depression. His research was important as it went against the prevalent racist tenor of public opinion (and scientific research that continued well into the 1950s), according to which only those peoples who had a sufficient 'degree of introspection and verbalization' could develop depression, such as the Jewish people or the Protestant Hutterites (Littlewood and Lipsedge 1982: 65–66). Other peoples, foremost 'the Black', were stereotyped as 'happy-go-lucky', 'feckless child[ren] of nature', 'unburdened by the heavy responsibilities of civilization', with 'irrepressible high spirits', 'little self-control' and an 'apparently boundless sexual appetite'. (ibid.) Kleinman provided important evidence in favour of interpreting depression as a universal biological malfunction, a 'disease' that affected all populations. He achieved this by accounting for the different complaints presented by patients in the U.S.A. and Taiwan as 'illness' experiences. The signs and symptoms of the illness were different but the disease the same. Symptoms of feeling unhappy and unworthy among Caucasians arose from a process of 'psychologizing' dysphoric affect but feelings of an oppressed chest and dizziness, as observed among Taiwanese, were attributed to a 'somatization' of distress.[9]

Kleinman's notions of 'illness' and 'disease' were instantly criticized (Frankenberg 1980, Taussig 1980, Young 1982), even, to a certain extent, by the author himself (Kleinman 1988). However, both notions continue to figure prominently in the ethnomedical literature (e.g. Waldstein and Adams 2006). Accounts of 'illness' have been criticized for focusing too narrowly on the individual's experience as elicited by a physician during a clinical consultation, and for insufficiently attending to social, historical, economic and political processes that shape cultural perceptions and the sickness experience. By contrast, the definition of 'sickness' as relating to 'socially recognisable meanings' of biological dysfunction (Young 1982: 210) expresses a social critique. However, again, ethnomedicine tends to overlook this definition of sickness, which intrinsically is critical of the existent social order, and continues to use sickness as a vague blanket term.

Kleinman's notion of 'disease' was at the time not as loudly criticized as his understandings of 'illness', although today the term 'disease' no longer refers to the 'biological dysfunction' itself but to the biomedical knowledge about it. The sociology of science and STS (science and technology studies) have evidently affected medical anthropological thinking and today the term 'disease' generally designates the sickness event in terms of 'external modern medical criteria', much in the sense it long had had in Lewis (1976: 129). The biomedical sciences consider diseases to arise from biological processes that affect all populations. Accordingly, there is a tendency among medical anthropologists to view diseases as universal entities that affect human beings in identical ways, even though the social idioms in which they are experienced may differ. However, this understanding of the interface of the biological and social is based on a modern European understanding of personhood and disease, which became prevalent with the rise of hospital medicine in Europe (Foucault [1963] 1976) but has since been heavily contested.

The disorder that lent itself to a sustained critique of 'disease' as a universal biological entity was the 'menopausal syndrome'. Lock (1993) found that the Japanese women she worked with did not talk about the hot flashes that epitomized menopause in North America because they did not have the bodily experience of them, or if they did, then not to the same degree. Lock (1993: 373) attributed these culture-specific differences in symptom reporting to different physical experiences: 'If we are to move beyond the usual mind-body dichotomy that sees either culture as dominant and biology as essentially irrelevant or, conversely, biology as an immutable base and culture as a distortion, then it is essential that we acknowledge the plasticity of biology and its interdependence with culture.' Biologies are not universal but vary with locality, and are affected by culture. When Lock coined the term 'local biologies', she spoke of sickness as a biological process, shaped by local cultural practices, understood in terms of the explanations favoured by local biological sciences. The notion of local biologies did away with the mind-body dichotomy intrinsic to the notions of 'disease' and 'illness', and, like the notion of 'sickness', attended to the power relations intrinsic to medical knowledge production.

Depression is a 'mental condition', menopause a newly discovered 'syndrome', but even a prototypical 'germ disease' like malaria varies with locality. This finding of recent biomedical research is generally underplayed in the social sciences, and yet, if one takes account of the varied biological manifestations of a biomedically-identified disease (Hsu 2009), new possibilities arise in order to explain other peoples' medical practice in more 'realist' ways.[10] In the case of the 'germ disease' malaria, for instance, recent research in the biomedical sciences highlights the fact that we can no longer equate the fever episodes directly with the taxonomies of the species that is the pathogen.[11] Nowadays, the biomedical-recognized aspects of malaria are thought to arise from the interplay of at least four biological factors: parasite, host, environment and co-morbidity.[12] These not only determine the severity of the sickness event but also its varied manifestations in intermittent fevers, convulsions, joint pains, flu-like symptoms, anaemia and listlessness. Accordingly, the wide-ranging culturally understood effectiveness of plants with anti-malarial properties may have a more 'real' basis than anthropologists and ethnobotanists usually accord them.

Until very recently, it was almost a sacrilege within medical anthropology to admit to genetic differences or physiological processes within the phenotype (which to biologists are self-evident), and to speak of biological realities that are species- or race-specific or particular to an individual's life history, and which vary with geographic locality, ecology, climate, weather and seasons, just as the cultural perception and experience of them may vary. Furthermore, it was highly suspect for any medical anthropological study on the cultural constructedness of sickness and the body politic to show any interest in the constitutive biological processes. There are good reasons for this, as anthropological research has historically fed into a racializing and racist discourse, despite the fact that genetic diversity within a single ape species, like that of the chimpanzees, in one single geographic African region is greater than the genetic diversity among all humans worldwide (Jobling et al. 2004: 217–22). Lock (1993) was one of the first to insist that medical anthropology cannot ignore recent advances in the biomedical sciences. [13]

Empiricism, Objectivity and the Epistemic Virtue of Maintaining Detached Subject-Object Relations

It would be an epistemological fallacy to consider the 'empirical knowledge' that the natural sciences and biomedical research produce to be the only kind of knowledge that a 'realist' position (in the anthropologist Brian Morris's sense) could produce in regard to humans-in-the-environment. Of course 'empirical knowledge' has its place in anthropology, but the 'empiricist' stance on which the scientific method relies, which produces this 'empirical knowledge', has its limitations, as argued here, even for those who do not consider everything humans experience to be a mere cultural construct. What is contested here is merely one aspect of the general empiricist principle that the world out there can be known through sense perception. This one aspect is that 'empirical knowledge', which is meant to be 'objective', must be derived in a subject-object relation, where the scientific human investigator, ideally, is detached from the object of investigation, the 'natural world'. [14]

In a project termed 'collective empiricism', which outlines three kinds of sight, Daston and Galison (2007: 378–79) have convincingly demonstrated that the word 'objectivity' has multiple layers of meaning, 'more than a mille-feuille'. On the one hand, 'critics have attacked it [objectivity] as a fraud, an impersonal mask that veils the very personal and ideological interests it purports to suppress, or as a crime and arrogant attempt to play god by pretending to a view from everywhere and nowhere'. On the other hand, the scientists themselves adhere to at least two different epistemic virtues of objectivity, which Daston and Galison dub 'mechanical' and 'structural', each with 'different metaphysical, methodological and moral commitments'. Daston and Galison argue that no one ever made an attempt to erase completely the 'scientific self' wedded to the epistemic virtues of approximating truth, objectivity and judgment. Rather, they argue, 'its practices, like all techniques of the self, cultivated certain aspects of the self at the expense of others' (Daston and Galison 2007: 381).

The epistemic virtue of 'being true-to-nature', which continues to be the predominant paradigm in botany and ethnobotany, required the scientific self to develop synthetic perception and selective memory and to acquire the skill of drawing botanical specimens as ideal types. The epistemic virtue of 'mechanical or structural objectivity' required the hard-working scientist, equipped with either a camera or with mathematical formulae, to resist wishful thinking, to attend to the particular, and to calculate or record mechanically. Finally, the epistemic virtue of 'trained judgement', that in Daston and Galison's (2007: 314, 363, 371) view supplemented the previous two virtues, considered the scientific self as an expert, who can trust well-schooled intuitions and who recognizes family resemblances in recurrent patterns between families of objects. As Daston and Galison (2007: 381) note, these modes of 'plumbing nature's types' - registering its appearances and intuiting its patterns - had one goal: 'a faithful representation of nature'. It arose through engagement with the natural environment in a subject-object relation and required a clear separation between the observer and the observed.

The problem with this empiricist understanding of perception is its insistence on the detachment of the observer from the object as the ideal mode of acquiring knowledge about it, when, for instance in the context of ethnobotany, it is blatantly apparent that the application of plants in medical practice makes them part of a nexus: a nexus of human beings in social relations interacting with plants that in turn are interacting with culturally-sensitized bodies in a culturally-modified natural environment and in socially-specific moments. Attempting to account for a nexus of interrelatedness by treating interrelatedness as a problem and 'noise', when it is crucial to this nexus, appears to be a fundamentally flawed epistemic attitude. Rather, we should find methods of exploring human-environment interactions in ways other than those required by the empiricist stance that dominates the natural sciences, which is that the observer be detached from the object observed.

Admittedly, botanists will respond that although natural scientific methods may be counterintuitive, they yield the most accurate knowledge possible on human-plant-applied-to-maintaining-health interrelations. Well aware of Schroedinger's dictum that any observation in particle physics is distorted by observation, they justify their methods by stressing that their findings are the best possible approximations to reality. Natural scientists who produce such 'empirical' knowledge do not see a need to question its philosophical assumptions and only in exceptional cases, as in Grimley Evans', do they inquire into the sociology of how it is produced.

However, the application of plants in medical practice poses epistemological and ontological problems for medical anthropologists, in particular, for critical medical anthropologists.[15] For them, there is no knowledge about other human beings, themselves, and the environment that does not rely on a culture-specific form of interaction. The negotiated intersubjective knowledge that makes up these social realities encapsulates knowledge about biological realities, which is not detached, out there, but here, in hand. This knowledge arises in negotiation with the materiality of the plants and the human bodies with which they are put in interaction (and such interaction with biological realities, in turn, affects sociality). Geissler and Prince, in particular, stress that practices pertaining to plants make them part of social life and generate particular forms of sociality. The activities they describe, and the attitude with which people undertake them, are the result less of reflection and ratiocination than of 'doing'. Grandmother, mother and child are engaging in a habit of doing something that to them falls into the realm of what one could call 'common sense'.

Scott Atran on Common Sense, Empiricism and the Nominalist Fallacy in Ethnobiology

As already noted, Roy Ellen is puzzled that medical anthropology pays scant attention to the work of ethnobiologists. He speaks of a 'lack' within medical anthropology. It would appear, as outlined above, that the epistemological premises in each field, rather than the cultural practices themselves, provide the main obstacle. Medicinal ethnobotany and ethnomedicine tend to treat knowledge about plants in medical practice as 'empirical knowledge', but medical anthropology has always engaged with questions of knowledge production in a critical way.

17

One could argue that the domain specificity of the biological reality explains the divergence. The biological reality of the plant world – it presents itself in persistent discontinuities that invites the researcher to group plants into clearly bounded categories – differs from that of diseases that always arise from complex host-environment interdependencies. A realist (in Morris's or Latour's sense) could argue therefore that the dominant research agendas differ in ethnobotany and medical anthropology. A sociologist of knowledge would additionally point out that from the very beginning medical anthropology drew its rationale from its claim of complementing the biomedical knowledge of biological processes and aimed at competence in accounting for the social, cultural, political and economic aspects of sickness. The narrative turn in medical anthropology gained such currency not least because it alluded to a different ontology – truth as constructed through narrative – for explaining illness events that prevail in industrialized countries (such as chronic pain, which poses as yet unresolved problems to biomedicine, if not philosophically insurmountable ones).

By contrast, ethnobiological research was among the earliest to provide evidence against the strong programme of cultural relativism and social constructivism (e.g. Diamond 1966; Berlin et al. 1974; Hunn 1977; Berlin 1992; Ellen 1993; Berlin and Berlin 1996). With hindsight, the engagement of ethnobiology with difference, namely lists of indigenous and Linnaean botanical terms of modern plant taxa, led to conclusions that emphasize cognitive continuities between different peoples. People all around the world consider different kinds of plants to 'fall into groups within groups' and form distinctive morpho-behavioural gestalts. Many folk taxa largely conform to the modern genera, and those of flowering plants and vertebrates often coincide even at the species level.[16] Atran (1990) has made this point forcefully, with overwhelming data and detail, reinforced by cognitive anthropological arguments. In contrast to the variability of the biological manifestations in the human body that may trigger the perception of a sickness episode, research on ethnobotanical taxa emphasizes cognitive universality and cross-cultural continuities.

Atran refers to 'common sense' as a pan-human mode of thinking. Common sense evidently is at the core of ethnobiology, and, as is argued here, it is an issue also in medical anthropology. It is also implicit in all the various projects of this volume. As erudite as

Harris' exposition on plant exchanges may appear, the reasons for explaining them appeal to common sense. Common sense is also central to Hsu's critique of the 'natural herb'. Barbira Freedman elaborates on common sensical gender relations and Geissler and Prince's account on the practices of child care is steeped in common sense. Grimley Evans' critique of the unreflected enthusiasm about a CAM remedy appeals as much to common sense as it calls for an improvement in treatment evaluation, while the findings of Weckerle, Blumenshine and Timbul on caffeine-containing plants represent a prime example of common sense in Atran's sense. It would appear that in this volume common sense arises as a theme in the context of exploring the social configurations into which enskilled practices of the everyday are enfolded, rather than from the zeal to find the pan-human cognitive schemas that drives so many ethnobiological studies. And yet, despite the emphasis on practice here and on cognition there, on the everyday here and on the expert there, one senses that overlaps may be possible.

When Atran (1990: 1–3) uses common sense to refer to 'ordinary thinking', one may see continuities to the concerns of several authors in this book. However, Atran then continues by defining common sense as 'what, in all societies is considered ... a manifestly perceivable empirical fact'. Common sense accordingly includes statements pertaining to 'an innately-grounded, and species-specific, apprehension of the spatio-temporal, geometrical, chromatic, chemical, and organic world in which we ... live.' Atran insists that 'common sense remains valid only as long as it is restricted to the manifestly visible dimensions of the everyday world, that is, to phenomenal reality'. He contrasts common sense with speculative reason, reflection and experimentation. He stresses that 'in this scenario, common sense does not preclude, but neither does it include, any magical, mythico-religious, metaphorical or other "symbolic" elaboration'. This is certainly a useful definition of common sense for the project Atran thereafter embarks on, where he highlights continuities between different folk biologies and, in a tour de force of the history of what today would broadly fall into the realm of botanical knowledge, leads the reader to the emergence of modern scientific taxonomy. However, for our purposes Atran's definition of common sense is not very useful.

To a Luo mother or Chinese doctor, and I would claim even to a modern Western scientist, there is no manifestly perceivable empirical fact that does not convey what Atran would call a metaphorical or symbolic message. People who use plants in medical practice do not distinguish between fact and symbol in the way an idealized scientist would do. When the Dinka said to Godfrey Lienhardt (1954) that some men are lions, this was common sense. But it was not a manifestly perceivable empirical fact to the ethnographer. Nor was it said in a figurative way. Lienhardt deplores the limited conceptual toolkit of the anthropologist who can only differentiate between literal and metaphorical meaning. He also doubts the usefulness of invoking a *mentalité primitive*. There are problems of translation, no doubt, but Lienhardt goes further and wishes to find other devices for explaining this Dinka statement.[17] Along similar lines, his brother Peter Lienhardt (1968: 58) highlighted in his discussion of sorcery on the Swahili coast the observation that acts of murder are attributed to sorcery and magic, regardless of whether they were committed by ultimately physical means – for instance, by cutting the victim's throat with a knife (a manifestly perceivable empirical fact) – or by using medicines at a distance (which leave no traces to the uninitiated observer). The point of reminding us of these classical anthropological works is that anthropology has long held that common sense does not coincide with empirical fact and that any anthropological study that distinguishes between a manifestly perceivable empirical fact and symbolic elaboration is ultimately untenable. Ellen (2006: S9) is acutely aware that the interrelationships between what he calls 'mundane' and 'symbolic' 'are often far from clear'.[18]

Nevertheless, Atran's allusion to common sense strikes a chord, in particular when he speaks of the innately grounded species-specific apprehension of the world we live in. He alludes here to commonalities of human beings in their dealings with and perception of the world, which they derive from what empiricists call the condition of being human. Common sense evidently has a wide semantic stretch. It refers to: (a) diverse but culturally unquestioned conventions; (b) knowledge that is considered basic to all humans; and, as will be argued in more detail below, (c) a practical enskilment of the human organism into the environment, such that a unity ensues which is taken for granted in an unreflected way and which may or may not be culture-specific or pan-human. Atran's notion of common sense, in line with that in the cognitive sciences, refers to (b): a genetically conditioned mode of plant recognition that he considers to be pan-human.

Ellen (2006) does hint at common sense as an enskilment of humans-into-the-environment when he outlines the limits of ethnobiological classification, drawing almost exclusively on lexicography and ethnolinguistics, and when he comments that practical and embodied ethnobiological knowledge is difficult to transform into written knowledge. Ellen even mentions 'knowledge and enskilment' and speaks of 'the relationship between cognition as a mental activity and the learned body routines which act on and in the world but are not necessarily simply the enaction of mental processes' (Ellen 2006: S8). This comes close to Lave's (1988) insight that grand cognitive schemas cannot account for the particular instances of arithmetic problem solving that occur in everyday life, actions which she found to be nested into culturally-structured settings. However, while Lave stresses that cognition is a complex social process that involves mind, body, action and setting, Ellen falls back into the nominalist fallacy (that naming something defines its essence) when in the following sentence he considers the above approach to enable a 'more accurate modelling of real-world categories'. But categories are in the mind not in the world out there! For medical anthropologists who learnt about narrative theory, Ellen's statement has unreflected, idealistic overtones.

The Anthropological Study of Material Culture and Bruno Latour's 'Realistic Realism'

In order to make sense of how plants become part of medical practice, the medical anthropologist turns here to inspiration from research on material culture, which does not appear to be as entrenched in scientism as ethnobiology (and the sort of nominalism just encountered). Plant materials applied in medical practice are after all material culture: due to culture-specific preparations they are turned into cultural artefacts.

Plants have materiality in that 'they are part of substantial ties, emerging from relations and establishing or rebuilding relations'.

21

Geissler and Prince (in this volume) are clearly drawing on insights from the anthropological study of material culture when, rather than highlighting tensions between the material properties of the plant as known through the natural sciences and their perception in social practice, they discuss how people perceive plants and become practically engaged with them. They evidently account for the plants' materiality in a manner that, as Tilley (unpubl.: 2) outlined in a response to Ingold, consists of exploring 'landscapes, contexts, movements, social and political strategies'.

If medical treatment is intended to transform the patient's status from ill to healthy, the preoccupation with material transformations that one finds among anthropologists of material culture promises to provide further insight. The enchantment of magic results from the artist's ability 'to make what is not out of what is, and to make what is out of what is not' (Gell 1999: 174). The shaman's powers can make manifest the cause of an underlying affliction through a stone or feather, extracted from underneath the patient's skin. The immaterial is transformed into the material.

The material also derives its importance from the immaterial. Miller (2005) ruminates on the way in which the soul's immortality is expressed in the monumental materiality of the Egyptian pyramids. Engelke (2005) discusses how honey becomes holy as it is imbued with the immateriality of the Pentecostal Holy Spirit. He contrasts the materiality of the pebble, which can be found anywhere, is easily replaced and is special-because-it-is-not, the materiality of water, which is scarce, but multi-vocalic in meaning, even outside the Christian context, and powerful precisely because of this, with the materiality of the sweet and sticky holy honey in Pentecostal healing among the Masowe Chishanu in Zimbabwe. This sticky sweetness, he suggests, makes honey highly desirable not merely for spiritual but also for more mundane, material reasons.

To be sure, what medical anthropologists are confronted with is not always easily categorized as either material or immaterial. The stuff that causes good fortune and luck in Mongolia, into which a medical anthropologist can read a cultural logic for explaining differences in health status,[19] would at first approximation appear immaterial and merely indexed by materials: a hair from the child's first hair cutting, a piece of umbilical cord kept in a family chest, contained and separated, for the purpose of maintaining relatedness (Empson

2007). By maintaining family relations and relations to one's place of origin in this indexical way, an individual is sure to thrive. One can go even further. In some people's daily practice, fortune is not only indexed by the material but material stuff in and of itself. As Holbraad (2007) notes in his exploration of what constitutes the power of the powder that in Ifá divination seances makes present the divine, the anthropology of *mana*-concepts cannot be buried yet. Holbraad suggests conceiving of them in a Latourian manner as both concepts and things (i.e. ontological hybrids). Life forces, ancestral presence, spiritual efficaciousness all assert themselves through a sort of motion that need not be immaterial, much like wind is 'air in motion' (*cf.* Hsu and Low 2008). Apart from the performative power of words (Tambiah 1968), it is perhaps the materiality of the breath in the speaking of secret spells that brings into motion the power in plants, as recorded in so many ethnographies (e.g. Bellman 1975).

Medical anthropology has disappointingly little to say on material culture in the medical field (Hsu 2002), despite recent efforts (e.g. Luedtke 2007), except for the currents that come together in science and technology studies (STS), but those do not generally address questions relevant to the application of plants in medical practice, nor do they take an interest in how spiritual powers become instantiated in the material world.

Among the currents of medical anthropology that do address material medical culture belongs the anthropology of pharmaceuticals. However, it is curiously uninterested in the materiality of drugs: it emphasizes meaning (Etkin and Tan 1994), socio-economic and cultural interpretation (Nichter and Nichter 1996), symbolic efficacy (Moerman 2002) and social efficacy (Whyte et al. 2003).[20] As good medical anthropologists, the anthropologists of pharmaceuticals have left the discussion of the drugs and their physiological effects to biomedicine, accounted for socio-cultural aspects, and thereby inadvertently reinforced the Cartesian dualism that has set the agenda for the medical anthropological project.

There is certainly important other medical anthropological research that aims at overcoming this Cartesian dualism: research on 'transcendental somatic states' and experiences of 'resonance' or 'true fellow-feeling' (Blacking 1977), the 'mindful body' (Scheper-Hughes and Lock 1987), 'overlapping, anaphoric combinatorial approaches and bodily routines' instead of codified knowledge (Parkin 1995), 'embodiment' and 'somatic modes of attention' (Csordas 1994, 2002), 'sensory attentiveness' (Desjarlais 1996), 'trans-individual systems of communication' (Seremetakis 1998), the 'body-in-mind' (Lambek 1998), and also much other research that often relies on Bourdieu's (1977, 1984) practice theory and Merleau-Ponty's phenomenology ([1945] 1962). However, Bourdieu's discussion of *habitus*, inspired by Panofsky's (1957) relating to architectural styles, is curiously disembodied, in contrast to the *habitus* and bodily routines described in Mauss ([1934] 1973). Ingold (2000a:170), exclaims: 'The embodiment of culture, in short, leads to nothing less than the disembodiment of the organism!'

Merleau-Ponty did emphasize immediacy between the self and its environment, and medical anthropology built on this insight in so far as it takes the body as a starting point for any exploration of the world. The body is taken as the foundation of human existence and as the generative principle through which the self apprehends the world. However, rather than focusing on the body-as-directly-related-to-the-world, as given in Merleau-Ponty's phenomenology, medical anthropologists have foregrounded the self and made the self-as-individual-body, detached from its environment, into a topic of research, much the same as it is in biomedicine.

It has been noted that anthropologists – and medical anthropologists in particular – draw almost exclusively on the phenomenology of Merleau-Ponty, to the exclusion of Husserl and others (Sugishita 2006). The study of material culture refers at times to Heidegger. Thus, Ingold (2000a:172–88) elaborates on Heidegger's notion of dwelling in his discussion of architecture and the built-up material environment, and Gosden (2007: 183) may ultimately be drawing on Heidegger (*cf.* Gosden 1994), when he suggests concentrating 'on time and temporality as a key aspect of the relationship between people and things': the stages of making a pot consist of 'sequenced negotiations' between human agents and the materials they work on, where the 'material nature' in interaction with a person's 'skills' create an end result. This process of 'transubstantiation' is paraphrased as 'the changing of objects into social relations' (Gosden 2007: 185). For Ingold, and Gosden, the starting point is the material world outside the body. The social and the mental world arise subsequently through the processes by which human beings engage in a bodily skilled manner with the material world.

While referring neither to Ingold's dwelling perspective nor to Gosden's transubstantiation, Rival's (2006, 2007) most recent work on 'historical ecology' and 'domesticating the landscape' takes a strikingly similar interest in humans as agents who nest themselves into their living environment of plants and animals, whose material appearance they thereby transform, genetically, and otherwise. However, in medical anthropology the self-in-its-natural-environment is usually only discussed in medical ecology (e.g. McElroy and Townsend 2004) and bioculturalism (e.g. Ulijaszek 2007).

The environments of the self with which critical medical anthropologists have engaged are often of an institutional kind: different niches of biomedicine and public health (e.g. Lindenbaum and Lock 1993, Good 1994, Young 1995, Nichter and Lock 2002, Mol 2002). Science and Technology Studies deserve to be mentioned at greater length here, as they have long highlighted the continuities between the self and the technological environment, and stress interdependencies between the self, material culture, society and the 'natural' environment. Latour (2000: 109) asks: 'what could it mean, according to mainstream social sciences, to provide a social explanation of a natural phenomenon?' His reply is a focus on the 'thing', which he defines as the 'assembly in charge of composing the common world' (Latour 2000: 120). So, if we treat plants as 'things in medical practice', would that mean that any medical-anthropological-cum-ethnobotanical research project advances into the limelight of a Latourian STS project?

Summarizing what Whitehead (1920) called a 'bifurcation of nature' and other arguments made in *Pandora's Hope* (Latour 1999), Latour (2000: 118) unveils the 'formidable political ploy' of the natural sciences to distinguish between primary and secondary qualities: 'Primary qualities define the real stuff out of which nature is made, particles, strings, atoms, genes, depending on the discipline, while secondary qualities define the way that people subjectively represent this same universe'. This, he points out, results in a political incapacitation of the ordinary persons' knowledge of the world: 'While what is visible, lived, felt, is, to be sure, subjectively essential but utterly inessential, since it is not how the universe is made up'. Scientists sum up the primary qualities of one Nature, while 'the secondary qualities ... divide us into multiple points of view which may be subjectively relevant but are objectively (in the traditional sense) irrelevant'. Although Latour does not call himself a phenomenologist, he thereby restores the validity of the ordinary person's perception of the environment, which will become central to the line of argumentation presented below. Latour emphasizes the political forces that are thereby freed.

Furthermore, Latour (2000: 109) discusses the fundamental flaw of the functionalist stance that sees in a social explanation the substitution of an 'object pertaining to nature' by one 'pertaining to society'. He (Latour 2000: 111–12) bitingly notes that 'one can become accepted in the salons of the social sciences, but only on the condition of not providing an explanation of what one deals with', 'namely what the *thingness* of this thing actually is'. As noted above, this certainly applies to many medical anthropologists. In contrast to the conceptual relativist and social constructivist, Latour (2000) does not consider science as just another language game, and in contradistinction to the scientific realist, he does not assume a gap between the world and the language about the world. He calls himself a 'realistic realist'. A social explanation, he suggests, consists of a translation process from the practices in the fieldwork terrain into a scientific language. 'The translators at work', as Stalder (2000) notes in a book review of *Pandora's Hope*, 'are ontological hybrids in the sense that they are simultaneously an object that is belonging to the world and a concept that is belonging to the word'. One such hybrid that is used by natural scientists is the pedocomparator. It is an object in that it is a suitcase full of specimens of soil and it is simultaneously a scientific concept in being 'an abstraction of the continuous soil variations in discrete bits of information, packed, ordered, and precisely numbered in the suitcase'. Another 'ontological hybrid' that Latour (1999: 192) describes in an attempt to tackle the social scientific problem of whether 'guns kill people' or 'guns do not kill, people kill people' is the 'object institution', which treats humans and their artefacts as one single entity. If Latour's 'realistic realism' is applied to the discussion of plants in medical practice, human beings and the plants they use are conceived as forming a unity, and this 'object institution' or 'corporate body', in turn, constitutes the starting point for a social scientific explanation.

Latour is certainly not alone in advocating that the ontological gap between concepts and the material world is not as large as philosophy would have it. In his articles about basket making and weaving, Ingold (2000a, 2000b) aims at dissolving the gap between learnt human activity and innate animal behaviour. Ingold does not speak of 'ontological hybrids'. The theoretical concept he elaborates is that of 'enskilment'. A skill, he says, 'cannot be regarded simply as a technique of the body' (Ingold 2000a:352). 'Skill, in short, is a property not of the individual human body as a biophysical entity, a thing in itself, but of the total field of relations constituted by the presence of the organism-person, indissolubly body and mind, in a richly structured environment' (Ingold 2000a:353). Ingold evidently also treats the artefact and human being as a single entity, but he does not call himself a 'realistic realist'. Rather, he aligns himself with ecology: 'that is why the study of skill, in my view, not only benefits from, but *demands* an ecological approach' (Ingold 2000a:353). We will return to this Ingoldian ecological approach later.

Farquhar and Lock (2007: 12) argued for integrating Latourian STS into medical anthropology when they outlined as future research agenda 'a materialism of lived bodies': 'All these recent efforts could be said to be seeking a new style of materialism, neither reductive and economistic nor sealed off from the traditional humanistic concerns of signification, subjectivity, and ethics.' Farquhar and Lock consider the social constructivist studies necessary and important for 'denaturalizing' generally held assumptions but these need to be complemented with 'new empirical research'. Farquhar and Lock (2007: 11) state: 'the problematic of perceiving bodily life in its actual empirical and material forms invites scholars to see social multiplicity more clearly and to adjust our actions more sensitively to the depths at which human being varies'. Notably, however, Farquhar and Lock do not endorse Latour's realistic realism, but advocate an empiricist stance.

Any medical anthropologist with realist inclinations will welcome Farquhar and Lock's call to attend to materiality in medicine, but their suggestion of 'perceiving bodily life' in an 'actual empirical and material form' (Farquhar and Lock 2007: 11) seems to invoke precisely the Cartesian dualism that they aim to overcome. Many authors confuse 'empiricist' with 'realist' endeavours. As already stated, acknowledgement of empirical data certainly has its place in critical medical anthropology. However, when it comes to the perceptions of bodily life it is questionable whether those are always best approximated through empirical data (elicited through scientific methods of detached observation and objectification). When it comes to questions of perception, and to 'perceiving bodily life', the empiricist stance is limited and may even be misleading.

The Ecological Critique of the Empiricist Stance on Perception

The idea that the self is intrinsic to and inseparable from perception, which phenomenology emphasizes, goes diametrically against the empiricist paradigm of perception. This is of particular interest to the researcher confronted with plants in medical practice, considering that the empiricist principle of perception is the dominant paradigm in the natural sciences, cognitive anthropology and ethnobiology. The empiricist paradigm posits that perception is initiated by external stimulation, and is hence a passive process: as the real world sends out different stimuli, sensory receptors are stimulated, sensations are felt, then transported to the brain, and there processed into perception. Psychophysical research of the nineteenth century on 'passive touch' is an example *par excellence* of an empiricist programme that was revolutionized by phenomenologists. In particular, the phenomenologist psychologist David Katz (1884–1954) stressed the importance of the hand and its active exploration of surfaces, arguing that it was the active engagement with the environment that elicited stimuli.[21]

One could claim that even an empiricist considers the self to be an integral aspect of perception and category formation if the self is located in the brain: stimuli from the external world impress themselves on the sense receptors, generating sensations that are transported to the brain, which then processes these sensory inputs, based on the individual's store of knowledge that, as philosophers of the Enlightenment period had it, was either innate knowledge, experientially accumulated knowledge or knowledge about the world derived from rational inference. Gibson ([1979] 1986: 25) caricatures this model of passive perception: 'it is supposed that sensation occurs first, perception occurs next, and knowledge occurs last, a progression from the lower to the higher mental processes'. It continues to be the predominant model in psychology. Most recently, it also has found entry in the anthropology of the senses.

28

Hinton et al. (2008: 139) declare in the first sentence of *The Medical Anthropology of Sensations*: 'In psychological theory, sensations are the first experiential responses to stimuli that ultimately lead to (or become incorporated into) more elaborate perceptions of objects and events.'

However, such empiricist understanding of perception and category formation has long been criticized from within psychology. Gibson's ([1979] 1986) *Ecological Approach to Visual Perception* radically revises our thinking about visual perception, and perception in general. He emphasizes that human beings are animals in an environment and that the animal's perceptual system is attuned to the environment such that the animal can avoid danger, orient and reproduce itself. Apart from invoking this otherwise undifferentiated Darwinian axiom, which is that the behaviour and morphology of organisms have the function to ensure reproduction and the continuation of the species, there is little that a biologist has learnt about perception which Gibson does not question. Perhaps, the most baffling is that Gibson does not consider sensation as an intermediary for perception. He rejects the assumption that perception is based on the inputs of the sensory channels, subject to cognitive processing (Gibson 1986: 238). This viewpoint and related ones are upheld and reinforced, he says, by generalizing the findings of 'peephole observation' to ordinary perception (Gibson 1986: 168). He contends that laboratory experiments may not yield results which are relevant to real life. Natural visual perception does not happen just in the head, and certainly not in a head that is made immobile as in the laboratory. Rather, Gibson speaks of a perceptual system, which involves 'eyes in the head on a body supported by the ground' (Gibson 1986: 1). This perceptual system includes the striated musculature, locomotion and manipulations with one's hands, an ensemble which in his view is indispensable for making the perceptual process happen but which, in turn, also depends on perception (Gibson 1986: 223).[22]

Natural vision does not just happen in the head. Nor does it happen in a state divorced from self-awareness. It involves the organism's constant awareness of the environment and of itself in it. Gibson provides an anatomical reason for explaining why the human organism has a heightened self-awareness in visual perception: the frontal positioning of the eyes. While their frontal positioning is usually thought to have evolved because of evolutionary hunting advantages due to stereoscopy, Gibson downplays the stereoscopic effects of frontal positioning. Instead, he stresses that the frontal positioning of the eyes produces a reduced visual field in comparison to that of animals with lateral eyes. A reduced visual field increases the observer's self-awareness.[23] This self-awareness is an integral part of perception: what is visually perceived, simultaneously and directly, are both the physical properties and the meanings they have relative to the animal. Gibson speaks of affordances that point both ways, to the environment and the observer in it.[24]

By conceiving of the organism-in-the-environment as a unit, and by postulating a direct and unmediated connectedness between the self-conscious organism and the environment, Gibson can overcome the dichotomy intrinsic to the empiricist understanding of perception which differentiates between sensation as a physical process and perception as the meaning-making mental process. People may have visual sensations but these may be quite unrelated to the perceptual process, Gibson claims. He vehemently rejects the idea that natural vision is based on an information-enriching process of a series of flat pictures that appear 'like pan cakes' on the retina. Rather, natural visual perception involves 'picking up', 'differentiating' and 'extracting' information from the flowing array of the light in which an organism is immersed and which reflects from the surfaces in its surroundings.[25]

Visual perception as 'information pickup' makes a clear-cut separation between perception and what in Gibson's (1986: 258, 263) view are 'non-cognitive kinds of awareness' such as fantasy, fiction, dreams and hallucinations, while it closes the supposed gap between perception and knowledge. The ecological understanding of direct perception calls for a new theory of cognition. Indeed, when Gibson emphasizes that visual perception arises from an active engagement with the environment, which involves locomotion and manipulation, he reminds us that cognition resides in doing, that cognitive categories are formed in social practice and through interaction with the material environment. Perceiving is doing, and this in constant awareness of a self that is interested in what the environment can provide for it.

Thomas Reid on Common Sense: Neither 'Believing' Nor 'Knowing' but 'Taking for Granted'

As shown above, the empiricist understanding of so-called 'passive' perception, which is that the real world sends out stimuli that are impressed on the sense organs which, in turn, produce sensations that are then processed into perception in the brain, has been criticized from various angles: Heidegger's 'being-in-the-world', Merleau-Ponty's body as a generative principle of perception, Katz's research on the role of the moving hand in active touch and Gibson's ecological approach to visual perception. These authors all emphasize that perception relies on a direct connectivity between an organism and its surroundings, which the organism actively explores. In this context it is noteworthy that, the British empiricists John Locke (1632–1704), George Berkeley (1685–1753), David Hume (1711–1776) and their theories of perception were already criticized two centuries earlier by a contemporary of theirs: Thomas Reid (1710–1796), who is known as a 'realist' (someone who holds that there are physical things existing outside the mind) and for his work on common sense.[26]

Reid is also known for decoupling sensation from perception. He considered sensation to have an ontologically entirely different status from perception. While there are ambiguities in Reid's writings on this subject (see Van Cleve 2004: 114–19), there are many passages where he rejects the empiricists' assumption that sensation is an intermediary stage of perception (strikingly similar to Gibson). Madden (1986: 261) explains: 'Sensation, which has nothing in common with perception, suggests perception to the mind because the mind is so constructed to interpret it in that way. Thus, the sensation and the native capacity in the mind together result in the completely new act of the mind, perception, which is an immediate apprehension of, and belief in, the existence of properties inhering in objects.' For Reid 'perception is a new mental act'; it 'may be suggested by a sensation but is not mediated by it' (Madden 1986: 261). Reid 'repeats endlessly the claim that perception is a function of our nature or constitution and is not a matter of passive sensation, as the British empiricists would have it'. However, 'he also repeatedly

31

insisted that how this comes about we haven't the slightest idea' (Madden 1986: 261). Madden stresses that Reid's nativistic ideas about perception make him a 'natural realist'.

Noteworthy for our purposes is the fact that Reid and Gibson independently came to conceive of humans as being directly cued into their environment. Both reject sensations as intermediaries in the process of perception. Reid did not systematically investigate how the native capacity in the mind, together with sensations, triggered the perceptual process, while Gibson alludes to a Darwinian axiom. Furthermore, both stress that the perceiver's self-awareness is an intrinsic aspect of the perceptual process. This allowed Reid to solve a well-known empiricist problem of perceptual relativity by differentiating between real and apparent magnitude, where the apparent magnitude is a function of the relation between the object and the perceiver (Van Cleve 2004: 103). Of course a contemporary researcher would not want to adopt Reid's philosophy in every aspect. His writings, which predate Darwin, remind us that a researcher can adopt a realist position and work on human-environment interactions without instantly submitting to either the empiricist understanding of passive perception or the Neo-Darwinian biocultural programme. Notably, the two botanists Harris and Weckerle discuss data that lends itself to a bioculturalist argument but neither has accorded it centre stage. Rather, both deal with the way in which the people themselves experience and perceive the plants, and with socio-political power relations, historical accident and technological development in the light of how they affected knowledge production and instituted new daily routines, themes that are central to critical medical anthropology.

Reid's realism also led him to invoke common sense. This was, however, the weakest aspect of his philosophy (Wolterstorff 2004: 78).[27] Perhaps common sense is a problem which philosophers may identify but which anthropologists may more successfully investigate? Since its beginnings, anthropology has been concerned with 'beliefs' and 'modes of thought', a theme that also resurfaced in different guises (technologies of persuasion, styles of knowing) in the sociology of knowledge and in critical medical anthropology. The anthropologist's recourse to the notion of 'belief' has since been critiqued by many authors, who incidentally understand the term in very different ways. Needham (1972) reminded us that peoples' activities are not grounded in belief as a credo that entails certainty and faith, but for Good (1994) belief expressed a lack of other people's objective knowledge and certainty: we have knowledge, they have beliefs. Important here is that the debates surrounding 'belief' highlight differences in modalities of knowing, as does the notion of 'common sense'.

Reid's comments on common sense are often interpreted, as Atran (1990: 3) did, as a foundation of all thought and practice. However, is that what Reid actually meant when he invoked the principles of common sense? As already noted, his principles of common sense are probably 'the least carefully formulated part of his philosophy' (Wolterstorff 2004: 78). It therefore comes as no surprise that some commentators have misconstrued commonsensism as 'essentially a faith in oneself – a conviction that a human being by proceeding cautiously, is capable of knowing the world in which it finds itself' (Chrishom 1998: 453). Chrisholm's words 'faith' and 'knowing' are evidently misplaced here, particularly following a recapitulation of Needham's and Good's comments on them. Wolterstorff's (2004: 89) comments are more insightful. According to him, Reid understood the principles of common sense in at least two ways. Reid can indeed be interpreted to have defined them as 'first principles in our reasoning', a philosophical idea that was not very original and can be traced to Aristotle. However, Reid's common sense can also be interpreted as 'things we all do and must take for granted in our everyday lives', which apparently was 'not at all traditional' (Wolterstorff 2004: 89). One can go a step further here and argue that Thomas Reid's writings on common sense remind us that 'taking-for-granted' is not a kind of knowledge but falls into the domain of practice.

Rehabilitating Common Sense as a Practical Stance of Taking the Human-in-the-Environment as a Continuum

Common sense is often misunderstood to designate a self-confident position of 'I know most of what I think I know' (Cardinal et al. 2004: 33). Gramsci accused conservative politicians who were opposed to social change of invoking common sense in this sense and the cognitive sciences currently uphold common sense in this sense as a 'first principle in our reasoning'. As Wolterstorff intimates, common sense in this sense expresses a philosophical idea that can be traced to Aristotle. However, as argued here, 'taking for granted' may primarily refer to an attitude of the person engaged in doing things rather than of the person who claims to reflect on things and know.

First, it is important to distinguish between the attitudes of 'taking for granted' and 'believing'. As Wolterstorff (2004: 88) notes, they are different propositional attitudes: 'We take for granted all sorts of things that we never bring to the point of being something we believe; one does not have to believe something to take it for granted. Taking a proposition for granted is a different propositional attitude from believing it; one can do the former with respect to a certain proposition, without doing the latter.' For Woltersdorff, this propositional attitude of common sense is a mode of thought: he speaks of it as a 'line of thought' when he states that Reid's 'things-taken-for-granted line of thought' was not at all traditional (Wolterstorff 2004: 89). However, what if we go a step further, and, inspired by Reid, rehabilitate common sense as an attitude that refers to human beings involved in practice, rather than in reflections of the mind?

In other words, 'taking for granted' may be as much a mode of doing as a mode of thinking, just as 'trying out' is a form of social action. Perhaps, in certain situations of ordinary life, human beings are prompted into this attitude of engaging with the environment by doing, rather than by deliberating over what could be done and, perhaps, they have the disposition to be prompted into this attitude of doing in a 'taking-for-granted' fashion only in those situations. Reid seems to have had such situations in mind, of unreflectively doing things, when he invoked the notion of common sense. In these situations human beings act in a way that would suggest they are in direct connection with the environment and form a continuum with it.

Atran's understanding of common sense has elsewhere been attacked in a richly documented re-examination of what can be said both for and against a thesis of cross-cultural universals and the contrary thesis of cultural relativity (Lloyd 2007). However, Lloyd's critique refers to common sense in much the same Aristotelian sense as Atran, namely as propositional knowledge: a first principle in our reasoning. The difference is that Atran makes claims to universality where Lloyd does not. However, Lloyd does not attend to the materiality of the living world and the implications this may have for being in it. Nor does Lloyd focus on the indeterminacy between human-environment interactions, perception and cognition.

Our discussion of common sense, by contrast, does so. It aims to rehabilitate and elaborate on Reid's realist notion of common sense in a way that points in the same direction as Ingold and Latour. To do this, we have to reiterate that common sense is not a self-confident propositional attitude derived from reliance on factual knowledge, which in the empiricist sciences relies on humans interacting with nature in subject-object relations, where the scientific self, as an ideally detached 'subject', makes natural processes to 'objects' of investigation. Latour and Ingold have in their own languages both hinted that the chasm between the subject and the object, the word and the world, the human being and the artefact is not as large as the contemporary sciences intimate. In a similar vein, let us rehabilitate the notion of common sense as pointing to a human disposition that arises in certain situations where the practice-based modes of human interaction with the material environment happen in a 'taking-for-granted' manner. In those situations where practice relies on common sense, the human-beings-interacting-with-the-material-environment and, in our case, the-plant-materials-of-the-environment-in-interaction-with-human-beings form a continuum.

The propositional attitude of 'taking for granted' that this understanding of common sense invokes is similar to that of 'trying out' in so far as it consists of doing rather than knowing. Recent research on how people take the natural phenomenon of wind for granted, integrate it into their everyday practices of hunting, mourning, dancing, dreaming or healing, and experience it accordingly (Hsu and Low 2008), may highlight new directions for medical anthropologists and ethnobotanists wishing to explore the 'taking for granted' that implicates plants into medical practice. It brings to mind Ingold's (2000a) notion of enskilment, Latour's (1999) hybrid ontologies, and, building on Ingold and Latour, Grasseni's (2007) ecology of practice. Latour emphasizes that the generally assumed gap between the concept and the thing is a social construct; Ingold stresses that all cultural forms that skilled practice results in are intrinsic to the thing-in-relation-to-the-agent; and Grasseni, elaborating on both,

35

argues that cognition and skill develop in the course of social actors acquiring and applying techniques that incorporate the material world into a web of social hierarchies and relations. Accordingly, a herbal drug's therapeutic effectiveness is neither solely a function of plant chemistry nor of the culture-specific theory of the practitioner who applies the plant, nor of the expectations of the patient. Rather, it results from a skilled practice of putting practitioner-patient-plant-in-the-environment into interaction.

Concluding Remarks

According to the above explorations, the interface between ethnobotany and medical anthropology has not been much explored, less because of disinterest in or inaccessibility of the cultural practices observed, but rather because of differences in the dominant epistemologies within these two sub-disciplines of anthropology. Recent developments in ethnobiology and cognitive anthropology have led to research that produces observations interpreted in the light of pan-human cognitive schemas (although there are some voices that stress the nested knowledge of situated practice). Medical anthropology, with its emphasis on cultural, social and symbolic meanings, and its emphasis on the cultural constructedness of many medical phenomena, has not actually engaged with the socio-cultural problems that the materiality of medical cultures poses (although, again, there are some exceptions).

As suggested here, if common sense is understood as a term that describes a situation-specific practical stance of engaging with the material world, it is likely to attract the attention of both ethnobiologists and medical anthropologists as a theme worth exploration. It certainly raises questions of knowledge production in daily practice-based interactions with it. Critical medical anthropologists may furthermore draw on inspiration from the anthropological study of material culture and incorporate ecological thinking that takes human-beings-in-their-environment as a whole into their research, rather than leaving ecological concerns to medical ecologist and bioculturalist researchers alone, which ultimately explain social processes in a Neo-Darwinian framework. Perhaps, medical anthropologists and ethnobotanists may find ways along these lines to engage with the 'phytotherapeutic realities' Roy Ellen speaks of, and 'the health practices of most people on our planet'.

Acknowledgements

I warmly thank Stephen Harris, Geoffrey Lloyd, David Parkin, Michael Stanley-Baker, Koen Stroecken, Katherine Swancutt, and, in particular, Carla Nappi and Inge Daniels who alerted me to recent debates in the philosophy of science and the study of material culture.

Notes

1. The project began in the third year after the master's course in medical anthropology had been instituted at the University of Oxford, where, between January and March 2003, the editors organized a research seminar series on 'Plants, Health and Healing', to which Françoise Barbira Freedman, Sir John Grimley Evans, Michael Heinrich and Caroline Weckerle contributed. Wenzel Geissler and Ruth Prince joined later. Michael Heinrich's contribution has since been published online (Heinrich 2005).

2. For anthropologists, Brian Morris's (1997) definition of 'realism', as opposed to the 'idealism' of the strong cultural constructivist programme, suffices here: 'Realism entails the view that material things exist independently of human sense experience and cognition' (p.318). In philosophy, realism often has a bad press, particularly 'naïve realism' (Cardinal et al. 2004:88). An exception is Latour (1999), who calls himself a 'realistic realist'. The multiple meanings of 'realism' and 'empiricism' will require more nuanced definitions (see note 14 below).

3. Ethnomedicine is not as troubled by the social modes of scientific/medical knowledge production as medical anthropology has been since its inception (see section 'Disease, Illness, Sickness and Local Biologies' in this chapter). Within public health, ethnomedical and applied research certainly have their merits. However, medical anthropologists find it difficult to engage with the preoccupations of ethnomedical researchers because of the latter's continued adherence to a rather ethnocentric social analytic toolkit.

4. A researcher interested in a realist interpretation (which needless to say is impossible to give with any certainty for such an ancient text and which therefore relies on educated guesswork) may be interested to know that

ticks, which attach themselves to the soft tissue of the anus and are full of blood, exude a red liquid (see Hsu, chapter 2 in this volume).

5. Farquhar and Lock (2007) refer to 'Cartesian common sense' and 'bourgeois common sense' in a derogatory way, which makes the notion of 'common sense' appear extremely reactionary, but Gramsci was, in fact, more nuanced and ambivalent.

6. The notion of empiricism is discussed in note 14 below.

7. Epistemology is a field of philosophy interested in how knowledge is generated, whereas ontology is a field of philosophy interested in questions of what constitutes 'being'. Both are buzz words in anthropology, with accordingly vague meanings.

8. Ethnomedicine, like ethnobotany, is far less concerned with epistemological and ontological questions.

9. Although Kleinman's (1980) concept of disease as a universal biological substratum, onto which was grafted illness as a culture-specific experience, should overcome racist science, it is difficult not to read a deprecating tone into his analysis of the illness experience: 'In Chinese culture, suppression, lack of differentiation, minimization, displacement and somatic substitution are the dominant mechanisms employed by individuals. In the United States, expression, differentiation, vigilant focusing are the dominant cognitive coping strategies for managing affect, at least among the middle-class Caucasians' (p.172). His later writings contain important revisions of this position (e.g. Kleinman 1988).

10. The term 'realist' is used here in the wide sense in which the anthropologist Brian Morris (1997) used it (not in the philosophical sense of scientific realism, see van Fraassen 1980:7–8). Importantly, it refers here both to knowledge produced through the empirical natural sciences (grounded in an empiricist stance towards perception and theory) and to knowledge derived from the experience of immersing oneself in the world (as posited by the phenomenologist stance on perception).

11. Plasmodium malariae Feletti and Grassi causes the 'quartan', i.e. four-day fever cycles; Plasmodium vivax Feletti and Grassi is known as the 'benign tertian' because it produces fevers in cycles of three days, without being lethal; and Plasmodium falciparum Welch causes the 'malignant tertian' which can be fatal.

12. A) Parasite factors: malaria is caused by four different Plasmodium species (Plasmodium ovale Stephens, in addition to the three mentioned in note 11 above), each of which has a distinctive geographic and ecological distribution. Within each Plasmodium species, there is strain variation, whereby some strains are more pathogenic than others to certain humans. B) Host factors: human blood types and haemoglobin variants can have a large influence on the expression of the disease; a well-known example is

sickle-cell anaemia which is protective of malaria. C) Environmental factors: in regions where malaria is endemic, adults whose immune system allowed them to survive childhood present with flu-like symptoms, joint pains and anaemia. In environments with relatively fewer infected mosquitoes and low malaria transmission rates, cases of morbidity and their severity rises disproportionately compared to places where transmission rates are higher. D) Co-morbidity: depending on other infections, the immune response may be weakened, and hence the sickness may manifest more severely. Furthermore, it appears that malaria facilitates a wide range of other infections, so that in some areas deaths secondary to malaria (indirect malaria mortality) can be at least as great as mortality directly attributed to malaria (cf. Warrell and Gilles 2003).

13. Nevertheless, the biomedical establishment currently favours genetic research at the expense, for instance, of epidemiological research on environmental factors (Doll, quoted in Darby 2003:378).

14. 'Empiricism is not a single, specific philosophical position' (van Fraassen 2002:13), and it is used in such different ways that one is inclined to avoid the term. However, since the words 'empiricist' and 'realist' occur in anthropological polemics, and this essay concerns the relation between the natural world of plants and our engagement with them, a footnote on the term 'empiricism' is warranted, even if it comes across as dilettante. One generally understands empiricists to adopt the cherished attitude of deriving rules of practice from observation and experience of the natural world. However, the notion of empiricism in the 'empiricist postulate' I mention can be more narrowly defined. It is a definition, though, as van Fraassen (2002:34) emphasizes, which arises from a position of the late nineteenth century that favoured Kant's transcendental idealism: historians of philosophy then created a narrative which pitted the rationalists on the continent against the empiricists on the British Isles, before Kant came onto the scene and demonstrated that they were equally mistaken. Leibniz was the rationalist who considered concepts to be derived from innate ideas (a marble block); Locke, the empiricist, argued that they derived from sense data: sensations were thought in the course of our experiencing the world to furnish the blank slate (*tabula rasa*) that is our mind (van Fraassen 2002:34). This 'empiricist' postulate that sense stimuli give rise to perceptions, which in turn lead to concept formation, continues to be the main paradigm in empirical psychology, and it is this aspect of empiricism, in particular, that is questioned here.

In the seventeenth century, the Enlightenment empiricists who set the foundations for this model of how sensation affects perception and cognition claimed philosophical superiority over the 'realists', whom they considered to be conservative adherents of the Aristotelian tradition that explained regularities in nature through 'substantial forms of different natures' (van Fraassen 1980:1). Since the reasons for these observed regularities were thought to be inherent to the substantial forms of natures, philosophers who had nativist ideas were called realists (e.g. Thomas Reid). Accordingly, any biologist who attributes primacy to the genetic make-up of organisms would be a realist, although contemporary biologists adhere to an empiricist theory that denies the reality of Aristotelian causal properties. Indeed, natural scientists are Aristotelian, says Latour (1998), but for another reason: because of their epistemic insistence on the validity of knowledge production in subject-object relations. Therefore, in the twenty-first century natural scientists can usually be attacked as being both realists and empiricists, and therefore, perhaps, the two terms are easily confused. The point I wish to make is that not every realist need adhere to the empiricist postulate of perceiving the environment.

15. The term 'critical medical anthropology' is confusing because it is used by medical anthropologists who have a Marxist orientation (and who rarely question the empirical knowledge production of the natural sciences) and by medical anthropologists who draw on literary criticism (who do question empiricist modes of knowledge production). Both are 'critical' of the current order of society and aim at providing a social critique.

16. Biologists often recognize complex single Linnaean species, whilst folk taxonomies recognize many more. In some cases modern research has split single Linnaean taxa into taxa recognized by folk taxonomies, for example, in the Mexican legume genus *Leucaena* (Hughes 1998) and in the Costa Rican skipper butterfly *Astraptes* (Hebert et al. 2004).

17. He hints at the possibility that serial analogies may provide the clue to the problem (Lienhardt 1954:106).

18. The research Ellen invokes in support of this is by anthropologists whose main contributions are either outside ethnobiology or went beyond it: Fox (1971), Rosaldo (1972), Ellen (1993), Healey (1993), Rival (1998).

19. Research presented at the conference 'Economies of Fortune and Luck: Perspectives from Inner Asia and Beyond' on 5–7 June 2008 made clear to medical anthropologists not merely how normative the term 'health' is but, worse still, how impoverished their conceptual toolkit is for accounting for differences in health status.

20. Van der Geest and Whyte (1989) focus on drugs as things but their discussion centres on meaning: the metaphoric and metonymic meanings of being 'thingy'. An exception is perhaps to be found in research on indigenous notions of compatibility (e.g. *hiyang*) between drugs and individual bodies, which relates the perceived materiality of medicines to sociality (e.g. Hardon 1994).

21. Empiricist psychophysicists of the nineteenth century applied sensory stimuli to the skin in order to identify sense receptors and their distribution. These physical structures were then thought to correspond to different sensations of touch (but this assumption has proved to be untenable in the light of the skin's many different tactile perceptions). The phenomenologists' research on 'active touch' went diametrically against the view that stimuli are impressed on sense organs. As a result, the Pacinian corpuscles, whose anatomical structure had long been known without the psychophysicists being able to identify their function, were found to be receptors of vibration, which is a sensation/perception caused by movement and 'active touch' (see Hsu 2000:261–63, and references therein).

22. Gibson's ideas have direct resonances with David Katz's stress on the importance of the hand's movements for tactile perception, but Gibson's bibliography suggests that he came to his conclusions independently. Leder (1990:17) remarks that many phenomenologists, among them Erwin Straus, noted that 'the classical distinction between perception and movement is in fact highly artificial, dividing in reflection what is always united in lived experience'.

23. Frontal eyes are generally thought to have evolved in predators for 'depth perception', but precisely because none of the experiments on depth perception for selecting suitable pilots in the Second World War predicted their success or failure in the real world, Gibson started to design experiments that led him in entirely new directions. The evolutionary advantage of frontal eyes is thus less 'depth perception' than 'self-awareness'. (If one takes Gibson's idea further, frontal perception may have evolved in predators, like cats, because it was an advantage for them to have greater self-awareness during the hunt. Primarily for this reason of greater self-awareness, it may have been further developed in social animals, like primates.)

24. The affordances of the environment are what frontal vision offers the animal, what it provides or furnishes, either for good or ill. Gibson's notion of affordances comes strikingly close to Straus's observation that things may be either 'alluring' or 'frightening', and either attract or repulse the perceiver, but Erwin Straus is not mentioned in Gibson's bibliography.

25. The notion of 'surfaces', which features so centrally in Gibson's theory, is reminiscent of the vocabulary of phenomenologists. However, again, Gibson's bibliography indicates no debt to phenomenology.

26. Naturally, it is difficult for an anthropologist without any appropriate training to appreciate the writings of any philosopher of the Enlightenment period, such as Reid's *Inquiries into the Human Mind on the Principles of Common Sense* (1764) and *Essays on the Intellectual Powers of Man* (1785). No claim can be made that his own ideas are accurately presented here. For this, with regard to his theory of perception, see for instance Nichols (2007).

41

This essay draws on select contemporary philosophers, whose comments on Reid's writings were most inspiring for developing the argument that common sense is a form of doing (a situation-specific form of social action in which humans interact with aspects of the environment, such as with plants as recognized, prepared, applied and appreciated in medical practice, in unmediated, but enskilled ways).

27. Does this suggest that the realist position is not without logical problems? Can an idealist argue in a logically more consequential way? It leads to conclusions, however, that Reid found at odds with common sense (Van Cleve 2004:104).

References

Atran, S. 1990. *Cognitive Foundations of Natural History: towards an Anthropology of Science*. Cambridge: Cambridge University Press.

Bellman, B.L. 1975. *Village Curers and Assassins: on the Production of Fala Kpelle Cosmological Categories*. The Hague: Mouton.

Berlin, B. 1992. *Ethnobiological Classification: Principles of Categorization of Plants and Animals in Traditional Societies*. Princeton: Princeton University Press.

Berlin, B., D.E. Breedlove and P.H. Raven. 1974. *Principles of Tzeltal Plant Classification: an Introduction to the Botanical Ethnography of a Mayan-speaking People of Highland Chiapas*. New York: Academic Press.

Berlin, E.A. and B. Berlin. 1996. *Medical Ethnobiology of the Highland Maya of Chiapas, Mexico*. Princeton: Princeton University Press.

Blacking, J. 1977. 'Towards an Anthropology of the Body', in J. Blacking (ed.), *The Anthropology of the Body*. London: Academic Press, pp. 1–28.

Bourdieu, P. [1972] 1977. *Outline of a Theory of Practice*. Cambridge: Cambridge University Press.

——— [1979] 1984. *Distinction: a Social Critique of the Judgement of Taste*. London: Routledge.

Boyer, P. 1996. 'What makes Anthropomorphism Natural: Intuitive Ontology and Cultural Representations', *Journal of the Royal Anthropological Institute* 2: 1–15.

Cardinal, D., G. Jones and J. Hayward et al. 2004. *Epistemology: the Theory of Knowledge. (Philosophy in Focus)*. Philadelphia: Transatlantic Publ.

Chrisholm, R.M. 1998. 'Commonsensism', in E. Craig (ed.), *Routledge Encyclopedia of Philosophy*. London: Routledge.

Crehan, K. 2002. *Gramsci, Culture and Anthropology*. London: Pluto Press.

Csordas, T.J. 1994. *Embodiment and Experience: the Existential Ground of Culture and Self*. Cambridge: Cambridge University Press.

——— 2002. *Body/Meaning/Healing*. New York: Palgrave Macmillan.

Darby, S. 2003. 'A Conversation with Sir Richard Doll', *Epidemiology* 14: 375–79.

Daston, L. and P. Galison. 2007. *Objectivity*. New York: Zone Books.

Desjarlais, R.R. 1996. 'Presence', in C. Laderman and M. Roseman (eds), *The Performance of Healing*. London: Routledge, pp. 143–64.

Diamond, J.M. 1966. 'Zoological Classification System of a Primitive People', *Science* 151: 1102–04.

Ellen, R. 1993. *The Cultural Relations of Classification: an Analysis of Nuaulu Animal Categories from Central Seram*. Cambridge: Cambridge University Press.

———— 2006. 'Introduction', in R. Ellen (ed.), *Ethnobiology and the Science of Humankind. Special Issue. Journal of the Royal Anthropological Institute*: S1–S22.

Empson, R. 2007. 'Separating and Containing People and Things in Mongolia', in A. Henare, M. Holbraad and S. Wastell (eds), *Thinking Through Things: Theorising Artefacts Ethnographically*. London: Routledge, pp. 113–40.

Engelke, M. 2005. 'Sticky Subjects and Sticky Objects: the Substance of African Christian Healing', in D. Miller (ed.), *Materiality*. Durham: Duke University Press, pp. 118–39.

Etkin, N.L. 1996. 'Ethnopharmacology: the Conjunction of Medical Ethnography and the Biology of Therapeutic Action', in C.F. Sargent and T.M. Johnson (eds), *Medical Anthropology: Contemporary Theory and Method*. Revised Edition. Westport: Praeger, pp. 151–64.

———— 2006. *Edible Medicines: an Ethnopharmacology of Food*. Tuscon: University of Arizona Press.

———— and M.L. Tan. 1994. *Medicines: Meanings and Contexts*. Quezon City, Philippines: Health Action Information Network.

———— and P.J. Ross. 1991. 'Recasting Malaria, Medicine and Meals: a Perspective on Disease Adaptation', in L. Romanucci-Ross, D.E. Moerman and L.R. Tancredi (eds), *The Anthropology of Medicine*. New York: Praeger, pp. 130–58.

Farquhar, J. and M. Lock. 2007. 'Introduction', in M. Lock and J. Farquhar (eds), *Beyond the Body Proper: Reading in the Anthropology of Material Life*. Durham: Duke University Press, pp.1–16.

Foster, G.M. and B.G. Anderson. 1978. *Medical Anthropology*. New York: John Wiley.

Foucault, M. [1963] 1976. *The Birth of the Clinic: an Archaeology of Medical Perception*. London: Routledge.

Fox, J.J. 1971. 'Sister's Child as Plant: Metaphors in an Idiom of Consanguinity', in R. Needham (ed.), *Rethinking Kinship and Marriage*. London: Tavistock, pp. 219–52.

Frake, C.O. 1961. 'The Diagnosis of Disease among the Subanun of Mindanao', *American Anthropologist* 63: 113–32.

Frankenberg, R. 1980. 'Medical Anthropology and Development: a Theoretical Perspective', *Social Science and Medicine* 14B: 197–207.

Gell, A. [1992] 1999. 'The Technology of Enchantment and the Enchantment of Technology', in E. Hirsch (ed.), *The Art of Anthropology: Essays and Diagrams*. London: Athlone Press, pp. 159–86.

Gibson, J.J. 1986. *The Ecological Approach to Visual Perception*. Hillsdale, NJ: Lawrence Erlbaum Associates.

Good, B. 1977. 'The Heart of What's the Matter', *Culture, Medicine and Psychiatry* 1: 25–58.

——— 1994. *Medicine, Rationality and Experience: an Anthropological Perspective*. Cambridge: Cambridge University Press.

Gosden, C. 1994. *Social Being and Time*. Oxford: Blackwell.

——— 2007. 'Holism, Intelligence and Time', in D. Parkin and S. Ulijaszek (eds), *Holistic Anthropology: Emergence and Convergence*. Oxford: Berghahn, pp. 182–93.

Gramsci, A. 1971. *Selections from the Prison Notebooks*. Edited by Q. Hoare and G.N. Smith. London: Laurence and Wishart.

Grasseni, C. 2007. 'Introduction', in C. Grasseni (ed.), *Skilled Visions: Between Apprenticeship and Standards*. New York: Berghahn, pp. 1–19.

Green, E.C. 1999. *Indigenous Theories of Contagious Disease*. Walnut Creek: Altamira Press.

Hardon, A.P. 1994. 'People's Understanding of Efficacy for Cough and Cold Medicines in Manila, the Philippines', in M.L. Tan and N.L. Etkin (eds), *Medicines: Meanings and Contexts*. Quezon City: Health Action Information Network, pp. 47–67.

Healey, C. 1993. 'Folk Taxonomy and Mythology of Birds of Paradise in the New Guinea Highlands', *Ethnology* 32: 19–34.

Hebert, P.D.N. et al. 2004. 'Ten Species in One: DNA Barcoding Reveals Cryptic Species in the Neotropical Skipper Butterfly *Astraptes Fulgerator*', *Proceedings of the National Academy of the USA* 101: 14812–17.

Heinrich, M. 2005. 'Safety of Traditional Remedies, in Ethnopharmacology', in E. Elisabetsky and N.L. Etkin (eds), *Encyclopaedia of Life Support System (EOLSS)*. Oxford: EOLSS Publishers.

Hinton, D.E., D. Howes and L.J. Kirmayer. 2008. 'Editorial', in D.E. Hinton, D. Howes and L.J. Kirmayer (eds), *The Medical Anthropology of Sensations. Special Issue. Transcultural Psychiatry* 45: 139–41.

Holbraad, M. 2007. 'The Power of Powder: Multiplicity and Motion in the Divinatory Cosmology of Cuban Ifá (or *Mana*, Again)', in A. Henare, M. Holbraad and S. Wastell (eds), *Thinking Through Things: Theorising Artefacts Ethnographically*. London: Routledge, pp. 189–225.

Hsu, E. 2000. 'Towards a Science of Touch, Part I: Chinese Pulse Diagnostics in Early Modern Europe', *Anthropology and Medicine* 7: 251–68.

——— 2002. 'Medical Anthropology. Material Culture, and New Directions in Medical Archaeology', in P.A. Baker and G. Carr (eds), *Practitioners, Practices, and Patients*. Oxford: Oxbow, pp. 1–15.

——— 2009. 'Diverse Biologies and Experiential Continuities: Did the Ancient Chinese Know that *qinghao* had Antimalarial Properties?', in F. Wallis (ed.), *Medicine and the Soul of Science: Essays by and in Memory of*

Don Bates. *Special Issue. Canadian Bulletin of Medical History* 26 (1): 203-13.

——— and C. Low. 2008. *Wind, Life, Health: Historical and Anthropological Approaches*. Oxford: Blackwell.

Hughes, C.E. 1998. *Monograph of Leucaena (Leguminosae - Mimosoideae)*. Ann Arbor, Michigan: American Society of Plant Taxonomists.

Hunn, E.S. 1977. *Tzeltal Ethnozoology: the Classification of Discontinuities in Nature*. New York: Academic Press.

Ingold, T. 2000a. *Perception of the Environment: Essays in Livelihood, Dwelling and Skill*. London: Routledge.

——— 2000b. 'Making Culture and Weaving the World', in P. Graves-Brown (ed.), *Matter, Materiality and Modernity Culture*. London: Routledge, pp. 50–71.

——— 2007. Materials against Materiality. Archaeological Dialogues 14 (1): 1-16.

Jobling, M.A., M.E. Hurles and C. Tyler-Smith. 2004. *Human Evolutionary Genetics*. New York: Garland.

Kleinman, A. 1980. *Patients and Healers in the Context of Culture: an Exploration of the Borderland between Anthropology, Medicine and Psychiatry*. Berkeley: University of California Press.

——— 1988. *Rethinking Psychiatry: from Cultural Category to Personal Experience*. New York: Macmillan/ Free Press.

Lambek, M. 1998. 'Body and Mind in Mind, and Body and Mind in Body: Some Anthropological Interventions in a Long Conversation', in M. Lambek and A. Strathern (eds), *Bodies and Persons: Comparative Perspectives from Africa and Melanesia*. Cambridge: Cambridge University Press, pp. 103–23.

Last, M. 1981. 'The Importance of Knowing about Not Knowing', *Social Science and Medicine* 15B: 387–92.

Latour, B. 1999. *Pandora's Hope: Essays on the Reality of Science Studies*. Cambridge: Harvard University Press.

——— 2000. 'When Things Strike Back: a Possible Contribution of 'Science Studies' to the Social Sciences', *British Journal of Sociology* 51: 107–23.

Lave, J. 1988. *Cognition in Practice: Mind, Mathematics and Culture in Everyday Life*. Cambridge: Cambridge University Press.

Leder, D. 1990. *The Absent Body*. Chicago: University of Chicago Press.

Lewis, G. 1975. *Knowledge of Illness in a Sepik Society*. London: Athlone.

Lienhardt, G. 1954. 'Modes of Thought', in E.E. Evans-Pritchard (ed.), *The Institutions of Primitive Society: a Series of Broadcast Talks*. Oxford: Basil Blackwell, pp. 95–107.

Lienhardt, P. 1968. *The Medicine Man: Swifa Ya Nguvumali by H. bin Ismail*. Oxford: Oxford University Press.

Lindenbaum, S. and M. Lock. 1993. *Knowledge, Power, and Practice: the Anthropology of Medicine and Everyday Life*. Berkeley: University of California Press.

Littlewood, R. and M. Lipsedge. 1982. *Aliens and Alienists: Ethnic Minorities and Psychiatry.* 3rd edition. London: Routledge.

Lloyd, G.E.R. 2007. *Cognitive Variations: Reflections on the Unity and Diversity of the Human Mind.* Oxford: Oxford University Press.

Lock, M.M. 1993. *Encounters with Aging: Mythologies of Menopause in Japan and North America.* Berkeley: University of California Press.

Luedtke, T. 2007. 'Spirit and Matter: the Materiality of Mozambican Prophet Healing', *Journal of Southern African Studies* 33: 715–31.

Madden, E.H. 1986. 'Was Reid a Natural Realist?', *Philosophy and Phenomenological Research* 47: 255–74.

Mauss, M. [1934] 1973. 'Techniques of the Body', *Economy and Society* 2: 70–88.

McElroy, A. and P.K. Townsend. 2004. *Medical Anthropology in Ecological Perspective.* 4th edition. Boulder: Westview Press.

Merleau-Ponty, M. [1945] 1962. *Phenomenology of Perception.* London: Routledge.

Miller, D. 2005. 'Materiality: an Introduction', in D. Miller (ed.), *Materiality.* Durham: Duke University Press, pp. 1–50.

Moerman, D. 2002. *Meaning, Medicine and the 'Placebo Effect'.* Cambridge: Cambridge University Press.

Mol, A. 2002. *The Body Multiple: Ontology in Medical Practice.* Durham: Duke University Press.

Morris, B. 1997. 'In Defence of Realism and Truth: Critical Reflections on the Anthropological Followers of Heidegger', *Critique of Anthropology* 17: 313–40.

Needham, R. 1972. *Belief, Language and Experience.* Oxford: Basil Blackwell.

Nichols, R. 2007. *Thomas Reid's Theory of Perception.* Oxford: Oxford University Press.

Nichter, M. and M. Lock. 2002. *New Horizons in Medical Anthropology.* London: Routledge.

Nichter, M. and M. Nichter. 1996. *Anthropology and International Health: Asian Case Studies.* Amsterdam: Gordon and Breach.

Panofsky, E. 1957. *Gothic Architecture and Scholasticism.* London: Thames and Hudson.

Parkin, D. 1995. 'Latticed Knowledge: Eradication and Dispersal of the Unpalatable in Islam, Medicine and Anthropological Theory', in R. Fardon (ed.), *Counterworks: Managing the Diversity of Knowledge.* London: Routledge, pp. 143–63.

Pelling, M. 1993. 'Contagion/ Germ Theory/ Specificity', in W.F. Bynum and R. Porter (eds), *Companion Encyclopaedia of the History of Medicine.* London: Routledge, pp. 309–34.

Pool, R. 1994. 'On the Creation and Dissolution of Ethnomedical Systems in the Medical Ethnography of Africa', *Africa* 64: 1–20.

Reid T. 2002. *Essays on the Interllectual Powers of Man.* Edinburgh: Edinburgh University Press.

——— 2002. *An Inquiry into the Human Mind: on the Principles of Common Sense*. University Park: Pennsylvania State University Press.

Rival, L. 1998. *The Social Life of Trees: Anthropological Perspectives on Tree Symbolism*. Oxford: Berg.

——— 2006. 'Amazonian Historical Ecologies', in R. Ellen (ed.), *Ethnobiology and the Science of Humankind. Special Issue. Journal of the Royal Anthropological Institute*: S79–S94.

——— 2007. 'Domesticating the Landscape, Producing Crops and Reproducing Society in Amazonia', in D. Parkin and S. Ulijaszek (eds), *Holistic Anthropology: Emergence and Convergence*. Oxford: Berghahn, pp. 72–90.

Rosaldo, M.Z. 1972. 'Metaphors and Folk Classification', *Southwestern Journal of Anthropology* 28: 83–100.

Scheper-Hughes, N. and M.M. Lock. 1987. 'The Mindful Body: a Prolegomenon to Future Work in Medical Anthropology', *Medical Anthropology Quarterly* 1: 6–41.

Seremetakis, N.C. 1998. 'Durations of Pain: a Genealogy of Pain', in J. Frykman et al. (eds), *Identities in Pain*. Lund: Nordic Academic Press, pp. 151–68.

Stalder, F. 2000. 'Beyond Constructivism: towards a Realistic Realism. A Review of Bruno Latour's *Pandora's Hope*', *The Information of Society* 16(3): 245-47.

Sugishita K. 2006. 'Transgression for Transcendence?: on the Anthropologist's (Dis)engagement in the Politics of Meaning', in U. Rao and J. Hutnyk (eds), *Celebrating Transgression: Method and Politics in Anthropological Studies of Culture*. Oxford: Berghahn, pp. 53-70.

Tambiah, S.J. 1968. 'The Magical Power of Words', *Man* 3: 175–208.

Taussig, M.T. 1980. 'Reification and the Consciousness of the Patient', *Social Science and Medicine* 14B: 3–13.

Tilley C. unpubl. Materiality in Materials. (Response to Ingold, no date). 3 p.

Ulijaszek, S. 2007. 'Bioculturalism', in D. Parkin and S. Ulijaszek (eds), *Holistic Anthropology: Emergence and Convergence*. Oxford: Berghahn, pp. 21–51.

Van Cleve, J. 2004. 'Reid's Theory of Perception', in T. Cuneo and R. van Woudenberg (eds), *The Cambridge Companion to Thomas Reid*. Cambridge: Cambridge University Press, pp. 101–33.

van der Geest, S. and S. Whyte. 1989. 'The Charms of Medicines: Metaphors and Metonyms', *Medical Anthropology Quarterly* 3: 345–67.

van Fraassen, B.C. 1980. *The Scientific Image*. Oxford: Oxford University Press.

——— 2002. *The Empirical Stance*. New Haven: Yale University Press.

Waldstein, A. and C. Adams. 2006. 'The Interface Between Medical Anthropology and Medical Ethnobiology', in R. Ellen (ed.), *Ethnobiology and the Science of Humankind. Special Issue. Journal of the Royal Anthropological Institute*: S95–S118.

Warrell, D.A. and H.M. Gilles. 2002. *Essential Malariology*. 4th edition. London: Hodder Arnold.

Whitehead, A.N. 1920. *The Concept of Nature*. Cambridge: Cambridge University Press.

Whyte, S. R., S. van der Geest and A. Hardon. 2003. *Social Lives of Medicines*. Cambridge: Cambridge University Press.

Wolterstorff, N. 2004. 'Reid on Common Sense', in T. Cuneo and R. van Woudenberg (eds), *The Cambridge Companion to Thomas Reid*. Cambridge: Cambridge University Press, pp. 77–100.

Young, A. 1976. 'Internalizing and Externalizing Medical Belief Systems: an Ethiopian Example', *Social Science and Medicine* 10: 147–56.

———— 1982. 'The Anthropologies of Illness and Sickness', *Annual Review of Anthropology* 11: 257–85.

———— 1995. *The Harmony of Illusions*. Princeton: Princeton University Press.

HISTORY
Editorial Introduction
Stephen Harris et al.

Despite the central role of plants in our health and happiness, we largely overlook them. Landscapes apparently devoid of humans or other mammals, although teeming with plant life, are regularly dismissed as barren. Yet plants often have long histories of associations with man. Beyond the role of plants as fuel, shelter and food, humans discovered how to harness plant chemistry as medicine. Ethnobotany, the study of the interactions between humans and plants, is integral to human natural history.

The value of different medicinal plants to different cultures must have been discovered on numerous occasions and that knowledge passed from generation to generation. Furthermore, as humans investigated their environments and moved plants around, such information may have been transported with the plants, not revealed, left behind, forgotten, ignored or new information discovered. As medicinal plants were moved between different contexts, the cultural and social frameworks in which they were used may have varied, leading to differing indigenous and non-indigenous responses to these plants. Medicinal plants, and the indigenous knowledge about them, are cultural and biological assets. However, today, such knowledge is widely known to have an explicit commercial value within a framework created by the tension between scientific and anthropological approaches to ethnobotany.

The importance of medicinal plants means they may be moved as humans migrate. Furthermore, humans may learn to use non-native plants. The relationships between humans and non-native plants are complex, often confounded by social, political, as well as medicinal needs. Concerns over the use of non-native plants are associated with the separation of use and knowledge and the influence on drug efficacy. These concerns may be played out in entire countries or empires, or in individual communities or families.

In his article 'Non-Native Plants and Their Medicinal Uses', Stephen Harris brings a botanical point of view to the issue of plants as human medicines and takes a broadly-based historical perspective to consider the means by which plants have been moved accidentally and deliberately by humans. A case study of the famous antimalarial quinine, isolated from the bark of the Andean tree *Cinchona*, illustrates how important medicinal plants can be as they are moved by humans from the wild in their region of origin to areas of cultivation where they might be more easily protected, controlled and exploited. However, this case study emphasizes that users of a plant may be separated from the people that have traditional knowledge of it and hence may misunderstand the plant. Correct identification, and understanding of the variation within a medicinal plant species, is crucial to understanding its basic biology and how to use it most effectively.

Historical knowledge about plants, particularly in Western cultures, has usually been investigated through the examination of manuscript and printed sources. However, such investigations rarely involve detailed, comparative, scholarly analyses of the sources. Irrespective of the difficulties of correlating names in such documents with modern plant names, the process is potentially flawed since it is biased; it largely ignores traditional knowledge. The knowledge contained in such sources is that of the literate, yet much traditional knowledge is likely to have been held by peoples with an oral tradition. This 'unrecorded' knowledge about medicinal plants is easily lost or only recorded piecemeal and out of context, leading to value knowledge being dismissed as 'old wives' tales' or ignored.

The article on '*Qing hao* 青蒿 (Herba *Artemisiae annuae*) in the Chinese *Materia Medica*', which Elisabeth Hsu wrote after several consultations with one of the few specialists of Chinese pharmacotherapy, Frédéric Obringer, and with the assistance of several Chinese scholars who cracked some difficult translation problems, discusses transformations of cultural practices involving similar plant materials. She highlights the fact that the Chinese herbal drug *qing hao*, which today has been proven to contain the highly effective anti-malarial artemisinin, was not initially considered for acute fever episodes. She demonstrates that early texts recommended it for the treatment of festering wounds caused by weapons or parasites (presumably as an antiseptic) or as a food additive, that it was not merely hailed for its fragrance, but also for its appetite-enhancing and vitality-engendering qualities. However, thousand years after its earliest known records, *qing hao* gained prominence within the genre of the *materia medica* as a remedy against intermittent fevers. Hsu explains these different recommendations in the light of how the plant was prepared. She argues against the concept of 'natural herbs' and emphasizes that herbal remedies are cultural artefacts which humans developed in close interaction with other humans and the plant materials. Although Hsu emphasizes that plants are prepared and consumed in culturally specific practices, she concludes her article, just like Harris, by stressing the importance of plant taxonomy and the insights it provides about the plant's qualities which must remain of foremost interest also to the social and cultural anthropologist.

1. Non-Native Plants and Their Medicinal Uses

Stephen Harris

Humans rely on plants for food, medicine, shelter, energy and beauty. Bread wheat is the product of ten thousand years of domestication. The Egyptian *Ebers Papyrus* (c. 1550 BCE) refers to knowledge of medicinal plants that dates back to at least 3000 BCE. Substances extracted from hallucinogenic plants have enabled man to encounter his gods. Wood and coal have been humans' primary sources of shelter and energy. The beauty of plants has inspired the transformation of landscapes. The scientific investigation of plants and their conservation has been justified, and is still justified, by the explicitly anthropocentric objectives of medicine and agriculture (Wilson 1988, Groombridge 1992).

Historically, the investigation of plants has been approached from two, often diametrically opposed, viewpoints: the philosophical and the applied. In Western culture, the philosophical approach to botany had its origin in Greece, particularly the work of Aristotle (384–322 BCE) and Theophrastus (370–285 BCE), although much of Greek botanical philosophy only survived beyond the European mediaeval period in Arabic culture (Morton 1981). The collection of facts about plants was relegated to applied studies, particularly early medicine. For almost 1,500 years, the work of the Greek Dioscorides (c. 40–90 CE) held sway in Europe as the ultimate source of practical knowledge on medicinal plants (Morton 1981), used by the gatherers of medicinal plants. The reputations of herbalists and druggists were poor because of the manner in which they surrounded their crafts in superstitions and mysteries, for example, the rigmarole associated with harvesting mandrake (*Mandragora officinarum*; Thompson 1934). Even Theophrastus ridiculed such superstitions in *Enquiry into Plants*.

Plants, and the biologically active compounds that they contain, have always been an important part of medicine, whether in heterodox or orthodox systems. The plants that are used may be indigenous to an area, or man may introduce plants into an area accidentally or deliberately; the latter types of plants are defined as non-native.[1] Native and non-native plants (whatever their mode of introduction) have historically always been used side-by-side, whether as food or as medicines. An indication of the importance of introduced species is provided by the case of wheat, a native of the Middle East, yet today one of the world's major cereal crops.

When lists of medicinal plants in *materia medica* have been prepared, there has been a tendency to either overlook non-native species in favour of native ones or else not recognize them as non-native.[2] Some authors have explicitly recognized that non-native species are an important component of *materia medica* (e.g. Hu 1990, Summer 2000). Parrotta (2001) detailed 545 plant species used in the Indian medical traditions of Ayurveda, Siddha and Unani. About thirty per cent of the species were not native to India in historical or prehistorical times. In a smaller investigation of medicinal plants used in the Assam (India), Dilip and Bikash (2003) cited medicinal plants that included the guava (*Psidium guajava*[3]), native to the New World, and onion (*Allium cepa*) and garlic (*Allium sativum*), both from northern temperate regions. Hutchen (1992), in an analysis of native American herbs, describes 124 species of which approximately forty-four per cent are non-native to North America (e.g. *Arnica montana* from Europe, *Eucalyptus* from Australia and *Taraxacum* from the Old World).[4] In a dictionary of African traditional medicine (Neuwinger 2000), containing many hundreds of species, there are examples of species introduced to Africa being used, e.g. orange, (*Citrus x aurantium*) from Asia, passion flower (*Passiflora foetida*) from the New World, *Mirabilis jalapa* from the New World, and groundsel (*Senecio vulgaris*) from north temperate regions. Similarly, poisons from introduced plants are used in Africa, for example, extracts of *Capsicum* and *Nicotiana* as fish poisons (Neuwinger 1996).[5] The neem tree (*Azadirachta indica*), which is native to India, is widely exploited in Africa for purposes ranging from an anti-malarial and the cure of skin ulcers and syphilitic sores to a pesticide (Neuwinger 2000). In a listing of the Chinese *materia medica*, Hu (1990) identified eighty-nine non-native species in a *materia medica* of many thousands of species (Hu 1980). The non-native species included *Acacia catechu* from tropical Asia, *Aquilaria* from South East Asia, *Carica papaya* from South America and *Ricinus communis* from Africa.[6] In a survey of Luo mothers, undertaken near Lake Victoria (Kenya), Geissler et al. (2002) recorded eighty plant species used in medical remedies, of which fifteen per cent were non-native, e.g. *Melia azedarach* (native to South Asia), *Thevetia peruviana* (native to the New World) and *Psidium guajava*.

Many non-native species are used in similar ways to the species in its native range. However, some introduced species find alternative uses in their non-native ranges. For example, *Hypericum perforatum* (native to Europe, western Asia and North Africa) has become very popular as a mild anti-depressant, although this property was first noticed in its non-native range. In Europe, there are few records of *Hypericum perforatum* having traditional uses as an anti-depressant (Allen and Hatfield 2004: 104–106).

The occurrence of non-native plants in *materia medica* is not a recent phenomenon. The *Ebers Papyrus* (Ebbell 1937), describes some 150 identifiable species, including non-native species to Egypt (e.g. *Boswellia* sp., *Aloe* sp.). The Assyrian herbal of King Asshur-bani-pal (reigned 699–626 BCE) includes names of some 200 species of which 140–150 can be identified with reasonable confidence; included in this list are examples of non-native species, e.g. rice (*Oryza*) from southeast Asia, *Commiphora* probably from Arabia, turmeric (*Curcuma longa*) probably from India (Thompson 1949).[7]

Theophrastus (300 BCE) discusses Greek medicinal plants in *Enquiry into Plants*, including introduced medicines such as Cinnamon and Cassia (*Cinnamomum* species) and *Papaver somniferum*. In Rome, Pliny provides details of the medicinal plants used (Jones 1951, 1956), although this was derived mainly from Greek authors. Greek pharmacology was incorporated into Dioscorides' *Materia medica*, a compilation of hundreds of entries that includes examples of introduced species being used, including *Piper nigrum* (pepper) from India, *Ferula persica* from the Middle East, and *Boswellia carteri* (frankincense) from East Africa (Gunther 1934).

In western Europe, from the Roman period until the late seventeenth century, one of the main sources of knowledge about medicinal plants was the herbal.[8] The majority of these herbals were based on Dioscorides' work, which had an enormous hold on the medical imagination for many hundreds of years (Arber 1986). However, the herbal tradition became corrupted by continual copying of errors from earlier sources, and the insistence that northern Europe plants could be equated with the plants described by Dioscorides from the Mediterranean and more distant lands (Arber 1986). Thus, the printed herbal became increasingly remote from real plants, with many of those described being either unidentifiable or fantastical.[9]

In European medicine, apothecaries and pharmaceutical chemists delivered plant-based medicines directly to the user (Holloway 1991). For example, in early seventeenth century Europe, Peruvian bark (*Cinchona* species), was in great demand as a cure for malaria, and efforts were made both to protect the quality of the imported bark and the secret of its preparation (Hobhouse 1999). The sale of the Peruvian bark 'secret' to Louis XIV, in 1679, made the Cambridge quack Richard Talbor a very rich man. Talbor's secret was that he had bought all the best Peruvian bark in England and served the ground powder in wine. He had recognized that in order for it to be effective as a cure for malaria, Peruvian bark had to be from the correct source and the active ingredients had to be dissolved. For most of the twentieth century, in the U.K. at least, the link between plants and medicine was less obvious. By the end of the century, there was a resurgence of general awareness of plants as a potential source of medicinal compounds, whether through the perception that orthodox medicine was failing, that heterodox medical systems existed, that plant products could be a commercial asset or as a justification for biodiversity conservation. Statistics associated with the use of natural products in modern medicine are impressive, for example, in 1993 more than half of prescriptions in the U.S. contained at least one major component that was either derived or synthesized from a natural source (Grifo et al. 1997). Furthermore, ten Kate and Laird (1999) estimate that forty-two per cent of sales of the top-selling drugs worldwide were natural products or natural product derivatives. Of approximately 120 pharmaceutical products derived from plants, about seventy-five per cent were discovered through the study of traditional medicinal use (Farnsworth et al. 1985).

In 1985, Farnsworth and Soejarto made an astounding claim; over \$8 billion was spent in community pharmacies in the U.S.

on prescription medicines and about twenty-five per cent of these medicines contained active principles extracted from just forty angiosperm species,[10] of which only three (*Podophyllum peltatum, Rhamnus purshiana, Veratrum viride*) were native to North America. Farnsworth and Soejarto's estimate did not include the so-called 'botanical medicines', i.e. those plants not recognized as official drugs by the Federal Drug Administration (58 species) or those that were components of 'herbal teas' (*c.* 300 species).[11]

The focus of this paper is non-native, i.e. introduced, plants ('the footprint of colonization') and their use as medicines. Firstly, a case study of the anti-malarial *Cinchona* will be presented in order to illustrate how important introduced species can be as medicinal plants. Following this the definition of non-native plants will be considered, together with the means by which plants can be moved, both accidentally and deliberately. The reasons for the importance for the distinction between native and non-native are considered, together with an argument for the importance of accurate identification in medicinal ethnobotany.

Cinchona – a Case Study of a Medicinal Plant Introduction

Quinine, traditionally one of the most valuable medicines in western Europe, was, until it was artificially synthesized in 1945, extracted from the bark of the Peruvian bark[12] tree (*Cinchona*). The myth of the discovery of quinine is a familiar one. In 1638, the Condesa de Chinchón was dying from an intermittent fever (malaria) in Lima, and, in desperation, a Jesuit priest suggested that the Viceroy might try an indigenous remedy that he had used successfully (Honigsbaum 2001),[13] although whether the indigenous people of the region knew about the bark as a febrifuge is disputed (Haggis 1942, Jaramillo-Arango 1949, Brockway 1979). The bark proved effective, the Condesa recovered, and following her return to Spain, the story became widespread and the rush for Peruvian bark started (Honigsbaum 2001). Indeed, the genus from which the bark was derived, *Cinchona*, was named by Linnaeus (1753) in honour of the Condesa, although he made an orthographic error with her name. For over a century, very little was known about the tree from which the bark came, there was dispute over its efficacy as a malaria treatment and prejudice with regard to its application.[14]

The genus *Cinchona* is essentially Andean, with only one widespread species reaching the mountains of southern Central America and the coastal range of Venezuela (Andersson 1998). Taxonomically, the genus has a notorious reputation, with more than 330 names published for the 23 species currently recognized. Despite the genus being monographed four times during the nineteenth century (Lambert 1821, de Candolle 1830, Weddell 1849, Kuntze 1878), there was no consensus over nomenclature or detailed information about *Cinchona* biology, especially for the species that produced quinine; the primary quinine alkaloid-producing species are *Cinchona pubescens* and *Cinchona calisaya*. Until the mid-nineteenth century, the only supplies of the raw bark were from diverse sources (and hence species) in the New World (Markham 1880). Both the British and Dutch were concerned about bark supply and funded major programmes to collect, often illegally, seed for cultivation in India and Indonesia, respectively. However, the sheer complexity of the taxonomy and the paucity of detailed information make the early literature on *Cinchona* cultivation and quinine production difficult to interpret unambiguously.

European, and particularly British, justifications for the introduction of Peruvian bark outside of its native range has always been stated in terms of the need to conserve the resource and intervene in the apparently wasteful practices used in the Andes for harvesting *Cinchona* (Anonymous 1931), where mature trees were felled to collect the bark. Hooker (1839), the son of the Director of Kew, made clear that coppicing was the most appropriate method for maintaining productivity and promoting growth of *Cinchona*. This seems to have been overlooked by his father, when the scheme for introducing *Cinchona* to British India was promoted (Brockway 1979). Other indicators, such as the fact that the Andean Republics exported *c.* 900,000 kg of bark in 1860, might also have indicated that *Cinchona* was not on the verge of extinction (Markham 1862). The search of Peruvian bark is an evocative story (e.g. Duran-Reynals 1946, Taylor 1943, Honigsbaum 2001, Markham 1880, Rocco 2003) but, for current purposes, it is necessary only to highlight the main themes. The primary users (Europeans) of quinine were separated from their source of supply, which led to actions being taken that

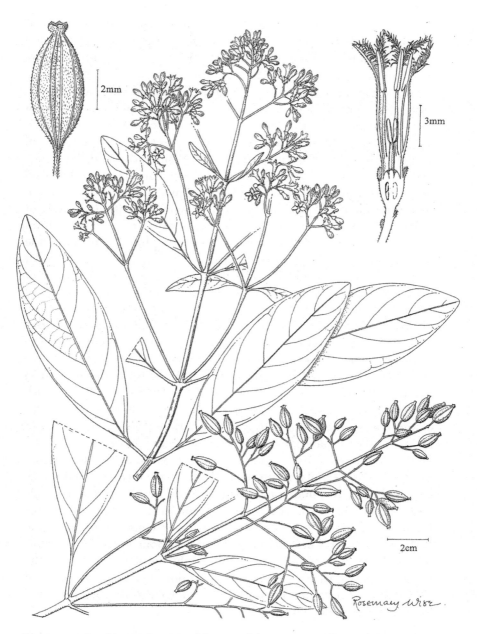

2mm

3mm

2cm

Rosemary Wise.

Figure 1.1: *Cinchona calisaya* Wedd., one of the commercially important sources of quinine. This species is highly variable and shows complex patterns of variation. Pen and ink drawing by Rosemary Wise

had, at best, dubious legality. Furthermore, poor understanding of the biology of the genus and its complex patterns of variation led to a poor understanding of both the taxonomy of the genus and the active principles.

Numerous adventurers and scientists went to the New World, either independently or sponsored by European powers, to search for *Cinchona* and bring material back for cultivation. However, only three expeditions, those of Hasskarl, Spruce and Ledger, will be highlighted here to illustrate the problems faced and the issues raised. In 1853, the Dutch botanist Justus Charles Hasskarl arrived on the Peruvian-Bolivian border, disguised as a German businessman, searching for *Cinchona* and illegally procured plants and seeds of *C. calisaya*; the plants died but the seeds were transferred to Java. However, they grew poorly and contained very little active principle (c. 0.4 per cent). In contrast, *C. calisaya* collected by the botanist Hugues Algernon Weddell in 1851 from Bolivia contained five per cent active principle.[15] In 1860, the Amazonian explorer Richard Spruce, collected seeds and plants of *Cinchona pubescens* from Ecuador at the behest of the civil servant and explorer Charles Markham, after securing the rights to collect the seeds from the local landowner (Spruce 1908). This material was dispatched to Kew and, in 1861, 463 healthy plants reached India for establishment in plantations (Markham 1880). Following problems associated with climatic conditions and disease, the trees grew and became a source of quinine in India until the early twentieth century.[16] The other major source of material was the businessman Charles Ledger, who in 1865 obtained a forty pound bag of *Cinchona calisaya* seeds from Bolivia. This material was offered to the British who turned it down as they had their own material growing in India. The Dutch grudgingly took one pound of the seed and transported it to Java, where they found that it contained up to thirteen per cent active principle. Ledger had illegally collected his material in Bolivia, since the export of *Cinchona* was a Government monopoly. Similarly, efforts by the British, after Spruce's successful expedition, to collect in parts of Ecuador were not encumbered by the knowledge that material was being illegally collected (Markham 1880).

> It was stated to me that the Government of Ecuador[17] has passed an edict prohibiting the exportation of either seeds or plants of the quina tree, under the penalty of 100 dollars for every plant, and for every drachm[18] of

seed. However, after consulting with Mr Mocatta,[19] I undertook to go to Loxa and make a collection of seeds of the C. Condaminea.[20]

Letter from Robert Cross to Secretary of State for India, dated 9 November 1861 (PBB 1852-1863)

In *Cinchona* bark, there are four important biologically active compounds (quinidine, cinchonidine, quinine, cinchonine), which are together known as quinine alkaloids (Camp 1949). There are great differences in the levels of these compounds in bark across the range of the genus, within populations of a species and even within the same tree. Such differences may have been responsible for the arguments over the efficacy of Peruvian bark when it was first introduced to Europe. Different sources of the bark, whether from species or populations, had different amounts of active principle, and, in the absence of extract standardization, it was impossible to predict the efficacy of a particular bark extract. This was one of the reasons behind the complex taxonomy that grew in the genus; individuals with slightly different morphology and levels of active principles were given different names. Quinine content appears to be one reason why Ledger's collections were so successful; they contained more alkaloids than any other material being grown.

The difficulties of growing non-native species can also be great, particularly if conditions (e.g. climate or soil) are not correct or if disease breaks out; this was the experience of the British when trying to establish Spruce's collections in India (Brockway 1979, Anonymous 1931). The establishment of plantations in India was limited by problems such as the wrong seed being planted, the climatic conditions (rainfall and soil) being wrong and the presence of parasites. In addition to these biological problems, there also seem to have been political and personality clashes among the main protagonists in the introduction (Honigsbaum 2001).

The case of Peruvian bark raises three general issues that are common to the use of non-native plants:

i.   The users of a resource may be separated from the people that maintain traditional knowledge of it (e.g. Europeans misunderstood why indigenous peoples used coppicing).[21] This may mean that the user does not use or grow the resource in the most effective way, or the resource may be exploited without any benefits being passed back to the holder of the traditional knowledge. This has implications for intellectual property rights and associated benefit-sharing.[22]

ii. Correct identification and an understanding of a plant's basic biology is crucial (e.g. the complex taxonomy of the genus *Cinchona*), together with knowledge of how to prepare products from it most effectively, since closely related species may produce different qualities and quantities of active principles.

iii. Intraspecific variation may be important in the plant's cultivation and for the efficacy of its products, since within a species plants from different parts of its range may have amounts of active principle (e.g. variation in *Cinchona* alkaloid levels).

What is a Non-Native Plant?

Clearly, if one is to focus on non-native plants then it is necessary to be able to separate them from native plants. In some cases, the task is a simple one. For example, the chilli pepper (*Capsicum annuum*) is found in the Old World but it is clearly non-native, since the genus' natural distribution is restricted to the New World (Heiser 1995). Furthermore, if one excludes the possibility of pre-Columbian contact between the Old and New Worlds, this species must have been introduced after 1492. However, in other cases the situation is much more uncertain. Deadly nightshade (*Atropa belladonna*), an important source of atropine, is considered native over much of the British Isles but appears to be introduced in some areas because of cultivation (Preston et al. 2002). Common ragwort (*Senecio jacobaea*), which is widely cited in early herbals for the relief of rheumatic pains, is common over much of the British Isles as a native of sand dunes; however, the grassland habitat in which it is common today is the result of introduction through agriculture (Harper and Wood 1957).

Thus, the definition of a non-native plant is associated with what is meant by the term 'native' and what is understood by both the pattern and the process of introduction. In the context of Europe, and specifically the British Isles, a native is defined as 'one which evolved in the U.K. or arrived before the beginning of the neolithic (c. 10,000 BP)' (Preston et al. 2002). Unfortunately, without clear criteria for the determination of native status, an observer can be misled. *Agave americana* is found commonly throughout the Mediterranean region and gives every appearance of being native. However, the genus is of New World origin and *Agave americana* was introduced in the region into Spain around 1492 whence it spread throughout the Mediterranean (Sauvaigo 1899).

The problem of the identification of introductions has a long history and was clearly presented by de Candolle (1886). De Candolle emphasized the difficulty of separating native from non-native since it was necessary to combine the skills of the botanist, archaeologist, palaeontologist, historian and philologist. Webb (1985) proposed eight criteria that could be applied to the definition of nativity, based on fossil and historical evidence, ecological and geographical data, patterns of reproduction and genetic diversity, and frequencies and methods of known introductions. It is rare that all these sources of information are available and for there to be absolute proof that a species is introduced. Of course, if one produces a hypothesis that a species is introduced then it is important that there is a mechanism of introduction (Cronk and Fuller 2001). The problem becomes all the more difficult when one considers the case of floras that are less well known than that of the European flora, when the introduction events are ancient or potentially frequent and when migration distances are short.

The problem of ancient events and deciding whether a species is introduced or native is illustrated by tamarind (*Tamarindus indica*). The name would suggest, as Linnaeus believed, that this species comes from India but it is also found in eastern Africa. Theophrastus made the earliest western records of *Tamarindus indica* from Bahrain (Hort 1916), but the species is apparently native to tropical Africa, whence it was introduced to Asia by Arab traders in prehistoric times (National Academy of Sciences 1979). However, the evidence is equivocal, with authors suggesting a native distribution in Africa (e.g. Dalziel 1937) or Africa, Arabia and western India (Irvine 1961), whilst others (e.g. Verdcourt 1979) suggest that it is indigenous to Africa and India. The problem of trying to decide upon the native range is compounded by *Tamarindus* being a monotypic[23] genus with no close extant relatives.

There are at least two distinct steps when one considers an introduced species: the physical process of the introduction and the consequences of that introduction. Consider the case of the opium poppy (*Papaver somniferum*), a source of opiates, which was introduced into the British Isles as a painkiller. The introduction was deliberate, human-mediated and has occurred on many occasions since the Roman occupation (Purseglove 1968). *Papaver somniferum* is now widely cultivated in gardens and escaped across much of the U.K. (Preston et al. 2002), although it is regarded as a casual.[24] Other introduced plants that are used for medicinal purposes, such as horse chestnut (*Aesculus hippocastanum*) which was introduced in the sixteenth century (Lack 2000), forms stable populations which are maintained in their own right and have effectively become naturalized.[25]

How are Plants Moved?

Humans may move plants deliberately or accidentally; animals and diseases may be moved in similar manners (Crosby 1986). Generally, the deliberate movement of a plant has some economic (e.g. *Triticum aestivum* from the Near East to the rest of the world) or social (e.g. *Rhododendron ponticum* from Turkey into the U.K.) benefit, whilst accidental movement is usually an unforeseen consequence of other activities, such as man's animals (e.g. *Senecio inaequidens* from South Africa to Europe in wool) or his means of transport (e.g. *Plantago major* from Europe entered North America by ship soon after settlement started in the early 1600s). The easiest way for plants to be moved from one place to another is as seeds but other routes are possible[26] (Ridley 1930).

The last century has seen the development from the mere recording of these so-called botanical 'carpet baggers', to an understanding of how they spread and interact with local floras. Large numbers of species can be introduced; for example, Hayward and Druce (1919) recorded 348 species growing around a wool processing factory in Scotland, whilst at a similar factory near Montpellier, more than 500 non-native species were recorded (Thellung 1912). Similarly, wars may move large numbers of species, for example, during the Franco-Prussian war a 'siege flora' of grasses and legumes from southern France and Algeria developed around Paris (Sykora 1990). Williamson (1996) has estimated that about ten per cent of introductions will become naturalized, and of these ten per cent are likely to cause ecological damage. It is naturalized species, and those which are cultivated, that are often of interest as medicinal plants, since they often colonize habitats that are associated with man, e.g. road side margins and waste ground.

Common plants are used for the treatment of day-to-day conditions (Geissler et al. 2002). Except in the case of 'special' medicines, rare plants tend not to be used.[27] An example of a plant that has been very successful as one of these introductions is *Plantago major*, or the 'White-man's footprint' as it came to be known among Native Americans. This species has spread to most regions of the world with suitable climates. Furthermore, *Plantago major* has been incorporated into local medical practice in its introduced range; for example, the seeds and husk are used for gastric complaints in Himachal Pradesh (India) (Chauhan 1999), North America (Hutchen 1992) and China (Hu 1980).

Deliberate plant movements were occurring in the Ancient World. In 1495 BCE, the Egyptian Queen Hatchepsut[28] sent a team to the land of Punt[29] for frankincense (*Boswellia* spp.; Naville 1898); this is the first known government-sponsored plant collecting expedition. Other classical sojourns to introduce plants include the Assyrian Sargon (reigned 722–705 BCE) who created parks specifically to grow non-native plants (Morton 1981). Furthermore, conquest brought not only the 'carpet-baggers' but also many unknown or underutilized species. Thus, following the Roman Conquest of Britain, trees, such as figs and apples, were introduced to bring 'variety, charm, colour and usefulness' (Lemmon 1968: 2). The movement of cultivated apples by the Romans is a more complex story involving the Greek, Central Asian and Chinese cultures (Juniper and Mabberley 2006).

In the Middle Ages, plants from the Middle East were introduced to European monastery gardens following the Crusades, e.g. *Cydonia oblonga* and *Saponaria officinalis* (Lemmon 1968). In the same period, the economic and medicinal value of products, such as pepper (*Piper nigrum* and *Piper longum*), cinnamon (*Cinnamomum*) and nutmeg (*Myristica fragrans*),[30] meant that there was a great stimulus to introduce these plants beyond their native ranges, again to maintain supply (Purseglove 1968). Much of the early interest involved the maintenance of trade routes from the West to the East. However, the establishment of botanic gardens led to significant changes in the institutional organization for deliberate plant introduction.

Initially, these gardens were a means for surgeons to have access to, and control over, the sources of their medicines (Brockway 1979, Rickett 1956). By 1545, there were gardens at Padua, Florence and Pisa, and by 1621 at Leiden, Leipzig, Montpellier, Heidelberg and Oxford. The surgeons of Louis XIII were responsible for the formation of the *Jardin des Plantes* in Paris in 1635, and the Physic Garden in Edinburgh (later the Royal Botanic Garden) was established in 1690. However, by the eighteenth century, the king of Spain explicitly recognized the economic imperative of introduced plants when he engaged Hipólito Ruiz and José Pavon to explore Peru (Dahlgren 1940). Similarly, other European colonial powers recognized the strategic importance of plant resources for food and medicines and increased their interests through the establishment of botanic gardens in the tropics (Brockway 1979). For example, following the establishment of the Royal Botanic Garden Kew in 1759, gardens were established in St. Vincent (1766), Jamaica (1779), Calcutta (1787) and Penang (1796). Such gardens had key roles in the transfer of tung oil (*Aleurites*) seeds, ipecacuanha (*Psychotria ipecacuanha*), coffee (*Coffea*), rubber (*Hevea brasiliensis*) and tea (*Camellia sinensis*) (Smartt and Simmonds 1995). Furthermore, the increasing importance of horticulture, particularly in seventeenth-century Europe, saw the establishment of the Royal Horticultural Society in 1804 by Joseph Banks and John Wedgewood, the original aim being to collect both useful and ornamental plants (Juma 1989).

One of the greatest limitations to the deliberate introduction of species was transportation technology. Plants often had to remain alive for very long periods in the hostile environment of a ship at sea, as there were no means of high-speed transportation. In 1823, Nathaniel Bagshaw Ward, an amateur naturalist and general practitioner from the dockland of East London, made the necessary transportation breakthrough; the Wardian Case[31] (Ward 1852). Before the Wardian Case, approximately ninety-nine per cent of plants imported to the U.K. from China were lost; after the Wardian Case losses were reduced to fourteen per cent (Brockway 1979). It is said that Hooker imported into Kew six times as many exotics in fifteen years as had been sent in the previous century, and enabled the British to move economically important plants into her colonies (Brockway 1979).

Does it Matter to a User Whether a Medicinal Plant is Native or Introduced?

Plants vary morphologically and chemically across their ecological ranges and may vary from season to season (Briggs and Walters 1997). These differences may be due to the plant's genotype[32] or may be the product of the interaction between the genotype and the environment.[33] Thus, plants from the same area may look similar but produce very different levels of active principles. If a plant in its native range has a large geographical or ecological range, then the importance of variation in genotype and environment can have consequences for the introduction and utilization of a species. These simple issues of genetic and environmental variation lead to two reasons about why it is important to be concerned whether a medicinal plant is native or not.

Firstly, it has already been pointed out that plants may be introduced deliberately or accidentally, and introductions may occur from a native area or an area where the plant has been previously introduced. In each of these cases, introduction involves a sample of a species' total genetic variation. That is, genetic variation is reduced in the introduced population compared to the native population. Although this issue appears rather esoteric for users of introduced medicinal plants, it is crucial and has been recognized for years by agriculturalists (Frankel et al. 1995), particularly with respect to the problem of disease resistance among introduced species.

Deliberate, planned introductions may involve plants that are best adapted to a particular part of the introduced area and usually are associated with how the plant can be utilized. However, as has been shown in the case of *Cinchona*, serendipity over the choice of introduced material, in the absence of detailed knowledge, is important; the quantity and quality of quinine alkaloids in *Cinchona* varied in different parts of the native range. Historically, pharmacists have expended much effort in obtaining plant material from specific regions of the world, in order to ensure that drugs were of a consistent and reliable quality (Jackson 1965). For example, Greenish (1929) describes in detail the best sources and times of collection of such drugs as *Aconitum napellus*. Nevertheless, deliberate introduction is no guarantee that a particular plant will be utilized by people in the introduction area.

In contrast, accidental introduction is likely to mean that the introduced material could have come from any part of the species' natural range. Furthermore, in the introduced range, knowledge of the medicinal properties of the species may be acquired from the native area or by comparison with species that are already used. In the former case, the randomness of the introduction may mean that the introduced species has reduced (or no) activity compared to the native range. If knowledge of the plant's medicinal uses is derived '*de novo*', then it probably does not matter if the plant is introduced.

Secondly, the use of introduced plants means that the supply of medicinal plants can be ensured, albeit at the risk of poor yields of the active principles or the probability of disease eradicating the species. This was recognized by Hatchepsut (Harlan 1992) and was an important factor in introducing tea from China to India (Watt 1908) and rubber from Brazil to Sri Lanka (Jackson 2008). At a more local level, a plant that is cultivated in a garden is available for most of the year, hence the development of monastic and botanic gardens.

The points are well illustrated in the case of the story of Peruvian bark discussed earlier. Successful exploitation of Peruvian bark by the British and the Dutch in their respective colonies illustrates the importance of variation, knowledge and supply in relation to non-native plants. The *Cinchona* seeds (with their high alkaloid content) that were sampled in Bolivia by Ledger, using knowledge provided by the indigenous Bolivian Manuel Incra Mamani,[34] were grown in Java (where access to the supply could be maintained). These plantations were the basis of the Dutch quinine monopoly until 1939. In the post-war years, synthetic anti-malarials have become important for the prevention and cure of malaria and the value of extracts from *Cinchona* bark diminished.

The Importance of Accurate Identification

Research into medicinal plants, whether introduced or native, requires that one has access to accurate identifications. The medicinal plant literature is full of lists of species that apparently have some medicinal value. Yet the value of these lists is often diminished by lack of information, such as a reference to voucher material,[35] details of where the material was collected, which parts of the plants are used, and how the material was harvested and prepared. Due to the genetic and environmental variation, just because a species is claimed to have a medicinal property, it is no guarantee that the sample collected will have those properties.

Voucher material of medicinal plants becomes important if the differences between species are subtle, meaning that accurate identification is difficult. This may be especially true for introduced plants, which may be unfamiliar. For example, Chauhan (1999) produced a list of rare medicinal plants in Himachal Pradesh (India), which contained at least eighteen introduced species. This list is significant for two reasons. Firstly, definitive records of difficult to identify species, such as *Chenopodium album*, *Mentha arvenis* and *Thymus serpyllum*,[36] are given without apparent reference to critically identified herbarium material. Secondly, these introduced species were rare. A general impression is that non-native species are common and that they are often weeds. Rare medicinal plants often attract the concern of biologists interested in conservation, yet as Chauham (1999) has shown rare plants may be introduced and of much less conservation concern than endemic species. Therefore, before decisions are made in the context of medicinal plant conservation, it is important to ascertain both the identity of the plant and whether it is native or non-native. The anthropologist would greatly enhance the value of their work if the botanical material that they collected were treated with the same care and rigour that is applied to other information that they collect. Martin (1995) and Alexiades (1996) give details of the preparation of plant material for identification and permanent deposit in botanical collections. Furthermore, ethnobotanists also have a responsibility to ensure that publication of their data does not compromise the intellectual property rights of their informants, since publication may decouple traditional knowledge and access to information.

Conclusion

Plants have been moved between areas for thousands of years, both accidentally and deliberately. Many of these unplanned experiments, both deliberate and accidental, have failed, although some have been spectacularly successful. Non-native species have been incorporated into *materia medica* from around the world, and this trend continues. However, the importance of non-native plants in indigenous *materia medica* has not been appreciated. It is important to understand the extent of non-native species used in a *materia medica* because: (i) users of a medicinal plant may be separated from the people that maintain the traditional knowledge of it, especially if the introduction event was accidental; (ii) intraspecific variation may be important for the plant's cultivation and for the efficacy of its products; and (iii) correct identification and an understanding of a plant's basic biology are crucial for its effective use.

Anthropologists should be encouraged to collect ethnobotanical data in a rigorous manner and to consider the routes by which the plants utilized by indigenous cultures have come to be where they are. In this way, important new insights may be obtained as to how information about plants is acquired.

Notes

1. Crosby (1986) gives an account of the impacts of species introduced from temperate regions into the tropics and the effects these had on indigenous peoples.
2. Lists of medicinal plants have been produced for across the world. However, in many there is little critical evaluation of either the plant identification or information that is presented regarding use. Such problems limit potentially useful traditional knowledge about medicinal plants. Furthermore, there are entire groups of organisms for which traditional medicinal knowledge is either absent or exceedingly limited, e.g. bacteria, fungi and marine organisms.
3. An appendix of all the scientific names mentioned in the text, together with their family, common names and native area, is provided at the end of the chapter.
4. Hutchen (1992) illustrates an additional issue in current and past *materia medica*; the confusion generated by common names and the absence of recognised synonymies (Morton 1981). In Hutchen's (1992) entry on *Castanea dentata*, this scientific name is equated with the common names Chestnut, American Chestnut, Spanish Chestnut, Horse Chestnut and Sweet Chestnut and the species is claimed to have a distribution of North America, Western Asia and southern Europe. *Castanea dentata* (American Chestnut) is native to North America; it does not have a European or Asian distribution. The other common names cited are applied to the European

and Asian species *Castanea sativa* (Chestnut, Spanish Chestnut, Sweet Chestnut) or *Aesculus hippocastanum* (Horse Chestnut), a species unrelated to *Castanea*.

5. *Nicotiana* is an example of one of the most successful poisons that has been transported worldwide and assimilated into most cultures.

6. Hu's (1990) list underestimates the number of non-native species used in the Chinese *materia medica* of Hu (1980). For example, non-native species such as *Acacia senegal* (native to Africa), *Plantago major* (native to temperate Europe and Asia), *Tussilago farfara* (native to temperate Europe and Asia), *Laurus nobilis* (native to the Mediterranean), *Digitalis purpurea* (native to temperate Europe and Asia) and *Tagetes erecta* (native to the New World) are excluded. Hu (1990) provides a fascinating insight into the movement of medicinal plants into China between 100 CE and 1840, and indicates that at least one non-native species was incorporated in the Chinese *materia medica* every twenty years during this period.

7. Matching ancient plant names with modern plant names is problematic in the absence of either good illustrations or actual specimens. Most identifications in ancient manuscripts have been based on philological evidence and/or information about the plant uses.

8. An herbal is a document containing the names and descriptions of herbs, or plants in general, together with their properties and uses.

9. The modern herbal first appeared in 1530 with the publication of Otto Brunfels' *Herbarum vivae eicones*. Whilst the text was second-rate and typical of the botany of the time, Hans Weiditz's naturalistic woodcut illustrations were a revelation. It is clear that Brunfels never studied the plants he mentioned in the field, and indeed appeared not to realise that floras varied from region to region. In contrast, Weiditz had studied plants in the field. In Bock's *New Kreütter Buch* (1539) it is clear that the author had made direct observations of the plants about which he wrote. In Fuchs' *De historia stirpium* (1542), the best parts of Brunfels' and Bock's works were fused to produce a masterpiece comprising about 500 plants growing in Germany, including maize (*Zea mays*), introduced from the New World.

10. For example, European *Digitalis* species, Asian *Papaver somniferum*, *Carica papaya*, *Cinchona* species, *Colchicum autumnale*, *Plantago* species, *Rauvolfia serpentina*, *Rheum* species and *Ricinus communis*.

11. Of the fifty-eight species not recognized as official drugs by the FDA, eighty-eight per cent were introduced, for example, *Acacia senegal*, *Cinnamomum camphora*, *Melaleuca quinquenervia* and *Olea europaea* (Farnsworth and Soejarto 1985). The species native to North America cited by Farnsworth and Soejarto (1985), include *Arctostaphylos uva-ursi*, *Hamamelis virginiana* and *Populus balsaminifera*.

71

12. Numerous common names have been applied to the source of quinine, including Fever bark, Jesuits' bark, Spanish bark, Bark of barks and Indian bark. The common name 'Peruvian bark' will be used here, despite the most efficacious sources of bark not coming from Peru.

13. Honigsbaum (2001) is one of the best single introductions to the complex history of *Cinchona* and its cultivation. Markham (1880) gives a fascinating account of the issues associated with the introduction of quinine, as they were perceived by one of the main architects of the introduction of *Cinchona* into British India. Spruce (1908) provides an exceptional account of the difficulties of collecting *Cinchona* seed in Ecuador. Brockway (1979) discusses the role of the Royal Botanic Garden at Kew in the introduction of *Cinchona* to British India.

14. Disputes over the efficacy of *Cinchona* were associated with the problem that barks from different parts of the *Cinchona* distribution have different amounts of compounds effective against malaria and the high price of the bark encouraged adulteration. Prejudice over the use of *Cinchona* was based on its association with Jesuits and the general prejudice against Catholics, especially in Britain and northern Europe. Indeed, legend has it that Oliver Cromwell, Lord Protector during the British Commonwealth, refused Jesuits' Bark as a cure for his, ultimately fatal, malaria, because it was a 'Popish remedy' (Honigsbaum 2001).

15. 7,000 plants were raised from Weddell's seeds in Java but all the effort went into propagating nearly one million plants from Hasskarl's seeds. It was only realised later that a mistake had been made over which material to propagate (Honigsbaum 2001: 119).

16. The official records of the introduction of *Cinchona* to India are contained in the Parliamentary Blue Books (published by the Her Majesty's Stationery Office) from 1852 to 1870. These provide a fascinating insight into the difficulties of introducing a high-profile economic species to an area outside its native range. Markham (1862) provides an early, if self-aggrandising, account of the same events. The Indian plantations gradually fell into ruin as manufactures preferred to important Peruvian bark from Java because of its higher content of active principles.

17. A law was introduced in May 1861 that made it illegible to export *Cinchona* plants.

18. A drachm is a measure of weight equal to approximately 3.9 gram. In the case of *Cinchona*, this corresponds to approximately 1,400 seeds.

19. The British vice-consul.

20. The modern name is *Cinchona officinalis*.

21. A management practice where the tree is cut close to its base and regrowth is promoted. This practice is applied to a very wide range of species and was well known to Europeans, for example, for the management of hazel.

Coppicing became a management tool used by the British in their Indian plantations (Honigsbaum 2001).

22. The commercialization and patenting of plant-derived medicinal products has been the focus of much international debate (ten Kate and Laird 1999), especially since the Convention on Biological Diversity recognized the rights of indigenous and local communities to benefit from their traditional knowledge.

23. A monotypic genus is a genus that contains only a single species.

24. A casual species does not form stable and persistent populations in the British Isles, and new populations must be re-established from time to time.

25. A naturalised species is one that is introduced to an area but grows and lives as if it is a native.

26. Non-seed routes for plant introduction include plant fragments that can root and bulbs (i.e. asexual methods).

27. The use of rare plants in medicine is a particular concern of conservationists concerned with medicinal plants, and plant conservation efforts are often broadly justified in terms of the potential for the discovery of new medicinal plants (Groombridge 1992).

28. The exploits of the leader of the expedition, General Neshi, are recorded in friezes at the temple of Deir el-Bahri (Naville 1898).

29. The exact location of Punt is unclear but it is probably the Horn of Africa (Naville 1898).

30. The long-term consequences of British and Dutch involvement in the nutmeg trade were immense. Run, the only island in the Banda Islands which had nutmeg, was finally exchanged by the British for the fledgling Dutch Colony of Long Island, New York, in 1667. The nutmeg trade from the Moluccas was eventually destroyed by the introduction of nutmeg to other parts of the tropics and the British lost the American War of Independence (Milton 1999).

31. A Wardian Case is essentially a closed box with glazed sides that protects the plant from unfavourable conditions and allows light in. If the box is well made, then a humid climate is created inside that enables seedlings or cuttings to grow. Ward (1852: 87) saw a role for his cases in 'their application to the relief of the *physical* and *moral* wants of densely crowded populations in the large cities'. The Wardian case was to become part of the Victorian and Edwardian house as the terrarium (Allen 1984).

32. The genotype is the genetic constitution of an individual.

33. The interaction of genotype and environment produces the phenotype, that is, the overall appearance of the plant. For example, if two plants with identical genotypes are grown in different environments, for example, at high and low altitudes, there may be differences in the overall appearance

of the plant (phenotype) that can only be associated with the environment in which they were grown.

34. Mamani was beaten to death in 1877, apparently for his part in Ledger's illegal export of *Cinchona* seed.

35. Voucher material is a plant specimen that is pressed, dried and permanently deposited in a herbarium (collection of dried plants). These specimens provide the link between the material that the author saw in the field, the name applied and the conclusions drawn in the paper. Good practice demands that voucher specimens are always prepared. Permanent collections also provide a means of identifying medicinal plants known only from partial material, e.g. stems, flowers or seeds.

36. Species in the genera *Chenopodium*, *Thymus* and *Mentha* are difficult to identify due to morphological variation and hybridization. However, correct identification of the species level is important since the medicinally active principles vary from species to species (especially in *Mentha* and *Thymus*).

References

Alexiades, M.N. 1996. *Selected Guidelines for Ethnobotanical Research: a Field Manual*. New York: New York Botanical Garden.

Allen, D.E. 1984. *The Naturalist in Britain: a Social History*. Princeton: Princeton University Press.

—— and G. Hatfield. 2004. *Medicinal Plants in Folk Traditions. An Ethnobotany of Britain and Ireland*. Cambridge: Timber Press.

Andersson, L. 1998. *Memoirs of the New York Botanical Garden. Vol. 80. A Revision of the Genus Cinchona (Rubiaceae-Cinchoneae)*. New York: The New York Botanical Garden.

Anonymous. 1931. 'Introduction of *Cinchona* to India', *Kew Bulletin of Miscellaneous Information* 1931: 113–17.

Arber, A. 1986. *Herbals*. Cambridge: Cambridge University Press.

Briggs, D. and S.M. Walters. 1997. *Plant Variation and Evolution*. Cambridge: Cambridge University Press.

Brockway, L.H. 1979. *Science and Colonial Expansion. The Role of the British Royal Botanic Gardens*. New Haven: Yale University Press.

Camp, W.H. 1949. '*Cinchona* at High Altitudes in Ecuador', *Brittonia* 6: 394–430.

Chauhan, N.S. 1999. *Medicinal and Aromatic Plants from Himachal Pradesh*. New Delhi: Indus Publishing Company.

Cronk, Q.C.B. and J.L. Fuller. 2001. *Plant Invaders: the Threat to Natural Ecosystems*. London: Earthscan Publications Ltd.

Crosby, A.W. 1986. *Ecological Imperialism. The Biological Expansion of Europe, 900–1900*. Cambridge: Cambridge University Press.

Dahlgren, B.E. 1940. *Travels of Ruiz, Pavon and Dombey in Peru and Chile (1777–1778)*. Chicago: Field Museum of Natural History.

Dalziel, J.M. 1937. *The Useful Plants of West Africa*. London: The Crown Agents for the Colonies.

de Candolle, A.P. 1830. *Prodromus Systematis Naturalis Regni Vegetabilis 4*. Paris: Treuttel and Würtz.

———— 1886. *Origin of Cultivated Plants*. London: Paul Trench.

Dilip, K. and D. Bikash. 2003. 'Medicinal Plants Used by the Sonowal Kacharis of Brahmaputra Valley, Assam, India', *Journal of Tropical Medicinal Plants* 4: 115–22.

Duran-Reynals, M.L.A. 1946. *The Fever Bark Tree: the Pageant of Quinine*. Garden City, New York: Doubleday and Company.

Ebbell, B. 1937. *The Papyrus Ebers. The Greatest Egyptian Medical Document*. London: Oxford University Press.

Farnsworth, N.R. and D.D. Soejarto. 1985. 'Potential Consequences of Plant Extinction in the United States on the Current and Future Availability of Prescription Drugs', *Economic Botany* 39: 231–40.

Farnsworth, N.R. et al. 1985. 'Medicinal Plants in Therapy', *Bulletin of the World Health Organisation* 63: 965–84.

Frankel, O.H., A.H. Brown and J.J. Burdon. 1995. *The Conservation of Plant Biodiversity*. Cambridge: Cambridge University Press.

Geissler, P.W. et al. 2002. 'Medicinal Plants Used by Luo Mothers and Children in Bondo District, Kenya', *Journal of Ethnopharmacology* 83: 39–54.

Greenish, H.G. 1929. *A Text Book of Materia Medica Being an Account of the More Important Crude Drugs of Vegetable and Animal Origin*. London: J. and A. Churchill.

Grifo, F. et al. 1997. 'The Origins of Prescription Drugs' in F. Grifo and J. Rosenthal J. (eds), *Biodiversity and Human Health*. Washington DC: Island Press, pp. 131-63.

Groombridge, B. 1992. *Global Biodiversity. Status of the Earth's Living Resources*. London: Chapman and Hall.

Gunther, R.T. 1934. *The Greek Herbal of Dioscorides. Illustrated by a Byzantine, A.D. 512; Englished by John Goodyer, A.D. 1655*. Oxford: University Press.

Haggis, A.W. 1942. 'Fundamental Errors in the Early History of *Cinchona*', *Bulletin of History of Medicine* 10: 586–92.

Harlan, J.R. 1992. *Crops and Man*. Madison: American Society of Agronomy.

Harper, J.L. and W.A. Wood. 1957. 'Biological Flora of the British Isles. *Senecio jacobaea* L.', *Journal of Ecology* 45: 617–37.

Hayward, I.M. and G.C. Druce. 1919. *The Adventive Flora of Tweedside*. Arbroath: T. Buncle and Co.

Heiser, C.B. 1995. 'Peppers', in J. Smartt and N.W. Simmonds (eds), *Evolution of Crop Plants*. London: Longman Scientific and Technical, pp. 449–51.

Hobhouse, H. 1999. *Seeds of Change. Six Plants That Transformed Mankind*. London: Papermac.

Holloway, S.W.F. 1991. *Royal Pharmaceutical Society of Great Britain 1841-1991. A Political and Social History*. London: The Pharmaceutical Press.

Honigsbaum, M. 2001. *The Fever Trail: the Hunt for the Cure for Malaria*. London: Macmillan.

Hooker, W.D. 1839. *Inaugural Dissertation Upon the Cinchonas, their History, Uses and Effects*. Glasgow: Glasgow University Press.

Hort, A. 1916. *Theophrastus. Enquiry into Plants. Volume 1*. London: William Heinemann.

Hu, S.-Y. 1980. *An Enumeration of Chinese Materia Medica*. Hong Kong: The Chinese University Press.

––––––– 1990. 'History of the Introduction of Exotic Elements into Traditional Chinese Medicine', *Journal of the Arnold Arboretum* 71: 487–526.

Hutchen, A.R. 1992. *A Handbook of Native American Herbs*. London: Shambhala.

Irvine, F.R. 1961. *Woody Plants of Ghana with Special Reference to Their Uses*. London: Oxford University Press.

Jackson, B. 1965. 'From Papyri to Pharmacopoeia – the Development of Standards for Crude Drugs', in F.N.L. Poynter (ed.), *The Evolution of Pharmacy in Britain*. London: Pitman Medical Publishing Company Ltd., pp. 151–94.

Jackson, J. 2008. *The Thief at the End of the World. Rubber, Power, and the Seeds of Empire*. London: Duckworth Overlook.

Jaramillo-Arango, J. 1949. 'A Critical Review of the Basic Facts in the History of Cinchona', *Journal of the Linnean Society of London* 53: 272–309.

Jones, W.H.S. 1951. *Pliny. Natural History Books 21–23*. Cambridge: Harvard University Press.

––––––– 1956. *Pliny. Natural History Books 24–27*. Cambridge: Harvard University Press.

Juma, C. 1989. *The Gene Hunters: Biotechnology and the Scramble for Seeds*. Princeton: Princeton University Press.

Juniper, B.E. and D.J. Mabberley. 2006. *The Story of the Apple*. Portland, Oregon: Timber Press.

Kuntze, C.E.O. 1878. *Monographie der Gattung Cinchona*. Leipzig: Pöschel and Treple.

Lack, H.W. 2000. 'Lilac and Horse-chestnut: Discovery and Rediscovery', *Curtis's Botanical Magazine* 17: 109–41.

Lambert, A.B. 1821. *An Illustration of the Genus Cinchona*. London: Longman.

Lemmon, K. 1968. *The Golden Age of Plant Hunters*. London: Phoenix House.

Linnaeus, C. 1753. *Species Plantarum*. Holmiae: Laurentii Salvii.

Markham, C.R. 1862. *Travels in Peru and India While Superintending the Collection of Chinchona Plants and Seeds in South America, and Their Introduction into India*. London: J. Murray.

––––––– 1880. *Peruvian Bark: a Popular Account of the Introduction of Chinchona Cultivation into British India 1860-1880*. London: J. Murray.

Martin, G.J. 1995. *Ethnobotany. A Methods Manual*. London: Chapman and Hall.

Milton, G. 1999. *Nathaniel's Nutmeg. How One Man's Courage Changed the Course of History*. London: Sceptre.

Morton, A.G. 1981. *History of Botanical Science: an Account of the Development of Botany from Ancient Times to the Present Day*. London: Academic Press.

Naville, E. 1898. *The Temple of Deir El Bahari*. London: Egyptian Exploration Society.

National Academy of Sciences 1979. *Tropical Legumes: Resources for the Future*. Washington, DC: National Academy of Sciences.

Neuwinger, H.D. 1996. *African Ethnobotany. Poisons and Drugs. Chemistry, Pharmacology and Toxicology*. London: Chapman and Hall.

———— 2000. *African Traditional Medicine. A Dictionary of Plant Use and Applications*. Stuttgart: Medpharm Scientific Publishers.

Parrotta, J.A. 2001. *Healing Plants of Peninsular India*. Wallingford, Oxon.: CABI Publishing.

PBB. 1852-1863. *Parliamentary Blue Book, Cinchona. 1852–1863*. London: Stationery Office.

Preston, C.D., D.A. Pearman and T.D. Dines. 2002. *New Atlas of the British and Irish Flora*. Oxford: Oxford University Press.

Purseglove, J.W. 1968. *Tropical Crops. Dicotyledons. Vol. 2*. London: Longmans.

Rickett, H.W. 1956. 'The Origin and Growth of Botanic Gardens', *The Garden Journal of the New York Botanical Garden* 6: 133–35, 157–59.

Ridley, H.N. 1930. *The Dispersal of Plants Throughout the World*. Ashford, Kent: L. Reeve and Co., Ltd.

Rocco, F. 2003. *The Miraculous Fever-tree. The Cure That Changes the World*. London: HarperCollins Publishers.

Sauvaigo, E. 1899. *Flora Mediterranea exotica. Enumération des plantes cultivées dans les jardins de la Provence et de la Ligurie*. Nice: Imprimerie J. Ventre et Cie.

Smartt, J. and N.W. Simmonds. 1995. *Evolution of Crop Plants*. London: Longman Scientific and Technical.

Spruce, R. 1908. *Notes of a Botanist on the Amazon and Andes: Being Records of Travel on the Amazon and its Tributaries as Also to the Cataracts of the Orinoco During the Years 1849–1864, 1817–1893 Vol. II*. London: Macmillan.

Summer, J. 2000. *The Natural History of Medicinal Plants*. Portland, Oregon: Timber Press.

Sykova, K.V. 1990. 'History of the Impact of Man on the Distribution of Plant Species', in F. di Castri, A.J. Hansen and M. Debussche (eds), *Biological Invasions in Europe and the Mediterranean Basin*. Dordrecht: Kluwer Academic Press, pp. 37–50.

Taylor, N. 1943. *Cinchona in Java: the Story of Quinine*. New York: Greenberg Publisher.

ten Kate, K. and S.A. Laird. 1999. *The Commercial Use of Biodiversity. Access to Genetic Resources and Benefit-sharing*. London: Earthscan Publications Ltd.

Thellung, A. 1912. 'La Flore Adventice de Montpellier', *Mémoire Société National Sciences Naturelle Mathématique Cherbourg* 389: 57–728.

Thompson, C.J.S. 1934. *The Mystic Mandrake*. London: Rider and Co.

Thompson, R.C. 1949. *The Assyrian Herbal*. London: Luzac and Co.

Verdcourt, B. 1979. *A Manual of New Guinea Legumes*. Lae, Papua New Guinea: Office of Forest, Division of Botany.

Ward, N.B. 1852. *On the Growth of Plants in Closely Glazed Cases*. London: John von Voorst.

Watt, G. 1908. *The Commercial Products of India*. London: J. Murray.

Webb, D.A. 1985. 'What are the Criteria for Presuming Native Status?', *Watsonia* 15: 231–36.

Weddell, H.A. 1849. *Histoire Naturelle des Quinquinas ou Monographie du genre Cinchona*. Paris: Victor Masson.

Williamson, M. 1996. *Biological Invasions*. London: Chapman and Hall.

Wilson, E.O. 1988. *Biodiversity*. Washington DC: National Academy Press.

Appendix

Table 1.1: Species, families, common names and native areas of the plants mentioned in the main text

Species	Family	Common name	Native area
Acacia catechu (L.) Willd.	Fabaceae	Catechu	South Asia to China
Acacia senegal (L.) Willd.	Fabaceae	Gum acacia	Sub-Saharan Africa
Aconitum napellus L.	Ranunculaceae	Monk's hood	Northern Europe
Aesculus hippocastanum L.	Sapindaceae	Horse chestnut	Balkans to Himalayas
Agave americana L.	Agavaceae	American agave	Southern North America and Mesoamerica
Aleurites species	Euphorbiaceae	Tung	Southern China
Allium cepa L.	Alliaceae	Onion	Mediterranean
Allium sativum L.	Alliaceae	Garlic	Mediterranean
Aloe species	Aloaceae	Aloe	Old World Tropics
Aquilaria species	Thymeleaceae	Agarwood	Indomalaysia
Arctostaphylos uva-ursi (L.) Spreng.	Ericaceae	Bearberry	Circumpolar
Arnica montana L.	Asteraceae	Arnica	Northern and Central Europe
Atropa belladonna L.	Solanaceae	Deadly Nightshade	Mediterranean
Azadirachta indica L.	Meliaceae	Neem tree	Indomalaysia
Boswellia carteri Birdw.	Burseraceae	Frankincense	Somalia
Camellia sinensis (L.) Kuntze	Theaceae	Tea	Southern and southwest China

Species	Family	Common name	Native area
Capsicum annuum L.	Solanaceae	Chili pepper	Mesoamerica
Carica papaya L.	Caricaceae	Papaya	South America
Castanea dentata (Marshall) Borkh.	Fagaceae	American chestnut	North America
Castanea sativa Mill.	Fagaceae	Sweet chestnut	Mediterranean to Caucasus
Chenopodium album L.	Amaranthaceae	Fat Hen	North temperate region
Cinchona calisaya Wedd.	Rubiaceae	Peruvian bark	Northern Andes
Cinchona officinalis L.	Rubiaceae	Peruvian bark	Northern Andes
Cinchona pubescens Vahl	Rubiaceae	Peruvian bark	Northern Andes
Cinnamomum camphora (L.) J.Presl	Lauraceae	Camphor	Southern China
Citrus x *aurantium* L.	Rutaceae	Orange	Southeast Asia and Southern China
Coffea sp.	Rubiaceae	Coffee	Ethiopia
Colchicum autumnale L.	Liliaceae	Autumn crocus	Europe to North Africa
Commiphora species	Burseraceae	Myrrh	Horn of Africa
Curcuma longa L.	Zingiberaceae	Turmeric	India-Malaysia
Cydonia oblonga Mill.	Rosaceae	Quince	Balkans to Caspian
Digitalis purpurea L.	Plantaginaceae	Foxglove	Mediterranean
Eucalyptus species	Myrtaceae	Eucalyptus	Australasia
Ferula persica Willd.	Apiaceae		Central Asia
Hamamelis virginiana L.	Hamamelidaceae	Witch hazel	North America
Hevea brasiliensis (A.Juss.) Muell.Arg.	Euphorbiaceae	Rubber	South America

Species	Family	Common name	Native area
Hypericum perforatum L.	Hypericaceae	St John's wort	Mediterranean to Central China
Laurus nobilis L.	Lauraceae	Bay tree	Mediterranean
Mandragora officinarum L.	Solanaceae	Mandrake	Mediterranean
Melaleuca quinquenervia (Cav.) S.T.Blake	Myrtaceae	Melaleuca	East Australia, southeast New Guinea, New Caledonia
Melia azedarach L.	Meliaceae	White cedar	Asia to Australia
Mentha arvensis L.	Lamiaceae	Field mint	Eurasia
Mirabilis jalapa L.	Nyctaginaceae	Marvel of Peru	Mexico
Myristica fragrans Houtt.	Myristicaceae	Nutmeg	Spice Islands
Nicotiana species	Solanaceae	Tobacco	South America
Olea europaea L.	Oleaceae	Olive	Mediterranean
Oryza species	Poaceae	Rice	Asia
Papaver somniferum L.	Papaveraceae	Opium poppy	Near East to Central Asia
Passiflora foetida L.	Passifloraceae	Passion flower	Tropical America
Piper longum L.	Piperaceae	Long pepper	Tropical East Himalayas
Piper nigrum L.	Piperaceae	Black pepper	Southeast Asia
Plantago major L.	Plantaginaceae	Common plantain	Eurasia
Podophyllum peltatum L.	Berberidaceae	May apple	Eastern North America
Populus balsaminifera L.	Salicaceae	Balsam poplar	Northern North America and temperate Asia
Psidium guajava L.	Myrtaceae	Guava	New World

Species	Family	Common name	Native area
Psychotria ipecacuanha (Brot.) Stokes	Rubiaceae	Ipecacuanha	Brazil
Rauvolfia serpentine (L.) Kurz	Apocynaceae	Rauwolfia	Indomalaysia
Rhamnus purshiana DC.	Rhamnaceae	Cascara sagrada	Western North America
Rheum species	Polygonaceae	Rhubarb	China and Central Asia
Rhododendron ponticum L.	Ericaceae	Rhododendron	Eastern Mediterranean
Ricinus communis L.	Euphorbiaceae	Castor Oil	Ethiopia-Egypt
Saponaria officinalis L.	Caryophyllaceae	Soapwort	Eurasia
Senecio inaequidens DC.	Asteraceae	South African Ragwort	South Africa
Senecio jacobaea L.	Asteraceae	Common Ragwort	North temperate Old World
Senecio vulgaris L.	Asteraceae	Groundsel	North temperate Old World
Tagetes erecta L.	Asteraceae	African marigold	Mesoamerica
Tamarindus indica L.	Fabaceae	Tamarind	East Africa
Taraxacum species	Asteraceae	Dandelion	North temperate Old World
Thevetia peruviana (Pers.) K.Schum.	Apocynaceae	Yellow oleander	Tropical America
Thymus serpyllum L.	Lamiaceae	Thyme	Eurasia
Triticum aestivum L.	Poaceae	Wheat	Transcausacia to Caspian region
Tussilago farfara L.	Asteraceae	Coltsfoot	North temperate Old World
Veratrum viride Aiton	Melanthiaceae	False hellebore	Eurasia

2. *Qing hao* 青蒿 (Herba *Artemisiae annuae*) in the Chinese *Materia Medica*

Elisabeth Hsu (in consultation with Frédéric Obringer)

Artemisia annua L. (Asteraceae), 'sweet wormwood', is one of the few plants of ethnobotanical interest that contains a biomedically acknowledged, highly effective chemical compound: artemisinin or *qing hao su* 青蒿素, which is currently recommended as an anti-malarial by the WHO (World Health Organisation). Modern Chinese scientists identified this molecule over thirty years ago after purifying a plant extract composed of plants used to produce the traditional Chinese medical drug called *qing hao* 青蒿 (Herba *Artemisiae annuae*). A drug of this name had been been known to Chinese physicians for more than two thousand years. However, while the literature on the recently identified anti-malarial substance *qing hao su* (artemisinin) is vast, research into the history of the age-old Chinese medical drug and plant *qing hao* (literally, the blue-green *hao*) is scarce, if non-existent. This article is the first to present knowledge about *qing hao* from antiquity to 1596 in one genre of Chinese medical writings, the *materia medica* (*ben cao* 本草).

The aim of this article is threefold. The first is ethnobotanical. It has to be borne in mind that 'herbal' medicines are not 'natural' herbs but cultural artefacts that are produced and used in culture-specific ways. It is well known that the plant materials used for producing any drug are harvested in particular seasons, at particular times of the day, often from specific places, sometimes after bespeaking the plant. Furthermore, choices have to be made about the use of the different parts of the plant, their specific form of preparation, their mixing with other ingredients, their dosage, and their mode of application. Moreover, agreement has to be reached about their effectiveness, whereby common sense, aesthetics, numerology, spells

83

and incantations, availability of the plant and other ingredients as well as other practical issues may play a role. This article will provide documentation of culturally-specific activities that led to the production and application of the Chinese medical drug *qing hao* which will highlight why in many contexts one should think of *qing hao* as a 'drug' rather than as a 'natural herb'.

Second, the article contributes to the history of medicine in China in that it provides a longitudinal study on one particular drug within the Chinese *materia medica*. To date there are barely any studies of the kind, not least because of methodological problems. On what grounds can we postulate the identity of an entity in the *materia medica* over two thousand years? This study will address the problem by proceding linguistically in the first instance. It will attend to trends of changing attitudes in the physicians' description and use of the drug known by the name *qing hao*, or its synonyms, and the living kinds whence it was derived. Painstaking care has been taken to be as comprehensive as possible in providing verbatim translations of all entries found on *qing hao* within the *materia medica* before the posthumous publication of Li Shizhen's 李時珍 (1518–1593) encyclopaedic *Ben cao gang mu* 本草綱目 (Classified Materia Medica) in 1596. Li Shizhen's is a landmark publication in the history of the Chinese *materia medica* and also in the history of *qing hao*.[1]

Third, the article aims to provide practical information for those researchers who wish to see *qing hao* cultivated at a low cost in the poverty-stricken countries where malaria is endemic, and who seek a contemporary ethnobotanical application of this ancient drug. To be sure, this article is not a practical guide, but since the *materia medica* recorded information taken from the medical genre of formularies (*fang ji shu* 方劑書) at the latest from the Song dynasty, 960–1279 CE, onwards, it contains detailed practical information on how to prepare and apply the drug. In particular, one observation, which is that the fresh plant should be soaked in water, wrung out, and its juice ingested in its raw state (rather than making a herbal tea from dried leaves), may have far-reaching implications for future ethnobotanical recommendations (Hsu 2006a, 2006b, Wright & al. 2010).

The very last section of the article explores to what extent a lexical item like *qing hao*, which in the Chinese *materia medica* designates both a living kind and the drugs derived from it, can be related to a modern botanical species name. Needless to say, any retrospective imputation of referential meanings into a linguistic term is a tricky undertaking. Although ethnobotanical research has provided justification for postulating cross-cultural continuities in plant identification over the centuries (Atran 1990), any issues relating to common sense remain largely unresolved. Moreover, it is not certain to what extent this general ethnobotanical principle applies to the specific case of *qing hao*. The genus *Artemisia* comprises over four hundred species (Wright 2002), and *Artemisia annua* is easily confused with other species, so that even today the drug *qing hao* has been identified in different regions of China, with their different ecologies, as being composed of plant materials from a variety of different species (Yang and Feng 1993: 221).

The Anti-Malarial Artemisinin

Artemisia annua provides a rare success story of ethnomedicinal plant preparations. Science has now revealed that this commonly known plant has pharmacologically active substances with anti-malarial properties against which, so far, no very significant resistance has arisen (McIntosh and Olliaro 2007). In the early 1970s, Chinese scientists isolated and identified artemisinin (Yu and Zhong 2002), which is also found in lesser quantities in *Artemisia apiacea* Hance and *Artemisia lancea* Vaniot. Artemisinin is the most powerful, but not the only, anti-malarial substance in these three species (Willcox et al. 2004). The Chinese brands Artesunate, Artemether and Co-tecsin, which contain pure artemisinin or one of its derivatives, are classified as Western medical drugs (Hsu 2009b), although to date none is produced according to GMP (good medical practice) standards (Phillips-Howard 2002) and counterfeits are frequent, particularly in Southeast Asia (Newton et al. 2001).

The anti-malarial properties of artemisinin and its derivatives arise from their impact on red blood cells, which during a malarial fever episode are infected with the protozoan *Plasmodium*. Artemisinin and its derivatives can affect an 'explosion' of these red blood cells, thereby destroying the *Plasmodium* habitat (Sriram et al. 2004). Artemisinin clears fever in between six and forty hours, which is faster than any other anti-malarial (Hien and White 1993, White 2008), and therefore its indication for cerebral malaria has long been recognized (Li et al. 1982). However, since artemisinin and its derivatives do not affect the schizontic liver stages of the *Plasmodium* cycle, they cannot be used as prophylactics.

The WHO was slow in recognizing the effectiveness of artemisinin for more than twenty years after their isolation (WHO 1994) and only recently has a policy been issued that recommends combination therapies of artemisinin and a more conventional anti-malarial that controls recrudescence (WHO 2006), such as mefloquine (Nosten et al. 2001) or amodiaquine (Duffy and Mutabingwa 2004).[2] This is the most recent milestone in the long history of *qing hao*.

Hao in the Early Chinese Literature and Problems of Nomenclature

Shennong, the Divine Husbandman, who was one of the three legendary emperors of China's Golden Age, tasted all herbs and accordingly the first comprehensive *materia medica* is entitled *Shennong's Canon of Materia Medica* (*Shennong ben cao jing* 神農本草經).[3] Legend has it that this work is many thousands of years old. However, historians of Chinese medicine agree that it was only during the Eastern Han dynasty (23–220 CE), when this work was compiled, that the *materia medica* became a field of scholarly inquiry.[4] The *Shennong ben cao jing* was lost, at the latest by the Southern Song dynasty (1127–1279), but has been reconstructed from quotations in later works (Ma 1990: 251). *Qing hao* is given there as a synonym of the drug called *cao hao* 草蒿, which means 'herbaceous *hao*'. *Cao hao* remained the main name of the drug in most of the *materia medica* works for eleven hundred years, until Li Shizhen (1518–1593) in his compilation *Ben cao gang mu* of 1596 made *qing hao* the main name and *cao hao* its synonym.

The above highlights one of the first problems the historian of Chinese pharmacotherapy encounters: the wealth of synonyms provided for a particular drug and plant. Chinese *materia medica* consist of long lists of drugs (*yao* 藥), each discussed in a separate entry that records their names, properties, preparation and applications.

These drugs are derived mostly from plants, but also from minerals and animals. The names of the drugs are often identical to those of the living kinds whence they are derived, but not always. These two ways of using a name can be encountered in discussions of *qing hao*. According to many ancient *materia medica* texts, the drug called *qing hao* was harvested from the plant with the same name. However, according to the contemporary pharmacopeia of the People's Republic of China (*Zhonghua renmin gongheguo yaodian* 1995: 169), the drug *qing hao* is mainly harvested from the plant called 'yellow blossom *hao*' (*huang hua hao* 黃花蒿). What figures as a drug is a derivative from a living kind that may or may not have the same name, and a living kind may or may not overlap with a Linnaean species. Depending on the geographical distribution of the living kind, it may be known by different names; depending on the preparation of the drug, drugs derived from the same living kind may take on different names. As already said, Chinese 'herbal' medicines are not 'raw' herbs but highly sophisticated cultural artefacts.

The word *hao* 蒿, which later commentators identified as *qing hao*, occurs in the earliest work of Chinese literature, the *Book of Songs* (*Shi jing* 詩經), from 1000–600 BCE. The text passage reads: 'You, you, is the deers' sound, as they graze on the *hao* in the wilderness' (*you you lu ming, shi ye zhi hao* 呦呦鹿鳴 食野之蒿). The commentator to the *Shi jing*, Lu Ji 陸璣 (third century CE) identifies this *hao* as *qing hao*.[5] The same term *hao* also occurs in the lexicographic work *Er ya* 爾雅 (Examples of Refined Usage) of the third century BCE. Again, a third-century CE commentator, Guo Pu 郭璞 (276–320), identifies the *hao* in question as *qing hao*.[6] In other words, what in the early non-medical literature was called *hao* was identified by commentators of the third century ce as *qing hao*.[7]

According to the *Er ya*, the plants *hao* were also called *qin* 菣. In fact, the term *qin* is identified as being specific to a certain region. Another third-century commentator, Sun Yan 孫炎, explains: 'Between the lands of Jing and Chu, one says *hao* are *qin*' (*Jing Chu zhi jian, wei hao wei qin* 荊楚之間 謂蒿為菣).[8] The Mawangdui manuscripts of the second century BCE, which date to approximately the same time as the *Er ya,* also provide a specific name for the plant in Jing.[9] This suggests that *qin* was the Jing name for the plant identified by the Chinese scholarship of the third century CE as *qing hao*.

Qing hao in the Mawangdui Manuscripts (168 BCE)

The term *qing hao* itself occurs for the first time in the Mawangdui manuscripts, which were unearthed from a tomb that was closed in 168 BCE. Among the forty-two manuscripts found in that tomb there was one that listed recipes for fifty-two different kinds of ailments. One of those was for treating so-called '[female] haemorrhoids' ([*pin*] *zhi* 牝痔). It mentions *qing hao*.

> [Female] haemorrhoids that have entered the opening [of the anus] for one *cun* [2.31 cm]:[10] in appearance and kind they are like lice on oxen three [x] [x]. When one is defecating, they ooze and expel blood; when one is not defecating, they go upwards [inside the anus].
>
> The recipe for them is: take five *dou* [5 x 2 litres] of urine, use it to boil two bunches of sweet wormwood (*qing hao*), seven golden carps (*fu yu*) the size of a hand, a six *cun* [6 x 2.31 cm] piece of smithed cinnamon (*gui*), and two pieces of dried ginger (*jiang*). Bring this to the boiling point ten times. Remove [the liquid] and put it [the medicine] in a jar. Bury [the jar] under a sitting mat. Make an opening. Use it to fumigate the haemorrhoids. When the medicine becomes cold, stop. Fumigate three times a day. If the throat gets choked, drink the medicinal broth, and do not drink anything else.
>
> Recipe for the medicinal broth: take two *sheng* [2 x 0.2 litres] of smithed dried stalks of *qu* [not further identifiable]. Take two *dou* [2 x 2 litres] of yams (*shu luo*) juice, use it to soak them and make a broth. Drink it. When the illness ends, stop. As to *qing hao*, in Jing its name is [*qin*].[11] As to *qu*, in Jing its name is *luru*. Its leaves can be brewed but get sour; its stalks have thorns. Excellent.[12]

The above text passage refers to a theme that will be encountered throughout the later *materia medica* literature: *qing hao*, together with other ingredients (seven golden carps, six pieces of smithed cinnamon and two of dried ginger), is soaked in urine. According to this particular text, it is then boiled, but not according to others. Particularly in those cases where the recommendation was to soak the plant but not to heat it, one may hazard a guess based on biological considerations. Urine is generally not infested with the harmful microbes found in contaminated water, which cause serious if not lethal diseases like typhoid or cholera. In some

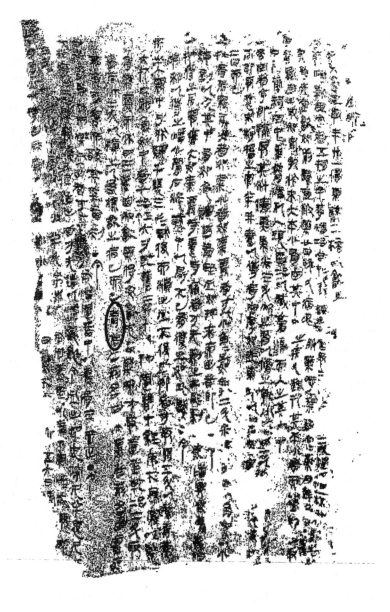

Figure 2.1: The Chinese characters *qing hao* 青蒿 in a Mawangdui medical manuscript (second century BCE)

cases, it may have been a better solvent than water for extracting pharmacologically active ingredients from the plant. Furthermore, cultural considerations may have played a role, as in cases where the recommendation consists of the numerologically striking 'seven' measures of a 'seven'-year old toddler's urine.

A plant identified by contemporary sinologists as *qing hao* is also mentioned in another Mawangdui recipe 'For purging the centre and increasing *qi* 氣 (breath, air, vapour)' (Chu zhong yi qi 除中益氣): 'Another [recipe]. Take two portions of *jun gui* (curled cinnamon), four of *xi xin* (asarum), one of *qiu* (wormwood), one of oyster, and two of Qin *qiao* (Qin zanthoxylum). Use a three-fingered pinch after the meal. It makes a person strong.'[13]

The plant in question is called *qiu* 萩, which modern sinological scholarship has identified with *qing hao*: Harper (1998: 272) refers to Xu Shen's 許慎 (c. 55–c. 149 CE) discussion of *qiu*.[14] However, if one takes seriously the debates of the third century CE, and the commentary on them from a Late Imperial Chinese natural historian, it is evident that *qiu* was described as having white leaves, while *qing hao* was recognized as such on the grounds of its blue-green ones (as spelt out clearly at the latest by the Song dynasty, see p. 101).[15] Therefore, we doubt the likelihood that the above Mawangdui passage which mentions *qiu* refers to *qing hao*.

To recapitulate, *qing hao* as a compound word is for the first time mentioned in the Chinese literature in the Mawangdui medical manuscripts. The recipe in question recommends soaking *qing hao* with other ingredients in urine before boiling it and using it for the fumigation of haemorrhoids. These haemorrhoids may have been called 'female haemorrhoids' because they oozed blood, like women menstruate blood. In their appearance, they resembled lice.[16] Perhaps this resemblance with lice explains why *qing hao* was recommended for treating 'female haemorrhoids', because according to the later *materia medica*, *qing hao* was considered to kill lice.

Qing hao in the Early *Materia Medica* up to the Tang Dynasty (618–907)

It is generally accepted that the earliest reference to *qing hao* in the Chinese *materia medica* is in the *Shennong ben cao jing*. It is mentioned among the 'drugs derived from herbaceous plants' (*cao yao* 草藥) as a synonym of *cao hao* 草蒿 (herbaceous *hao*). It quoted in two other works that predate the Tang dynasty but are now lost. One is the *Informal Records of Eminent Physicians* (*Ming yi bie lu* 名醫別錄), an anonymous work of the third century CE (that Li Shizhen erroneously attributed to Tao Hongjing 陶弘景); the other is *Notes to the Canon of the Materia Medica* (*Ben cao jing ji zhu* 本草經集注) by Tao Hongjing (456–536) from around 500 CE.[17] Based on quotations in later works, the first three *materia medica* texts on *qing hao* have been reconstructed as follows:

> The herbaceous *hao* [*cao hao*]. Its flavour is bitter, cold. It treats *jie* itches, *jia* itches,[18] and ugly wounds. It kills lice and lingering heat between bones and joints. It brightens the eyes. Another name is *qing hao*, another name is *fang kui*. It grows in river waste lands.[19] (*Shennong ben cao jing, juan* 4, p. 341)

> Without poison. It grows in Huayin.[20] (*Ming yi bie lu, juan* 3, p. 149)

> It is everywhere, this one is today's *qing hao*, people even take it mixed with fragrant vegetables for eating it.[21] (*Ben cao jing ji zhu, juan* 5, p. 363)

The entry emphasizes the usefulness of *cao hao* for treating sores and wounds. It also mentions the idiom 'lingering heat between bones and joints', which comes curiously close to the common term of the 'bone breaker' and may have referred to the patient's subjective experience of malarial fevers in regons where malaria is endemic.[22] At the end of the quotation, Tao Hongjing recommends *qing hao* as a food supplement, which is in line with the *Shi ming* 釋名 (Explanation of Names) by Liu Xi 劉熙 of 200 CE that mentions *xiang qi hao* 香氣蒿 (fragrant smell [*qi*] *hao*) among the foodstuffs.[23] As we will see below, *qing hao*'s wound healing properties were well known up to and during the early Tang dynasty (618–907), and its life-enhancing qualities as a food supplement were stressed from the late Tang onwards.

Most obviously, the treatment of 'ugly wounds' was already known to Ge Hong 葛洪 (284–363) in the fourth century, although it was as late as in 1061/62 that a *materia medica* recorded this, namely the *Ben cao tu jing* 本草圖經 (Illustrated Canon of the *Materia Medica*) by Su Song 蘇頌, which is known to us only through quotations from Tang Shenwei's 唐慎微 (c. 1056–1136) *Zheng lei ben cao* 証類本草 (*Materia medica* Corrected and Arranged into Categories) of *c.* 1082:

In the most ancient recipies, it [*qing hao*] was mostly used on its own. Mr. Ge, when treating wounds caused by metal knives, in their early stages took raw *qing hao*, pounded it with a pestle, and applied it on top of them. He took silk to pack[24] the wound, the bleeding stopped, and they healed.[25] (*Ben cao tu jing*, quoted in *Zheng lei ben cao, juan* 10, p. 20b)

Ge Hong's knowledge of dressing wounds is remarkable; wounds caused by metal knives must have been rather deep. In his view, they could only be treated in the early stages (when, in biomedical terms, the infection had not yet spread). Notably, *qing hao*, in its fresh and raw state, was used on its own.

This point is elaborated in the *Xin xiu ben cao* 新修本草 (Newly Revised Materia Medica) of 657–659 by Su Jing 蘇敬 (seventh century) and his team, who were the first to compile a *materia medica* by government request. The *Xin xiu ben cao* recapitulates verbatim Tao Hongjing's *Ben cao jing ji zhu* (i.e. all three paragraphs in the first quotation above), and adds the following sentence:

It is said that this *hao*, if in its fresh state crushed and applied on to wounds from metal [weapons], largely stops the bleeding, causes the growth of flesh and stops pain. [It is proven to be] excellent.[26] (*Xin xiu ben cao, juan* 10, p. 271–72)

Again, fresh *qing hao* treated wounds (translated into biomedical jargon, it was appreciated for its haemostatic, dermatogenic and analgesic qualities). In addition, other works of the Tang dynasty recommended treating wounds with fresh *qing hao*.[27]

In a similar vein, the use of presumably fresh but chewed *qing hao* was recommended for treating bee stings in the *Bu que zhou hou bai yi fang* 補闕肘后百一方 (Hundred and One Formulae for Amplifying those Kept in one's Sleeve) of c. 500 CE by Tao Hongjing. This is a formulary which elaborated on Ge Hong's *Zhou hou bei ji fang* 肘後備急方 (Emergency Formulae kept in one's Sleeve) of the fourth century, but is now lost:

Bai yi fang: When a bee has stung a person, chew it, apply it on top of the wound. One instantly recovers.[28] (quoted in *Zheng lei ben cao. juan* 10, p. 20b)

Apart from being used for treating wounds, *qing hao* was also recommended as a fragrant fresh food supplement in Tao Hongjing's *Ben cao jing ji zhu*. This may explain why the first book-length treatise on dietary therapy, the *Shi liao ben cao* 食療本草 (*Materia*

Medica for Successful Dietary Therapy) of 721–739, included an entry on it, although its author, Meng Shen 孟詵 (621–713) did not refer to Tao Hongjing. This *materia dietetica* on the interface of pharmacotherapy and cooking details for the first time in the history of *qing hao* elaborate procedures of drug preparation. It too is lost and known to us only through mediaeval manuscript fragments and quotations in other works.

[i] They say *qing hao* is cold, enhances *qi*, causes growth of head hair, can make the body feel light, supplement the interior and prevent ageing, brighten the eyes, and halt wind poison. If crushed and applied on top of a wound, it stops bleeding, and causes the growth of flesh. The one that is white in colour when it sprouts in early spring, this one, with fragrant vinegar, is made into pickles that enhance the person's [well-being].[29]

[ii] For treating bone steaming, take one *liang* [41.3 g.] of urine to soak it over night, dry it, turn it into powder and make a pill. It entirely eliminates [feelings of] exhaustion arising due to heat/fevers.

[iii] Also, in cases of daemonic *qi*, take the seeds, make them to powder, use wine to ingest them with a square inch spoon. One recovers.

[iv] Burn into ashes, drench in juice, blend with lime, simmer [or fry]. It treats ugly wounds and scarred moles.[30] (*Shi liao ben cao*, quoted in *Zheng lei ben cao, juan* 10, p. 20b)

The procedures of drug preparation outlined above are very elaborate, and highlight that the application of *qing hao* is a culturally highly specific phenomenon. Notably, treatment recommendations for different disorders depended on the method of drug preparation.[31] The first paragraph elaborates on *qing hao*'s longevity-enhancing qualities, which so far had only briefly been mentioned with the idiom 'it brightens the eyes' in the *Shennong ben cao jing*; and, in line with other Tang works, it refers also to *qing hao*'s wound healing effects. The second paragraph speaks of 'bone steaming' and 'exhaustion due to heat/fevers', reminiscent of the 'lingering heat between joints and bones' cited in the *Shennong ben cao jing*.[32] The fourth paragraph takes up another well-known theme from the *Shennong ben cao jing*, the treatment of wounds, but in a more elaborate manner than was previously the case. The daemonic *qi*, however, which is mentioned in the third paragraph, is entirely new to the discussion of the drug *qing hao* in the *materia medica*.

The early *materia medica* did not recommend *qing hao* for treating daemonic *qi* and related disorders, but other Tang dynasty works did so, such as, for instance, Chen Zangqi's 陳藏器 *Ben cao shi yi* 本草拾遺 (*Materia Medica*: Supplements) of the eighth century, also lost and also quoted in the *Zheng lei ben cao*. The *Ben cao shi yi* is noteworthy for yet another reason. It details two interesting forms of drug preparation for treating such acute episodes of daemonic *qi*. One involves 'wringing out' (*jiao* 絞) the plant and ingesting the expressed juice, the other dissolving *qing hao* powder in urine.

> [i] *Hao* controls daemonic *qi*, *rigor mortis* possession disorders,[33] *fu lian*,[34] the blood *qi* of women, an abdomen that feels full inside and is intermittently cold and hot, and chronic diarrhoea.
>
> [ii] In autumn and winter, use the seeds, in spring and summer, use the sprouts, together pound them with a pestle, wring out the juice, and ingest.
>
> [iii] Alternatively, dry it in the sun and make it into a powder, and apply it in urine. If one feels cold, use wine to boil it.
>
> [iv] Also, burn it into ashes, wrap them in paper eight to nine times. For drenching them, take its juice, mix with lime. It eliminates and stops the [growth of] superfluous flesh and black moles.[35] (*Ben cao shi yi*, quoted in *Zheng lei ben cao, juan* 10, p. 20a)

It is difficult to know precisely what kind of conditions 'daemonic *qi*' (*gui qi* 鬼氣), '*rigor mortis* possession disorders' (*shi zhu* 尸注) and 'harbouring and connecting' (*fu lian* 伏連) described. As Li Jianmin (1999) has argued, they arise in contexts where victims are polluted by the dead.[36] Regardless of their precise identification, we note again that the therapeutic recommendation changes in relation to how *qing hao* is prepared.[37] However, it is not only different drug preparations that are mentioned, but also different parts of the living plant (the seeds and sprouts). This is an observation we will return to in the following section.

To summarize, in particular three applications of *qing hao* stand out during the Tang dynasty, each involving a range of culture-specific drug preparations: its wound treatment (with crushed fresh *qing hao* or with its ashes blended in lime); its life enhancing qualities and use in treating lingering heat (as a food supplement: as fresh fragrant herb or as a processed prickle); and its regulation of possession-related disorders and convulsions (either as a fresh juice or as powder in urine).

Qing hao in the *Materia Medica* of the Five Dynasties (907–960)

During the time of the Five Dynasties physicians appear to have become increasingly interested in the plant as a living kind, whence the drug was derived. This is at least the impression one gains from Song dynasty (960–1279) quotations of two *materia medica* compilations dating to the Five Dynasties that are now lost: Han Baosheng's 韓保昇 *Shu ben cao* 蜀本草 (*Materia Medica* from the Kingdom of Shu) and Da Ming's 大明 *Rihuazi ben cao* 日華子本草 (*Materia Medica* of Master Sun Rays). Thus, the *Zheng lei ben cao* quotes the *Jiayou ben cao* 嘉祐本草 that quotes the *Shu ben cao* that, in turn, quotes a certain *Tu jing* 圖經 (Illustrated Canon), which is concerned mainly with the living kind:[38]

> The *Tu jing* says: it is said that the leaves resemble the *yin chen hao* (perennial *hao*), but the back of the leaves is not white. It is about four *chi* [4 x 31.2 cm] high. In the fourth and fifth month collect the sprouts and dry them in the sun. East of the Yangtze, people call it *xin hao* because its smell resembles that of a *xin*-cat.[39] The people here call it *qing hao*.[40] (*Shu ben cao*, quoted in *Zheng lei ben cao, juan* 10: 20a)

In contrast to the above Tang dynasty works, the *Shu ben cao* pays much attention to the living kind. It describes the plant by the colour of its leaves, by its overall height, and by comparing it to other kinds of plants. The *Rihuazi ben cao* also attends to the living plant, in that it differentiates between specific applications of its different parts.

> [i] *Qing hao* supplements the centre and enhances *qi*, it makes the body feel light, supplements the overworked [i.e. those who are in a state of utter exhaustion]. It conserves the complexion and causes growth in body- and head hair; the head hair remains black and does not grow old. In addition, it eradicates garlicky hair [strings of black and white hair].

> [ii] If one has heartache and is yellow from heat/fevers, pound it raw with a pestle into juice, and ingest it together with applying it [externally].

> [iii] In cases of diarrhoea, to food and drink add its powder, a five *qian* [5 x 4g] spoon full.

[iv] If you burn it into ashes, blend with lime and fry, it treats ugly and poisonous wounds; in addition use also the stalks.[41]

[i] It is also said: the seeds are sweet, cold, without poison.

[ii] For brightening the eyes and opening the stomach [i.e. enhancing one's appetite], use them stir-fried.

[iii] For treating the overworked, use them steeped in the urine of healthy adult men.

[iv] For treating ugly wounds, sore skin, wind papules and for killing lice, fry and wash them.[42]

[i] It is also said: the *chou hao* (stinking *hao*) seeds are cool, without poison. They treat the overworked/exhausted, guide the *qi* downwards, open the stomach, stop night sweats and pernicious *qi* and daemonic poison.

[ii] Another name is *cao hao*.[43]

The *Rihuazi ben cao* entry is sub-divided into three sections that concern parts of the living kind: there is one on *qing hao*, one on *qing hao* seeds, and one on *chou hao* 臭蒿 seeds (stinking *hao* seeds). Their seeds are both cold/cooling and 'without poison', and the *qinghao* seeds are in addition sweet. Importantly, the *Rihuazi ben cao* speaks of two different kinds, named *qing hao* and *chou hao* (stinking *hao*), while *cao hao* is given as a synonym. It thus foreshadows a distinction Li Shizhen will make between *qing hao* and *huang hua hao* (yellow blossom *hao*) in 1596, where the *Rihuazi ben cao*'s description of the 'stinking *hao*' provides the basis for what Li Shizhen will call the 'yellow blossom *hao*'.

In summary, the quotes from the Five Dynasties *materia medica* literature point to an increased interest in the living plant, whence the drug *cao hao* or *qing hao* was derived. They also suggest an increased awareness of part-specific usages of the plant. However, since the works from the Five Dynasties mostly survived in Song dynasty quotations, it is possible that their preoccupation with the plant as a living kind reflects an interest that was particularly pronounced during the Song dynasty.

Qing hao in the *Materia Medica* of the Song Dynasty (960–1279)

The Song dynasty *materia medica* is most remarkable for extensively describing the living kinds and newly incorporating information from the genre of formularies *(fang ji shu)*. Several Song dynasty entries on *qing hao* begin with a discussion of the characteristics of the plant and end with formularies on how to apply the drug.

Thus, the entry of the *Ben cao tu jing* (Illustrated Canon of the *Materia Medica*) composed by Su Song in 1061/62 and lost already during the Song dynasty, begins with a detailed description of the plant and ends with an outline of drug preparations.

[i] The *Tu jing* says: *cao hao* is just *qing hao*. It grows in Huayin's river wastelands. Now it is everywhere.

[ii] In spring it grows sprouts, its leaves are extremely fine and tender; sometimes people take it mixed with various fragrant vegetables and eat it. At the height of summer, it is three to five *chi* [3–5 x 31.2 cm] high. After autumn time, it opens fine pale yellow blossoms. After the blossoms fall down, it immediately grows seeds, as big as millet grains. During the eighth and ninth month one collects the seeds, dries them in the shade.

[iii] The roots, stalk, seeds and leaves all enter the medicine. Use the dry ones for roasting to make a drink; its fragrance is especially good.

[iv] *Qing hao*, another name is *fang kui*. Always when preparing the seeds, do not prepare the leaves, when preparing the roots, do not prepare the stalks. If the four are put together, they turn around and cause illness. If one gets children's urine to steep them in it, it is excellent. It treats bone steaming and exhaustion due to heat/fevers.[44] (*Ben cao tu jing*, quoted in *Zheng lei ben cao, juan* 10, p. 20b)

To facilitate the reading of the above quotation from the *Ben cao tu jing*, we have divided it into four paragraphs. The first repeats knowledge from the *Shennong ben cao jing*. The second contains detailed observations of *qing hao* as a plant. The third and fourth paragraphs specify which parts of the plant can be used.[45] Notably, paragraph three refers to *cao hao* with as synonymous with *qing hao*, and paragraph four to *qing hao* as synonymous with *fang kui*.

The fourth paragraph also takes up a theme encountered already earlier: the plant *qing hao* should be steeped in urine. This is in line with the recommendation in the Mawangdui text, the *Shi liao ben cao*, the *Ben cao shi yi* and the *Rihuazi ben cao*. Whereas the Mawangdui text recommended subsequent boiling for treating so-called 'female haemorrhoids', none of the four *materia medica* of the Tang and Song do so when they recommend using it for treating 'bone steaming and exhaustion due to heat/fevers'. It appears as though many physicians had become acutely aware of *qing hao*'s effectiveness in its fresh and raw state, but not all, as becomes clear in the following quotation, where it is likely that the recommendation was to reduce the urine by means of boiling it:

> According to the *Hai shang fang* by Cui [Yuan]liang,[46] it [*qing hao*] treats daemonic *qi* and bone steaming: take five great *dou* [5 x 6 litres] of clarified urine of a young boy, five *dou* [5 x 2 litres] of *qing hao*, ideally plants with seeds of the eighth and ninth month, cut finely; mix the two components together, put them into a big pot, heat on a fast fire, reduce to three great *dou* [3 x 6 litres]; eliminate the residue, wash the pot and dry it, filter the juice again, put it in the pot, heat on a low fire, reduce to two great *dou* [2 x 6 litres]; take the bile of the gall bladder of ten pigs and mix it [into the liquid]; heat [and reduce] to one great *dou* and a half [9 litres]; take out of the fire, leave to cool and put in a new porcelain jar. At the time of wishing to apply them, take two or three *liang* [2–3 x 41.3g] of licorice, toast them, pound them to powder and heat them; mix and pound them in a mortar with a thousand turns of the pestle; make them to pills, and flush down twenty pills on an empty stomach with porridge; increase gradually to thirty pills and stop.[47] (*Ben cao tu jing*, quoted in *Zheng lei ben cao*, juan 10, p. 20b)

The *Ben cao tu jing* thus began with a description of the living kind, then described Mr Ge Hong's method of wound dressing (quoted above) and ended with quotations from a formulary on how to prepare the drug. *Cao hao* and *qing hao* referred both to the plant as living kind and to the cultural artefacts derived from specific parts of it.

The most important work of the *materia medica* in the Song dynasty is Tang Shenwei's *Zheng lei ben cao* of around 1082. It is a compilation that quotes many texts that are now lost. The *Zheng lei ben cao* entry on *cao hao*, which is preceded by two illustrations – a northern and a southern *cao hao*, the former in blossom (or with seeds, the illustration is not clear enough to state with certainty), the latter without[48] – is structured as follows: it first quotes verbatim the *Shennong ben cao jing*, the *Ming yi bie lu* and Tao Hongjing's comment to those quotations in the *Ben cao jing ji zhu*. This is

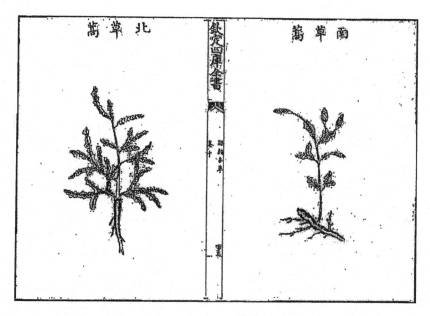

Figure 2.2: The two illustrations of *cao hao* 草蒿 in the *Zheng lei ben cao*
(*Materia medica* corrected and arranged in categories) of 1082. Depicted are a
northern (*bei* 北) and a southern (*nan* 南) *cao hao* (unrelated to what is said in
text)

followed by a quotation from the *Xin xiu ben cao*, to which is added
a comment from Chen Zangqi's *Ben cao shi yi*. Thereafter, comes the
quotation from the *Tu jing* as quoted in the *Shu ben cao* in a quotation
from the *Jia you ben cao*. Then, the *Er ya* and the *Shi jing*, and the
various commentaries on the quotations from these ancient texts are
presented. Three quotations from the *Rihuazi ben cao* follow, as does
the above long entry from the *Ben cao tu jing*. There then follows a
quotation from the *Leigong bao zhi lun* 雷公炮炙論 (Treatise on Lei
Gong's Methods of Drug Preparation), date unknown, by Lei Xiao
雷敩,[49] the *Shi liao ben cao* (quoted above), the *Bai yi fang* (quoted
above), and the *Dou men fang* 斗門方 (Formularies from the Lock
Gate) of the seventh to tenth century.

The two formularies, which both contain recommendations to use
children's urine, outline elaborate procedures of drug preparation:

Leigong 雷公 says: generally speaking, all that affects only the centre
is marvellous, when you reach your knees, lift up your head, when you
reach the waist, bend your head. When using seeds, do not use leaves;

when using roots, do not use stems. If the four are put together, they
turn around and cause inveterate illnesses. Pick an indefinite amount of
leaves, use seven measures [cannot be further specified] of seven-year old
children's urine, soak the leaves during seven days and seven nights, filter,
dry, and use them.[50] (*Leigong bao zhi lun*, quoted in *Zheng lei ben cao*,
juan 10, p. 20b)

Dou men fang: To treat emaciation due to overexertion in men and women,
heat up together *qing hao* cut into small pieces, three *dou* [3 x 6 or 2 litres]
of water, five *sheng* [5 x 0.6 or 0.2 litres] of children's urine; reduce to two
sheng and a half [1.5 or 0.5 litres], eliminate the residue, put it into a pot,
simmer until it becomes a paste. Make pills as big as the seed of *wu tong*
(*Firmiania simplex*); on an empty stomach, while lying down, with warm
wine, swallow down twenty pills.[51] (*Zheng lei ben cao, juan* 10, p. 20b)

In summary, the Song dynasty *materia medica* on *qing hao* is
remarkable in two respects. First, it provides detailed descriptions
of the living kinds, whence the drug with the same name is derived.
Secondly, it includes quotations from formularies, usually towards
the end of an entry on a drug, which outline complex procedures of
drug preparation.[52] Although the names are identical, their materiality
differs: plants are living kinds; drugs are highly sophisticated cultural
artefacts.

The Botanical Description of *Qing hao* by the Song Scholar Shen Kuo (1031–1095)

At the very end of the entry on *cao hao*, the *Zheng lei ben cao* edition
of 1249 contains a strikingly detailed description of the living kind
qing hao. It is a quotation from the *Ben cao yan yi* 本草衍義 (Dilations
upon *Materia Medica*), which was compiled in 1116 by Kou Zongshi
寇宗奭, thirty-four years after the first publication of the *Zheng lei
ben cao*:

Cao hao is now *qing hao*. It is everywhere. It can be obtained in very
early spring. People pick it for using it as a vegetable. The roots are red,
the leaves fragrant. Today people call it *qing hao*. There is also one that
can be distinguished from it, but it is within the same category; it can be
distinguished due to its blue-green colour. In Shaanxi, between Sui and
Yin, there is *qing hao* in the midst of bushels of *hao*, sometimes there
are one or two clumps that are especially blue-green in colour. The local

people call them 'fragrant *hao*' (*xiang hao*). The stalks and leaves are the same as those of the 'common *hao*' (*chang hao*), but the common *hao*'s colour is pale blue-green (*dan qing*), this *hao*'s colour is deep blue-green (*shen qing*) and blue-greener (*you qing*). Hence its smell (*qi*) is aromatic. I guess the one the ancients used was the deep blue-green one, they made it to the preferred one, how would it be otherwise, for how could a *hao* not be blue-green! (*Zheng lei ben cao, juan* 10, p. 20b) [53]

The *Ben cao yan yi,* strictly speaking, dates to the Jin dynasty (1115–1234) but the above quotation clearly reflects Song dynasty scholarship; Kou Zongshi had adopted into his *materia medica,* with barely any variation, an essay by Shen Kuo 沈括 (1031–1095) in the *Meng xi bi tan* 夢溪筆談 (Dream Pool Essays) of 1086, which provides a remarkably close botanical observation of the plant *qing hao*:

Figure 2.3: *Qing hao* 青蒿 in Shen *Kuo's Meng xi bi tan* of 1086

The categories (*lei*) of *hao* are very numerous. Consider, for instance, the category *qing hao.* There are two kinds, one is yellow and one is blue-green. There is the one that the entire *materia medica* literature refers to as *qing hao,* yet I fear there is another one that can be distinguished from it. In Shaanxi, between Sui and Yin, there are blue-green (*qing*) *hao* in midst of bushels of *hao,* sometimes there are one or two stocks that are especially blue-green in colour, the local people call them 'fragrant *hao*' (*xiang hao*). The stalks and leaves are the same as those of the 'common *hao*' (*chang hao*), but while the common *hao*'s colour is [bright] green (*lü*), this *hao*'s colour is blue-green and emerald (*qing cui*), just like the colour of pine and juniper. In the depth of autumn, when the other *hao* are yellow, this one alone is blue-green; its smell (*qi*) is quite aromatic. I guess [this is] the one the ancients used, they considered this one the preferred one. [54] (*Meng xi bi tan,* paragraph 502 , p. 873)

Shen Kuo's description differentiates between two kinds of *qing hao*: one is blue-green (*qing*) in colour throughout summer and autumn, the other is green (*lü*) and turns yellow (*huang*) in autumn. The kind with blue-green and emerald leaves, which Shen Kuo called 'fragrant *hao*' (*xiang hao* 香蒿), was the one that in his view the ancients valued.[55] We will return to these observations of the living kind in the very last section of this chapter, when in the context of discussing practical applications of this textual knowledge, we explore possible modern botanical identifications.

Qing hao in the *Materia Medica* of the Jin (1115–1234) and Yuan (1271–1368) Dynasties

Whereas the treatment of wounds figured prominently in the Tang *materia medica,* and the description of living kinds in the Song *materia medica,* the *Zhen zhu nang bu yi yao xing fu* 珍珠囊補遺藥性賦 (The Pearl Bag with Rhapsodies on the Properties of Drugs), which some attribute to Li Gao 李杲 (1180–1251), is remarkable for mentioning 'bone steaming' and 'heat/fevers due to exhaustion' in the most prominent position of its brief entry on *cao hao,* with synonym *qing hao.*[56] This is the first time in the history of *qing hao* that a *materia medica* entry accords it such importance in treating heat and, by implication, presumably fevers.

In retrospect, one may interpret this as a hint that by the Jin dynasty (1115–1234) and Yuan dynasty (1271–1368), physicians had become acutely aware of *qing hao*'s effectiveness in treating fevers (which with hindsight, we may now guess, must have included malarial ones, Hsu 2009a). Historians of China have demonstrated that the innovative agricultural techniques of producing wet rice during the Song dynasty not only provided the nutritional basis for a drastic increase in population density,[57] but also led to an increase in malaria (e.g. Miyasita 1979) and increased government efforts of controlling it, not least, by means of requesting the compilation of useful *materia medica* (e.g. Obringer 2001).[58]

However, other *materia medica* of the Jin and Yuan periods contain only sparse information on *qing hao* or ignore it altogether. Thus, it is mentioned neither in the *Zhen zhu nang* 珍珠囊 (The Pearl Bag), composed by either Zhang Yuansu 張元素 (twelfth century) or Li Gao 李杲 (1180–1251), nor in the *Tang ye ben cao* 湯液本草 (*Materia Medica* of Decoctions) of 1298 by Wang Haogu 王好古, nor among the 153 kinds mentioned in the *Ben cao yan yi bu yi* 本草衍義補遺

(Additions to the Dilations on the *Materia Medica*) by Zhu Zhenheng
朱震亨 (1282–1358).

Qing hao in the *Materia Medica* of the Ming Dynasty (1368–1644)

We will focus on two Ming dynasty works, namely the *Ben cao meng quan* 本草蒙筌 (Enlightenment of the *Materia Medica*) of 1565 by Chen Jiamo 陳嘉謨 (fl. 1565) and the *Ben cao gang mu* by Li Shizhen of 1596. Both works stand out for providing further information on the living kind *cao hao* (or *qing hao*), and on the processes of transforming it into a cultural artefact.[59] Furthermore, Ming dynasty *materia medica* provide, for the first time in its history, lists of what in ethnobiology are known as 'covert categories'.[60]

The *Ben cao meng quan* is remarkable because it presents knowledge of other *materia medica* in its very own words, in phrases of four to five characters each:

> *Cao hao*, that is *qing hao*. The flavour is bitter, the *qi* is cold. It is without poison. In mountain valleys and in river wastelands, it grows everywhere. The leaves, seeds,[61] roots, and stalks together can enter the medicine. In spring and summer time, collecting and using the stalks and leaves is appropriate. Put them into children's urine and simmer to a paste. They drive away bone steaming and heat from overexertion. In their raw state pound them with a pestle, let them rot, and wring out the juice. They repulse heart ache and yellowness due to heat/fevers. For superfluous flesh and swollen boils, burn them to ashes, drench them to a thick sauce and paste them on. For diarrhoea and daemonic *qi*, grind them to powder, regulate them with rice, drink and swallow. If one uses it in autumn and winter, take the roots and seeds. The seeds must be stir-fried, the roots chewed. They cure wind papules and *jie* itching, they stop depletion-discomfort and night sweats, they open the stomach and brighten the eyes, they ward off the evil and kill lice.[62] (*Ben cao meng quan, juan* 2, p. 129)

In the above quotation, which summarizes the different usages of *cao hao*, one sentence – which again highlights that Chinese medical drugs are cultural artefacts resulting from lengthy procedures of preparation – is of particular interest. It concerns the preparation of raw *qing hao* leaves and stalks for the treatment of heart ache and yellowness due to heat/fevers: in their raw state one should pound them with a pestle, let them rot, and wring out (*jiao*) the juice. A variation of this procedure was already mentioned in the *Ben cao shi yi*, and its possible relevance for the extraction of chemical compounds with anti-malarial properties will be highlighted in the discussion.

In respect to living kinds, the *Ben cao meng quan* is remarkable for at least two other reasons. First, the illustrations which are embedded within the text of the expanded 1628 edition, called *Tu xiang ben cao meng quan* 圖像本草蒙筌 (Illustrated Enlightenment of the *Materia Medica*), are worth mentioning because they diverge from the text in interesting ways. Thus, there are four pictures of *hao*: *cao hao* (herbaceous *hao*), *qing hao* (blue-green *hao*), *jiao hao* 角蒿 (horn *hao*) and *bai hao* 白蒿 (white *hao*). Although the text discusses *cao hao*, as being synonymous with *qing hao*, the illustrations depict *cao hao* and *qing hao* as two very different plants.[63] Evidently, the term *cao hao* was considered vague and referred to a drug derived from different plants. In full awareness that illustrations often diverge from *materia medica* descriptions (Haudricourt and Métailié 1994), the two separate illustrations of *cao hao* and *qing hao* are noteworthy because they hint at a later historical development, which eventually led to the demise of the term *cao hao* and to a fuller appreciation of *qing hao*.

Second, in contrast to all *materia medica* mentioned so far, the *Ben cao meng quan* presents the entry on the drug *cao hao* in a list of different *hao*, namely *yin chen hao* 茵陳蒿 (perennial *hao*; *Artemisia capillaries* Thunb.), *cao hao* (herbaceous *hao*; *Artemisia apiacea* and *Artemisia annua*), *bai hao* 白蒿 (white *hao*; *Artemisia sieversiana* (Ehrh.) Willd.), *xie hao* 邪蒿 (evil *hao*; *Seseli seseloides* (Fisch. and Mey. *ex* Turcz.) M.Hiroe), *mu hao* 牡蒿 (male *hao*; *Artemisia japonica* Thunb.), *jiao hao* 角蒿 (horn *hao*; *Incarvillea sinensis* Lam.), *lin hao* 蔯蒿 (no literal translation possible), *tong hao* 茼蒿 (ditto; *Chrysanthemum coronarium* L.), *ma xian hao* 馬先蒿 (in front of the horse *hao*; *Pedicularis resupinata* L.).[64]

In the first instance, the above list may appear problematic to an anthropologist or historian insofar as Chinese names of living kinds are equated to modern botanical species. However, this is often done in ethnobotany in the understanding that the botanical name provides a rough approximation of the living kind. A realist position allows for the possibility that there may be some overlap in the plants denoted

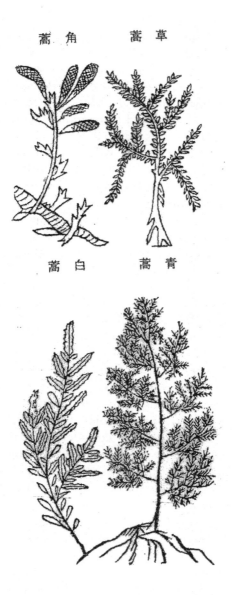

角蒿　　草蒿

白蒿　　青蒿

Figure 2.4: *Cao hao* 草蒿 in the *Tu xiang ben cao meng quan* (Illustrated enlightenment of the *materia medica*) of 1628. Depicted are on the top row a *cao hao* (resembling the southern *cao hao*) and a *jiao hao* 角蒿 (resembling the northern *cao hao*), to which have been newly added in the lower row a *qing hao* 青蒿 and a *bai hao* 白蒿 (only loosely related to what is said in text)

by a modern botanical species name and the Chinese names of living kinds, although the connotations of the names as linguistic items and other meanings implied by these terms do not coincide. Chen Jiamo was not a modern botanist, but according to modern botany, most *hao* in his list fall into species of the genus *Artemisia*. His list also contains *hao* that modern botany identifies as belonging to the genera *Pedicularis* (Orobanchaceae) and *Chrysanthemum* (Asteraceae) and to the family *Apiaceae*. Species within these taxa generally have leaves that are pinnate and fine, which, with the exception of *Pedicularis* species, are scented. In the reckoning of modern botanists, they are therefore easily confused with one another (*Pedicularis* species being the most likely not to cause confusion).

Georges Métailié (2001) has identified several lists of living kinds in Li Shizhen's *Ben cao gang mu* of 1596 forming 'covert categories'. Li Shizhen, in contrast with Chen Jiamo, is explicit that his entries are on kinds (*zhong* 種), rather than on drugs (*yao* 藥). As has already been said, these *zhong*-kinds cannot be equated to Linnaean species while there are overlaps between the plants they denote. The Ming dynasty authors who compiled those lists of living kinds evidently observed the plants from vantage points not entirely unrelated to those of modern botanists.

In the *Ben cao gang mu*, the *zhong*-kind is named *qing hao*, and *cao hao* is given as a synonym. This is the first time in medical history that *cao hao* figures as a synonym to *qing hao*, rather than vice versa. There appears to be a reason for this, although Li Shizhen is not explicit about it. It seems that he considered the term *cao hao* too vague. In its stead, he created entries on two *zhong*-kinds: one was *qing hao* (blue-green *hao*), and the other was given a new name, *huang hua hao* (yellow blossom *hao*).[65] Evidently, Li Shizhen did away with the entry on *cao hao* and instead differentiated between two different kinds: *qing hao* and *huang hua hao*.

The entry on *qing hao* in the *Ben cao gang mu* is extensive and repeats, with variations, much of what was said above; it is far too long to be presented here and deserves a separate study. Relevant for our discussion is merely an extract from the section in the 'Appended Recipes', which contains a wide range of quotations from formularies. Li Shizhen evidently expanded knowledge not only with regard to *qing hao* as a living kind but also in respect of the drug *qing hao* as a cultural artefact.

106

In this context, it is worth knowing that the *Ben cao gang mu* discusses every *zhong*-kind in various sections. For *qing hao* they are: *shi ming* 釋名 (Explaining the Names), *ji jie* 集解 (Grouped Explanations),[66] and *xiuzhi* 修治 (Preparing the Treatment). The third section, in turn, is subdivided into two subsections, one on the 'leaves, stem, roots and seeds', and one on the 'seeds' only. These subsections each comprise further sub-subsections on *qi wei* 氣味 (Quality and Flavour), *zhu zhi* 主治 (Main Therapeutic Indications), *fa ming* 發明 (Bringing Light; only given for the first subsection), and *fu fang* 附方 (Appended Formulae).[67]

The 'Appended Formulae' sub-subsection to the subsection on the use of 'leaves, stalks, roots and seeds' (*ye jing gen zi* 葉莖根子) claims to discuss four old formulae and fourteen new ones for treating the following disorders: emaciation due to overexertion in men and women, [feelings of shivering from] coldness and heat due to depletion and overexertion, daemonic *qi* due to bone steaming, vexating heat due to bone steaming, night sweats due to depletion and overwork, intermittent heat and coldness due to the intermittent fever illness, phlegm due to warmth factor intermittent fevers, bloody and slimy diarrhoea [literally: red and white diarrhoea], nose bleeding, blood in the stool due to haemorrhoids caused by alcohol consumption, wounds caused by metal [weapons] and bruises from pouncing, teeth that are swollen and painful, poisonous bee stings, pus coming out of the ears, and rotten flesh inside the nose.

In consideration of the current use of *qing hao* as an anti-malarial, the formulae of only one of the above fourteen conditions are translated here, namely the three that are recommended for treating 'intermittent heat and coldness due to the intermittent fever illness' (*nüe ji han re* 瘧疾寒熱):

Formula from the *Zhou hou fang*: use one bunch of *qing hao*, two *sheng* [2 x 0.2 litres] of water, pound with a pestle to juice and ingest it.[68]

Formula from the *Ren cun fang*:[69] use *qing hao* picked at dawn on the fifth day of the fifth month, dried in the shade, four *liang* [4 x 41.3g] and one *liang* [41.3g] of the core of a cinnamon stalk, and grind it into powder. When the fever has not yet arisen, just before that, ingest two *qian* [2 x 4g] with wine.[70]

Jing yan fang (Formula based on the Experience [of Li Shizhen himself]): use *qing hao* picked on the *duanwu* day [the fifth day of the fifth lunar month], the leaves dried in the shade, the core of a cinnamon stalk and other ingredients, and grind into powder. Every time when ingesting, [use] one *qian* [3.69g]. Use hot wine if at the beginning one felt cold, use cold wine if at the beginning one felt hot. On the day when the fever arises, at the *wugeng* hour [11 am – 1 pm] ingest it. [71] (*Ben cao gang mu, juan 2*, p. 945)

Of these three formulae, the first one is most frequently cited. However, Li Shizhen did not cite it verbatim. In the original text, Ge Hong wrote in the chapter on 'Formulae for Treating all Intermittent Fevers of the Hot-Cold Type' of his *Formulae kept in one's Sleeve*:

Another formula: *qing hao*, one bunch, take two *sheng* [2 x 0.2 litres] of water for soaking it, wring it out for taking the juice, ingest it in its entirety. [72] (*Zhou hou bei ji fang, juan 3*, 'Zhi han re zhu nüe fang' 治寒熱諸瘧方16, p. 734-407)

Ge Hong makes it very clear that one should soak the plant in water, wring it out, use the juice of the plant in its entirety and ingest it. The water should not be boiled; there is no mention of making a tea or an infusion. Rather, the juice of the plant itself should be used, as also emphasized in other passages of the *materia medica*:

In autumn and winter, use the seeds, in spring and summer, use the sprouts, together pound them with a pestle and wring out the juice and ingest. Alternatively, dry them in the sun into a powder, and apply them in urine. (Quotation from the *Ben cao shi yi*)

In spring and summer time, collecting and using the stalks and leaves is appropriate ... In their raw state pound them with a pestle, let them rot, and wring out the juice. They repulse heartache and yellowness due to heat/fevers. (Quotation from the *Ben cao meng quan*)

Neither an infusion nor a decoction is recommended. Rather, the juice is to be extracted from the plant itself through wringing it out. This is an important observation that may have far-reaching ethnobotanical implications for the current usage of *qing hao* as a herbal anti-malarial. We will return to this practical issue in the end of the chapter.

With regard to the Ming *materia medica* discussed above, we note summarily first, that information derived from other genres was increasingly incorporated into the *materia medica*, such as, from the Song onwards, formularies, which outlined complex procedures of transforming parts of the living kind into cultural artefacts. Second, a trend emphasizing the botanical observation of living kinds was increasingly documented from the Five Dynasties onwards. Third, the presentation of *materia medica* knowledge was radically re-organized and re-ordered in the Ming. All three trends appear to have culminated in Li Shizhen's encyclopaedic work of 1596, as he attended to *zhong*-kinds, rather than *yao*-drugs, and discussed their natural history and medical applications in separate sections (the newly added *ji jie* and *fu fang* sections). Future research may or may not confirm whether these trends are manifestations of more general developments in the history of the Chinese *materia medica* or whether they are particular to the history of *qing hao*.

Summary

To summarize, the history of *qing hao* presented in this article is one of the first longitudinal studies of one particular drug in the Chinese *materia medica*. We have attempted to be comprehensive, which has inevitably resulted in translating quotations that repeated themselves. These quotations, which often outlined lengthy procedures of drug preparation, highlighted how misleading it is to call a Chinese medical drug like *qing hao* a 'natural herb'. It needs to be born in mind that herbal remedies are cultural artefacts. Recommendations for treatment vary depending on mode of preparation.

This longitudinal study of the term *cao hao* (with its synonym *qing hao*) highlighted several trends of its application that were specific to certain time periods, as well as the fact that overall its range of applications increased over the centuries.

A) Its external usages for treating wounds, lice (and 'female haemorrhoids' that looked like lice) as well as bee stings were emphasized already in the Han dynasty and stressed in the Tang dynasty. The recommendations varied but mostly the drug was applied either as crushed fresh plant or in the form of ashes mixed with lime.

B) Its vitality enhancing use was documented from the Tang onwards, being recommended as a food supplement, in pill form or as a fresh herb.

C) Its use for treating 'heat lingering in joints and bones' and 'exhaustion due to heat/fevers', which may sometimes have referred to chronic conditions caused by endemic malaria (Hsu 2009a), was mentioned already in the first *materia medica*, namely the *Shennong ben cao jing* of the first century CE. However, it was only in a post-Song dynasty *materia medica* of the twefth century that its fever-eliminating properties were accorded primary importance. Drug preparations varied and sometimes involved soaking the fresh plant in urine.

D) Its use against bouts of intermittent fever episodes was already recognized in the early fourth century by Ge Hong, but in a different genre, a formulary. It took more than one thousand years for Ge Hong's knowledge to become integrated into the *materia medica* until, finally, Li Shizhen quoted it in the *Ben cao gang mu* of 1596. The recommendation was to soak the fresh plant in water, wring it out, and ingest the juice.

The drug *cao hao* was also recommended for other conditions, sometimes in combination with other drugs, too many to detail here. Morever, several remarkable *materia medica* were published after the *Ben cao gang mu*, in the late Ming, the Qing dynasty (1644–1911) and the Republican era (1911–1949). Although some do contain interesting additional observations, it is impossible to gauge their importance without engaging in archival research. Methods of historiography thus terminate our study here. Finally, we will attend to the third point outlined in the introduction, which concerns the practical ethnomedical application of *qing hao* today.

Lexical Items in Texts and Their Referential Meanings

It needs to be borne in mind that ancient texts matter to anthropologists. In fact, the anthropological study of texts may become relevant even in applied anthropology. This is the case, in particular, when currents of so-called 'traditional medical', 'folk medical' or 'ethnomedical' knowledge, of which there are literary traces, continue to be relevant for contemporary medical practice. The reading of textual knowledge is fraught with difficulties, however, one of which concerns the referential meanings of the linguistic terms used. There are studies that focus mainly on sense relations, and stringency in argumentation is certainly enhanced by focusing only on constructed meanings.

However, the ethnobotanical literature (cited in the introduction) makes a case in favour of a realist position, even though it emphasizes that folk botanical kinds – also Chinese *zhong*-kinds – cannot be equated mindlessly to modern botanical species. This literature posits that ethno-botanical and modern botanical terms generally relate to an existent world ('reality') and refer to groups of living kinds between which there are overlaps.

Li Shizhen does not mention *cao hao* in his list of *hao*, but has instead the *zhong*-kinds *qing hao* and *huang hua hao*, taxa for which modern botany aimed at finding rough equivalents, *Artemisia apiacea* and *Artemisia annua* respectively. His list includes *yin chen hao* (perennial *hao*; *Artemisia capillaris*), *qing hao* (blue-green *hao*; *Artemisia apiacea*), *huang hua hao* (yellow blossom *hao*; *Artemisia annua*), *bai hao* (white *hao*; *Artemisia sieversiana*), *jiao hao* (horn *hao*; *Incarvillea sinensis*), *lin hao* (no literal translation possible), *ma xian hao* (in front of the horse *hao*; *Pedicularis resupinata*), *yin di jue* 陰 地厥 (no literal translation possible; *Botrychium ternatum* (Thunb.) Sw.), *mu hao* (male *hao*; *Artemisia japonica*). In the above list it is *huang hua hao*, not *qing hao* as is generally assumed, which refers to *Artemisia annua*.

The dictionary for Chinese medical drugs (*Zhongyao dacidian* 1986: no. 4182 and no. 2491) explains that the drug *huang hua hao* is derived from the plant material *Artemisia annua* and the drug *qing hao* from the plant material of *Artemisia apiacea*. It furthermore specifies, with regard to *qing hao*, that this drug is also derived from plant material of other species, namely *Artemisia annua* (*huang hua hao*), *Artemisia capillaris* (*yin chen hao*) and *Artemisia japonica* (*mu hao*). Likewise, the modern pharmacopeia of the People's Republic of China (*Zhonghua renmin gongheguo yaodian* 1995: 169) mentions *qing hao*, i.e. Herba *Artemisiae annuae*, as a drug that is derived from the plant *Artemisia annua*, which in modern Chinese botany is called *huang hua hao*.

Accordingly, *Artemisia annua*, whence artemisinin and its derivatives were extracted in the 1970s, is strictly speaking *huang hua hao*, not *qing hao*. However, the name *huang hua hao* was introduced into the Chinese *materia medica* as late as in 1596, while the terms *cao hao* and *qing hao*, which primarily designated the drug (*yao*) in question, have a long history. Clearly, *cao hao* and *qing hao* had a wider semantic field than *huang hua hao* and with hindsight one

111

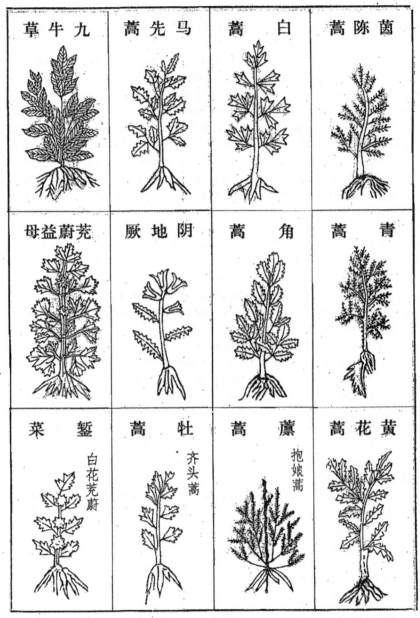

Figure 2.5: *Qing hao* 青蒿 and other *hao* 蒿 in the *Ben cao gang mu* (Classified *materia medica*) of 1596 (if depictions are read from left to right, and top to bottom, the sequence follows that given in the text)

would surmise that before 1596, they must have been derived from plant material inclusive of that which today is called *huang hua hao*, i.e. *Artemisia annua*.

Li Shizhen's entry on the *zhong*-kind *huang hua hao* (today equated with *Artemisia annua*) contains two sections, one on its seeds and one on its leaves. The entry on its seeds reproduces the *Rihuazi ben cao* quotation on the seeds of the 'stinking *hao*' (*chou hao*). The only difference is that Li Shizhen describes their flavour as pungent rather than cooling.

> Seeds <qi qualities and flavour>: pungent, cool, without poison.
>
> <main indications>: they treat the overworked/exhausted, guide the *qi* downwards, open the stomach, stop night sweats and pernicious *qi* and daemonic poison.[73]

To this Li Shizhen has added his own observations in an entry on its leaves:

> Leaves <*qi* qualities and flavour>: pungent, bitter, cooling, without poison.
>
> <main indications>: a child's fright fever due to wind and coldness.[74]

In the section on the 'Grouped Explanations, concerned with the natural history of the kind, he remarks:

> *Chou hao* (stinking *hao*), another name is *cao hao*. <[Li] Shizhen> says: The 'fragrant *hao*' (*xiang hao*) and the 'stinking *hao*' (*chou hao*) can be called *cao hao*. This *hao* is similar to *qing hao* but its colour green (*lü*) carries a dull yellow. Since its *qi* is pungent and smelly, one cannot eat it. People make use of pastes and yellow wine to modify it [its taste]. So it is.[75]

Li Shizhen's observation comes very close to Shen Kuo's as it differentiates *huang hua hao* from *qing hao* with regard to the leaves' colours: *huang hua hao* has [bright] green (*lü* 綠) leaves that carry a dull yellow while *qing hao* has blue-green (*qing* 青) leaves. This, incidentally, comes close to one of the main criteria that modern pharmacognocists use for distinguishing *Artemisia annua* from *Artemisia apiacea*. According to the standard dictionary on the Chinese *materia medica* (*Zhongyao dacidian* 1986: no. 4186 and no. 2491), the leaves of *Artemisia annua* are *lü*-green and those of *Artemisia apiacea* blue-greenish-green (*qing lü* 青綠).

113

Figure 2.6: *Huang hua hao* 黃花蒿 and *qing hao* 青蒿 as depicted in the *Zhi wu ming shi tu kao* 植物名實圖考 (Researches on the illustrations and authenticity of plant names) of 1846. Note the resemblance of *qing hao* with the *qing hao* in the *Meng xi bi tan* of 1086

The above dictionary information coincides with that in the *Flora Sinensis* (*Zhongguo zhiwuzhi* vol. 76, 1991: 60–63) insofar as the leaves of *huang hua hao* (*Artemisia annua*) are given as *lü*-green and the leaves of *qing hao* (*Artemisia carviflora* Buch.-Ham. *ex* Roxb. var. *carviflora*, of which *Artemisia apiacea* is a synonym) as blue-greenish-green (*qing lü*) or light green (*dan lü* 淡綠). In a similar vein, the *New Flora of Korea* (Lee 2006, vol. 2: 327) mentions that the main difference is that the leaves of the annual *Artemisia annua* become yellow in autumn, while those of the perennial *Artemisia apiacea* remain blue-green.

Discussion

This article gives a comprehensive, chronologically ordered overview of all the important *materia medica* entries on *cao hao*, with synonym *qing hao*, before 1596. It presents literal translations of *qing hao*'s diverse medical use over almost two thousand years, which provides ample evidence that the notion of 'natural herbs' is misleading, as

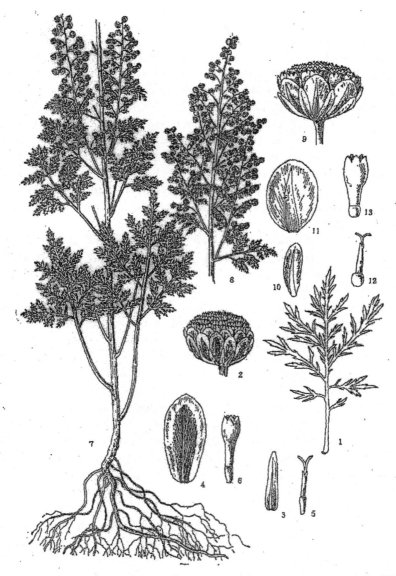

1—6.青蒿 Artemisia carvifolia Buch.-Ham. ex Roxb.; 1.中部叶, 2.头状花序, 3—4.外、中层总苞片, 5.雌花, 6.阴性花。7—13.黄花蒿 A. annua Linn.;7.植株一部分 ,8.茎上端一部分, 9.头状花序, 10—11.外、中层总苞片, 12.雌花,13.阴性花。(邓盈丰绘)

Figure 2.7: *Qing hao* 青蒿, *Artemisia carviflora* Buch-Ham. Ex. Roxb. (synonym to *Artemisia apiacea* Hance as mentioned in text); and *huang hua hao* 黄花蒿, *Artemisia annua* L., as depicted in the *Flora Sinensis* (*Zhongguo zhiwuzhi*)

many of these entries are concerned with drug preparations that turn living kinds into cultural artefacts.

The Chinese kind *qing hao* is generally equated with *Artemisia annua,* the plant whence the anti-malarial wonderdrug artemisinin is extracted, but this is strictly speaking erroneous, since modern botany identifies *Artemisia annua* as the 'yellow blossom hao' (*huang hua hao*) rather than the 'blue-green *hao*' (*qing hao*). However, considering that before 1596 the term *huang hua hao* did not exist and that throughout more than a millennium of Chinese medical history, the terms *qing hao* and *cao hao* were used in a vague and general sense, *Artemisia annua* must have been among the modern botanical species, whence the drugs *cao hao* and the synonymous *qing hao* were derived.

Li Shizhen, who did away with *cao hao* in 1596 and distinguished instead between *qing hao* and *huang hua hao,* paradoxically considered *qing hao,* which today is identified as *Artemisia apiacea,* rather than *Artemisia annua* as good for treating intermittent fevers. Li Shizhen's recommendation thus directly contradicts modern research: *Artemisia* sesquiterpenes, which modern researchers have identified as primarily responsible for the anti-malarial effects, occur up to twenty-one per cent in the oil-soluble liquid extractions of *Artemisia annua,* and to a much lesser degree in those of *Artemisia apiacea* (*Zhongyao dacidian* 1986: no. 4186 and no. 2491).

It is possible that giants of intellectual history get details wrong. If one were to grant Li Shizhen accuracy, nevertheless, one would have to take seriously the problem of extracting sesquiterpenes in 'traditional' procedures of drug preparations. Perhaps the traditional recipes recommended methods that made possible the extraction of the *Artemisia* sesquiterpenes, like artemisinin and its derivatives, in more substantial quantities from *Artemisia apiacea* than from *Artemisia annua.* It is also possible that, although artemisinin occurs in significantly larger concentrations in *Artemisia annua,* synergistic effects of various constituents within *Artemisia apiacea* played a role that has been underestimated. Or perhaps the current botanical identification is not straightforward after all. Experimental pharmacognosic research in laboratories could help to provide an answer to these questions.

Governments in countries where malaria is endemic have created their own *Artemisia annua* plantations, which enable them to produce locally low-cost drugs of the pure anti-malarial substance artemisinin and its derivatives. There is also the possibility of gardening plants in ways that would allow one to use them in their traditional mode (Willcox et al. 2004). The question that then arises concerns the most adequate 'traditional' usage. As seen above, there were many different ways in which the drug *qing hao* was prepared in Chinese medical history. Moreover, the accurate dosage would have to be determined, to prevent rapid emergence of drug resistance against *qing hao*.

Lay people from malaria endemic regions speak of *Artemisia annua* herbal teas, which consist of adding some dried leaves to two litres of water. As should be evident from the above, this knowledge is derived from a distorted reading of Ge Hong's writings. Hirt (2001, cited in Willcox et al. 2004: 46) recommends very specific dosages but, according to ancient Chinese writings it is not accurate to recommend an infusion by pouring one litre of boiling water on 5g of dried leaves for a 60kg adult. Given these dosages it is no wonder that recent clinical trials found that the administration of *Artemisia annua* herbal teas could not be recommended for general use (Müller et al. 2004, Räth et al. 2004)! If one takes seriously the authors of the premodern Chinese *materia medica*, the set up of all these current modern trials has to be questioned as they investigate the effectiveness of infusions made of boiled water poured over dried leaves rather than that of fresh juices.

According to Ge Hong of the fourth century, Chen Zangqi of the eighth century and Chen Jiamo of the sixteenth century, it is important to use the herb in its raw state, and not to boil it. The raw plant should be soaked in water (or in urine) for some time – one author speaks of the plant becoming lame – and thereafter the whole plant should be pounded or wrung out. For treating intermittent fevers, the juice that is wrung out from the whole plant should then be ingested in its entirety.

Acknowledgements

This article is based on papers presented at the Medical Anthropology Research Seminar of the Institute of Social and Cultural Anthropology, University of Oxford, in February 2004; the

Anthropology Unit, Tsinghua University, Taiwan, in March 2004; and the Wellcome Unit for the History of Medicine, University of London, in December 2004. I am much indebted to Frédéric Obringer who identified and fotocopied most of the *materia medica* quotations that I have translated for this article and who thereafter checked my translations; he also identified the time-period-specific measures. Chang Chechia, Academia Sinica, Taiwan, also checked some translations and resolved some bibliographical questions. I furthermore wish to thank Merlin Willcox for generously sharing his source material on *qing hao* and getting me started on its research back in 2002. Finally, my thanks go to Stephen Harris, Rebecca Marsland, David Parkin and David Rogers for their critical comments on my earlier drafts and to Rudolf Pfister, Mark Stanton and the typesetter for their work on unusual Chinese characters.

Notes

1. Our study, which relies on modern and Qing dynasty (1644–1911) editions of ancient texts, terminates in 1596 primarily for methodological reasons, as the innumerable printed *materia medica* of Late Imperial China would require archival research.
2. Artemisinin monotherapy often results in recrudescence if it is taken for fewer than seven days (Phillips-Howard 2002, White 2008), i.e. most *Plasmodium* are rapidly eliminated, but a few survive and these few reproduce until a parasitic load is reached that causes a new fever attack.
3. The term *ben cao* 本草 is best translated as *materia medica*. Pharmacopeias are proscriptive in character, but this is not true of the Chinese *ben cao* literature. See Unschuld (1986: 5, 11–16) and Sivin (1987: 179 ff.).
4. The dynastic history of the Eastern Han (*Han shu* 漢書 30, "Yi wen zhi" 藝文志, p. 1777) lists eleven titles of canonical prescriptions (*jing fang* 經方).
5. *Mao shi* 毛詩, *juan* 9.1, *Xiaoya* 小雅, 'Luming' 鹿鳴, p. 138a. See also Legge (1991: 246).
6. *Er ya* 爾雅, *juan* 8.13, 'Shi cao' 釋草, p. 2625c and p. 2626a.
7. Late Imperial Chinese scholarship found fault with this equation, however. See note 15 below.
8. Ibid. See also *Zheng lei ben cao* 證類本草, *juan* 10, p. 20a, and *Ben cao gang mu* 本草綱目, *juan* 15, p. 943.
9. On the manuscript, the Chinese character for the name is partially damaged. Harper (1998: 272), in accordance with Ma (1992: 515), suggests *qiu* 萩. Considering that throughout the *materia medica* the Jing name for *hao* is

qin 菣, we suggest filling the lacuna with *qin* 菣. The Mawangdui passage then reads: 'The name for *qing hao* specific to the region Jing is *qin* 菣.' See the section '*Qing hao* in the Mawangdui Manuscripts (168 BCE)' in this chapter.

10. All measures of length, volume, and weight changed over time. Throughout this article, the measures specific to the time period in which a quotation was written are given in square brackets. They are based on the tables in the appendix to the *Hanyu dacidian* 漢語大辭典 and Guo (1993).

11. As indicated above (note 9), the text is damaged here. We suggest that the lacuna reads *qin* 菣 rather than *qiu*萩.

12. '[牝]痔之入竅中寸 狀類牛幾三ㄨㄨ然 後而潰出血 不後上鄉(嚮) 者方 取弱(溺)五斗 以煮青蒿大把二 鮒魚如手者七 治桂六寸 乾薑(薑)兩果(顆) 十沸 抒置甕中 貍(埋)席下 為竅 以熏痔 藥寒而休 曰三熏 因(咽)敝 飲藥將(漿) 毋飲之 為藥漿方 取崫莖乾治二升 取薯(署) 苽(蓏)汁二斗以漬之 以為漿 飲之 病已而已 青蒿者 荊名曰[萩]崫者 荊名曰盧茹 其藥可亨(烹)而酸 其莖有朿(刺) 令'.
Translation modified from Harper (1998: 272–273). See Ma Jixing (1992: 510–516), Mawangdui Hanmu boshu zhengli xiaozu (1985: 54–55, CC 248–252). Ma and Harper contain detailed discussions on the animals and plants mentioned.

13. 取勺桂二 細辛四 荻一 戊厲一 秦朾(椒)二 指最(撮)以為後飯 令人強 Translation by Harper (1998: 346). See also Ma (1992: 709–10), Mawangdui (1985: 110, C112).

14. *Shuo wen jie zi* 说文解字 IB, 28b.

15. See Ma (1992: 515). In a commentary to the *Er ya* 爾雅 phrase '*xiao* is *qiu*' (*xiao, qiu* 蕭萩), the commentator Guo Pu 郭璞 says: *qiu* is indeed a *hao* (*qiu ji hao* 萩即蒿). Guo Pu quotes Lu Ji 陸璣 who specifies that *qiu* is like an 'oxtail *hao*' (*niu wei hao* 牛尾蒿), similar to the 'white *hao*' (*bai hao* 白蒿). Indeed, Lu Ji explicitly says *qiu* has white leaves and considers Xu Shen 許慎 mistaken to take *qiu* for a 'moxa *hao*' (*ai hao*艾蒿, i.e. mugwort). However, according to Hao Yixing 郝懿行(1757–1825), Xu Shen considered mugwort synonymous to *lai xiao* 蘱蕭, not *qiu xiao* 萩蕭, and Lu Ji was mistaken to consider this *qiu* an 'oxtail *hao*', because the 'oxtail *hao*' had green leaves and not white ones, while *qiu* had white leaves and was thus similar to 'moxa *hao*', i.e. mugwort (*Er ya, juan* 8.13, 'Cao shi' 草釋, p. 2629c and *Er ya yi shu* 爾雅義疏, vol. 2.1, 'Cao shi', p. 58a-b). The upshot of all these learned debates is that Guo Pu and Lu Ji of the third century agreed that *qiu* had white leaves. Hence, contrary to Ma Jixing, we contend that there is no scholarly reason to identify *qiu* with *qing hao*. It would appear reasonable to assume that the latter was called the 'blue-green *hao*' due to the colour of its blue-green leaves.

16. An educated guess about a possible referential meaning of these 'lice' is that ticks, which can infest the anus, turn white once they have sucked themselves full of blood, and therefore may have looked like lice (David Rogers, personal communication). In this case, the referential meaning of *pin zhi* 牝痔, usually translated as 'female haemorrhoids', would not be haemorrhoids in the biomedical sense but ticks filled with blood, i.e. blood-oozing, lice-like piles.

17. The bibliographical information on these two works is based on Ma (1990: 262, 267).

18. *Jie sao jia yang* 疥瘙痂痒. Itching that can affect toes and fingers. See, for instance, *jie jia* 疥痂 in *Ling shu* 靈樞10, p. 307, or *jie chuang* 疥瘡 in *Zhu bing yuan hou lun* 諸病源候論, *juan* 50, p. 1411.

19. 草蒿 味苦 寒 無毒 治疥瘙痂癢 惡瘡 殺蝨 留熱在骨節間 明目 一名青蒿 一名方潰陰 生川澤. *ze* 澤 is here rendered as 'wasteland', in accordance with Bodde ([1978] 1981). Today this is the ecological niche of *A. apiacea* and *A. annua*, rather than that of *ze* meaning swamps and wetlands.

20. 無毒 生華陰. Huayin is in Shaanxi province (Ma 1990: 263).

21. 處處有之 即今青蒿 人亦取雜香菜食之

22. This is said in full awareness that retrospective biomedical diagnoses are a tricky undertaking. In areas where malaria is endemic, it is called 'bone breaker' (a remark from the audience in the Medical Anthropology Research Seminar on 9 February 2004). See also Hsu (2009a).

23. See *Shi ming* 釋名, *juan* 4.13, p. 31a-b: '膲 *huo* is a *hao*. The fragrant smell *hao* is a *hao*'. (*huo hao ye, xiang qi hao hao ye* 膲 蒿也 香氣蒿 蒿也).

24. The 1249 edition of the *Zheng lei ben cao* 證類本草 has an obscure character, where the *Si ku quan shu* 四庫全書 edition, *juan* 10, vol. 740, p. 483, reads *guo* 裹, meaning 'to pack'. We are indebted to Chang Chechia 張哲嘉 for drawing our attention to this detail.

25. 古方多單用者 葛氏治金刃 初傷取生青蒿 搗傅上以帛裹創 血止即愈

26. 此蒿 生挪敷金瘡 大止血 生肉 止疼痛良

27. However, Sun Simiao's 孫思邈 (581–?682) *Qian jin yi fang* 千金翼方, *juan* 3, p. 32, which was published after 659, does not contain this information and repeats only the first two paragraphs of Tao Hongjing's 陶弘景 *Shennong ben cao jing ji zhu*[神農]本草經集注.

28. 百一方治蜂螫人 嚼青蒿傅瘡上 即差

29. This application of *qing hao* is also mentioned in the *Qi min yao shu* 齊民要術, p. 532 (fa 88), 'Zuo zuo ju fa' 作酢菹法 (Method for Making Pickled Vegetables). See also *Tian gong kai wu* 天工開物, *juan* 17, *shen qu* 神曲 (Superior Ferment), p. 427.

30. [i] 云青蒿寒 益氣長髮 能輕身補中 不老明目 煞風毒 搗傅瘡上 止血生肉 最早春便生 色白者是 自然香醋淹為菹 益人 [ii] 治骨蒸 以小便漬一兩宿 乾 末

為丸 甚去熱勞 [iii] 又 鬼氣 取子為末 酒服之方寸匕差 [iv] 燒灰淋汁 和石灰 煎 治惡瘡瘢胲

31. We have divided the text accordingly into meaning-based paragraphs. They hint at multiple textual layers in this brief quotation that, however, only detailed textual research can ascertain.

32. Notably, both texts referred to conditions that, *inter alia*, could have been caused by recurrent endemic malaria, but neither mentioned 'intermittent fevers' (*nüe* 瘧, *han re* 寒熱), a term which in some contexts might have designated acute fever episodes caused by malaria.

33. For *zhu* 注 'possession disorders', see Chao Yuanfang's 巢元方 *Zhu bing yuan hou lun* 諸病源候論 of 610, *juan* 24, p. 690–715.

34. For *fu lian* 伏連 lit. 'to harbour and connect', see Wang Tao's 王燾 *Wai tai mi yao* 外台秘要, *juan* 13, p. 358 and p. 752.

35. [i] 蒿主鬼氣尸疰伏連 婦人血氣 腹內滿及冷熱久痢 [ii] 秋冬用子 春夏用苗 並搗汁服 [iii] 亦暴乾為末 小便中服 如覺冷 用酒煮 [iv] 又燒為灰 紙八九重 淋取汁 和石灰 去息肉胲子

36. Some medical historians speak of contagion and communicable diseases, others of possession disorders. Some episodes may have manifested in convulsions, which, considering that *qing hao* contains an anti-malarial substance, may have been caused by cerebral malaria. This is said in full appreciation that there may be many other possible causes for the convulsions.

37. Note that paragraph four in both the *Shi liao ben cao* 食療本草 and the *Ben cao shi yi* 本草拾遺 recommended similar drug preparations for treating wounds: mixing the plant's ashes with lime.

38. The unabbreviated title is: *Shu chong guang Yinggong ben cao* 蜀重廣英公本草 (Shu's Revised and Enlarged *Materia Medica* of the Duke of Yingguo), which elaborates on the *Xin xiu ben cao* and a so-called *Tu jing* 圖經 (Illustrated Canon) of unknown date. Shu refers to the Five Dynasties kingdom in the region of present-day Sichuan, Yinggong refers to the Duke of Yingguo. This was Mr Li Ji, who was the Prime Minister in charge of the compilation of the *Xin xiu ben cao* 新修本草. The latter was also called *Yinggong ben cao* 英公本草 (*Materia Medica* of the Duke of Yingguo). Since the *Shu ben cao* 蜀本草 was already lost in the Song dynasty (Yan 1994: 1108), quotations from it mentioned in the *Zheng lei ben cao* are those from Zhang Yuxi's 章禹錫 *Jiayou ben cao* 嘉祐本草 (*Materia Medica* of the Jiayou Period) of 1061.

39. For *xin* 狁, see *Ben cao gang mu* 本草綱目, *juan* 51, p. 2875, on *li* 狸 (a wild cat, maybe *Felis bengalensis*), which likens it to a little wild cat.

40. 圖經云 葉似茵蔯蒿 而背不白 高四尺 許四月五月採苗 日乾 江東 人呼為狁蒿 為其臭似狁 北人呼為青蒿

41. [i] 青蒿補中益氣 輕身補勞 駐顏色 長毛髮 髮黑不老 兼去蒜髮 [ii] 心痛熱黃 生搗汁服并傅之 [iii] 瀉痢 飯飲調末五錢匕 [iv] 燒灰和石灰煎 治惡毒瘡并蟹 亦用

42. [i] 又云 子 味甘 冷 無毒 [ii] 明目 開胃 炒用治勞 [iii] 壯健人 小便浸用 [iv] 治 惡瘡疥癬 風癵(疹)殺蝨煎洗

43. [i] 又云臭蒿子 涼 無毒 治勞 下氣 開胃 止盜汗及邪氣鬼毒 [ii]又名草蒿

44. [i] 圖經曰草蒿 即青蒿也 生華陰川澤 今處處有之 [ii] 春生苗 葉极細嫩 時人 亦取雜諸香菜食之 至夏高三五尺 秋後開細淡黃花 花下便結子 如粟米大 八 九月間採子 陰乾 [iii] 根莖子葉並入藥用 乾者炙作飲香尤佳 [iv] 青蒿亦名方 潰 凡使子勿使葉 使根勿使莖 四者若同 反以成疾 得童子小便浸之 良 治骨 蒸熱勞為取

45. However, as very often in compilations of pre-modern scientific works, these two thematically ordered statements, which are juxtaposed, contradict each other. *Materia medica* were the work of compilers who assembled knowledge from many different strands of medical learning rather than that of authors who wrote a tightly argued prose. These works presented knowledge in a thematically ordered way, and given the plurality of opinions they recorded, it is inevitable that some statements would contradict each other.

46. The *Hai shang jing yan fang* 海上經驗方 (Experience-based Formulae from the Sea) by Cui Xuanliang 崔玄亮 (c. 761–827). In this quotation, Yuan 元 is given for Xuan 玄.

47. 崔[元]亮海上方 療骨蒸鬼氣 取童子小便五大斗 澄過 青蒿五斗 八九月揀帶 子者最好 細剉 二物相和 內好大釜中 以猛火煎 取三大斗去滓 淨洗釜令乾 再瀉汁安釜中 以微火煎 可二大斗 即取豬膽十枚相和 煎一大斗半 除火待冷 以新瓷器盛 每欲服時 取甘草二三兩熟炙 搗末 以煎和搗一千杵為丸 空腹粥 飲下二十丸 漸增至三十丸止

48. *Zheng lei ben cao* 證類本草, *juan* 10, p. 740-482; in the edition of 1249, *juan* 10, p. 19b, both are called *cao hao* 草蒿.

49. The dates of Lei Xiao 雷斅 are unknown. The date of the book is an object of debate. The treatise was probably composed by various authors in different periods between the Song dynasty of the Five Dynasties (420–479) and the Song dynasty (960–1279; Liu and Sun 2002: 155).

50. 雷公云凡使唯中為妙到膝即仰 到腰即俛使子勿使葉使根勿使莖四件若同 使齜(翻)然成痼疾 採得葉不計多少 用七歲儿童七箇溺浸七日七夜後漉出 曬(晒)乾用之

51. 斗門方治丈夫婦人勞瘦 青蒿細剉 水三斗 童子小便五升同煎 取二升半去滓 入器中煎成膏 丸如梧桐子大 空心 臥以溫酒吞下二十丸

52. In this context, we note that almost all the quotations from the *materia medica* translated above are in Tang Shenwei's 唐慎微 *Zheng lei ben cao* 證類本草. In other words, the *Zheng lei ben cao*'s entire entry on *cao hao* 草蒿, synonymous with *qing hao* 青蒿, of the c. 1082 edition, has been translated in this article. The difference lies in the sequencing of the quotations.

While it is difficult to know what Tang Shenwei's rationale was, this article has presented the quotations in chronological order.

53. 草蒿今青蒿也 在處有之 得春最早 人剔以為蔬 根赤葉香 今人謂之青蒿 亦有所別也 但一類之中又取其青色者 陝西綏銀之間有青蒿 在蒿叢之間 時有一兩窠 迴然青色 土人謂之為香蒿 莖葉與常蒿一同 但常蒿色淡青 此蒿色深青 猶青 故氣芬芳 恐古人所用以深青者為勝 不然 諸蒿何嘗不青

54. 蒿之類至多 如青蒿一類 自有兩種 有黃色者 有青色者 本草謂之青蒿 亦恐有別也 陝西綏銀之間有青蒿 在蒿叢之間 時有一兩株 迴然青色 土人謂之香蒿 莖葉與常蒿悉同 但常蒿色綠 而此蒿色青翠 一如松檜之色 至深秋 餘蒿並黃 此蒿獨青 氣稍芬芳 恐古人所用 以此為勝

55. Shen Kuo's 沈括 observations are similar to those of modern botanists when they differentiate between the colours of the leaves of the two *Artemisia* species called *A. apiacea* and *A. annua*. According to modern botany, the annual species' leaves turn yellow in autumn.

56. *Zhen zhu nang bu yi yao xing fu* 珍珠囊補遺藥性賦, *juan* 3, p. 55.

57. This is the topic of many specialist studies; the classic reference is Bray (1984), see in particular pp. 113–29, 495, 598 (footnote a).

58. For reasons that are not entirely transparent, this entry on *cao hao* also contains information on the herb *xuan fu hua* 旋覆花 (suddenly inversed blossom; *Inula japonica* and/or *I. linariifolia*), with the name *jin fei* 金沸 (the boiling of gold), that was used for 'abating acute attacks of cough due to phlegm' (*dun tan sou zhi feng* 鈍痰嗽之鋒).

59. In many other works of the Ming dynasty, such as for example the *Ben cao pin hui jing yao* 本草品匯精要 of 1505 by Liu Wentai 劉文泰 (fl. 1488–1505), which entirely reorganizes the presentation of knowledge within an entry on a drug, one does not find much new information. There are only slight variations in wording, in the sequencing of citations, and in the attribution of the quotations to previous works.

60. 'Covert categories' arise from a comparison of folk taxa with modern biological taxa. They are 'categories' that appear to exist tacitly in people's minds and are not made explicit through linguistic labeling but which curiously overlap with modern taxonomies (Berlin et al. 1968).

61. The word *shi* 實 instead of *zi* 子 is used.

62. 草蒿 即青蒿 味苦 氣寒 無毒 山谷川澤 隨處有生 葉實根莖並堪入藥 春夏採用莖葉為宜 入童便熬膏 退骨蒸勞熱 生搗爛絞汁 卻心痛熱黃 瘧肉腫癤 燒灰淋濃湯點 泄痢鬼氣 研末調米飲吞 秋冬用之 取根與實 實須炒過 根乃咀成 愈風疹疥瘙 止虛煩盜汗 開胃明目 闢(閉)邪殺蟲

63. In a similar vein, the perenniel *hao* is depicted twice, namely as that from Jiangningfu (Jiangningfu *yin chen* 江寧府茵陳) and that from Jiangzhou (Jiangzhou *yin chen hao* 絳州茵陳蒿), but only one kind is discussed in the text.

64. The Linnaean identification of these kinds is based on the *Zhongyao dacidian* (1986), although there are controversies. For instance, *xie hao*, n° 1752, *Seseli seseloides* (Apiaceae), is given by Wu (1990: vol. 3, p. 375) as *Artemisia apiacea*.

65. In 1596 Li Shizhen 李時珍 added *huang hua hao* to a list of well-established kinds: the *Shennong ben cao jing* 神農本草經 had classified *yin chen hao* 茵陳蒿 as an upper grade drug, *ma xian hao* 馬先蒿 as a middle grade drug, and *bai hao* 白蒿 and *cao hao* 草蒿 as lower grade drugs. *The Ming yi bie lu* 名醫別錄 of 510 mentioned *mu hao* 牡蒿 for the first time, the *Xin xiu ben cao* 新修本草 of ca 660 *jiao hao* 角蒿, and the *Tu jing ben cao* 圖經本草 of 1062 *yin di jue* 茵地厥.

66. The newly introduced section on 'Grouped Explanations' contained many citations from non-medical genres, such as arboricultural literature, poems, philosophical essays, encyclopaedias, and others. Georges Métailié has studied them and their contribution to natural history extensively.

67. Li Shizhen 李時珍 was certainly not the first to reorganize the presentation of knowledge on a kind; his most notable precursor in this respect was Liu Wentai, but their entries on kinds were divided into very different sections.

68. 肘後方 用青蒿一握 水二升 搗汁服之

69. *Sun shi ren cun tang jing yan fang* 孫氏仁存堂經驗方 (Formulae of Experience from the Benevolence Remembrance Hall by Master Sun), date and author unknown. See *Ben cao gang mu* 本草綱目, *juan* 1, p. 17. The measures are given for a Tang dynasty work, but since the date of the work is unknown, they must be treated as very rough approximations.

70. 仁存方 用五月五日天未明時採青蒿陰乾四兩 桂心一兩 為末 未發前 酒服二錢

71. 經驗方 用端午日採青蒿葉陰乾 桂心等分 為末 每服一錢 先寒用熱酒 先熱用冷酒 發日五更服之 切忌發物

72. 又方 青蒿一握 以水二升漬 絞取汁 盡服之

73. 子<氣味> 辛 涼 無毒 / <主治> 治勞 下氣 開胃 止盜汗及邪氣鬼毒

74. 葉 <氣味> 辛 苦 涼 無毒 / <主治> 小兒風寒惊熱

75. 臭蒿一名草蒿 <[李]時珍曰> 香蒿臭蒿通可名草蒿 此蒿與青蒿相似 但此蒿色綠帶淡黃 氣辛臭不可食 人家採以罨醬黃酒曲者是也

References

A. Modern Sources

Atran, S. 1990. *Cognitive Foundations of Natural History: Towards an Anthropology of Science*. Cambridge: Cambridge University Press.

Berlin, B. D.E. Breedlove and P.H. Raven. 1968. 'Covert Categories and Folk Taxonomies', *American Anthropologist* 70: 290–99.

Bodde, D. [1978] 1981. 'Marches in the *Mencius* and Elsewhere: a Lexicographic Note', in C. Le Blanc and D. Borei (eds), *Essays on Chinese Civilization*. Princeton: Princeton University Press, pp. 416–25.

Bray, F. 1984. *Agriculture*, in J. Needham (series editor), *Science and Civilisation in China*, vol. 6, part 2. Cambridge: Cambridge University Press.

Duffy, P.E. and T.K. Mutabingwa. 2004. 'Drug Combinations for Malaria: Time to ACT?', *Lancet* 363: 3–4.

Guo Zhenzhong (郭正忠). 1993. *San zhi shisi shiji Zhongguo de quanheng duliang* 三至十四世紀中國的權衡度量 (Weights and Measures in China, from the Third to the Fourteenth Centuries). Beijing: Zhongguo shehui kexue chubanshe.

Harper, D. 1998. *Early Chinese Medical Literature: The Mawangdui Medical Manuscripts*. London: Routledge.

Haudricourt, A.G. and G. Métailié. 1994. 'De L'Illustration Botanique en Chine', *Etudes Chinoises* 13: 381–416.

Hien, T.T. and N. White. 1993. 'Qinghaosu', *Lancet* 341: 603–08.

Hsu, E. 2006a. 'The History of *Qinghao* in the Chinese *Materia Medica*', *Transactions of the Royal Society of Tropical Medicine and Hygiene* 100: 505–08.

Hsu, E. 2006b. 'Reflections on the "Discovery" of the Anti-malarial *Qinghao*', in J. Aronson (ed.), *Future Developments in Clinical Pharmacology. Special Issue. British Journal of Clinical Pharmacology* 61: 666–70.

Hsu, E. 2009a. 'Diverse Biologies and Experiential Continuities: Did the Ancient Chinese Know that *qinghao* had Antimalarial Properties?', in F. Wallis (ed.), *Medicine and the Soul of Science: Essays by and in Memory of Don Bates. Special Issue. Canadian Bulletin of Medical History* 26 (1): 203-13.

Hsu, E. 2009b. 'Chinese Formula Drugs (*zhongchengyao*) – an Alternative Modernity? The Case of the Anti-malarial Substance Artemisinin (*qinghaosu*) in East Africa', in E. Hsu and G. Stollberg (eds), *Globalizing Chinese medicine. Special Issue. Medical Anthropology* 28 (2): 111-40.

Lee, Y.N. (李永魯). 2006. New *Flora of Korea* (韓國植物圖鑑). Seoul: Kyo Hak.

Legge, J. 1991. *The Chinese Classics. Vol. 4: The She King*. Taipei: SMC Publishing.

Li Jianmin. 1999. 'Contagion and Its Consequences: the Problem of Death Pollution in Ancient China', in Y. Otsuka et al. (eds), *Medicine and the History of the Body*. Tokyo: Ishiyaku EuroAmerica, pp. 201–22.

Li, G.Q. et al. 1982. 'Clinical Studies on Treatment of Cerebral Malaria with *Qinghaosu* and its Derivatives', *Journal of Traditional Chinese Medicine* 2: 125–30.

Liu Zuyi (劉祖貽) and Sun Guangrong (孫光榮). 2002. *Zhongguo lidai mingyi mingshu* 中國歷代名醫名術 (The Famous Arts of Eminent Physicians the History of China). Beijing: Zhongyi guji chubanshe.

Ma Jixing (馬繼興). 1990. *Zhongyi wenxianxue* 中醫文獻學 (Study of the Chinese Medical Literature). Shanghai: Shanghai kexue jishu chubanshe.

Ma Jixing (馬繼興). 1992. *Mawangdui gu yishu kaoshi* 馬王堆古醫書考釋 (Explanation of the Ancient Medical Documents from Mawangdui). Changsha: Hunan kexue jishu chubanshe.

Mawangdui Hanmu boshu zhengli xiaozu 馬王堆漢墓帛書整理小組 (eds). 1985. *Mawangdui Hanmu boshu* 馬王堆漢墓帛書 (The Silk Documents from a Han Tomb at Mawangdui). Vol 4. Beijing: Wenwu chubanshe.

McIntosh, H.M., and P. Olliaro. 2007. Treating Severe Malaria. Cochrane Database of Systematic Reviews Library, http://www.thecochranelibrary.com

Métailié, G. 2001. 'The *Bencao gangmu* of Li Shizhen: an Innovation in Natural History?', in E. Hsu (ed.), *Innovation in Chinese Medicine*. Cambridge: Cambridge University Press, pp. 221–61.

Miyasita, S. 1979. 'Malaria (*yao*) in Chinese Medicine During the Chin and Yuan Periods', *Acta Asiatica* 36: 90–112.

Müller, M.S. et al. 2004. 'Randomized Controlled Trial of a Traditional Preparation of *Artemisia annua* L. (Annual Wormwood) in the Treatment of Malaria', *Transactions of the Royal Society of Tropical Medicine and Hygiene* 98: 318–21.

Newton, P. et al. 2001. 'Fake Artesunate in Southeast Asia', *Lancet* 357: 1948–50.

Nosten, F. et al. 2000. 'Effects of Artesunate-Mefloquine Combination on Incidence of *Plasmodium falciparum* Malaria and Mefloquine Resistance in Western Thailand: a Prospective Study', *Lancet* 356: 297–302.

Obringer, F. 2001. 'A Song Innovation in Pharmacotherapy: Some Remarks on the Use of White Arsenic and Flowers of Arsenic', in E. Hsu (ed.), *Innovation in Chinese Medicine*. Cambridge: Cambridge University Press, pp. 192–213.

Phillips-Howard, P. 2002. 'Regulation of the Quality and Use of Artesiminin and its Derivatives', in C.W. Wright (ed.), *Artemisia*. London: Taylor and Francis, pp. 309–21.

Räth, K. et al. 2004. 'Pharmacokinetic Study of Artemisinin after Oral Intake of a Traditional Preparation of *Artemisia annua* L. (Annual Wormwood)', *American Journal of Tropical Medicine and Hygiene* 70: 128–32.

Sivin, N. 1987. *Traditional Medicine in Contemporary China: a Partial Translation of* Revised Outline of Chinese Medicine (1972) *with an Introductory Study on Change in Present-day and Early Medicine*. Ann Arbor: Center for Chinese Studies, University of Michigan.

Sriram, D. et al. 2004. 'Progress in the Research of Artemisinin and its Analogues as Antimalarials: an Update', *Natural Product Research* 18: 503–27.

Unschuld, P.U. 1986. *Medicine in China: a History of Pharmaceutics.* Berkeley: University of California Press.

White, N.J. 2008. '*Qinghaosu* (Artemisinin): the Price of Success', *Science* 320: 330–34.

WHO. 1994. *The Role of Artesiminin amd its Derivatives in the Current Treatment of Malaria 1994–1995.* Report of an informal consultation convened by the WHO in Geneva 27–29 September 1993. WHO/MAL/94.1067.

WHO. 2006. Facts on ACTs (Artemisinin-based Combination Therapies), January 2006 Update. http://www.rbm.who.int/cmc_upload/0/000/015/364/RBMInfosheet_9.htm, sourced on 19 September 2008.

Willcox M. et al. 2004. '*Artemisia annua* as a Traditional Herbal Antimalarial', in M. Willcox et al. (eds), *Traditional Medicinal Plants and Malaria.* Boca Raton: CRC Press, pp. 43–59.

Wright, C.W. 2002. *Artemisia.* London: Taylor and Francis.

Wright C.W., Linley P.A., Brun R., Wittlin S. and Hsu E. 2010: 'Ancient Chinese Methods Are Remarkably Effective for the Preparation of Artemisinin-Rich Extracts of Qing Hao with Potent Antimalarial Activity', Molecules 15 (2): 804-812.

Wu Zhengyi (吳征鎰). 1990. *Xinhua bencao gangyao* 新華本草綱要 (Essentials of the New China *Materia Medica*). 3 vols. Shanghai: Shanghai kexue jishu chubanshe.

Yan Shiyun (嚴世芸). 1990–1994. *Zhongguo yiji tongkao* 中國醫籍通考 (Comprehensive Examination of Chinese Medical Books). Shanghai: Shanghai zhongyi xueyuan chubanshe.

Yang Zhaoqi (楊兆起) and Feng Xiu'e (封秀娥). 1993. *Zhongyao jianbie shouce* 中藥鑒別手冊 (Handbook for identifying Chinese medical drugs), vol. 2. Beijing: Kexue chubanshe.

Yu H.W. and Zhong S.M. 2002. '*Artemisia* Species in Traditional Chinese Medicine and the Discovery of Artemisin', in C.W. Wright (ed.), *Artemisia.* London: Taylor and Francis, pp. 149–57.

Zhongguo zhiwuzhi 中國植物志 (*Flora Sinensis*). 1991. Zhongguo kexueyuan zhongguo zhiwuzhi bianji weiyuanhui 中國科學院中國植物志編輯委員會 (eds). Vol. 76. Beijing: Kexue chubanshe.

Zhonghua renmin gongheguo yaodian 中華人民共和國藥典 (Pharmacopeia of the People's Republic of China). 1995. Zhonghua renmin gongheguo weishengbu yaodian weiyuanhui 中華人民共和國衛生部藥典委員會 (eds). Guangdong: Guangdong keji chubanshe.

Zhongyao dacidian 中藥大辭典 (Great Dictionary of Chinese Medical Drugs). 1986. Jiangsu xinyi xueyuan 江蘇新醫學院 (eds). Shanghai: Shanghai keji chubanshe.

B. Premodern Sources

Ben cao gang mu 本草綱目 (Classified Materia Medica). Ming, 1596. Li Shizhen 李時珍. 4 vols. Renmin weisheng chubanshe, Beijing, 1977–1981.

Ben cao meng quan 本草蒙筌 (Enlightenment of the *Materia Medica*). Ming, 1565. Chen Jiamo 陳嘉謨. References to *Tu xiang ben cao meng quan* 圖像本草蒙筌 (Illustrated Enlightenment of the *Materia Medica*). Punctuated and annotated by Wang Shumin 王淑民 et al. Renmin weisheng chubanshe, Beijing, 1988.

Ben cao pin hui jing yao 本草品匯精要 (Essentials of the *Materia Medica*, Classified by Grades). Ming, 1505. Liu Wentai 劉文泰. Renmin weisheng chubanshe, Beijing, 1982.

Ben cao yan yi bu yi 本草衍義補遺 (Additions to the Dilations on the *Materia Medica*). Yuan. Zhu Zhenheng 朱震亨 (1282–1358). In Zhou Ximin 周喜民 (ed.), *Jin Yuan si da jia yixue quanshu*金元四大家醫學全書 (The Complete Medical Books of the Four Great Jin and Yuan Scholars). 2 vols. Tianjin kexue jishu chubanshe, Tianjin, 1994.

Er ya 爾雅 (Examples of Refined Usage). Zhou, third century BCE. Anon. References to *Er ya zhu shu*爾雅注疏, in *Shi san jing zhu shu*十三經注疏 (Commentary to the Thirteen Canons), vol. 2.

Er ya yi shu 爾雅義疏 (Dilations on the Meaning of the *Examples of Refined Usage*). Qing. Hao Yixing 郝懿行 (1755–1823). Shanghai guji chubanshe, Shanghai, 1983.

Han shu 漢書 (History of the Former Han). Han, first century. Ban Gu 班固. Zhonghua shuju, Beijing, 1962.

Huangdi nei jing 黃帝內經 (Yellow Emperor's Inner Canon). Zhou to Han, third century BCE to first century CE. Anon. References to *Huangdi neijing zhangju suoyin* 黃帝內經章句索, edited by Ren Yingqiu 任應秋. Renmin weisheng chubanshe, Beijing, 1986.

Ling shu 靈樞, see *Huangdi nei jing* 黃帝內經.

Mawangdui Hanmu boshu zhengli xiaozu 馬王堆漢墓帛書整理小組 (eds). 1985. *Mawangdui Hanmu boshu* 馬王堆漢墓帛書 (The Silk Documents from a Han Tomb at Mawangdui), vol. 4. Wenwu chubanshe, Beijing.

Meng xi bi tan 夢溪筆談 (Dream Pool Essays). Song, 1086. Shen Kuo 沈括. References to *Mengxi bitan jiaozheng* 夢溪筆談校證, annotated by Hu Daojing 胡道靜. 2 vols. Shanghai guji chubanshe, Shanghai, 1987.

Ming yi bie lu 名醫別錄 (Informal Records of Eminent Physicians). Three Kingdoms, third century CE. Anonymous. Edited by Shang Zhijun 尚志鈞. Renmin weisheng chubanshe, Beijing, 1986.

Qi min yao shu 齊民要術 (Essential Techniques for the Peasantry). Northern Wei, 535. Jia Sixie賈思勰. References to *Qi min yao shu ji zhu* 齊民要術集注, annotated by Miao Qiyu 繆啟愉. Nongye chubanshe, Beijing, 1982.

*Qian jin yao fang*千金翼方 (Appended Prescriptions Worth a Thousand). Tang, 650/659. Sun Simiao 孫思邈. Ziyou chubanshe, Taipei, 1994.

[Shennong] Ben cao jing ji zhu 神農本草經集注 (Notes to Shennong's Canon on *Materia Medica*). Liang, *c*. 500. Tao Hongjing 陶弘景, annotated by Shang Zhijun 尚志鈞 and Shang Yuansheng 尚元勝. Renmin weisheng chubanshe, Beijing, 1994.

Shennong ben cao jing 神農本草經 (Shennong's Canon on *Materia Medica*). Han, first century CE. Anon. References to *Shennong bencaojing jizhu* 神農本草經輯注, annotated by Ma Jixing 馬繼興. Renmin weisheng chubanshe, Beijing, 1995.

Shi ji 史記 (Records of the Historian). Han, *c.* 90 BCE. Sima Qian 司馬遷. Zhonghua shuju, Beijing, 1959. See also: *Shiki kaichû kôshô* 史記會注考證.

Shi jing 詩經 (Book of Songs). Zhou, 1000–600 BCE. Anonymous. References to *Mao shi zheng yi* 毛詩正義. In *Shi san jing zhu shu* 十三經注疏 (Commentary to the Thirteen Canons), vol. 1.

Shi ming 釋名 (Explanation of Names). Han, 200 CE. Liu Xi 劉熙. *Si bu cong kan* 四部叢刊. Shangwu yinshuguan, Shanghai, 1929.

Shuo wen jie zi 說文解字 (Discussing Patterns and Explaining Words). Han, 121 CE. Xu Shen 許慎. References to *Shuo wen jie zi zhu* 說文解字注, commentated by Duan Yucai 段玉裁. Qing, 1776–1807. Shanghai guji chubanshe, Shanghai, 1981.

Tang ye ben cao 湯液本草 (*Materia Medica* of Decoctions). Yuan, 1298. Wang Haogu 王好古. References to *Jiegu laoren Zhenzhunang ji qita san zhong* 潔古老人珍珠囊及其他三種 (The Pearl Bag by Zhang Yuansu and Three Others of the Kind). Zhonghua shuju, Beijing, 1991.

Tian gong kai wu 天工開物 (Exploitation of the Works of Nature). Ming, 1637. Song Yingxing 宋應星, annotated by Zhong Guangyan 鐘廣言. Zhonghua shuju, Hong Kong, 1978.

Wai tai mi yao 外台秘要 (Arcane Essentials from the Imperial Library). Tang, 752. Wang Tao 王燾. Renmin weisheng chubanshe, Beijing, 1955.

Xin xiu ben cao 新修本草 (Newly Revised Materia Medica). Tang, 657–659. Su Jing 蘇敬. Shanghai guji chubanshe, Shanghai, 1985.

Zheng lei ben cao 證類本草 (*Materia Medica* Corrected and Arranged in Categories). Song, *c.* 1082. Tang Shenwei 唐慎微. References to *Chong xiu Zhenghe jing shi zheng lei bei yong ben cao* 重修政和經史證類備用本草. Facsimile of the 1249 edition. Renmin weisheng chubanshe, Beijing, 1957. And to *Siku yixue yeshu congshu* 四庫醫學叢書, annotated by Cao Xiaozhong 曹孝忠. Shanghai guji chubanshe, Shanghai, 1991.

Zhen zhu nang 珍珠囊 (The Pearl Bag). Jin, twelfth century. Zhang Yuansu 張元素 or Li Gao 李杲. References to *Jiegu laoren zhenzhunang ji qita san zhong* 潔古老人珍珠囊及其他三種 (The Pearl Bag by Zhang Yuansu and Three Others of the Kind). Zhonghua shuju, Beijing, 1991.

Zhen zhu nang bu yi yao xing fu 珍珠囊補遺藥性賦 (Pearl Bag, with Rhapsodies on the Properties of Drugs). Jin, twelfth century. Zhang Yuansu 張元素 or Li Gao 李杲. Punctuated by Wang Zijie 王子接. Qing, eighteenth century. Shanghai kexue jishu chubanshe, Shanghai, 1958.

Zhou hou bei ji fang 肘後備急方 (Emergency Recipes kept in one's Sleeve). Jin, fourth century. (340 CE?). Ge Hong 葛洪. *Si ku quan shu* 四庫全書 (Collection of the Works from the Four Storehouses). References to

Wen yuan ge Si ku quan shu 文淵閣 四庫全書. Shangwu yinshuguan, Taibei, 1983.

Zhu bing yuan hou lun 諸病源候論 (Treatise on the Origins and Symptoms of Medical Disorders). Sui, 610. Chao Yuanfang 巢元方. References to *Zhubing yuanhoulun jiaozhu,* annotated by Ding Guangdi 丁光迪. Renmin weisheng chubanshe, Beijing, 1991.

ANTHROPOLOGY
Editorial Introduction
Stephen Harris et al.

Trial and error must have played a significant part in the discovery of the healing properties of plants. Clues to the biological activities of some plants may have come from observations of animals, yet the observation that a particular species has certain biological activities is only one node in a network of interactions that lead to a plant being described as medicinal. Complete knowledge of the properties and efficacy of a medicinal plant can only be obtained through multidisciplinary investigations. Detailed observations and experimentation are necessary since the active principles in plants are not absolutes. At one dosage, and applied in a certain manner, a plant extract may be efficacious; at another it may be lethal.

Medicinal plants tend not to be given as simples but rather as mixtures, which may require complex formulae and elaborate preparation. Ayahuasca, the psychoactive preparation used by numerous Amerindians, is an elaborately prepared drink with one major ingredient (*Banisteriopsis caapi*). However, at least 100 other species, which increase the psychoactive properties of ayahuasca mixtures, are known to have been added at different times and in different places throughout Amazonian South America. Clearly, medicinal plant discovery and the understanding of their properties influence the physical and mental landscapes involved in the contexts in which they are utilized.

In the article 'Shamanic plants and gender in the Healing Forest', Françoise Barbira Freedman explores the known but unexplained male bias in Amazonian shamanism in terms of the transgendering that characterizes shamans' relations with spirits, mediated by plants and animals in the forest as cosmos. The plants used by Lamista Quechua shamans in the Peruvian Upper Amazon, in contrast with plants used by hunters and plants which are accessible to all, are associated with spirit owners, called 'mothers'. Using examples, Barbira Freedman addresses the little studied gendering of shamanic plants, most of which are paired as male and female and consistently contrasted with reference to colour, shape, habit, location and spirit owners. She argues that these gendered oppositions are central to the understanding and treatment of sickness by Upper Amazon shamans. Many plants have been shown to be pharmaco-active, but it is the dynamic interaction between paired plants and cosmological domains that constitutes the foundation of shamanic knowledge and power, mirroring the local polarities of upland forest and flooded lowlands as sites of male and female power sources. In contrast with seduction and predation for hunters and warriors, male shamans seduce and tame spirit allies like women. Shamanic agency in Amazonia is predominantly male not just because men control social relations outside residential and territorial units, but also because these relations are conceived of as mastery over cosmic reproductive powers with which female bodies are innately imbued.

Wenzel Geissler and Ruth Prince provide another fine-tuned ethnography of a particular locality in East Africa. Their article 'Persons, plants and relations: treating childhood illness in a western Kenyan village' explores some herbal medicinal practices around small children that they observed in a family in Uhero, a Luo village in western Kenya. They argue that people's knowledge about childhood illnesses and about the collection, preparation and effects of herbal medicines relies upon specific imaginations and practices of relatedness. Knowledge about medicines, and medicines' capacity to elicit bodily transformations, may not be located *within* entities, such as in the knowledgeable woman's mind or in the biochemical properties of the plants. Rather, they may be situated *between* entities or emerge from the interactions of entities. Crucial to transformational bodily processes is the engagement with others, human and non-human, through shared substance and physical nearness. Children's vital capacity itself emerges from relations; bodily health consists in the flows of substance between body and environment; and the potency of plants to heal resides in a web of interactions between the women of a village, between people and place, between living and dead, and between bodies and their environment. These traits of herbal medical practice in Uhero suggest that herbal remedies, for example in central-eastern Africa, do not simply represent an 'ethnobotany' or 'ethnopharmacology' with its specific 'pharmacopoeia', i.e. a set of potent medicinal substances, which nevertheless functions according to the same logic as biomedical pharmaceutics. Medicinal knowledge does not necessarily fit into itemized inventories that map the Linnaean botanical classification upon standardized inventories of disease. More importantly, medicines cannot be taken for granted as 'powerful things' that heal subjects equipped with instrumental rationality. The plants used in the cases examined are not just powerful tools, 'things' handled by knowledgeable actors, akin to western pharmaceuticals in the hands of biomedical doctors. Instead, they are part of substantial ties, emerging from relations and establishing or rebuilding relations.

3. Shamanic Plants and Gender in the Healing Forest

Françoise Barbira Freedman

Introduction

Shamans are experts who have agency in promoting, maintaining and restoring the connection between the bodies and souls of humans in an animated cosmos. This underlies the culturally understood notion of health in Amazonia. Healing implies the dissolution of body boundaries in order to extract or project material or immaterial entities that are markers of relationships with cosmic entities. Human social identity and personhood are remodelled again and again in function of contact, wanted or unwanted, with cosmic entities throughout the life cycle. 'Master plants' (Spanish: *plantas maestras*; Quechua: *mamayuk*) with psychotropic properties, handled specifically or preferentially by shamans, facilitate the opening of 'doors of perception' as tools of diagnosis and also in the treatment of sickness. Throughout Amazonia, tobacco (*Nicotiana rustica*) is the main shamanic plant tool used for acting on body boundaries as a male catalyst of 'master plants' owned/controlled by 'mother/guardian spirits' (Spanish: *madres*; Quechua: *mamakuna*); these are generically conceptualized as female although some of the spirits can be male or have both male and female personae. The paradox that in Amazonia women are often declared to have innate shamanic abilities, yet the large majority of shamans are male, needs to be examined in the light of the relation between shamanic medicinal plants, gender and shamanic agency in modifying bodies.

In this chapter, I discuss Amazonian notions of gender in relation to the classification and use of shamanic plants in the Peruvian Upper Amazon. This, surprisingly, has not been addressed in the anthropological literature in spite of the importance that local shamans and ordinary people attribute to the gendering of plants.

135

I argue that male shamans need to transcend their ordinary male identity in order to enter into relationships of both seduction (quasi-affinity) and taming (quasi-consanguineal closeness) with plant spirits as allies in the cosmos, and that in order to achieve this they display behaviours and engage in activities consigned to the female gender in the visible human world. If, as I argue, polarities of gender are central to the understanding of embodied kinship and to the relation between the visible and the invisible in Amazonia, then these gendered polarities, and how they are acted upon in shamans' androgynous bodies to enable their agency in the cosmos, must be brought to the fore. In those Amazonian societies in which plant medicine plays a main part in shamanic healing, as among all the Forest Quechua in the Upper Amazon (in Colombia, Ecuador, Peru and Bolivia), if not in other parts of Amazonia, the 'healing forest' (Schultes and Raffauf 1996) is a gendered forest.

My main ethnographic reference for the discussion of shamanic plant gendering in the Upper Amazon is to the Lamista Quechua, one of several Quechua-speaking forest minorities in northwest Amazonia. The Lamista Quechua are an ethnic aggregate of Amazonian people pacified by Spaniards around the frontier fort of Lamas in the seventeenth century. Like other Forest Quechua, the Lamistas have preserved a separate historical cultural identity through asymmetrical ethnic relations with the dominant society. Lamas, strategically located on the eastern slopes of the northern Andes of Peru before the rapids of the Huallaga river, the first southern tributary of the Amazon, has been a site of colonization, trade and shamanic exchanges between Andeans and Amazonians since pre-Incaic times. During the colonial period, the Lamista Quechua were reputed as makers and traders of curare arrow poison and as specialists in tree bark medicine (Spanish: *palos*). Like their Jivaroan neighbours, more particularly the Aguaruna, the Lamista Quechua can be described as egalitarian with respect to both political and gender relations but with a marked male dominance in political and shamanic activities (Descola 1986). I did anthropological field research among them for two years in 1975–1977, then for one year in 1980–1981, and since the end of the Shining Path guerrilla movement in 1995, I have visited them several times. Moreover, I conducted fieldwork with Lamista migrants near Iquitos. The languages used in research were Spanish and Quechua (San Martin dialect).

136

Why Should Female Shamans be Exceptional in Amazonia?

The realm of shamanic power in Amazonia is believed to be completely dominated by men, according to Atkinson (1992; general) and Kensinger (1995; Cashinahua). However, Perruchon (2003; Shuar) and Colpron (2006; Shipibo) argued differently, and Colpron has offered ethnographic evidence on Shipibo female shamans that differs significantly from previous scanty mentions of female shamans in the South American Lowlands. The relative absence of female shamans in Amazonia and more widely in South America has been explained in various ways. The dominant argument is that female shamans are more common in agrarian societies (Vitebsky 1995: 33, 38–39), where a spirit-possession type of shamanic practice and spirit mediumship are predominant.[1] However, in societies where spiritual power is actively achieved and shamans actively engage in summoning spirits, as is the case among hunters or hunters/horticulturalists, male shamanism prevails (Atkinson 1992). The shared underpinnings of shamanism and gender in the Amazon and in the Andes, which have surprisingly hardly been addressed in the respective literature on the two regions (Glass-Coffin 1998, 1999; Langdon and Baer 1992), challenge the hunter/agriculturalist differentiation. In the Andes, women have been associated with 'marginal, peripheral, degraded, passive or reactive forms of shamanism' (Glass-Coffin 1998: 140). In neither post-conquest Amazonia nor the Andes can centrality and marginality be generalized, as in both regions shamanism is politically but not socially, and economically but not symbolically, marginalized.

Historical explanations are also found wanting. The extent to which Christian interference, whether during the colonial period east of the Andes or since the rubber boom in the Lowlands, has modified the role of women in Amazonian shamanism is not clear. Marie Perruchon's (2003) study of gender and shamanism among the Shuar of western Amazonia explores the asymmetrical access to the shaman's role in a society where there is theoretically no differentiation between male and female shamans. She hypothesizes that gender relations have been altered through recent historical changes in Shuar society following the arrival of Catholic Salesian missionaries. Hispanic Catholics made the source of shamanic power male and rejected the idea that women could possess spiritual power, as they saw spiritual leaders as intrinsically male. Perruchon (2003: 176) sees the 'androcentric ideology' of Salesian missionaries as 'probably very influential' on the fact that female shamans are a diminishing category in Shuar society. Little evidence, however, is offered to support this view, either from historical sources or from comparative ethnographies. Perruchon's view would be supported by an increase in the number of female shamans following the recent reclaiming of a more authentic indigenous lifestyle by the Shuar and other forest indigenous populations in Ecuador, but this has as yet not been documented. Colpron's (2006) detailed ethnography of the Shipibo-Conibo supports Perruchon's (2003: 327, 343, 362) statements, that approximately one woman in every ten to twelve is a shaman, and that there is no perceived difference between female and male shamanic power. My own reckoning for the Lamista Quechua would be more conservative, with less than one per cent of women known to be shamans and a ratio of no more than one female to fifteen male shamans.

Why should other ethnographies of the region, including monographs written by women, have ignored the existence of female shamans? The definition and transmission of shamanic identity, agency and gendered identities may be relevant. When women engage in shamanism in the Upper Amazon, they are usually related to male shamans through ties of kinship, or affinity, or both. Shamans' wives or sisters may 'know' the plants used by their male shaman relatives, their chants, spells and modes of preparation and application. In some groups, women can become curers but do not take *ayahuasca* (Siskind 1973, on the Sharanahua). Some female shamans develop skills of their own, but competition with men outside their local kin group is only possible for those indigenous women who have migrated in ethnically mixed areas of settlement. The three Lamista Quechua female shamans who taught me aspects of their art admitted the limits of their agency in relation to the male shamans with whom they were closely related. They were able to remove pathogenic darts from the bodies of patients but could not send darts to enemies like their male counterparts.

Although seventy per cent of Amazonians now live in towns, and most shamanic activity takes place in urban environments (albeit with regular access to forest areas), the use of shamanic plants associated with cosmological referents continues to apply to urban shamanism (Barbira Freedman 1999). There is a proliferation of mixed-blood female folk healers in Amazonian towns, but female shamans proper, who use *ayahuasca* and/or other Amazonian psychotropic plants to treat patients, continue to be exceptions (there are no more than five in the town of Iquitos compared to the over 100 male shamans in 2007). In the Peruvian Upper Amazon, all the female shamans I interviewed, whether indigenous or of mixed blood, mediated or mediate their relationships with plant spirits through the networks of male shamans to whom they were or are related through ties of kinship, affinity or patronage. While this is not remarkable, it hints at a bar to accessing full-fledged shamanic power for Amazonian women in relation to their male relatives and patrons. As argued here, this barred access is best explained in the context of gendered medicinal plant use and modes of entry to the spirit world.

Herbalists, Hunters, Poison-Makers and Shamans

'All Indians are users of plant medicines' (Spanish: *todo indio es purguero*). This statement, which urban mixed-blood dwellers in Upper Amazon towns frequently make about forest people they label as 'Indians', is associated with fear. *Purga*, purgative, the colonial Spanish word for shamanic plant medicine as differentiated from common medicinal plants, denotes the use of plants that not only have a purging effect but are also psychotropic, inducing dreams or visions. The most basic distinction about plant use in the Upper Amazon is therefore an ethnic one. Non-Indians are users of 'simple plants' (local Spanish: *plantas sencillas*) – medicinal plants that can be applied directly for treatment by non-experts, including all women. In contrast to 'master plants', 'simple plants' do not have associations with the spirit world in the form of the 'mother spirits' that animate them. They do not require expert knowledge or power, nor do they confer knowledge or power on those who use them.

Besides this broad herbalist use of medicinal plants to which they do not attribute much importance, Indians use plants under three main rubrics: hunting, poison-making and shamanism. Unlike the use of 'simple plants' by either Indians or non-Indians, the use of plants in hunting, poison-making and shamanism requires expert handling by individuals following a long observance (at least half a year) of ritualized prescriptions and proscriptions. With the exception of powerful shamans whose affinity with animal species could be compromised by killing, all Indian men practice hunting from a young age until their mature years and use specific plants to sharpen their senses, their skills and their bravery. When this is insufficient and hunters are plagued by bad luck, they may prepare psychotropic brews to strengthen and seek visions of the incident or action that is at the origin of their bad luck.

The specialized role of poison-maker, transmitted in a male line through apprenticeship, is now dying out as there is less demand for dart poison or *curare*. With few exceptions (Balée 1994), the societal role of poison-makers has been little studied in Amazonia. The Lamista Quechua were one of few specialized groups who traded their *curare* in the Upper Amazon and until recently exchanged it for blowguns with the Aguaruna (Scazzocchio 1977). Although some of the plants that are most valued in the treatment of severe pathologies are both poisons and medicines, like the Malpighiaceae used in the making of *curare*, only confirmed male shamans can treat patients with these dangerous plants. All hunting poisons and the strongest fish poisons are dangerous to prepare and involve plants that are in some cases barred from use by non-expert men and, to my knowledge, are always barred to women. They are deemed to be powerful but not necessarily perceived as 'master plants' which link humans to entities in the spirit world.

The specificity of male shamanic agency, as distinct from poison-makers and hunters on the one hand, and herbalists and other healers, such as bonesetters, on the other, is not cut and dried. Experienced shamans have the most inclusive power. However, the agency to prepare vision-inducing brews is mostly reserved for men – only exceptionally for Lamista Quechua women – who have apprenticed themselves to older men in order to gain experience and knowledge of plants with powerful and often dangerous effects. These are the specialists I refer to as shamans in this chapter. Differences in degree between herbalists and shamans rest on agency, by which I mean the ability to transform actively and shape phenomena and inter-subjective relations with visible effects. Symbolic efficacy, the social recognition of which is the measure of shamanic power anywhere in the world, implies both an interpretation of the root causes of phenomena and the ability to act at this causal level to bring about desired changes.

While some herbalists have enough cognitive understanding of the cosmology of the Upper Amazon to diagnose causes of illness, they do not have the visionary power that is at the source of shamanic agency. This is only conferred by a prolonged personal relatedness with the mother spirits of 'master plants'. Poison-makers stand out as pragmatic specialists whose skills overlap with those of shamans but who are not concerned with the relations between humans and spirits. Continuities and discontinuities between the male activities of hunting, poison-making and shamanic activities, open to both men and women, can be elucidated in relation to gender.

Greene's (1998: 641) concise description of South American shamanism aptly refers to the fact that shamans address sickness not just as a physical condition of individual bodies but also as an inherently socio-political and cosmological condition. Sorcery, from within or without local communities, intersects with the actions of spirits, dead ancestors and natural forces to cause sickness. In their classic introduction to shamanism in South America, Langdon and Baer (1992) compare and contrast a multiplicity of shamanisms with respect to social authority. Although in some parts of Amazonia shamans can assume political leadership or priesthood, this is not the case among the Lamista Quechua or the majority of indigenous peoples of the Upper Amazon (see Hugh-Jones 1995 on the differentiation between horizontal and vertical forms of shamanism). Distinctions between the role of shaman and what Vitebsky (1995: 121) called 'shamanship' are helpful in accounting for the fact that there is a continuum of specialization among shamans, to which seniority, recovery from a serious illness and long periods of apprenticeship are most relevant. Whether they officiate in life-cycle rituals and lead annual cycle festivities or not, Amazonian shamans' power is founded on their life-giving strength. For Santos-Granero (1986: 257), 'in lowland South America political power and the ritual of production are two sides of the same coin'. This links back to Eliade's (1964: 323) classic references to shaman's tasks as increasers of game, facilitating births, reading omens and acting as intermediary between humans and spirits. Lamista shamans are explicit about their role as reproducers of plants, animals and

141

human society in the cosmos. Their agency and mediation in the cosmos are starkly differentiated from the physiological, unmediated way in which women have babies. Notwithstanding this, shamanic songs allude to the ways in which male shamans emulate women's reproductive powers. Shamans, of either sex, intervene with the spirits, the masters of game animals and cosmic elements in order to maintain or recreate harmony and balance. However, this is a thankless and constant task. In order to keep boundaries safe in society (bounded bodies, boundaries between the human and spirit worlds), shamans must transgress them, fighting enemies without respite. Alliances with spirits are precarious in the same way that neither marital relations nor political alliances are secure, requiring frequent shamanic intervention to repair and strengthen them.

All along the Upper Amazon arc that extends from Bolivia to Colombia, pre- and post-Hispanic exchanges between Andean and Amazonian populations resulted in the historical development of extensive medicinal floras that incorporated non-local plant species and integrated exogenous concepts of health and disease. The rise of the medical system called Vegetalismo in the Peruvian Upper Amazon in the late nineteenth century (Barbira Freedman 1999) contributed to formalize the differentiation between shamanic 'master plants' and 'simple plants' (Luna 1986). The local appellation of plants with mother-spirits as 'master plants' connotes the use of these plants by shamans to gain further knowledge and expand their art. Mother-spirits endow the plants they own/control/animate with a power that humans can muster but that is also dangerous to them if their bodies are not adequately prepared by special diets.[2] Chemical research on plants-with-mother spirits in the last two decades has identified a high incidence of alkaloids and other chemicals that substantiate the relative power and importance attributed to these plants. Although a reductionist explanation can be offered, namely, that most shamanic plants include compounds which act upon the central nervous system and therefore entail risks, this does not represent indigenous understanding. Local shamans consider a plant's relative value or efficacy not in terms of its intrinsic medicinal properties but in terms of its association with the spirit world. 'Master plants' that constitute the shamanic *materia medica* (Spanish: *el vegetal*), such as for instance *ayahuasca* (*Banisteriopsis caapi* and various plant admixtures), are valued over and above medicinal plants of recognized great utilitarian worth,[3] such as the wound healing dragon's blood (*Croton lechleri*). The attribute of souls to plants in the context of Amazonian animism is too complex an issue to address in this chapter. While all *plantas maestras* have souls, some culturally important plants, such as manioc and maize, are also endowed with souls. 'Simple plants', however, do not have souls.

The training of Upper Amazon shamans aims to identify those 'master plants' that will give them access to spirit 'allies' (Spanish: *espiritus aliados*, Quechua: *supay* + possessive suffix) in visions and dreams. These allies, with a connotation of 'helpers' or 'assistants' (Spanish: *ayudantes*), confer agency on shamans for the purpose of healing or harming humans. If the support of allies is lost, so is the particular agency that they enabled. There is a parallel between the support that the spirit masters of game animals give to hunters so that they find game, and the power that mother-spirits of 'master plants' confer on shamans. This parallel invites an engagement with debates on predation and seduction in Amazonian anthropology. The fact that Amazonian women do not hunt with spears, blowguns or guns, relying mostly on machetes to debunk and kill animals, needs to be considered. The predatory imagery of shamanism is predominantly male, drawn from both hunting and warfare. Shamans heal by removing pathogenic 'darts' from patients' bodies and they harm or kill by sending 'darts' into their enemies' bodies. Hunting also involves the seduction of the game animals that are to become prey, with an imagery of sexual seduction. The power of attraction that draws game to hunters and spirits to shamans has become generalized as luck in love and fortune in the urban shamanism of the Upper Amazon. *Pusanga*, originally referring to hunting magic among the Shuar, has become as a generic name for all plants and amulets used to retrieve or increase luck, ensure seduction or neutralize it when its misuse has caused harm. Like hunters, shamans use *pusanga* plants and objects to protect themselves and to enhance their seductive appeal to spirits. The luck magic known as *pusanga* thus highlights the close relation between seduction and predation in hunting and shamanism. Shamans treat hunters affected by loss of luck; they also use *pusanga* plants for treating men or women suffering from misfortune and persistent bad luck associated with gender relations. Unlike 'simple plants', which are not gendered, *pusanga* plants, like 'master plants', are paired as male and female counterparts. Shamanic treatment

143

using these plants relies on the visionary power and spirit allies they confer, in contrast with urban folk healers who use *pusanga* plants as if they were 'simple plants'.

In order to counter the harmful agency that caused illness (whether that of a malevolent shaman, a molested spirit or a disturbed cosmic element), shamans acting as healers and restorers of social and cosmic harmony need to 'see' the causes in plant-induced visions or dreams. On the basis of their visions, they then activate their embodied power/knowledge (Quechua: *yachay*) with the support of their plant spirit allies in order to 'put right' what was 'twisted' or 'deviated'. Only plants with 'mother spirits' procure access to the immanent dimension of 'soul' and the spirit world where the causes of human fortune and misfortune can be acted upon. While in other parts of Amazonia, biochemical stimulation is sought directly from plants (tobacco, *ayahuasca*, *Virola* species) or from animals (toads, ants) to achieve direct contact with spirits, in the Upper Amazon a particular symbolic medical system has developed around an elaborate knowledge of plants and their effects. This development took place during the colonial period, reaching a peak with the *vegetalismo* in the first half of the twentieth century, but symbolic associations between plants, animals and power may have already been used in pre-Hispanic times. In this system, mastery consists in gaining a personal understanding of, and consequently agency over, empirical and symbolic connections between aspects and elements of the cosmos, all of which are neither animated or unanimated in a fixed way, nor male or female, nor separated or connected with the human world. For Amazonian Quechua shamans, and shamans in a few other indigenous populations in the Upper Amazon (Witoto, Siona, Secoya, Muinane), 'master plants' are selected for both their empirical and symbolic properties. These properties are not differentiated in the perception of local shamans: plants can both be good to think with and good to use. The cosmopolitan ethnobotanical divide between the empirical and symbolic components of Amazonian shamanic plant knowledge is not acceptable to Amazonian shamans.

Once shamans have harnessed the support of particular 'mother spirits', their power becomes ambivalent and can be used for healing or harming, restoring balance or destroying it. In order to attain this ambivalence, shamans must transcend the most symbolically important polarity in the cosmos: gender. They do so not only by transgressing gender boundaries, assuming a different gender identity from that of their birth when acting in the cosmos, but also through ingesting plants classified and paired as male or female. The Amazonian cosmos is also made up of domains permeated with gender symbolism.

Transformation, Gender and Androgyny in Amazonia

In their comparison of gender in Amazonia and Melanesia, Gregor and Tuzin (2001) comment on how gender roles and their attendant ideas about sexuality appear as templates for many other domains of culture: 'Ritual systems, cosmology, leadership, warfare, concepts of self and images of the human body, kinship and perceptions of the environment are all gendered: thought of and conceived in terms that are linked to masculinity, femininity and human sexuality.' Pertinently, Gregor and Tuzin (2001: 8–9) note that Lindenbaum (1984: 222) could have been referring to Amazonia when she observed that: 'Papua New Guineans live in a gender-inflected universe in which the polarities of male and female articulate cosmic forces thought to be located in the human body; indigenous theories of human reproduction contain within them an implicit recipe for social reproduction.' In the Upper Amazon, where journeys to both the Andes and to the Lowlands are part of the collective consciousness of the landscape (even if they are not regular occurrences for all people), polarities of high and low, dry and wet, hard and soft, are pervaded with male/female complementary oppositions. Shamanic power draws on the qualities of these gendered environments: each shaman needs to create his or her own dialectical mastery of polarities and seeks experiential knowledge of 'master plants' that illustrate and reveal contrasting properties, thereby confirming and expanding the systemic aspects of Upper Amazon shamanic plant medicine.

Not surprisingly, human sexuality, associated not only with procreation and pleasure but also with illness and symbolic contamination, looms large in the understanding and use of shamanic 'master plants'. Avoidance of any contact with women of reproductive age is one of the most stringent aspects of shamanic training, together with the avoidance of salt. Human sexual avoidance underlies any activity involving access to the spirit world, which in contrast is characterized by a hyper-sexuality. The shamanic ascesis (Quechua: *sasiku*) can be seen as a more stringent extension of the rules that apply to hunters and poison-makers before they go hunting or make poison. Unlike hunters and poison-makers, however, shamans need to transcend and gain mastery over the most dangerous and polluting aspects of femaleness: menstruation and childbirth. Although there is no ritual practice of bleeding penises in Amazonia, comparisons have been made between symbolic procreation and parturition in Melanesia and in Amazonia (Hugh-Jones 2001). Menstruating and childbearing women are polluting to men in general, particularly to male shamans, and above all to spirits. To my knowledge, female shamans either suppress manifestations of their female identity if they are of menstruating age or they mostly take up shamanism after the menopause. Colpron (2006) confirms this in describing how Shipibo female shamans who still menstruate must hide and actively attempt to suppress their female body odours [using tobacco, *piri piri* (*Cyperus* species)] in order to practice shamanism. Among the Quechua Lamista, a menstruating or lactating woman would absolutely be barred from ingesting 'master plants' as a patient, let alone as a practitioner. Breaches of taboos related to sexuality are frequent explanations for illnesses of women, men and children who then require shamanic intervention. In order to perform these treatments, male shamans must have integrated female sexual attributes into their own bodies, after having made themselves soft by means of fasting and inactivity in seclusion. Female shamans enter shamanism as a praxis that is mostly defined from a male perspective. The interdependence between human shamans and cosmic entities is negotiated on the basis of male agents incorporating female sexual and reproductive powers, while female agents need to suppress them in order to acquire a quasi-male agency. The transgendering of male shamans and of spirits who can change their gender identity in specific encounters, or over time, is extremely fluid, supporting the 'transformational' quality of Amazonian cosmologies highlighted by Rivière (1989). Lamista Quechua shamans present the transcending and harmonizing of gendered opposites in the cosmos as the main purpose of their shamanship: their role is to constantly 'put straight', 'bring back into line' the lives of individuals and of their communities

146

through a dynamic balance that they activate as an embodied process. Individual male shamanic transgression of gender boundaries in the Upper Amazon, using 'master plants' as the means to this end, can be compared to collective forms of male transgendering in Amazonia in male rituals of initiation and cyclical social reproduction rituals in other parts of Amazonia. Anthropological interpretations of war feuds and head-hunting as predation, followed by a progressive (female-like) taming and incorporation of enemies through a variety of rituals that involve women (Overing and Passes 2000; Taylor 2000), indicate more complex ways of turning gender boundaries inside out in order to reinforce group fertility.

Female shamans have to transcend gender through a sublimation of the innate capacities of their bodies which are blander when it comes to accessing the spirit world and activating the cosmic forces of reproduction. They enter the shamanic career as putative men and practice as shamanic healers and sometimes sorceresses on the understanding that they hide their gender identity (as culturally constructed in Amazonia). Female shamanism cannot be defined or practiced separately from male shamanic transgendering, paradoxically emulating it in their interactions with both male shamans and the spirits. The incantations (Quechua: *icaro*) that they chant in shamanic sessions do not differ from those of men. Although it is often said in the Upper Amazon that women have more natural ability to shamanize than men, the symbolic system through which they need to filter this ability is defined from a male perspective. Female shamans enter an arena of alliances and enmities in which there is no possible neutral position. As one Lamista female shaman put it, having set foot 'in this football pitch we cannot get out and the game is relentless, never-ending'. This is a first explanation of the relative invisibility of female shamanism in the anthropological literature, not only because in the Upper Amazon female shamans are few and far between among male shamans but also because the arena of shamanism is defined in terms of a male symbolic appropriation of female reproductive powers.

McCallum (2004) has signalled eloquently the risks of essentializing gender and sexuality in Amazonian ethnographies.[4] It is not only the androgyny of Amazonian shamans but also their transformative powers and interaction with animals and spirit entities that have challenged anthropological thinking about gender, sexuality and personhood beyond the comparative sphere of Melazonia (i.e. Melanesia and Amazonia). Rather than fixed categories, shamans engage with attributes of sex as part of a perspectival world that allows many permutations of form and identity according to the position of the subject.[5] Perruchon (2003: 28) found that Shuar male shamans made love to a female Tsunki and female ones to a male Tsunki anaconda, whereby both Tsunki were conceived of as the archetypal first Shuar shaman. The archetypal first shaman, for the Lamista Quechua as for many other Amazonian Amerindian forest people, is the rainbow anaconda, perceived as either male or female or androgynous.[6]

When asked whether the souls of women and men are the same, Lamista Quechua people hesitate. Many are not sure and comment on the greater vulnerability of women's over men's bodies to cosmic entities, particularly in the vicinity of water. There is a consensus that women's souls are more easily possessed by water spirits because their bodies are softer and less bounded, particularly during menstruation, childbirth and nursing when bodies are open and leaky. Irrespective of the greater permeability of women's bodies, for the Lamista Quechua a healthy body is generally speaking a bounded body. Sickness is understood as an intrusion that is remedied by loosening boundaries, removing pathogens and sealing the body anew. In the Upper Amazon, the training of male shamans includes the use of 'master plants' to contact, channel and harness the powers attributed to the moon and the rainbow associated with the female gender. Visions of, and identification with, the anaconda, the mother spirit of the water, are obtained through a 'study' of water master plants (a long process of familiarization while dieting in isolation), resulting in a very concrete knowledge of these plants' ecologies, their patterns of reproduction, their interaction with animals which live from them in various ways or disperse their fruit and seeds, and also their symbolic associations with other beings in the cosmos. This is done while ingesting the plants and experimenting with their effects under the supervision of a more experienced shaman, and also by engaging in extensive observations in the plants' habitats. It is the combination of experiential knowledge, personal observations and transmitted lore that constitutes shamanic knowledge/power, or *yachay*.[7] As shaman apprentices gain increasing familiarity with the animal mother spirits of the plants, they acquire and come to master the perspectives of these beings: in the case of the water, otters (Spanish: *lobo de rio*, species: *Pteronura brasiliensis* and *nutria*, species: *Lontra longicaudis*), river dolphins (Spanish: *bufeo, boto*, species: *Inia geoffrensis*) and caymans (Spanish: *lagarto*, species: *Caiman crocodilus yacare*) are seen as the children (closely related and obedient) of the giant green anaconda Yaku Mama (*Eunectes murinus*), mother-owner of the water cosmic domain. The challenge that shamans face is to embody these perspectives, when desired, without losing their own personal human identities. When common mortals are accidentally overcome by animal entities to the point of losing their human perspective (an occurrence that women are more vulnerable to in the case of water spirits), shamans need to use their knowledge of the 'master plants' related to water and sing the corresponding chants in order to bring the victims back into their human bodies.

Rather than seeking explanations for the scarcity of Amazonian female shamans in connection with social and political gender relations, both anthropological arguments and local ethnography point to cosmological epistemology as a locus of analysis. Lamista Quechua shamans describe their work as maintaining the balance of sexual power in the cosmos, by maintaining polarities inscribed in landscapes and journeying metaphorically between the poles they claim control of. The greater power they claim, the more distant and significant the polarities of reference are, extending outside the Amazon region. Although it is relevant that men travel through the forest/cosmos as hunters and shamans (the same Quechua word *puri-ku* is used for both physical and shamanic travel) and that they take overall responsibility for relations with the outside world beyond the local community, it is necessary to further elucidate perceived gender differences in the essential shamanic requirement of de-centring and re-centring bodies and perspectives. In the following section I offer a few examples of the gendering of plants in the polarized cosmic domains of the water and the upland forest as a basis for discussion.

Gendered Plants in the Wet Lowlands and the Montane Forest

Far from representing 'botanical metaphors', shamanic plants heal or kill, or both; heal and kill, bind or separate; or both, bind and separate. They are material instantiations that are essential to the social reproduction of persons. Shamanic plants mediate growth, life cycles and the restoration of integral identity and body/soul boundaries. While in some parts of Amazonia, shamans only use a few plants besides tobacco for maintaining or restoring balance between the human and spirit worlds, in the Upper Amazon and all along the foothills of the Andes bordering the Amazon basin shamanic practice involves about two hundred 'master plants' with three hundred or more medicinal plants that have no recorded 'mother spirits' but that can be adjoined to 'master plants' in shamanic visionary brews and in remedies. In spite of the historical interest in medicinal plant use by the Hispanic missionaries and chroniclers, until recently little interest was paid to shamanic plant knowledge other than that of herbalism. What constitutes a shared medicinal flora has been and continues to be decided by individuals and is transmitted through time and in space. In the region, it consists partly of esoteric shamanic knowledge, owned only by those who have engaged on an experiential training, and partly of shared communal medicinal knowledge. This combination is still present in the compilation of the Lamista Quechua medicinal flora published by the local expert Grimaldo Rengifo (2005). The encyclopaedias of medicinal plants compiled by local biologists in the wake of the Rio Biodiversity Convention in 1992 list uses of plants per region but do not take into account local perceptions of plant mother spirits. Some mention the vernacular gendering of some plants but none elaborates on the generalized perception of plants in gendered pairs. The invisibility of local categories in the representation of Upper Amazon plant knowledge in the published literature and in most of the local 'botanical gardens' is best attributed to the dominance of cosmopolitan botany.

The range of shamanic plants mastered by distinctive shamans varies a great deal. On average, a strong Lamista Quechua shaman has full knowledge of about fifteen to twenty 'master plants' and uses five or six additional plants consistently in his/her day-today practice. Learning about plants is part of the upbringing of indigenous children in a forest environment, together with learning about animals, weather patterns, and the wild crafting of forest resources. At the extreme urban end of the forest-urban continuum of contemporary Amazonian shamanism, however, it is now possible to come across shamans who use purchased *ayahuasca* and do not have any empirical knowledge of plants. Nevertheless, even though the Upper Amazon shamans with whom I am concerned here reside mostly in towns, they all have gained a personal knowledge of 'master plants' in their training and the majority of them know more about medicinal plant use than local herbalists.

Throughout the Upper Amazon there is a consensus that plants are paired and contrasted as male and female (Spanish: *macho y hembra*, Quechua: *ullku/warmi*) on the basis of descriptors associated with gender categories. In a minority of cases, gendering refers to related modern botanical species or to varieties of one species. In the majority of cases, gendering denotes a symbolic pairing of two different plant species. Although the gender descriptors are not used systematically within the medicinal flora of any one indigenous group, this pairing is widespread and broadly consistent through the Upper Amazon. Forest people are sensitive to the pairing of flowering trees in the forest canopy. Complementary gendered plants are always thought of in relation to each other, paying attention to their location and interaction on the ground, their differentiated uses and symbolic associations. Paired plants are cultivated together in plant gardens. I have found no evidence that male and female shamans use more plants of the same or of the opposite gender: both use either or both.

A cosmological feature not accounted for in Viveiros de Castro's (1998) perspectivism is the widespread use of Chinese box or Russian dolls patterns to encase levels of inclusion of particular phenomena. The most inclusive level of gender complementarity of plants in Upper Amazon shamanism is that between tobacco and all other 'master plants'. Tobacco is considered to be the male catalyst that enhances the effects of all other shamanic plants. Lamista Quechua shamans frequently assert that tobacco is the 'father of all plants', a male consort to the 'mother spirits' of all shamanic plants. Tobacco, the domestication of which is thought to have originated on the eastern slopes of the central Andes 7,000 years ago (Wilbert 1987), is the shamanic plant *par excellence* in South America. While

151

ayahuasca (*Banisteriopsis caapi*) has gained increasing dominance in Amazonian neo-shamanism through the twentieth century, tobacco continues to be the most important plant without which no shamanic activity can take place, be it a collective ritual or an individual healing séance (Barbira Freedman 2002).

Although most men and some Amazonian women smoke tobacco publicly, the healing or transformative activity of blowing tobacco on the bodies of patients is a shamanic prerogative that can be seen as an extension of the way in which hunters use tobacco as a source of protection in the forest, a means of defence against spirit attacks and a tool for taming spirits in wild forest areas. Tobacco is the botanical support of a paradigmatically male shamanic agency in the cosmos, enabling shamans to access the undifferentiated, transformative space in which the boundaries of human persons can be dissolved and redrawn. Tobacco dehumanizes hunters by disguising the human body odours detested by spirits throughout Amazonia. Upper Amazon female shamans all use tobacco in the same way as men shamans, donning large cigars to show their matching competence. As far as I know, all female shamans acknowledge the gendered complementarity between tobacco and the other 'master plants' whence they derive their knowledge/power.

Another general aspect of gender complementarity, which to my knowledge has been ignored in the literature, is related to colour symbolism in the Upper Amazon: black, red and white are dominant colours, to which are added iridescent and shiny blue/green. The iridescent quality, which all Quechua attribute to the rainbow, does not apply to plants, only to animals, such as the anaconda and certain boas. In the general colour symbolism of the Upper Amazon, white and white/red are mostly associated with the female gender, and black and black/red with the male. There is an overlap with healing for white and red, harming with sorcery for black, and shamanic ambivalence of healing and harming for black and red. The relation between colour and the organoleptic properties of Amazonian medicinal plants, particularly tree barks in the Upper Amazon, has been surprisingly ignored in the literature in spite of the importance that local people give to it in both their description and uses of plants.[8] Colour is relevant to my argument that plants are perceived and used in function of their attributed gender: a 'white' tree can be predicted to be associated with healing and the learnings of therapeutic shamanism, while its black or red counterpart are likely to connote ambivalent shamanic power or sorcery. In the Upper Amazon, a large number of tree species, if not the majority of them, are categorized on the basis of these three dominant colours and there is a general consensus about their spirit associations and the properties of their barks, roots and exudates where colour identification overrules odours, textures and tastes.

The gendered complementarity of paired plants in the Upper Amazon is rationalized in a number of ways that include observed aspects such as contrasting habits: crawler versus climbing plant (Mansoa alliacea sp. *ajo sacha*); shapes of leaves (Petiveria alliacea sp. *mucura*); colour (Jatropha sp. *piñon rojo, piñon blanco*); and sexual attributes (Spanish: *buceta*). Besides visible features, explanations are also offered in terms of associations with cosmic domains (wet lowlands/upland forest, Spanish: *del agua/de la altura*). For example, the *Capirona* tree (*Calycophyllum* species) is differentiated into *Capirona del agua* and *Capirona de la altura*, to which not only the Lamista Quechua but also other Upper Amazon forest people attribute contrasting characteristics and properties. It is claimed that only the upland forest *Capirona* is effective for treating malaria. Other explanations include associations with gendered spirits: male and female spirits of the water (Quechua: *yaku runa / yaku mama*), a domain epitomized by the giant anaconda, and male and female spirits of the upland forest (Quechua: *sacha runa /sacha mama*), a domain epitomized by the gold jaguar (*Panthera onca*). The symbolic logic that underlies these associations is inscribed in a cosmology described in piecemeal accounts of individual shamanic embodied experience. In Upper Amazon shamanism, the gendering of plants, juxtaposed with the complementary opposition of wet lowlands (feminine) and dry upland forest (masculine), may be seen as part of the canonic dualism which Lévi-Strauss has unveiled in its many complex facets in Amazonia. Shamans use polarities of space and gender in a dynamic way in the sense of what Peter Roe (1998) coined as 'dynamic Lowland South Amerindian dualism'. In his analysis of the jaguar in its gold and black manifestations, Roe argues that the jaguar is not just opposed to aquatic reptilian forms like the anaconda but that it also constitutes an internal dyad that locks contrasting aspects. While the gold jaguar (local Spanish: *tigre*) is a paragon of masculine Culture, associated with the sun, beneficial hunts and eagles, the black jaguar (Quechua: *yana puma*) represents a negative embodiment of feminine Nature, associated with the water (clouds and flooded forests), with the anaconda and with danger and evil. My argument is that the extreme poles, symbolized by the giant anaconda (androgynous but quintessentially female) and the jaguar (with male associations of predation in spite of the role of female jaguars as predators), are extremely difficult, if not impossible for women to access in the Amazonian cosmos, due to perceived differences in the capacities that male and female bodies have for transgendering.

Plants that are not gendered are placed outside the local symbolic system, either because they are Hispanic colonial (lavender, rue) or Chinese (ginger) imports, or imports from more recent colonists (garden decoratives used as good luck plants). The Lamista Quechua also traditionally used certain plants as boundary markers on the margins of local residence groups and these are not gendered. Medicinal epiphytes recently introduced from other parts of Amazonia as part of neo-shamanic curing have not been gendered in the Lamista Quechua flora, as there is no local traditional medicinal use of epiphytes. Lamista shamans are keen to experiment with new plants (e.g. noni [*Morinda citrifolia*] from the Pacific region in recent years) but plants imported from within Amazonia fit more readily in their symbolic medical system than exogenous plants.

Two tables are presented in what follows with a view to illustrating the gendering of plants and their cosmic associations. The water cosmic domain is generally associated with female plants and female reproductive functions and sexuality (Table 3.1), whilst the upland forest domain is generally associated with male plants and men's strength and virility (Table 3.2). According to the vernacular classification, female and male plants have their own attributes in each cosmic domain, irrespective of their habitat.

Water, the Female Domain of Amazonian Shamanism

In order to gain control in the transgression of boundaries between the human and spirit worlds, or the visible and the invisible, which is the hallmark of their power and craft, Amazonian shamans must also gain a metaphorical command of gender polarities in the cosmic domains of water, earth and sky. In the Peruvian Upper Amazon, this takes the form of shamanic journeying from the Andean foothills to Amazonian rivers (and more particularly to the lakes), in order to collect stones and shells of particular colours and qualities and enter into alliances with particular animals whose forms, habits and special characteristics are of symbolic interest. The behaviour of otters and pink dolphins as water mammals, the predatory powers of sting rays, jaguars and harpy eagles, and the magnetism of snakes are selected as features which humans can use to link to the cosmic domains and to master their dynamics. In the Amazonian cosmos, border areas and beings that cross over from one domain to another or link domains are given particular significance in assisting human shamans to perform their to and fro journeys to the spirit world. The rainbow and its animal counterpart, the anaconda, not only symbolize the connection between earth/water/forest and sky but also epitomize the shamanic bridging identity with a connotation of androgyny. Shamans who master the cluster of symbols and metaphors of the rainbow gain a greater ability to treat diseases attributed to the rainbow and underwater streams, both in the Amazon and in the Andean regions. 'Diseases of the rainbow' (Spanish: *enfermedades del arco*) affect women more specifically. Shamans who have mastered the use of plants associated with the rainbow develop a particular transgendered identity that entails a command of human female sexuality and reproductive processes. They have reached the apex of a shaman's career, discussed in more detail below.

The base of Lamista Quechua shamanic expertise is 'strong tree medicine' (Quechua: *sinchi palero yachay*) from barks that are only found, or are particularly strong, in the montane forest. Until a few decades ago, new shamans had to demonstrate the potency of their tree medicine among senior shamans in the same way as young Lamista men had to prove their physical strength before being allowed to marry. The path of tree medicine has not traditionally been open to women, nor has it been opened yet, as the barks of 'master plants' are said to require too much strength for women's bodies.

To be fully accomplished and gain a socially acknowledged control of the water domain, a Lamista Quechua shaman must furthermore travel either to the Lower Huallaga river to gain power from Cocama shamans or to the Ucayali river to gain power from Shipibo shamans.

There, he gains mastery of the 'knowledge/power of the water' (Quechua: *yaku yachay*), including the use of 'water plants' (Spanish: *plantas del agua*, as opposed to *plantas del monte*).[9] He does this with the help of a 'water wife', a female water spirit who helps him form affinal relations in the underwater world.[10] As shamans 'travel' in spirit through the underwater world from their homes along the waterways, they are thought to develop closer relations with underwater spirits, progressing from affinity to quasi-consanguineal ties as they consolidate relations with their underwater families. This path is open to women but the trickery of the male underwater consorts (Quechua: *yaku runa*) is greater than that of the mermaids. On their return, shamans endowed with water plant powers must set up residence near a river that is a tributary of a larger river with *urmana*, i.e. with access to a larger waterway, if not of the Amazon itself.

The highest rank in Upper Amazon shamanism is that of *banku*, which involves the capacity to divine the causes of illness and their treatments through the prolonged immersion of shamans in deep river pools, where they are in direct contact with water spirits and no longer require to ingest 'master-plants'. I am not aware that any woman has ever been recorded as having reached this status anywhere in Amazonia, even in old age. Female shamans can compete with men in the treatment of rainbow diseases up to the point that they risk losing their identity boundary and do not come back. Their ability to master the perspectives of cosmic beings is to a large extent mediated by the network of male shaman relatives (kin and affines) of which they are part. Shamans who have 'mastered the rainbow', controlling its symbolic associations with plants and animals across water and upland forest domains, also travel to the northern Andes to exchange shamanic knowledge and power with Andean shamans living near mountain lakes, thought to be connected to the Amazon waterways.

Mature shamans who embody the anaconda/rainbow have gained control of gender and a special expertise in identifying and resolving human illnesses (physical, psychological or both) in terms of liminality; in contrast to the unfortunate females or inadvertent males who have been seduced/captured by water spirits of the opposite sex. Mature shamans identify situations of inappropriate contact or transgression (for instance, a menstruating woman washing clothes in the river) when human bodies are not firmly bounded. Their task is to re-create and seal the appropriate placement of embodied perspectives that have been inappropriately conflated. This is done with the help of plants. To aim at separating the symbolic treatment from the plants' pharmaco-active properties would misrepresent local understandings of shamanic treatments. The plants that heal women's reproductive afflictions, such as disorders of menstruation, of pregnancy and childbirth and, more generally, of bleeding and uterine dysfunctions throughout the female reproductive cycle, not only have healing properties but are also used as 'master plants' to increase the receptivity of both male shamans and their female patients to the spirit world. They are typically plants of the water.

Water Plants

Shamans have secluded small gardens in which they cultivate or tend wild specimens of 'master plants', whose mother spirits have provided them with particularly valuable guidance in their quest for knowledge/ power. Shamans who develop expertise in water plants mostly live near a stream or river where they can be in close proximity to plants with perceived associations with water spirits, be they metaphorical or real (in that they are the foodstuffs of or provide an abode for the water boas or river mammals). Lamista shamans, who are mostly bark medicine experts, may live in upper forest communities where water plants cannot be found or cultivated as there are only small streams. In this case, shamans rely on the incantations that they have learnt from wet lowlands shamans whom they visit without actually using plants. When treating patients, these shamans of the upland forest re-live their journeys to the wet lowlands and their acquisition of water plant knowledge. Their declared intent in using particular water plants is to benefit their social network and accrue their power in relation to competitors.

The Lamista Quechua female shamans, and the female shamans of mixed blood whom I got to know during fieldwork, did not have their own special gardens to grow their familiar 'master-plants' nor did they tend plants in the forest like their male counterparts. However, some grew their own *ayahuasca* vines and other shamanic plants in their own backyards or gardens. Like other women, the Lamista female shamans I knew made and decorated water pots with cosmic symbols, with which they also decorated the belts they handwove for male kin. The symbolism of women's crafts in relation to shamanism and *ayahuasca* visions has been described by Ghebart-Sayer (1984) for the Shipibo. Water symbols, particularly stylized anaconda, are frequently represented on Lamista women's pots and belts. Lamista Quechua men did not interfere with the women's making of pots, even though the firing of large pots required considerable strength, due to the handling of large logs, while Lamista Quechua women accepted the ban on their proximity to the special areas where men grew shamanic plants and to the cooking pots, where medicines were prepared.

Figure 3.1: A female plant of the water

Figure 3.2: A male plant of the water

Table 3.1:[12] Gendering of water plants and their cosmic associations.

Pair	Vernacular name (gender)	Botanical name (family)	Parts used and colours	Mother spirits	Known active chemicals	Shamanic expertise required	Conditions treated
1	*Bohinsana* (f)	*Calliandra angustifolia* Spruce ex Benth. (Fabaceae) (synonym: *C. stricta* Rusby)	Shrub with red/white flowers.	Mermaid	Cyclooxygenase inhibitors and harmala alkaloids	Medium to high	Inflammatory conditions; Cancers of female reproductive organs; Long-term contraception; Immunity stimulant.
	Kori sacha (m)		Bark, root	Phosphorescent fish		Specialized water shamans	As an *ayahuasca* admixture or, by itself, for gaining shamanic understanding of water and rainbow diseases
2	*Caupuri* (f)	*Virola surinamensis* (Rol. ex Rottb.) Warb. (Lauraceae)	Tree. Red resin	Rainbow boa	Bufotenin, dimethyl triptamine beta-carbolines, harmines		For seduction of women; Treatment of women's mental disorders
	Caupuri (m)	*Banisteriopsis caapi* (Spruce ex Griseb.) C.V.Morton var. *caupuri* (Malpighiaceae)	Vine with black knotty stem	Anaconda	Beta-carbolines, harmine, tetrahydroharmine		For having strong visions (male shamans)

Pair	Vernacular name (gender)	Botanical name (family)	Parts used and colours	Mother spirits	Known active chemicals	Shamanic expertise required	Conditions treated
3	*Yawar piri piri* (f)	*Eleutherine bulbosa* (Mill.) Urban (Iridaceae)	Red rhizome			Herbalist/water shaman overlap	Female reproductive disorders; Childbirth aid; Abortive
	Yaku piri piri (m)	*Cyperus articulatus* L. (Cyperaceae)	White rhizome	Worm	Cyperones	Hunter/shaman overlap	Hunter's luck; Love magic; Abortive; Nerves; Anticonvulsant.
4	*Lupuna blanca* (f)	*Ceiba pentandra* (L.) Gaertn. (Malvaceae)	Tree. White bark	White owl		Strong shamans only	For all reproductive processes; Individual/ social fertility and reproduction
	Puka lupuna (m)	*Ceiba speciosa* (A.St.Hil.) Ravenna (Malvaceae)	Tree. Red bark	Naka-naka snake		Shamans versed in sorcery	For killing enemies by burying food remains in the hollow of this tree; For learning sorcery

There is a cross-cutting of gender, colour, declared medicinal usages and kinds of 'mother spirits' (see Table 3.1). In the pairs presented, the male plants appear to require greater shamanic agency. With the exception of the black *Caupuri* (*Banisteriopsis caapi* var. *caupuri*), all these water plants are characterized by white and red colours, which in combination connote healing and femaleness, in contrast to the red and black colour combination that signals ambivalent male power. Red on its own, as in the case of the *Puka lupuna* tree, can signify either the restoration of vital functions or their destruction by sorcery. With respect to the relation between shamans, gender and plants that are grown or tended, the type, size and habit of plants seem to be relevant. Female shamans grow in their gardens Cyperaceae that are herbaceous plants, and occasionally *Bubinsana* (*Calliandra angustifolia*), a leguminous shrub, but only male shamans can cultivate or tend arborescent shrubs or trees like *Caupuri*. *Lupuna* trees are tended in the wild but not cultivated.

Rainbow diseases are attributed to an intrusion of the cosmic water domain into the world of humans and almost exclusively affect women. This intrusion is attributed to inadvertently stepping on iridescent, still water by accidental, real or supposed exposure to differentiated qualities of rainbow (white rainbow, red rainbow, iridescent rainbow, moon bow). This exposure causes a range of symptoms that include various kinds of psoriasis, menstrual disorders, conditions that are diagnosed as herpes and other sexually transmitted diseases. The most feared rainbow disease is a phantom pregnancy that results in weight loss and can be fatal.

As far as I know, female shamans do not become experts in the treatment of typically female disorders, such as rainbow diseases. On the contrary, because these disorders are understood as a breach of personal boundaries, their treatment is rather entrusted to male shamans who have gained experimental control of female-like unbounded bodies through diet and familiarity with the water plants near water. Shamans with such a special expertise in plants associated with the rainbow, who are sought for the treatment of these conditions, will invariably chant the incantations that pertain to water plants while treating patients and may or may not use some of the water plants listed in Table 3.1. The aim of their treatment is to dissociate patients' bodies from lingering contact with the rainbow. Various water animals (water boas in particular) can also cause phantom pregnancies or cause sickness in babies taken out too soon near water. River pools and small lakes are a favourite place of intimacy for couples, as sexual relations often take place in secluded bathing spots rather than in houses. Fantasies and stories of the seduction of both men and women by water spirits are common, both in indigenous communities such as the Lamista Quechua and in popular lore and paintings throughout the Upper Amazon. These accounts are part of the aetiology of any illness in the region and serve to label unclear but incapacitating psychosomatic disorders.

In general, shamanic treatment consists in restoring the appropriate embodied perspective of the affected humans and the intruding cosmic entities. Yet in the shamanic treatment of pathologies related to the cosmic water domain, no clear patterns emerge with regard to the use of gendered pairs of water plants. Male shamans use any of the paired plants and sometimes explore experimentally the dynamic relation between the male and the female plant, and in this case will ensure they have access to both plants, whether they cultivate them or tend them in the wild. By contrast, the female shamans I worked with are more likely to use the female plants in the pairs, in accordance with their colour associations and their known therapeutic applications, at least in the cases of *Bobinsana*, *Piri piri* and *Lupuna*. It is of interest that the 'master plants' in Table 3.1 have bioactive chemical compounds that support, or at least do not contravene, the vernacular therapeutic usages cited. However, for local shamans the main interest of these plants is that by ingesting and experimenting with these compounds in their own bodies, they gain an understanding of the cosmic ecology.

The Upland Forest, the Male Domain of Amazonian Shamanism

For the Quechua Lamista, male power is linked to a hardened and firmly bounded body, impervious to intrusion from invisible pathogenic darts sent by malevolent shamans or by enemies who commission shamans to act as sorcerers. The qualities that are most valued are vigour, bravery and resistance to pain. Hunting luck and a beneficial relationship with spirit masters of game animals are most desirable to men. Their absence or deficiency in them is attributed to laziness, the moral scourge of all Amazonian boys and men. There are no Quechua Lamista male initiation ceremonies; the transition to manhood traditionally has been effected through head hunting and, more recently, through the hunting of a jaguar and military service in the Peruvian army, followed by marriage. Shamanic initiation is compared to rebirth after near-death experiences under the effect of psychotropic 'master plants'.

The Lamista Quechua's special area of shamanic expertise within the Upper Amazon is 'tree bark medicine' (path of the *paleros*), as practised by 'tree shamans' (Quechua: *kaspi*,[11] Spanish: *palo*). The tallest and largest trees are thought of as the 'grandfathers' of the forest and their combined stature and power give them a dominant place in the shamanic tree medicine. However, relative stature is only one marker of shamanic trees among others: the qualities of their roots (size, colour and texture), of their bark (degrees of outer roughness or smoothness assessed visually and by touch, external colour, colour and texture of the inner side of pealed bark, scent and taste), of their exudates known as milks (Spanish: *leche*) and blood (Spanish: *sangre*) and of their seeds (colour, shape and hardness) all constitute a vast array of ecological knowledge.

Lamista men pick up some of this knowledge as children from older relatives while walking in the forest, but they only develop it experientially as tree medicine if they ingest tree parts under the supervision of senior shamans. 'Tree bark medicine' typically consists of male strengthening decoctions and sexual tonics and enhancers for men, but some barks are used to treat fevers and other illnesses in the population as a whole. While there is an overlap between hunters and shamans in the preparation of invigorating bark tonics, shamans take responsibility for 'putting right' (Quechua: *kuskacha-y*) and re-ordering dysfunctions. The spread of sugar cane mills in the Upper Amazon during the nineteenth century contributed to standardizing the maceration of tree tonics in rum, as opposed to boiling the barks or roots in water as decoctions. Shamanic brews made with specific parts of trees are usually stronger than tonics and have potent effects, the description of which is used to discourage women from contemplating the *palero* shamanic path. While *ayahuasca* is said to be lenient to those who transgress dietary rules, gentle in its effects on human bodies and therefore suitable for female shamans, tree medicine is 'unforgiving' (Spanish: *no perdona*): slight errors in dosage or transgressions of rules to ensure correct and safe use by training shamans may result in insanity or even cause death.

Figure 3.3: A female plant of the upland forest

Figure 3.4: A male plant of the upland forest

Table 3.2: Gendering of upland forest plants and their cosmic associations

Pair	Vernacular name (gender)	Botanical name (family)	Parts used and colours	Mother spirits	Known active chemicals	Shamanic expertise required	Conditions treated
1	*Uchu sanango* (m)	*Tabernaemontana maxima* Duke and Vasquez (Apocynaceae)	Woody shrub with white flowers. Bark	*Chulla chaki* forest spirit	Unidentified alkaloids	Overlap hunter/shaman /poison-maker	Purgative; As an adjunct of *ayahuasca*, for gaining virility and endurance; Treatment of hunters; Convulsions and shock
	Chirik Sanango (f)	*Brunfelsia grandiflora* D.Don ssp. *grandiflora* (Solanaceae)	Woody shrub. Bark, root	Old wrinkled woman forest spirit	Acylated flavonol glycoside	Medium to strong shamans	Inflammatory conditions
2	*Ajo sacha macho* (m)	*Mansoa alliacea* (Lam.) A.Gentry (Bigoniaceae)	Shrub. Bark, leaf	Fox	Sulphur compounds	Overlap herbalist/ shaman	Inflammatory conditions; Counteraction for sorcery; Shamanic training
	Ajo sacha hembra (f)	*Mansoa hymenaea* (DC.) A. Gentry (Bigoniaceae)	Herbaceous plant. Leaves, roots			Shaman experts at curing sorcery-induced misfortune	Hunters' luck; Love magic; Purification of body and mind

3	Ayahuma (m)	Couroupita guaianensis Aubl. (Lecythidaceae)	Tree. Bark	Woman without a head		Tree shamans	Gain ancestors' strength for hunting skills; Febrifuge; Treatment of lack of resolve
	Chullachaki kaspi (f)	Remijia peruviana Standl. (Rubiaceae)		Lepidoptera forest spirit		Medium to strong shamans	Treatment of fevers with body pains; Learning to counteract sorcery and expanding one's awareness of cosmic dynamics
4	Huayruro macho (m)	Ormosia amazonica Ducke (Fabaceae)	Tree. Bark. Black and red seeds	Forest spirit with red cloak; Giant anteater (Piwi)		Strong shamans with ambivalent power	Cure laziness; Increase virile strength; Shamanic training
	Huayruro hembra (f)	Ormosia sp. (Fabaceae)	Tree. Red seeds	Old fairy		Strong shamans	Treatment of women's tumours that cause bleeding; Novices' choice of shamanic path, healing or sorcery
5	Remo kaspi (m)	Aspidosperma excelsum Benth (Apocynaceae)	Tree with buttress roots. Bark	Añuje forest rodent with hard penis	Indole alkaloids	All shamans	Male sexual dysfunctions, particularly impotence; Malaria
	Cumaceba (f)	Swartzia polyphylla D.C. (Fabaceae)	Tree. Bark	Fairy	Flavonoids; Isoflavones	Overlap hunters/shamans	Female reproductive disorders, particularly after childbirth; Malaria

A great deal of tree medicine knowledge revolves around the precise collection and use of sap and exudates (latex, resins). The colour and texture of the soft inner bark (white/red, fibrous/smooth, thick/thin) is also scrutinized, as squares of bark are cut out with a machete. The widespread symbolic opposition between blood and milk/semen is salient in Upper Amazon tree medicine. There is a difference between the coagulants that form when the barks of the male and the female trees are slashed with a machete: cuts in the former result in a thick, dark red/brown resin-like crust, whilst cuts in the latter ooze for much longer with a reddish sap. This may be the rationale for the use of female *Huayruro* bark in the treatment of women's tumours that produce dark and malodorous bleeding.

Huayruro, in particular, gender-crosscuts colour symbolism (Table 3.2). The black and red seeds of the male *Huayruro*, which are now widely used to make necklaces for the tourist trade in Amazonia, are one of the strongest markers of Lamista Quechua healer/ sorcerer ambivalence when worn as two crossed belts on the chests of shamans at the main annual feast of Santa Rosa in Lamas. In contradistinction, one female shaman I knew combined laces of red female *Huayruro* seeds with white laces to show her *bona fide* status as a healer who did 'not send disease darts' (Spanish: *no virotea*).

In the case of the male *Remo caspi* and the female *Cumaceba*, the pair shares the characteristics of having a smooth dark bark and an extremely dark wood. Indeed, the name of *Remo caspi* indicates that this is the wood of preference for making the hardest paddles, which do not break in river rapids. Cuts produce sap with contrasting colour; dark in the case of *Remo caspi* and magenta in the case of *Cumaceba*. The traditional preparation of both barks is in the form of a decoction of chips, which are boiled for the greater part of a day to achieve a liquid with the appearance and consistency that the shaman deems suitable for the condition of the patient treated. Bark decoctions are often used both orally and externally (as *lavados* on wounds or in sit baths for women's conditions). Shamans do not simply apply decoctions of medicinal tree parts as herbalists would. They are adamant that the 'medicine' resides in the incantations that have been granted to them by the 'mother spirits' of the trees while they were dieting in isolation and experimenting with the psychotropic effects of barks, roots, seeds, saps and resins.

167

Female shamans make use of herbaceous plants in the upland forests, such as for example, the male and female *Ajo sacha* domesticated and cultivated in home gardens in much the same way as female shamans tend to the herbaceous Cyperaceae among the water plants. Two of the female shamans I knew used the female *Cumaceba* for treating 'tumours' in women and postpartum disorders, and one had 'studied' the medicine of the female *Chullachaki caspi* tree.

'Tree bark medicine' (*paleros*) is only one of the shamanic resources in the upland forest. Another is the hotchpotch category of plants known as *sanango*, which includes trees, vines (Spanish: *soga*, Quechua: *waska*) and shrubs (no indigenous generic name). The commonality of *sanango* is their attributed therapeutic value: this may be an early Hispanic colonial category that became embedded in the shared medical practices of Upper Amazon mission territories, although I do not have supporting evidence to substantiate this at present. *Sanango* are organized in gendered pairs; the most common is that between *Uchu sanango* and *Chirik sanango* (Table 3.2), where the former is the 'male *sanango*', one of the classic Lamista 'master-plants' with combined purgative and psychotropic effects associated with virile strength and bravery, and the latter the 'cold *sanango*', which is used for treating inflammatory conditions. In this case, the male and female pairing crosscuts a hot and cold opposition, which is probably indigenous. Although Hispanic medicine emphasized hot/cold notions, these were already used throughout the Andes and possibly in some parts of Amazonia (Bastien 1989; Butt-Colson and de Armellada 1983; Foster 1987).

While Amazonian 'hallucinogenic plants' have attracted a great deal of publicity and generated considerable ethnobotanical research as 'entheobotany' (the study of the 'plants of the gods'), tree medicine has remained esoteric. Few urban shamans embark on this path of shamanism which has the reputation of being dangerous and demanding, and which is associated more with the acquisition of knowledge by way of dreams than by way of visions. For the Lamista Quechua, dreaming is a superior, more traditional source of insights gained from the 'master plants' and therefore it is greatly valued in spite of the increasing dominance of *ayahuasca* shamanism, which is vision based.

Gender Fluctuations

Both in the water and in the upland forest, relations with spirit owners of plant medicine are conceived of as a slow process from seduction to affinity and from affinity to the closest consanguineal bond, that of parent to child. In the cosmos all permutations are possible so that male shamans seduce spirits in an androgynous fashion, then address them as brothers-in-law (fathers-in-law, if the relation is through a mermaid in the underwater world) who are urged to follow them, and later on, they then address them as their children.

Table 3.3: Descriptors used in the Upper Amazon to differentiate male and female plants, with particular reference to gendered pairs.

Descriptor	Male plant	Female plant
Habit	Tall, erect, woody stem (vine, shrub) or trunk (tree)	Low, rambling, soft stem, branching out stem (shrubs)
Colour	Black, black and red, black and white, shiny	Red, red and white, white, dull
Texture	Rough, scaly	Smooth
Location	Upland forest or any forest area or raised banks	River banks, lakes, flooded valleys or areas where plants have roots in water
Size	Very large or very small	Smaller or larger than male counterpart
Symbiosis	Proximity or interaction	Proximity or interaction
Association with gendered spirits	Male forest spirits	Female forest and water spirits
Human-like sexual characteristics	Similarity with male genitals	Similarity with female genitals
Attributes of gender	Claws	No claws
Hot/cold associations	Hot	Cold
Sap or exudate characteristics	Dark sap or resin, certain types of latex	Red sap or resin, thin latex

The descriptors that are used in the Upper Amazon to differentiate male and female plants, with particular reference to gendered pairs, concern habit, colour, texture, location, size, forms of symbiosis, characteristics of the sap as well as human-like sexual characteristics, attributes of gender, hot/cold associations and association with gendered spirits (Table 3.3).

While the gender of particular spirits fluctuates according to the context and to the speaker, the gendering of shamanic plants in the Upper Amazon rests on a wider consensus in the region. Shamanic plant knowledge acquisition involves the understanding of the dynamic relations between gendered species and the engineering of balance among them.

There are some androgynous trees, such as *Uvos* (*Spondias mombin*), which comprises male and female parts: in the local system the bark of *Uvos* is considered to be male and its fruit female. The tree as a whole is also associated with femaleness and some of its parts have been shown to have pharmaco-active properties applicable to women's reproductive disorders.

By contrast, some plants are not gendered even though they are used in combination. For instance, the various plants that are labelled *ayahuasca* (several varieties of *Banisteriopsis* and *Brugmansia*) are paired with plants that activate the visionary quality of brews. These plants are generically called *chacruna*; the most commonly used species are two shrubs (*Psychotria viridis* and *Psychotria carthagenensis*) and a scandent vine (*Diplopterys cabrerana*). The triptamines contained in the *chacruna* are inactive when orally ingested unless they are exposed to monoamine oxidase inhibitors, which have been found in the ayahuasca plants. Enhancing the synergy of *ayahuasca* and *chacruna* is part of shamanic expertise. The absence of gendering of the *ayahuasca* and *chacruna* when they are used in combination is surprising, unless this absence is explained as appropriate for plants that together are vehicles to trigger visions through which trainee shamans study relations of all beings in the cosmos.

Occasionally, patients treated with tree medicine for a life-threatening condition receive the shamanic knowledge associated with the tree that cured them. In dreams, they are visited by spirit beings, in human or animal form, which 'teach' them incantations that will unlock the therapeutic power of particular trees. Sometimes these recovered patients also claim to have been shown how to collect and prepare the tree medicines. In the same way as shamans, they have acquired an embodied familiarity with a 'master plant' and accessed its animated hub of connections and meanings in the forest as cosmos. In order to become shamans, however, they would need to make this familiarity operational by activating social relations in the realm of the invisible. It is perhaps this aspect of Amazonian shamanism that makes the shamanic career most challenging for women.

Shamans who are specialists in the knowledge and use of particular 'master plants' are aware of their counterparts in gendered pairs and often have expertise of both plants. In order to claim this expertise, they need to obtain a dedicated incantation from the 'mother spirits' that own/control the plants in the cosmos. Incantations can be exchanged and purchased with money or labour among shamans, particularly during visits to ethnic groups with different plants and knowledge. Even then, though, the implication of owning an incantation is that a particular relation with a plant/spirit entity has been established and must be maintained appropriately in time.

While incantations take listeners to the primordial time when there was no separation between the visible world of humans and the animated cosmos, the process of social expansion characteristic of Upper Amazon communities is transposed in the spirit realm, in the forest as cosmos. Men in search of available areas of forest to create new colonies, which in the next generation will constitute local communities, need to 'tame' local forest spirits that dwell and own/control this non-humanized forest.

The process is one of female-like seduction and taming, rather than one of male predation. Shamans in their androgynous capacities are best qualified to act as founders of new forest colonies. Once tamed (the same Spanish word *amansar* is used for the taming of captured wild animals), the forest spirits are miniaturized as playful, child-like gnomes and roaming souls are either assimilated or redirected elsewhere. Lamista Quechua founding shamans are said to have guardianship over the delicate balance between the visible and the invisible realms in new forest colonies. They have it without assuming political authority. While it is clear that the pan-Amazonian spirit world surrounds and also reflects native societies (Viveiros de Castro 1998), the inflections of this spirit world on gender relations and gendered identities may deserve closer attention. In particular, further comments on gendered modes of relating with the 'mother spirits' of plants are required for an understanding of the local

171

concept of medicine/knowledge/power in Upper Amazon shamanism and its implications for men and women.

Discussion: What then is Plant-Induced Shamanic Agency in the Upper Amazon?

In their seduction of the spirit entities that own/control the plants which they use as vectors to gain power in the spirit world, male shamans keep their male identity but behave with female gender codes: they use sexual seduction, in a comparable way to hunters who seduce prey. Once a quasi-affinal relation has been secured, they tame and nurture spirits and the plants associated with them in the ways that women tame/look after/raise children, pets and domestic animals (Quechua: *wiwa*). In so doing, they recreate in themselves the androgyny of the archetypal shaman as rainbow-anaconda. Rather than leading a people, as in their capacity of founders of new local communities, they nurture, like women.

Women's relationships to spirits are far more complex as they must acquire cosmic knowledge within a symbolic system that is mainly constituted from a male perspective. Although they can use their fluid, permeable bodies and sexual identities to their advantage in the shamanic quest, this is also fraught with danger. The female shamans I have come across competed with male rivals from within their network of male shaman relatives. The few tales I heard about women engaged in shamanic feuds in the Upper Amazon concerned women of mixed ethnic origin and pointed to extraordinary situations. Female shamans must harden and seal their bodies, be vigilant at all times and prevent male teachers and thieves from stealing their embodied powers. Few female shamans are able to tend and use water plants that are most powerfully linked to fertility and reproduction, even if they have passed the menopause, because of their gender closeness to the world of the anaconda that male shamans need to control. Even fewer can engage with the full force of the upland strong trees.

Shamanic treatment requires a negation of human sexuality and gender in the human world, this in contrast to the hyper-sexuality and transgendering within the cosmos at large. A shamanic treatment intervention consists first of all in a loosening of the boundedness of

172

patients' bodies through a combination of diet (characterized by an abstinence from salt, fat and sexual relations) and plant preparations, which all are used in association with tobacco and specific incantations. Patients' bodies become soft, bland and thin as well as de-sexualized before the source of pathologies can be ascertained and made visible in the cosmos, and before body boundaries can be redrawn anew with a re-alignment of soul substance sealed by the shamanic incantations (Bahr and Haefer 1978).

Male shamans transcend gender categories in the cosmos; as they gain access to androgynous, transformative entities, they gain knowledge of/power over female powers of fertility and birth. Perruchon (2003: 42) notes the inconsistency between the androgynous shamanic ideology and the view was also volunteered to me by male Lamista shamans that women are potentially 'more powerful shamans than men'. There is a marked contrast between the raw, innate reproductive power of women and the gradually, painstakingly acquired integration, embodiment and control of this female power by male shamans as they become androgynous for the purpose of engineering balance between the polarized domains of the male/female, water/sky, this world, the underworld and the underwater world. Female shamans are constrained by this paradigmatic model of male transgendering, which to a large extent determines both the relations of the shamans with beings in the cosmos and their redrawing of body boundaries (theirs and their patients') as new nodes in webs of connections between humans, plants, animals, spirits and cosmic elements.

The pairing of gendered plants is indicative of the organizing power of gender among other dual oppositions in Amazonia. Rather than associating female plants with women and male plants with men, plant pairs in the Upper Amazon are best understood as enhancing the androgyny that male shamans strive to achieve in their quest for balance of the polarities. The minority of women who take up the shamanic path are constrained not so much by their more permeable bodies as by the logical necessity to suppress their ordinary female efficacy without being able to reclaim it in its entirety as a distinctively shamanic agency. This begs the question as to whether a female shamanic agency would be inherently impossible in Amazonian cosmologies. It would be the next question of choice.

Notes

1. Mapuche and Araucanians are notable exceptions to this general statement.
2. On the concept of *madre* in South America, both in the Amazon and the Andes, see Métraux (1967).
3. In North Amerindian Iroquoi 'plant medicine' nutritive or utilitarian plants are most valued by shamans; they are also plant experts.
4. The blurring of gendered activities has been emphasized in the writings of anthropologists from both the symbolic economy and the moral economy camps (Bamberger 1997; Mader 1997; Perruchon 2003; Rival 1998; Taylor 1996). Rather than representing dichotomized power relations between men and women (Ardener 1981) or even multiple discourses rationalizing both asymmetric and symmetric gender relations (Moore 1994), the features of Amazonian gender are embodied in ways that deserve further exploration (McCallum 2004)
5. Viveiros de Castro (1998) presents Amerindian perspectivism as an embodied process through which commonality of soul for all beings takes specific forms, affects and capacities in particular bodies. Each of these sets constitutes a perspective that defines personal identity at a particular point. In shamanism, to know is to embody the correct perspective corresponding to a being in the cosmos, with the implication of conquering his/her point of view and the dynamics of its placement and inter-relations with other beings in the cosmos. Although the Lamista Quechua also use a terminology of 'conquering', this chapter does not address the mechanics of embodiment through which shamans learn to assimilate multiple perspectives.
6. Kane (1994: 177) speaks of 'twisting fertility and mortality in its coils' (Tsunki, Shuar); for the Barasana, Romi Kumu, the female source of shamanic power and the prototype shaman, is sexually ambiguous (Hugh-Jones 1979: 125, 178). The Pemon term for shaman is *rato*, meaning 'water mother' (Fürst 1993: 402). Campbell (1989: 105) refers to a similar Wayapi term. The Mehinaku shaman is compared to an anaconda (Ripinsky-Naxon 1993: 92).
7. A Quechua term now denoting shamanic knowledge in 'vegetalismo' throughout the Upper Amazon, and in neo-shamanism.
8. Shepard (2004) offers the most comprehensive account so far on organoleptic properties of Amazonian plants as perceived by forest people. A discussion of these properties in relation to colour symbolism and gender lies outside the scope of this chapter.
9. Some of the water plants only grow in restricted areas of the Lamista Quechua territory near the Huallaga river.

10. Until recently Shipibo, Conibo and Piro shamans used to travel to the Huallaga to acquire 'tree medicine' from Lamista shamans in return. These exchanges of knowledge are still actualized in contemporary shamanic encounters staged by non-indigenous agents, including foreigners in international nongovernmental organizations.

11. The new accepted spelling of Quechua terms that has been officially recognized in Peru in the 1990s has replaced the previous Hispanic spelling, particularly replacing 'c' with 'k' and 'hu' with 'w'. In order to avoid confusion regarding plant vernacular names still listed in Hispanicized Quechua in books and articles, I have maintained the old spelling for plant names in this chapter.

12. Data in Tables 3.1 to 3.3 are mostly drawn from my longitudinal field research with Lamista Quechua shamans over twenty-five years, in collaboration with Peruvian botanists and biologists for identification of collected plants. Additional sources include Soukoup (1970) and Vasquez. Information on biochemical activity is drawn from Brack (1998) and Taylor (1998).

References

Ardener, S. 1981. 'The "Problem" Revisited' in S. Ortner and H. Whitehead (eds), *Sexual Meanings: The Cultural Construction of Gender and Sexuality*. Cambridge: Cambridge University Press.

Atkinson, M. 1992. 'Shamanisms Today', *Annual Review of Anthropology* 21: 307–30.

Balée, W. 1994. *Footprints of the Forest. Ka'apor Ethnobotany – the Historical Ecology of Plant Utilization by an Amazonian People*. New York: Columbia University Press.

Bamberger, L. 1974. 'The Myth of Matriarchy: Why Men Rule in Primitive Society', in M. Rosaldo and L. Lamphere (eds), *Women, Culture and Society*. Stanford, California: Stanford University Press, pp. 263–80.

Barbira Freedman, F. 1999. '"Vegetalismo" and the Perception of Biodiversity: Shamanic Values', in D. Posey (ed.), *Cultural and Spiritual Values of Biodiversity*. London: Intermediate Technology Publications, pp. 277–78.

——— 2002. 'Tobacco and Curing Agency in Western Amazonian Shamanism', in P.A. Baker and G. Carr (eds), *Practitioners, Practices and Patients: New Approaches to Medical Archaeology and Medical Anthropology*. Oxford: Oxbow, pp. 136–60.

Bastien, J.W. 1989. 'Differences between Kallawaya-Andean and Greek European Humoral Medicine', *Social Science and Medicine* 28: 45–51.

Berlin, B. 1992. *Ethnobiological Classification: Principles of Categorization of Plants and Animals in Traditional Societies*. Princeton: Princeton University Press.

Brack, A. 1998. *Diccionario Enciclopédico de Plantas Utiles del Perú*. Centro de Estudios Regionales Andinos "Bartolomé de las Casas", Cuzco.

Butt-Colson, A. and C. de Armellada. 1983. 'An Amerindian Derivation for Latin American Creole Illnesses and their Treatment', *Social Science and Medicine* 17: 1229–248.

Campbell, A.T. 1989. *To Square with Genesis: Causal Statements and Shamanic Ideas in Wayãpí*. Edingurgh: Edinburgh University Press.

Colpron, A.-M. 2006. 'Chamanisme Féminin "contre nature"? menstruation, gestation et femmes chamanes parmi les Shipibo-Conibo de l'Amazonie Occidentale', *Journal de la Société des Américanistes* 92: 203–35.

Descola, P. 1986. *La Nature Domestique, Symbolique et Praxis dans l'Ecologie des Achuar*. Paris: Editions de la Maison des Sciences de l'Homme.

Eliade, M. 1964. *Shamanism: Archaic Techniques of Ecstasy*. London: Routledge and Kegan Paul.

Foster, G. 1987. 'On the Origin of Humoral Medicine in Latin America', *Medical Anthropology Quarterly* 1: 355–93.

Furst, P.T. 1993. 'I Am Black Jaguar' Magical Spells and Shamanism among the Pemon', in G.H. Gossen (ed), *South and Meso-American Native Spirituality: From the Cult of the Feathered Serpent to the Theology of Liberation*. New York: Crossroad.

Ghebart-Sayer, A.G. 1984. *Cosmos Encoiled: Indian Art of the Peruvian Amazon*. Oxford: Blackwell Publishing.

Glass-Coffin, B. 1998. *The Gift of Life: Female Spirituality and Healing in Northern Peru*. Albuquerque: University of New Mexico Press.

―――― 1999. 'Engendering Peruvian Shamanism through Time', *Ethnohistory* 46: 205–38.

Greene, S. 1998. 'The Shaman's Needle: Development, Shamanic Agency and Intermediality in Aguaruna Lands, Peru', *American Ethnologist* 25: 634–58.

Gregor, T.A. and D. Tuzin. 2001. *Gender in Amazonia and Melanesia. An Exploration of the Comparative Method*. Berkeley, California: University of California Press.

Hugh-Jones, S. 1979. *The Palm and the Pleiades: Initiation and Cosmology in Northwest Amazonia*. Cambridge: Cambridge University Press.

―――― 1995. 'Inside-out and Back-to-Front: the Androgynous House in Northwest Amazonia', in J. Carsten and S. Hugh-Jones (eds), *About the House: Lévi-Strauss and Beyond*. Cambridge: Cambridge University Press, pp. 226–52.

―――― 2001. 'The Gender of Some Amazonian Gifts: An Experiment with an Experiment', in T.A. Gregor and D. Tuzin (eds), *Gender in Amazonia and Melanesia: An Exploration of the Comparative Method*. Berkeley: University of California Press.

Kane, S.C. 1994. *The Phantom Gringo Boat: Shamanic Discourse and Development in Panama*. Washington: Smithsonian Institution Press.

Kensinger, K.M. 1974. 'Cashinahua Medicine and Medicine Men', in P. Lyon (ed.), *Native South Americans: the Ethnology of the Least Known Continent*. Boston: Little, Brown and Co., pp. 283–88.

Langdon, E.J.M. and G. Baer. 1992. *Portals of Power: Shamanism in South America*. Albuquerque: University of New Mexico Press.

Lindenbaum, S. 1984. 'Variations on a Sociosexual Theme in Melanesia', in G. Herdt (ed.), *Ritualized Homosexuality in Melanesia*. Berkeley: University of California Press, pp. 337–61.

Luna, L.E. 1986. *Vegetalismo: Shamanism among the Mestizo Population of the Peruvian Amazon*. Stockholm, Sweden: Almqvist andWiskell International.

Mader, E. 1997. 'Las visiones y relaciones de género en la cultura shuar' in M. Perrin and M. Perruchon (eds), *Complementariedad entre hombre y mujer: Relaciones de género desde la perspectiva amerindia*. Quito: Ediciones Abya-Yala.

McCallum, C. 2004. *Gender and Sociality in Amazonia: How Real People are Made*. Oxford: Berg.

Métraux, A. 1967. *Religions et magies indiennes d'Amérique du Sud*. Ed. posthume établie par S. Dreyfus. Paris: Gallimard.

Moore, H. 1994. *A Passion for Difference: Essays in Anthropology and Gender*. Cambridge: Polity Press.

Overing, J. and A. Passes. 2000. *The Anthropology of Love and Anger*. London: Routledge.

Perruchon, M. 2003. *I Am Tsunki. Gender and Shamanism Among the Shuar of Western Amazonia*. Uppsala Studies in Cultural Anthropology No. 33, University of Uppsala.

Rengifo, G. 2005. *Plantas Medicinales de Lamas*. Tarapoto, Peru: Pratech.

Ripinsky-Naxon, M. 1993. *The Nature of Shamanism: Substance and Function of a Religious Metaphor*. Albany: State University of New York Press.

Rival, L. 1998. 'Androgenous Parents and Guest Children: The Huaorani Couvade', *Journal of the Royal Anthropological Institute* 4: 619–42.

Rivière, P. 1989. 'Men and Women in Lowland South America', *Man* 24(3): Correspondence.

Roe, P.G. 1998. 'Paragon or Peril?: the Jaguar in Amazonian Society: a Multi-Dimensional Analysis of a Dualistic Natural Symbol', in N.J. Saunders (ed.), *Icons of Power: Feline Symbolism in the Americas*. London: Routledge, pp. 171–97.

Santos Granero, F. 1986. *The Power of Love: The Moral Use of Knowledge amongst the Amuesha of Central Peru*. Atlantic Highlands, NJ: Athlone Press.

Scazzocchio, F. 1977. 'Curare kills, cures and binds: persistence and change of indigenous trade in the Peruvian Upper Amazon', *Cambridge Anthropology* III.

Schultes, R. and R.F. Raffauf. 1996. *The Healing Forest: Medicinal and Toxic Plants of the Northwest Amazonia*. Portland Oregon: Dioscorides Press.

Shephard, G. 2004. 'A Sensory Ecology of Illness and Therapy in two Amazonian Societies', *American Anthropologist* 106: 252–66.

Siskind, J. 1973. 'Visions and Cures among the Sharanahua', in M.J. Harner (ed.), *Hallucinogens and Shamanism*. New York: Oxford University Press, pp. 28–39.

Soukoup, J. 1970. *Vocabulario de los nombres vulgares de la flora peruana*. Lima: Colegio Salesiano.

Taylor, A.C. 1996. 'The Soul's Body and its States: An Amazonian Perspective on the Nature of Being Human', *Journal of the Royal Anthropological Institute* 2: 201–15.

———— 2000. 'Le Sexe de la Proie: Représentations Jivaro du Lien de Parenté', *L'Homme* 5: 309–34.

Taylor, L. 1998. *Herbal Secrets of the Rainforest*. Rocklin, California: Prima Health Publishing.

Vasquez, R. 1992. 'Sistemática de plantas medicinales de uso frecuente en el área de Iquitos' *Folia Amazónica* 4(1):61-76, Iquitos, Peru.

Vitebsky, P. 1995. *The Shaman*. Boston: Little Brown.

Viveiros de Castro, E. 1998. 'Cosmological Deixis and Amerindian Perspectivism', *Journal of the Royal Anthropological Institute* 4: 469–88.

Wilbert, J. 1987. *Tobacco and Shamanism in South America*. New Haven: Yale University Press.

4. Persons, Plants and Relations:
Treating Childhood Illness in a Western Kenyan Village
P. *Wenzel Geissler and Ruth J. Prince*

Introduction

This chapter is the result of long-term ethnographic fieldwork in Uhero,[1] a Luo village in western Kenya. We have lived in Uhero – first by ourselves and eventually joined by our children – for several extensive periods over the past decade (totalling around four years). In the end of our last two-year ethnographic fieldwork (2002), Uhero had 956 inhabitants distributed across 105 scattered patrilineal, virilocal homesteads. Most people of Uhero (*JoUhero*) engaged in subsistence agriculture (maize, millet, potatoes), some planted locally marketed cash crops, many of the men fished, and men and women engaged in short-distance fish trade. Many of the older people had lived and worked in towns before settling in their rural homes, and many of Uhero's youth moved between village and town, working or, more likely, looking for work. Most households relied on migrants' remittances for cash needs, such as schooling and medical care, but due to the declining Kenyan economy, these remittances were dwindling. Like most rural Luo, *JoUhero* found themselves, at the end of the century, in a disappointed, nostalgic mood, looking back at the lost promises of modernity, as well as the long-gone pre-colonial past, and without great expectations for the future.

The themes of our last long fieldwork concerned transformations of relatedness in the everyday life of a late-modern Kenyan village suffering from widespread illness and death, and specifically the concrete, bodily practices that constitute and negotiate substantial social relations. *JoUhero* understand physical touch and other material contact in relation to the concept of *riwo*, a *Dholuo* verb describing practices that momentarily merge persons, or their bodies, by sharing substance[2] (for a detailed account see Prince and Geissler 2010). In this understanding, momentary physical contact between humans, between humans and things, and between substances, has a transcendental quality, not in the sense of relating to another world, but going beyond, for an instance, the difference between one human and another. This transcendent moment between persons has transformatory and creative capacity. From it springs life and 'growth' (*dongruok*), which is conceptualized not as the creation *ex nihilo* of a new entity or as the expansion of an existing entity, but as a transformation, as an elicitation of something new out of the old, a movement from one form to another, rather than the creation or extension of one. Material contact in this sense is central to *JoUhero*'s concerns with social relations and with how things should be done in everyday and ritual situations, to sustain the growth of life. In these times of death – Uhero is in an area with high mortality, presumably due to HIV/AIDS[3] – growth is in doubt and there is little agreement among the villagers about how the continuity of life can be maintained. Elsewhere, we have explored controversial forms of creative touch, such as sexual intercourse, which tend to give rise to conflictual and explicit discourses (e.g. Geissler and Prince 2007; Prince 2008). In this chapter, we look instead at a largely consensual and implicit form of touch: treating young children with Luo plant medicines, which are understood as integral for nurturing and critical for the elicitation of children's growth.

'Luoland' – the Kenyan shore of Lake Victoria and its hinterland – is an economically (and for a long time politically) marginal part of Kenya; most people live, like *JoUhero*, in separate patrilineal rural homesteads from subsistence agriculture and fishing, and poverty and hunger are common. Nonetheless, Luo-speaking people have for over a century been intensely involved in the country's transformations under colonial occupation and changing post-colonial regimes. Political and religious orders were changed (e.g. Ogot 1963, Atieno Odhiambo 1974, Lonsdale 1977), intergenerational and gender relations were affected by labour migration, urbanization and capitalism (Parkin 1978, Cohen and Atieno Odhiambo 1989, 1992), and land use and tenure were altered by market production, title deeds and land sales, and population growth and class formation (Pala 1980, Hay 1982, Shipton 1989). These changes had, and continue to have, profound effects on understandings and practices of relatedness in Luo sociality, which we explore in detail elsewhere (Gessler and Price, 2010). Health and healing were of course affected by these changes, and we shall touch upon certain consequences of these wider social changes below. However, home-based herbal medicine is an astonishingly persistent trait of Luo everyday life. Despite changing gender relations, religious rupture, and the effects of capitalism on relations among people, natural resources and land, women continue to collect plants around their homes and prepare medicines for their children in their kitchens. Mothers bring plants from the village to the city to sustain their children and grandchildren, and little is talked about these practices. They are as taken-for-granted and unspoken-of as cooking and other domestic chores. Unlike much supposedly 'Luo culture' these days, this herbal medicinal knowledge is neither tangibly 'modernized' nor 'traditionalized'. Here and there, a few self-appointed (mainly male) 'herbal doctors' and some villagers (mainly from more fertile non-Luo areas) try to make money by selling dried plant materials and preparations on local markets. Some semi-industrialized packaged 'anti-viral' herbal remedies can be seen in the towns (Pool and Geissler 2005), and occasionally the spectre of a 'billion dollar ... global industry ... in traditional medicine' is raised by politicians or donors (e.g. Anonymous 2004). Yet, all this is largely irrelevant to what ordinary mothers do every day when they apply local plants to their children's bodies. Their practices are rarely verbalized, profoundly female and domestic, and, as we shall see below, inherently flexible, constituted in negotiations and conversations – spoken about rather than fixed in a rigid text of 'traditional knowledge'. The question is beyond the aims of this chapter, but it might be exactly this flexibility which makes Luo herbal medicine so relatively unaffected by wider social changes, sociality and reflections about both.

Plants, mostly used fresh after collection, constitute the principal medicinal resource of the mothers of Uhero;[4] rare remedies for serious illnesses, which will not be central to this chapter, might occasionally include other ingredients, such as salt or earth. Medicines that include other substances – ranging from the thatch of houses to human and animal body parts, from the pages of religious books to menstrual blood – are part of a completely separate conceptual domain. Even when such medicines are employed for healing purposes, the assumption is that the healer in question, referred to

181

as *ajuoga* ('diviner-healer' or 'witchdoctor', depending upon one's judgment), knows how to heal *and* to kill, and often these treatments are achieved for the price of another person's illness or death. It is possible that this distinction between 'innocent' and 'natural' plant remedies and pagan 'magic' – further associated with the difference between female and male, and local and alien healers – has been accentuated by Christian teachings since colonial occupation, some of which distinguished between the 'natural properties' of plants and dangerous 'pagan superstitions'. In any event, the two are completely distinct social practices in contemporary Uhero, and this chapter focuses on the former. To study the latter would imply looking at a different set of afflictions (serious illnesses of adults rather than infant illnesses), different diagnoses (divination rather than observation and conversations), different applications (involving marked ritual acts), and different practitioners (non-local *ajuoge* rather than local healers [*jothieth*] and village women).

Most women in Uhero, irrespective of their education, wealth and religious orientation, use plant remedies for their children and grandchildren.[5] Some *JoUhero*, notably born-again Christians, are suspicious about herbal medicines' potential association with ancestral power. Yet, even Christians who otherwise reject 'pagan' practices often argue that 'God made these plants to help our children to grow!' Plants are used by mothers in Uhero alongside Western pharmaceuticals, including self-administered injections,[6] and home-based herbal treatments alternate with visits to the hospital or dispensary within a characteristic 'pluralist' health care setting. In this article, we chose to focus on healing with plants, not only because of the theme of this volume, but also because we would argue that herbal medicine is the dominant form of medicinal care for young children (into which a limited range of Western pharmaceuticals are accommodated; see Prince et al. 2001). Furthermore, these omnipresent but implicit practices give insight into some fundamental aspects of *JoUhero*'s sociality, beyond issues of health and illness.

Everyday Treatment

We began learning about Luo plant medicines when we worked on a series of medical research projects, involving worm treatment among school-children (improving their growth and mental development, see Olsen et al. 2003), and psychometric studies about children's medicinal knowledge and cognition (see Sternberg et al. 2001) (for a catalogue of this work see Geissler & Pine 2009). Talking with children about worms and the body during breaks in the assessment of parasite loads, nutrition and cognitive capacity (Geissler 1998), the children revealed extensive knowledge of herbal remedies for abdominal illnesses (Prince et al. 2001). Exploring the bush together with them, we came to the homestead of Mr Okoth, whose inhabitants have since taught us about village sociality, including herbal medicines. In this chapter, we shall draw upon the everyday life of Mr Okoth's family and describe some of their medicinal practices, and how they conceptualize the body's composition and boundaries, its relation to the bodies of others and to the environment, and their knowledge and use of medicinal plants, and what this might tell us about their understandings of persons, relations and (medicinal) capacity.

Healing in the Home

Rebekka (b. 1944), Mr Okoth's first wife, takes care of her grandchildren with herbal medicines. She supplies her married daughters with plant materials and advice, and she treats her son's three children, who live with her. Infant illnesses fall into the category that *JoUhero* distinguish as 'everyday illnesses' (*tuoche* [sg. *tuo*] *mapilekapile* [*pilepile*, 'daily']) as opposed to serious illnesses, which are often referred to as 'death' (*tho*). Children's illnesses are usually mild but continually present, and women in Uhero tend to agree with Rebekka that 'a young child should at times be sick' ('*nyathi matin nyaka bed matuo*'), or 'small illnesses are good' ('*tuoche matindotindo gibeyo*'), because if a child never falls ill, it may eventually die of a serious illness (Prince et al. 2002). Accordingly, one 'should follow a child with Luo medicines so that it grows well' ('*iluori gi yiende nyaluo mondo nyathi adong maber*').

Medicine is a female domain, as underlined by the saying: '[Having] children teach[es] you medicines ('*nyithindo ema puonj yiende*'). Girls learn about medicinal plants once they begin taking care of children, and most women know medicines and treat children and grandchildren (see also Ominde 1952, Olenja 1991, Kawango 1995, Taylor et al. 1996, Amuyunzu 1998, Geissler 1999, Prince and Geissler 2001). Accordingly, the terms commonly used to designate herbal medicine are *yath agulu* (pot medicine), linking medicine to the domestic domain and female creativity, and *yath nyaluo*, 'the Luo daughter's medicine', which also draws attention to the genealogical, inter-generational quality of this herbal medicine, which we will return to below.

Herbal medicinal treatment is a continuous practice between people within the homestead, living in a close relationship, such as grandmothers, mothers and children. Prepared and administered alongside other everyday practices such as digging, collecting vegetables, water and firewood, cooking and eating, it brings the powers from the bush, the earth and the place to work within relations in the home. Herbal treatment is part of the bonds one enjoys with others, and is tied in with the practices of relatedness that sustain these. This is especially so within the family, where most herbal remedies are used, but even local healers are more like 'healing friends': social intercourse, conviviality and commensality are vital dimensions of the healing relationship, upon which depend not only one's trust in the healer, but also the healer's prowess, and the power of her plants.

Plant, Bush and Land

Figure 4.1 depicts the varying stages of a treatment: Little Mary (b. 1996) has occasionally had diarrhoea and rashes during the previous month, and Rebekka has decided to give her *fundo* (steambath). In the afternoon, Rebekka walks into the bush to collect the bark and roots of several trees, among which she considers the following to be essential: *ober* (*Albizia coriaria* Welw. *ex* Oliv.), *roko* (*Zanthoxylum chalybeum* Engl.), *akado* (*Euclea racemosa* Murr. ssp. *schimperi* [A.DC] White) and *ochuoga* (*Carissa edulis* [Forssk.] Vahl.); for a systematic presentation of the local medicinal plants, see Geissler et al. 2002; see also Johns et al. 1990. After digging out a piece of root, Rebekka covers the rest to allow the plant to heal and to prevent people from interfering with her medicine. Since the potency of medicines lies, at least partly, in the relation between the sick child and the land (and its dead and living people), which the plant establishes, the tree or bush from which the medicine was collected constitutes, for a while, a vulnerable point at which others can attack this relation. If someone wished to harm the child, she could 'work' (*tiyo*) on the plant and thereby on the medicine and the child's body.

Figure 4.1: Stages of everyday treatment: Rebekka Okoth gives Mary a steam bath

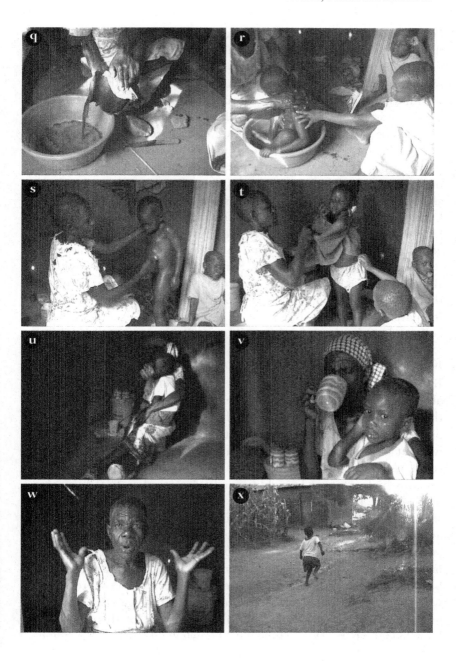

People were not specific on what they meant by 'work' but usually in this context it implied the use of evil 'medicines' to harm someone.

The plants Rebekka uses all grow within the village in a one-mile radius around the home, and she knows where to go in the thick bush to find what she needs. Unlike some of her younger co-wives, Rebekka is, after forty years of marriage, at home in this landscape. She no longer relies upon medicinal supplies and advice from her maternal home; she has herself become a 'parent of the plants/medicines' (*wuon yath*). During the many years of our acquaintance, Rebekka never mentioned buying plants as ingredients of her medicines, although even small local markets sell plant materials, such as the bark of larger trees, which for ecological reasons are scarce around Uhero. Asked about these market medicines, she expressed concerns about their uncertain origins and qualities (for her wider objections to commodification, see below). Sometimes when we travelled with Rebekka to her home area or to mutual friends, she picked plants that were not to be found in Uhero or asked her relations and friends for particular species, but most of the herbs she used were local, collected on the day she prepared the medicine.

Knowledge between Generations

Rebekka's ten-year-old grandson helps her collect medicine. Their abilities complement each other. She shows him plants and how to use them; he carries out heavy work, such as digging. Rebekka collects the parts she wants to use, knowing best how to cut bark, root or branch without lasting damage. Their collaboration is characteristic of the relationship between grandmothers and grandchildren, and of the way in which most medicinal knowledge is passed on to the younger generations. Learning medicines is usually embedded in intimately shared everyday life (which is common among alternate generations), and it occurs in practical work rather than through explicit teaching (see Prince and Geissler 2001). Usually knowledge of medicines is passed on across a wide generational gap, to grandchildren, because they live close to grandmothers and are considered 'free' with them.[7] This teaching of medicines by the oldest to the youngest in the home emphasizes the genealogical aspect of this medicinal knowledge; when asked where Luo knowledge of herbal medicines comes from, *JoUhero* would invariably say 'our grandmothers', and before that: 'the grandmothers' grandmothers'. When asked what a child should learn from grandmothers, all *JoUhero* would mention 'Luo medicines'. In this way herbal medicine becomes a token of historical continuity as well as of ethnic identity, since Luo think of themselves as sharing one set of original 'grandmothers' from their common patrilineal ancestor's homestead. The capacity of medicines derives partly from kinship links into the past and across the Luo people and their land.

In older ethnographic accounts, in biographical narratives of elderly Luo, and even in the nostalgic lyrics of contemporary Luo pop music (see Prince 2006), the close relationship between children and their grandparents, institutionalized in the role of the *pim*, a classificatory grandmother living with the children of a homestead in a special house, the *siwindhe*, is praised. The teaching of medicines and healing, among other intimate knowledge, such as that about sexuality, is central in this relationship (see Evans-Pritchard 1965: 230. Cohen 1985). Today, hardly any *JoUhero* recall the meaning of these terms, and yet most village children live for at least part of their youth in the house of a grandmother. Although urbanization and high rates of extramarital birth doubtlessly affect the co-residence of different generations, often children live with old women precisely because their parents reside in towns or they were born out of wedlock. Thus, despite profound social transformations, the learning about plant medicines remains embedded in the close and intimate everyday life of oldest and youngest in the village.

Healing and Other Bodily Relations

Children are also considered the most suitable apprentices of their old, post-reproductive grandmothers, because neither engage in sexual relations; this freedom of sexual entanglement is regarded as a prerequisite of medicinal capacity (see also Reynolds 1996). If they are touched by someone who has recently had sex, medicinal plants can lose their power or even become dangerous (see Geissler and Prince 2007). Therefore, a woman of reproductive age who wishes to help someone with a sick child would either take the mother to the plants in question, so she would be able to collect them herself, or send a (grand)child; in any case she would meticulously avoid handling the plants, to avoid later accusations of harming the child. This concern with the potency of sexual intercourse, or with the substance that arises from a bodily relation and is brought in touch with the plants, points to the critical importance of substantial relatedness for medicinal capacity and effects. The touch of a person who had intercourse merges the transformative, procreative capacity of the sexual union with the medicinal plant's transformative healing capacity, and the plant carries that confusion of forces to the sick child, potentially causing it harm.

This constitutes an instance of what – in many different everyday contexts – is called 'confusion' (*nyandore*): an illicit relating of relations. It is important to emphasize the particular inappropriateness of mixing with adjacent generations' sexual relations. In many, indeed most other instances, social practices including healing aim precisely at bringing together relations, extending and mending a web of substantial relatedness that continuously grows in width and complexity. One example from medicine use is the ingestion of earth with the herbal remedies for the treatment of *chira* (a serious illness associated with confused relations) (see Parkin 1978, Abe 1981, Geissler 2000, Prince and Geissler 2001). In many cases, this earth is to be taken from the site where the rules of relatedness were broken, for example from the place where one killed another person, or from the demarcation of land that one has secretly moved to one's advantage. In other words, 'confusion' can be due to illicit material relations or the infringement of relations. Healing with plant medicines, or through associated rituals, reconstructs such severed or inappropriate relations. It does not, contrary to the erroneous but widespread notion of 'cleansing' (e.g. Wilson 1960), erase the traces of 'polluting' relations. This logic of transformative relatedness, of which medicinal plants are a part, is different from that of purity and contamination, separation and danger.

Just like the potent substance of intercourse that interferes with the capacity of herbal medicines, plants themselves are bundles of relations, and their potency arises from these relations, not from their chemical (or spiritual) 'essence': plants emerge from the earth, which is the abode of the people of the past and of the future. As such, plant medicines are commonly conceptualized as gifts that link generations and give life and health, and their potency is at least partly derived from their role as a bridge between past, present and future life. These vertical relations between generations that are embodied in plants and that give life to infants, are incompatible with the horizontal (pro)creative ties between partners in bodily intercourse.

190

Such separations between different kinds of transformative practices of relatedness – in particular between vertical, intergenerational links and horizontal, gendered ones – are common throughout everyday social life in Uhero. For example, extramarital intercourse can kill a man's child when he comes home and holds it; similarly, an expecting woman, who did not confess her earlier unfaithfulness, cannot give birth to her child. Touching the substance of intercourse can also interfere with divinatory contact with the ancestors, as it confuses gendered horizontal and vertical lineal relations. More generally, the most powerful creative form of touch, bodily intercourse, can interfere with other 'touchy' transformations in women's everyday life: it makes one's pots crack in the kiln, or turns one's millet beer sour, messing up crucial, transformative moments.

Plants, the Past and the Home

Having returned home, Rebekka cleans the plant parts, stuffs them into a pot, seals its lid with cow-dung, and boils it on the cooking stones in her kitchen. Although, like most women in Uhero, she usually cooks in aluminium pots (*sufuria*), she prefers an earthen pot (*agulu*) for medicines, thus evoking the role of the past, and of past people, in what also is called 'pot medicine' (*yath agulu*). This term underlines the domestic nature of this medicine and the link between herbal remedies, cooking and women. It also associates plant medicines with the wider implications of pots in Luo culture: femaleness, womb, fertility; earth, moulding, creation, transformation; ancestors, spirits, links through time. Earthen pots are the products of female creativity. Making pots (*chweyo*, 'to mould', also used for the process of shaping the embryo and for the creative acts of God) is associated with some of the same customs as conception and childbirth.

Once produced, pots are containers in which creation occurs, notably food preparation and beer brewing, and containers of sacrifice and libation (where these are still practiced), as well as abodes for domesticated ancestral spirits (*juogi*). Pots are likened to the womb, and accordingly, beer brewing is associated with similar rules and prohibitions as sexuality.[8] Moreover, pots are made from earth and return to earth when they have been destroyed, following customary rules after the female owner's death, and earth is the ultimate origin and destination of life in what *JoUhero* usually call the 'earthly ways' of everyday life and healing. In this context, the *agulu* is more than a tool and more than a symbol of wider connections; it is a substantial link to the old people, the place, and the earth, whence medicines grow and derive their power.[9]

Touching the Other Body

When the medicine is ready, Mary, Rebekka's grandchild, comes with her siblings. Rebekka talks to them while she undresses Mary, places the pot in front of her stool, sits down with the naked child and, assisted by the other children, covers herself with the blanket before removing the lid. Mary and Rebekka joke in muffled voices about the heat, while the other children look on. After some minutes, grandmother and granddaughter emerge sweating from under the blanket. Rebekka pours some liquid from the pot into a cup and some into a basin, in which she places Mary. Gently, she washes the sweat off the child's body with the dark infusion, massaging the granddaughter who stands, with closed eyes, in the basin. She dries her, dresses her, and gives her a little of the liquid to drink after she herself has taken from it. Her older siblings also drink from the cup before they all run back to their mother's house. Rebekka covers the pot (the contents of which she will use on Mary for two more days) and proceeds to prepare dinner.

From collecting the plants to washing Mary, the treatment has taken four hours, but Rebekka evidently derived pleasure from the intense contact with Mary, just as the little girl enjoyed the attention given to her body. The intimacy between the one administering the treatment and its recipient is characteristic of domestic treatments, which often involve bodily closeness, mutual touch and sharing — whether in the steam under the blanket, during the herbal massage or drinking the bitter fluid from one cup. The healer works on the other body in order to alter its state, but touch is here more than an instrumental action in a subject-object relation, as in 'applying medicine' to a patient. Touch itself heals and brings comfort to the body, lends power to the medicines, and reflects back on the one who gives the medicine. 'Treating children is hard work!' Rebekka sighs, and adds: 'But treating children is *hera*'. *Hera*, commonly translated as 'love', designates here less an emotional disposition than concrete, material practices of relatedness: visiting, eating, talking, laughing together, sharing resources, providing or accepting a meal, or washing or treating a sick person (see Geissler and Prince 2004). Applying medicines to infants is a form of physical love in this sense; it recreates bodies by engaging them in immediate relations of touch and shared substance, and in intermediate relations with the place and its past, living and dead of the home.

The Composite, Porous Body

We turn now to some of the illnesses of infancy that Rebekka and the other women in Uhero struggle against with herbal remedies. This will help us to understand the relationality of *JoUhero*'s notions of persons and bodies, and the medicinal use of plants to nurture and protect infants, that arise from these.

Internal Divisions

Most children's illnesses are located in the abdomen. This makes sense from a biomedical viewpoint, because most young *JoUhero* are infected with worms, intestinal microbes or both (Geissler et al. 1998, Luoba 2003). However, when asked about worms (*njokla*, sing. *njoha*), many *JoUhero* express the view that the body needs some worms to maintain digestion and life in general; 'worms are life' (Geissler 1998, Prince et al. 2002). Likewise, other non-human living entities, such as maggots in the head (*kut wich*), influenced by the moon, are accepted within the body's confines (Ocholla-Ayayo 1976: 52–56). Even some internal organs are accorded some agency and independent capacity, such as *chuny* (the liver or, in some translations, the heart; for Christians also the soul).

Treatments between Inside and Outside

This appreciation of ambiguous inner agents that give life to the body (and occasionally trouble it), and that are linked to and influenced by outside influences, is critical to *JoUhero*'s understanding of illness and the body. Most children's illnesses are located in the belly and the skin, or in the relationship between inside and outside. Common illnesses of infancy combine different forms of diarrhoea with discoloured skin or hair, or rashes (Prince et al. 2001). *Yamo* is the origin, in the belly, of these and other illnesses such as, for example, small pimples (*yambe matindo*), boils (*yamo mokuot*), rashes on the head (*koko*), rashes associated with 'measles' (*ang'iew*) or rashes linked to 'chicken pox' (*nundu*).[10] Once *yamo* emerges, it should be allowed to move out of the body, whether as part of its natural course, or through the incision and squeezing of boils (*saro* and *thwinyo*), sweat in the steambath (*fundo*), mucus provoked by snuff (*fito*), or diarrhoea and urination induced with laxatives and infusions that 'wash one's belly' (*luoko iye*), such as with *ogaka* (*Aloe vera* (L.) Burm.). Accounts of such treatment often end with a characteristic climax: 'you diarrhoea and diarrhoea and – *bas!* – it is exhausted' (note the gesture accompanying this sentence in the last picture, Figure 4.1).

These treatments do not rid the body of the illness-agent, but restore bodily flows and exchanges between inside and outside, body and environment, for example through diarrhoea, urination, sweating, bleeding or sneezing. Body boundaries are constructed as permeable, and the course of an illness is determined by this permeability of one's surfaces and orifices, which medicines facilitate. In this understanding, illness and death result from impermeable body boundaries, from the cessation of vital processes of bodily flows and sharing, and from the force of illness being trapped inside the body. Thus, when a child falls ill, the treatment aims at eliciting the flows between the body and its surroundings, which constitute its being in the world. The importance of bodily flows for the child's life is evident in the rituals of 'taking the child outside' (*golo nyathi oko*), performed some days after the birth. These used to include a stage in which the child was placed on the ground until it had urinated, 'greeting' the world and affirming his bonds with it (for a similar ritual, see Taylor 1992: 96).

Hard skin and a stiff body are seen as harbingers of illness and small children – at particular risk of turning rigid – are regularly massaged (*rwayo*, n. *rwecho*) with oil and crushed plant materials, such as *ng'oche ng'oche* (*Senna bicapsularis* (L.) Roxb.) to ensure the flexibility and softness of flesh and skin. Apart from the physical effect of the oil on the skin, the clarified butter (*mo*) that used to be employed for this purpose also implied links to cattle, the principal expression of relatedness (and value) in a society proud of its pastoral origins (today, white petroleum jelly is used). Not yet quite in the world, infants easily refuse to engage with it and are sensitive to changes of environment. They need to 'get used' (*ng'iyo*) to their environment, implying a process of mutual adaptation and permeation. Thus, parents ought to take water from their original place of residence when they move, mix it with water in the new place and bathe the child; in this way, substantial flows between the body and different environments are merged, and the child is opened to its new environment.[11]

External Agents

Ancestral spirits (*juogi*) act in and on the child's composite body and link it firmly to earth, place and group, sustaining its life and potentially causing illness (Odhalo 1962, Hauge 1974, 1981, Ocholla-Ayayo 1976, 1980, Sindiga 1995). Some Christians, especially born-again 'saved' ones, do not appreciate this influence; they try to keep the 'old people' out of their children's lives, and avoid, among other measures, giving ancestral names with their implication of relatedness with the dead. However, this avoidance is more difficult than it would seem. Even if a child's parents choose purely Christian names, other relations will try to find out 'who the child is', i.e. whose dead person's traits she embodies and whose name she should bear. Others will employ the Christian name in much the same way in which they would have used the older ancestral naming (*juogi*-names): as a marker of shared qualities and substance between the child and another person (see Geissler and Prince 2004). Moreover, some Christians would justify their choice *not* to *juogi*-name their child with reference to the fact that their parents had not done this, and that it therefore might harm their children if they chose to do otherwise, thus drawing upon precisely the same logic as the older ancestral naming.

Apart from a recent, growing tendency among new evangelical churches, ancestral spirits are not usually exorcized, but are appeased with sacrifices and herbal medicines, or directed to somebody else (see Evans-Pritchard 1950, Whisson 1964, Abe 1981); therapy for *juogi* does not primarily enforce the person's boundaries against spirits and others, but on the contrary restores material continuity between them.[12] The agency of the spirit in one's body is not considered harmful as such; problems reside in twisted relations or disturbances of continuity between living and dead people. It is taken for granted that a person (and her body) is interfused with the forces of other, dead people, as evidenced by the importance for a child's health of naming her after the right people. A wrong name can cause sickness and death; the right name can entail shared bodily reactions against certain foods or places, and privileged social relations evoked by the name (Geissler and Prince 2004). The notion of 'possession' in the sense of 'Who owns this body – myself or another agent?' is thus of little relevance to *JoUhero*. The critical question is not who *owns* a person's body, but to whom she *owes* her life.

Living persons also contribute to a child's life and enter into relations of material continuity with it, most evidently in the flows of nurture, which commence with breast milk and soon include herbal medicines. Later, commensality and especially sharing food with siblings and parents becomes important to the child's continuous development and health, both in everyday food practices and in rituals in which substantial relations with living people are affirmed.[13] Such material relations with living people can also make children sick, as illustrated by the evil eye (*sihoho*): a woman's gaze fixes upon food that a child is eating (or a mother's breast), which therefore gets stuck in the child's stomach. To cure the child, she should share food with the evil-eyed woman, restoring the continuity that her gaze had broken (*hoso*).[14]

Even detached parts of the child's body continue to influence her well-being. The placenta (*biero*), an embodiment of the maternal relation, should be buried in order to tie the person to her place of belonging and ensure her well-being. This is often not done today, either because the mother gave birth in hospital or, more commonly, because she and her family have embraced the Christian struggle to rid themselves of ancestral, 'earthly' ties. However, even then the placenta must be safely disposed of in a latrine, to avoid a dog, or worse, a sorcerer interfering with it, which may kill the child or render it infertile. Likewise, the child's hair, nails or faeces, even her footprints, can be misused to damage her; in this context, hair, nails, faeces and footprints are also referred to as *biero*, underscoring the (metonymic) principle that their misuse shares.

The Porous Body

In contrast to biomedical germ theory and hygiene, where only the whole, bounded and single body is healthy, and intrusions equal sickness, most child-care practices in Uhero regard the presence of others within the body primarily as a source of vital force. The vital capacity of the child and its body does not reside in its essence, contained within its boundaries, but *between* the child and others. The result of such relational capacity is not an unfolding of a pre-existing potential inside a stable thing towards predetermined effects; rather, it is a less predictable occurrence between moving things (or persons); from the always contingent event of their encounter something new emerges. This transformative sense of capacity moves in space and time, from one to the other, from one state to another. By contrast, the capacity of a pharmaceutical drug, for example, is understood as a stable, inert potential – its effects are contained within the boundaries of its material substance. Our own research on bodies, worms, medicinal knowledge and cognition, with which we began our encounter with Luo medicine, was framed by this epistemological imaginary (Geissler and Prince 2009). Each of the entities under study – worms, bodies, minds - was imagined as distinct, individual, growing or diminishing in inverted proportion to the other: worms subtract bodily substance, reducing cognition; the absence of worms allow nutrients to be accumulated in bodily substance, which results in expanding minds. The underlying logic of zero-sum economy has certainly made inroads into some *JoUhero*'s understandings of, for example, formal education and wealth, but for most mothers, the notion of children's growth is not (yet) reduced to a matter of 'parental investment' and 'child development'.

Herbal Medicines as Relations

Within the biomedical understanding of body, mind and person, medicinal treatment is constructed as the end of illness; the death of the illness-agent is the aimed for, definite outcome of treatment. By contrast, the composite and porous constitution of the body and its capacities in Luo herbal medicine allows, indeed requires continuous re-negotiations of its being in the world. Worms curl up peacefully when they drink a herbal infusion, head-worms calm down when the child is given herbal snuff, other medicines return the sunken heart to its position or restore volatile ties with the spirits. Each relationship within and beyond the body provides entry points to meaningful action, which remains open-ended, as none of these agents is ever definitively appeased or removed. Medicines, though powerful, are imagined not primarily as weapons to destroy the agents of illness and defend the body, but as substances through which one gets in

197

contact with these agents, such as spirits or worms, restores relations and opens new pathways of growth.

Herbal medicines open up blocked passages and surfaces and restore continuity between inside and outside, and between one person and another. They can do this because they themselves are agents to which people relate, and are part of continuous relationships between living and dead persons and between persons and places. Medicinal plants create or restore bodily bonds of shared substance, because as they embody relations, they are more than inert matter or mere tools of medical action: they are others with whom one engages, rather than objects one utilizes. The ambiguity of their capacity is an expression of this agency.[15]

Ties with the Home and its Old People

Plant remedies can restore the continuity between body and world because, growing from the earth of one's place, they embody the potential of growth and the continuity between living and dead humans, and between humans and land. Ingested, inhaled or absorbed into the body, medicinal plants do more than symbolize the ancestors: they bring living and dead in touch with one another and this is where their capacity to elicit growth lies. Certain particularly powerful medicines grow close to the lake (an abode of spirits in which all ancestral force ends), in old homesteads and on graves, but within the logic according to which many Luo inhabit land, all land is an abode of past and future life, associated with the ambivalent capacities of life and death.

This 'earthly' (*mag piny*) thinking, as it is called by *JoUhero*, is evident in concerns with food. Food gives the body strength or blood, but this is not simply an appropriation and accumulation of matter that is added to the individual body (as in the scientific concept of 'nutrition'). Instead body and person become part of a place through eating the food (or other matter) of the land. Regular, everyday domestic food practices create consubstantiality and continuity between body, place and people. They contribute, for example, to the gradual transformation of young wives into members of their husbands' place and group, which is marked by shared meals of increasing intimacy between, among others, daughters-in-law and mothers-in-law. The emphasis on consubstantiality that transforms those involved and facilitates growth is particularly strong around ritual meals, such as those after funerals. Such meals are special in that they include meat, which is not common in the everyday diet: animals – ideally cows – are slaughtered for the purpose, in a particular location in relation to the homestead, the food is only touched by particular members of the family, and the animal is partitioned, cooked and consumed according to particular kin and affinal relationships. Both in everyday and ceremonial meals, commensality reinforces creative relations.

This relational implication of eating also means that certain illnesses of urban life (such as diabetes) are said to respond well to food from one's home. However, the ingestion of plants grown in one's home can also harm the eater. For example, it is dangerous to eat food that was grown on land that one comes from but that was sold to another group; here, the land-sale (a recent innovation) severs ancestral ties and creates a rift with one's (dead) 'old people', which, when ingested, can affect one's life and growth. The same logic prohibits, for example, a mother-in-law from eating food in her son-in-law's home before the latter has substantiated their affinal relationship by bridewealth gifts (including shared food). Underlying these effects of eating is the earth's capacity to elicit and interrupt growth, which is evident in the practice of earth-eating, considered normal especially during pregnancy (Prince et al. 1999, Geissler 2000). Mixed with medicines, earth can treat illnesses associated with ancestral forces, but earth can also kill; if, for example, earth has been ingested during an oath, a perjurer will be killed by it. Earth creates in these situations the capacity of substantial relations, which can facilitate or terminate flows of life. This conceptualization of ingestion as creation of continuity between body and environment (animated by ancestral forces and inhabited by living people) is important for the conceptualization of the capacity of herbal remedies. Plants are potent, because they emerge from the land – like grains, cattle and people – and carry with them the potent remainder of past relations, into which the body of an ill child is drawn through ingestion, inhalation or massaging with herbal remedies.

Since plants, like foodstuffs, derive their potency from their relations with place, people in a particular area have special ties to local herbal medicines. Young wives either rely on their mother-in-laws' medicinal advice or return to their parental home to obtain medicines for their children. Townspeople rely, in particular for their children's health, on medical supplies from their rural homes. Rural grandmothers send medicines or travel to their urban grandchildren to administer treatments, and Luo migrants in other areas of Kenya seek Luo healers' advice for illnesses that might be related to their home, since well-being, illness and healing ultimately centre on the powers of home.

Ties among the Living

Since the capacity of herbal remedies lies not in their inherent properties, but in their relations, *JoUhero*'s relationship to medicinal plants is not best described as one of 'ownership'. Despite the introduction of private property in land over the past three decades, medicines can be picked freely in the bush and are nobody's individual property. Individual and group rights to land have nothing to do with rights to medicines (see also Obado and Odera 1995: 158). Neither should herbal remedies be linked to personal profit. Many *JoUhero*, and especially Rebekka, were outraged over a neighbour's attempts to market, in the nearby town, medicines produced from wild plants: the neighbour dug out whole plants, leaving nothing to regenerate (as was the normal practice), boiled the medicines and bottled them. This extraction of plants from land and group, which cut their roots as well as their ties to local well-being and growth, and the transaction of their capacity, contained in bottles, available on the market, turning a local medium of relatedness into an object of exchange, seemed wrong to many *JoUhero*. Rebekka was certainly not opposed to a knowledgeable woman 'being given' a chicken (or even money in lieu of one) after treating a village child, but she resented the idea of 'payment' on a market: 'Who planted these medicines? Him? How can he ask for money?'

In accordance with this opposition to selling life-sustaining medicines, healers in Uhero did not usually demand payment (*chulo*) for their medicine, but 'just to be given something' (*miyamiya*). Only one of the many knowledgeable women in Uhero was reputed to talk about money before even treating, and even having fixed prices for certain treatments; she was not related to anybody in the village and came from a different ethnic group. Her alleged greed caused her interminable quarrels with the other villagers, and she was evicted on several occasions. Some (male) healers of wider reputation in neighbouring villages or farther afield were said to charge (high) fees, but these were rarely consulted by *JoUhero* (compared to the continuous mutual consultations among the women), and often their work was closer to the ambiguous activities of the healer-diviners, who cared for rare and highly personal afflictions.

The term *wuon yath* ('father or parent of the plant/medicine'), which designates the person who originally knew a particular plant or remedy, does not imply ownership as much as it indicates responsibility for a creative potential and genealogical attribution (in the sense in which a grandfather is not the 'owner' of his descendants). Medicinal knowledge is conceptualized not so much as individual cognitive property, but in terms of relations. Contrary to Western ideas of 'medicine men' as African medical experts, equivalent to doctors, Luo herbal medicines are not mobilized as part of a domain of exclusive knowledge but as a collective, communal resource of (mainly) women (see Olenja 1991, Kawango 1995, Prince et al. 2001, Geissler et al. 2002). Since no woman knows all medicines, discussions about medicines and mutual advice are part of the treatment. Sharing medicines and knowledge about medicines is an aspect of daily life within the homestead: co-wives, mothers and daughters-in-law, and grandmothers and grandchildren often show each other herbal remedies, linking and transforming the medicinal knowledges of several generations and different places. Of course, knowledge is not shared indiscriminately and completely. Secrets and the refusal to share knowledge is also part of this overall pattern of sharing, which is shaped by patterns of relatedness – both in the limited sense of kinship and affinity, and in a wider sense of friendship and affection among kin and non-kin – and associated to other forms of sharing, such as commensality, shared lifetime and shared experiences and situations (such as recent childbirth). If a person close to one, such as a grandmother, gives a grandchild the 'root' of a plant medicine (*tiend yath*, the knowledge of the plant and its location), this knowledge constitutes a gift, which remains tied to the person or group from which it originated (and this origin is often evoked in the course of treatment). Such relations to older and to dead people that are embodied in medicinal knowledge and in medicines are among the sources from which these remedies derive their capacity.[16]

The fact that medical knowledge is not the possession of individuals but owed to others, the old people in the earth, the relatives who taught one and with whom one shares them, and that medicinal relations are intimately interwoven with other material relations, was expressed in the mythical narrative that a knowledgeable woman told one of us (Ruth) about how she acquired her medicinal skills as a child. An old woman in the bush (an ancestress), whom she had washed, although she was dirty and smelly, had given her a medicinal plant and blessed it before she disappeared (Prince and Geissler 2001). Here, entering into a material relation with the woman through her body's dirt is the first step towards sharing powerful knowledge; the sharing of capacities is predicated upon bodily engagement. In a similar story about the acquisition of healing power, a father travelling home from Nairobi to get herbal remedies for his sick child shared his food with somebody on the train, who afterwards gave him a herbal medicine for the child; only after the stranger had alighted, did the father realize that he was one of his 'old people'. Herbal remedies are always owed to someone, part of what one shares with others, whether it is one's grandmother with whom one lived, or ancestors who appear in dreams. The place of sharing food or touching dirt in these and similar stories does not mean that medicine is 'exchanged' for food or kindness. Rather, a substantial relation is acknowledged by sharing food or touch and extended further through sharing healing capacity.

Reaching for Past Relations

One could say that plant medicines derive capacity from the *traces* of relations. Traces materialize past encounters in time; they are substantial, but often ephemeral. Unlike things-in-themselves, they witness the conditions of their creation, i.e. the substantial merging between different trajectories: like the imprint of a foot in the mud (which, as a trace, contains medical capacity in the sense of *biero*), the medicinal plant in the bush is a trace of past relations. Physical contact with these traces evokes the transformative capacity of consubstantiality, which is channelled into future relations: one's children and descendants. The capacity of traces, different from that inherent in things, is realized when they are brought together with something else, which releases the residue of a past relation into a new one. This capacity does not lie dormant inside the things, untouched by time, but is only existent in its momentary engagement with others, when it links the present to past and future occurrences.

202

The outcome of bringing a trace to work on a body is never certain, as one never controls all past constituents of a trace, unlike when one employs, for example, a pharmacological compound with a proven, inherent capacity to cause a specific effect.

Herbal medicines are engaged in relations. They work between people, or between humans and the outside, and they derive their potency from aspects, or traces, of the people with whom they interact. These relations are not static links between entities – lines connecting points on a map – but movements from one to the other that intersect and momentarily take form (as persons or as things) where they get in touch. The primary fact in this understanding is the overall 'forward movement' (*dhi nyime*), the flows or 'growth' (*dongruok*); from this movement, figures and forms arise. It is not things and persons that are given, but the growth that makes them alive. It is this growth that herbal medicines try to ensure. The expression 'the root of the plant/medicine', mentioned above, points to this generative relation rather than to the 'plant itself' or the 'name of the plant' (the real thing). This relation implicates the plant with the ground from which it grows, and with the person who gives it.

The association of 'the root of the plant' with the person who knows where to find the plant, the *wuon yath* (parent of the plant/medicine), who prepares and administers the medicine and who shows the 'root' to her descendant, underlines that medicinal knowledge itself is understood as a relational capacity rather than, say, a cognitive store of information. Knowledge is here a relation between living persons, land and place, and the people of the past, who are related to the plant as well as to living people. These material ties embody both the healing capacity of the plant, and they constitute the knowledge of the plant.[17] As the genealogical associations of the concepts of *tiend yath* (roots of plant/medicine), *wuon yath* (parent of the plant/medicine) and *yath nyaluo* (Luo daughter's plants/medicines) highlight, plant growth, medicinal knowledge and human life rely upon analogous and intertwined processes of creativity.

'You Just Try': Capacity, Hope and Surprise

Touch, with the implication of *riwo*, is a *contingent* practice in the full sense of the word. On the one hand, it implies physical nearness, the potential of consubstantiality, or *contiguity*, which this chapter has

203

explored so far by looking at the role of nearness and consubstantiality in healing, in understandings of the body and its well-being, and in the conceptualization of herbal medicines and their potency. On the other hand, and equally important, touch implies *contingency*. The encounter *between* two persons, any encounter, is also a contingent *event*, an indeterminate movement from one to the other, the outcome of which is never quite certain. This indeterminacy, this potential to surprise, is a source of the transformative creativity of touch. Unlike an instrumental, intentional *act*, performed by one upon the other in order to alter it, this occurrence always creates something more than what was intended, something new, unforeseen. In this sense, all social practices in Uhero are regarded as having a tentative aspect, an element of uncertainty.

Trying without Errors
This engagement with the unforeseeable is particularly evident in the context of medicine use. 'Trying', which Susan Reynolds Whyte suggested to be constitutive of the 'subjunctive mode' (Whyte 1997: 23) of African healing practices, such as the ones we are looking at here, is not so much a surrender to an 'insufficient' grasp of truth and certainty (e.g. lacking scientific diagnostic tools), but an integral part of the relational nature of healing, medicinal knowledge and medicinal capacity. In contrast to the notion of 'intentional subjects' or 'actors', who through rational action realize goals that were prefigured in their reasoning, human practice is here always indeterminate, always relying on something beyond the rational calculus of an actor, beyond intentionality. This 'beyond' is not an external subjectivity, such as 'God's will', but the element of imprecision that inheres to any human encounter.

The women in Uhero emphasize that treating children's illnesses means 'trying' (*temo*), much in the sense of Sisyphus' labours, pushing forward in an uphill struggle that one never wins. Never gaining security or stability, they try to keep up with the force of necessity, and draw upon contingent contacts with others – people's advice, medicines and care, but also upon unseen forces within and around the body – to restore life and facilitate growth. This notion of 'trying' acknowledges contingency and the absence of control, and suggests another relation between person, tool and task than that constituted by instrumental intentionality. In this last section, we want to illustrate this sense of trying, which pervades all uses of medicines in the homes of *JoUhero*, with a brief extract from a characteristic, never-ending kitchen conversation about child illness between NyaSakwa, Rebekka's youngest co-wife, and her mother-in-law, Mary, about the former's youngest, six-month-old daughter Ingeborg, who was named after Wenzel's 'mother' (Prince et al. 2002).

Open-Ended Relations

NyaSakwa and Wenzel were sitting in front of the kitchen. NyaSakwa's mother-in-law, Mary, passed by to find embers with which to light her pipe. Ingeborg was screaming on NyaSakwa's lap.

Mary (M): [lighting her pipe]: Why is my friend crying?

NyaSakwa (N): The worm [*njoka*] has followed her. She can't sleep [...]. He strangles her and she vomits and has *luya*.

M: Why don't you just start with those people's medicine for...

N: Which medicine?

M: ...for evil eye [*sihoho*]. The one they gave you earlier.

N: That woman refused to give my husband this medicine; do you think she would give it to me?

The first sentences of this encounter with the mother-in-law have already brought up two different aetiologies: the worm and evil eye. These are very different agents affecting the child's well-being, and they call for different remedies. Reference to 'the worm' implies probably a 'worm' (*njoka*) that is said to 'follow the child' (*luwo nyathi*), moving up its back, causing convulsions (which, for example, accompany cerebral malaria). This would ideally have been prevented by regular massaging with Vaseline and plant materials (e.g. crushed leaves of *Ng'oche ng'oche* [*Senna bicapsularis*]). 'Worm' could also simply refer to intestinal worms (*njokla*), which would have called for soothing and 'straightening' herbal teas (e.g. *Ong'ono* [*Capparis fascicularis* DC], *Okeke* [*Albizia coriaria*] or the commonest stomach remedy *Akech* [*Schkuhria pinnata* (Lam.) Thell.]; see Mwenesi 1995; Geissler 1998). 'Evil eye', by contrast, would have required sharing food with the evil-eye woman, herbal tea made from, for example, *Nyunyodhi* (*Leonotis nepetifolia* [L.] Ait.f.) or *Olulusia* (*Vernonia amygdalina* Del.), or the surgical removal of the evil-eye substance (see Prince and Geissler 2009). Yet, this does not seem to stir a debate about what the 'real' illness is. More alternatives were to follow in the course of this conversation and over the following days. Note also the taken-for-grantedness of the mother-in-law's unasked-for advice, which inserts itself into an ongoing, multivocal conversation about the baby and her illness. Before Mary passed by, and after she left, other women from the home and nearby had passed by and volunteered similar tentative advice. As NyaSakwa mentions, these continuous conversations about plant knowledge, healing and children do not imply that everybody shares everything. Although the acknowledged rule is that a childbearing mother should share her medicines with another mother, as they share the same responsibilities, personal sympathies doubtlessly influence whom one tells about a medicine and whom one might even show the plant itself, whereas conflicts and tensions can prevent sharing and mutual help.

Mary went on. In a characteristic manner, she shifted between different domestic concerns, and reminded a boy who was carrying maize to the mill, that he should bring her some flour:

M: Hey, you, my 'husband' [i.e., my grandson]! You are going to the mill, but where did you pluck your vegetables [i.e., you plucked them on my land, so you should share your maize with me!]?

N: I have also stayed hungry today! Nothing, since the funeral yesterday!

M: I cannot sleep on porridge alone, my dear. [...] The worms just go 'brrrrrrr'!

Wenzel (W): [to NyaSakwa, pointing at Ingeborg] So this is *luya*?

N: Yes, those white ones that swell on her head are *luya*.

W: So *luya* is the illness she suffers from?

N: No, *luya* is just sweat — just like you are perspiring now. These are just things of her body; this is not an illness.

As on other occasions, the ethnographer's search for illness-entities had failed. In this case, this was due to linguistic incompetence. Nevertheless, it raises the issue of whether the question: 'Is X the illness she is suffering from?' is meaningful under such circumstances. In everyday conversations, this question, or its affirmative answer, hardly ever figured. Instead, one would say: 'It could be X' or, much more commonly: 'Why don't you *try* (the medicine) Y?', suggesting a medicine, rather than a causal explanation or illness category.

Mary continued speaking to Ingeborg, for whom she felt a particular fondness due to the coincidence of her birth with the departure of our 'mother', Ingeborg, with whom Mary had often sat chatting and smoking. The association between Ingeborg junior and senior was constituted by naming, nickname joking, narratives about the older namesake that constantly surrounded the young child, and the reference to tobacco and shared smoking. Although light-hearted and joking, this connection carried a mutual responsibility, and Mary took a keen interest in her 'friend's' health. Meanwhile, Wenzel continued to try to 'pin down' the illness:

M: [to baby Ingeborg] My sweet friend, whom should I chat with if not you? Who would bring me tobacco?

W: [to NyaSakwa] So she is not ill? Why do you then treat her with medicine?

N: I try [*temo*] her with Luo medicine that she drinks.

W: Which medicine?

N: Luo. Of the pot [*agulu*].

W: Yes, sure, I mean: What is its name?

N: The name of that medicine?

W: Mmm.

N: I don't know; I just pluck it from the bush here.

N: [turns to Mary] How is that plant called? She drinks *ober*[18] and also ... this is for *wuoyo* [one of the illnesses of infancy associated with *yamo*], and I have also given her another one for *nala* [yet another illness of infancy].

These two new potential illnesses, *wuoyo* and *nala*, belong to the *yamo* complex, marked by intestinal and skin symptoms, from which most infant illnesses stem, and both would call for treatments along the lines of the steam bath (*fundo*), opening up blocked body boundaries and orifices. Again, the issue of which specific illness the child 'really' was suffering from was less important than the fact that she was treated. This underlined both the quality of healing as an aspect of maternal nurture, and the role of continuous trying to engage with some of the many forces that pervade the child and upon which her well-being depends. Meanwhile, Mary was distracted by a pot of boiling porridge on the hearth inside the kitchen hut. She called an older child:

M: Can one of you wash this calabash for me? I want to eat. Use soap!

N: [calls for Mary's attention] Mary, I ask you: that plant that you told me to massage her with yesterday [to restore the body's suppleness and permeability], can I mix it with any oil?

M: [to NyaSakwa] You just mix it with any oil that you can apply to her body. [...] [to the child taking the calabash] Here wash this! It is dirty and I want to take porridge. [to baby Ingeborg] What shall we do with you my dear friend? Don't you see, your son Wenzel [jokingly addressed as baby Ingeborg's 'son'] refuses to give me tobacco! He would just throw me away carelessly!

Talking to the infant, Mary expresses first her concern with the baby herself; then she turns the joking relationship with the child onto Wenzel, who is now positioned as Ingeborg's son: he should take care of his mother's friend Mary, supplying her with tobacco. This kind of fleeting and joking reference to mutual responsibilities is not only characteristic of joking relationships, but also of the playful way in which many relations are evoked and negotiated in everyday life, not least around medicines. Such relations are never as stable and binding as some kin-relations but they are not insignificant.

Looking into Ingeborg's mouth, Mary continued, addressing NyaSakwa:

M: What have you put on the child's tongue?

N: She has drunk medicine.

M: Is that what is stuck on the tongue?

N: Yes, her tongue was bad, and I usually give her that medicine for *nala*.

M: [to Ingeborg, laughing] My only friend! You see, nowadays I have no tobacco. [to NyaSakwa] You should have tried *atipa* for 'false teeth' (*Lak matwi*). *Nyunyudhi* can't be used for that.[19]

N: Mary, look now! It is her stomach that aches so much at night that she doesn't want anyone to touch her. [...]

M: Oh, my dear friend!

N: I am still looking for the medicine that I was searching in vain, when you saw me the other day. [...]

M: What medicine was that?

N: It grows up, behind your house. Where you cleared. You never showed me the root.

[Interruption by a visitor.]

More illnesses and plants were mentioned in passing. 'False teeth' was the fifth potential aetiology suggested in the course of five minutes, and again the question of what to do took precedence over the question of diagnosis or aetiology. The ethnographers, concerned with their little 'mother's' well-being, tried to contribute their own treatment suggestion.

W: [to NyaSakwa] Would you like me to take Ingeborg to [the government health post]?

N: I am tired of [the hospital]! Yes, this may well be malaria, but then, [at the hospital] ... You are just told about money. Here ten shilling, there ten shilling; you expect you will be given drugs, [...but] you are told 'there is no medicine, go and buy it from the shop'. And you have used your money. [...] I stopped going to the clinic. Better to use some of the medicine you have.

M: You Luos you are stupid! Just try [*tem atema*] pot medicines [*yiend agulu*] on this friend of mine! Long ago when there were no hospital medicines [*yiend osiptal*], weren't people growing well?!

In the framework of 'trying', the hospital appeared to have much less potential than the bush. Whereas the latter would always offer another medicine that could be tried, the hospital only seemed to have one kind of medicine for one illness – malaria – and this medicine was rarely available at that. As Mary's intervention shows, the contrast between hospital and the mother's kitchen is loaded with associations of historical change and identity, positioning the past 'Luo medicine', embedded in local relations and history, against the new, outside and ahistorical 'hospital medicine'. Mary continued to joke with Ingeborg:

M: [to Wenzel, pointing at Ingeborg]: You see, now she is looking at you? Are you seeing your mother's look? She is the one who has carried you and suffered!

W: Yes.

N: [trying to focus Mary's attention again] Look at the stomach! She pulls it in until it reaches her back. [...]. There is something pulling in the stomach. [...] That thing [the 'worm'] just follows the lower stomach up to the loins. [...]

M: Do this: take soap and massage her stomach [...] until the soap makes foam.

N: Just any ordinary soap?

M: There are these bar-soaps nowadays. [...] Massage her well! Do not throw this friend of mine away! My tobacco! [...] [Mary sends Wenzel to fetch embers for their pipes and both light up.]

N: [to Mary] Look at her stomach, now! If you touch that stomach of hers it is fighting.

M: Yes, you just massage her. It could be *okulbat* [another of the diffuse complex of infant illnesses].

N: I thought *okulbat* is when the body is cool and she sleeps and sleeps...

M: That's the one! [note NyaSakwa's earlier explanation that the child was hot and sleepless.]

N: ...but when the worms have just started to make brrrrr sounds, isn't it....?

M: Yes, probably it is just the worms.

N: It has begun inside her.

M: Just try that soap! And now leave me in peace; let me go and take a bath. [...]

The conversation had come to an inconclusive end. Any of its threads could be taken up at the next encounter. The ethnographer, however, was interested to see something happen. He asked Mary:

W: Mary, why don't you try to *treat* this child? [...]

M: But don't you see that I have treated her!? I said she should be massaged with soap!

W: Is soap a Luo medicine?

M: Yes.

N: If I could find Kaluma [industrially produced mentholated ointment], I could massage her with it, after massaging her with the soap. [...] I could mix Kaluma with that medicine you told me to use, couldn't I? It is difficult to massage her with the medicine and then with Kaluma. Wouldn't it be good to mix them? Or are the powers of these medicines not to be mixed [since one is from the shop and the other from home]?

Commodities such as industrial soap and petroleum jelly are freely combined with Luo plant medicines, often taking the place of clarified butter, which used to the only available oil that could be used for massaging and the external application of medicines. Such integration of non-plant substances from distant sources precedes the introduction of industrial products, as the well-established use of mineral salt from southern Luoland underlines. Even some semi-pharmaceutical products, such as various mentholated ointments, are applied interchangably or mixed with local plant remedies. However, as the above quotation also shows, 'pot medicines' from the bush are often deemed to be incompatible with 'hospital medicines' from shop or dispensary, as their perceived working mechanisms contradict each other. Thus, in the case of *yamo* related illnesses, herbal remedies are meant to 'bring out' the illness by opening the body by inducing sweat, rashes or diarrhoea. In contrast, injections 'keep the illness inside'; therefore, even Rebekka, who was otherwise very happy about biomedical treatments, argued that giving injections while doing *fundo* for *yamo*, as in the case above, was dangerous and to be avoided. In more than one case, she subverted our attempts to take an obviously ill child to hospital, delaying us by the necessary number of days, until she had finished the *fundo*.

M: Why don't you massage her with the Kaluma that you once had?

N: It was finished. I did not buy a new tin.

M: Then you are the one who makes the child sick! Is there no Kaluma in the shop?

N: This is what I wanted to come to you for. [...]

M: I don't have any money. [pointing at Wenzel]: You had better ask Wenzel!

N: Yes, isn't he her child who should be treating her? [to Wenzel] If your mother is sick aren't you the one who should treat her? [to Mary] He is Ingeborg's son and he doesn't want to treat Ingeborg! Well, that is up to him. [...]

M: Wenzel! Where is he? Is he there? Has he been lost?!

We heeded this call and took Ingeborg to hospital, but although she received her childhood vaccinations and treatment for malaria, she continued, like most infants, to be sick every now and then, and the women's long conversation about the children's health and medicines continued. This conversation was characteristic of the open-ended, tentative negotiation of herbal medicines in Uhero. Various potential illnesses were discussed, but it remained unclear (indeed, unimportant at this point) what the child's 'real' problem was; a range of medicines was suggested, and few were tried out immediately. In addition, the chronology of illness and treatment was unclear: there was no clear beginning and even weeks later, after a visit to the health post and treatment for malaria, there was no conclusion. Meanwhile, Ingeborg grew tall and fat.

Characteristically, this discussion of illness was embedded in other everyday concerns – notably those with food and its preparation – and evoked biological, affinal, classificatory and fictive kinship relations and related expectations and exchanges. It would be difficult to extract from this conversation a clear-cut trajectory from malfunction, through diagnosis and treatment, to restored health. This vagueness was even more marked when more than two women were involved in the discussion. Of course, one could still extrapolate from the above conversation that 'soap treats stomach ache caused by worms' – but this would produce a very specific representation of this encounter. More than the choice of the right tool was at stake here: care, responsibilities, affection. Talking and treatment belonged together and were both ways of trying, of deploying capacity through relations, as witnessed by Mary's offended retort to Wenzel's request for her to 'treat' the child: 'But don't you see I have treated her?!'

'Trying' is here not to be confused with a pattern of 'trial-and-error' (like that of doctors' prescription treatments in ill-equipped hospitals), nor is it due to a deficient causality, limited by insufficient means of establishing the truth. 'Trying' does not represent a not-yet-there, a lack of grasp. The women's questions aim less for the certainty of one truthful answer, but for an open path forward, with possibilities and opportunities for action. They do not search for the 'underlying reality' of body and illness, but constitute real everyday life by moving through it. 'If' is the condition of the next step forward, and as long as one moves, there is life.

Plants, Knowledge, Capacity

We have argued that in this western Kenyan village home, mothers' concerns with the bodily well-being of infants, their illnesses, the treatments for these, and the remedies prepared from local medicinal plants, are constructed in a 'relational' framework: the capacity of bodies, illness-agents, remedial action and medicinal plants is located in relations, rather than in the things-in-themselves. Likewise, the effects or transformations achieved by medicinal treatments are conceived of as relational, changing the ties between living and dead persons or between persons and their internal agents, and not simply 'restoring' diseased person's bodies to their individual wholeness and health. Strength, harm and the restoration of vitality are effects of relations: they are bonds that arise from temporarily shared substance. These fluid but material bridges – between humans, between them and the place they live in, between the living and dead and their material embodiments in things – constitute that which they relate. In an unlimited and ever-shifting web, relations are made and unmade, intentionally and unintentionally, and out of these movements, life takes its many, temporary shapes – and, most importantly, children grow. Healing practices to guard and restore life carefully intervene into this web, straightening links, disentangling others, and tying new ones.

Thus, practices of healing are not constructed as 'acts', in which inherent capacities – such as a grandmother's cognitive expertise or a plant's chemical properties – are brought to work, like inanimate tools, upon the child's body, understood as a bounded entity. Such (mis)understandings of herbal medicinal practice arise from particular (maybe 'Western') imaginations of knowledge and capacity that rest on an ontology of distinct entities; in this view, medicinal knowledge and pharmacological potency are 'properties' of respectively minds and plants, just as the health and ill-health of infants, in this view, arise from their individual bodies' vital capacity. By contrast, a relational understanding of life and well-being and of the capacity to create and maintain life results in another way of understanding and using medicines, which also is different from the underlying assumptions of much 'ethno-pharmacology'. The latter, and in particular bioassay-based pharmacognosy, transfers to new, 'ethnic' contexts the familiar idea that bodies and minds, diseases and disease agents, and plants and their biochemical constituents are distinct entities with inherent

213

properties and capacities. This assumption results in the expectation that ethno-diagnosis and ethnobotany will lead straight to potent medicinal plants, the chemical compounds of which can be isolated through laboratory-based assays.

The different foundation of herbal medicine that we explored here may be among the explanations for the failure of many ethnopharmacological surveys of African herbal medicines to identify marketable pharmacological compounds. With this we are not saying that Luo medicinal plants do not possess chemical properties, which may be remedial against certain illness conditions; occasionally, potent chemical compounds have indeed been found in African medicinal plants. Our argument is not that such scientifically measurable effects of chemical capacity do not occur, but that these are conceptually different from the relational notions of capacity and effect that we explored here.

The failure rate of ethnopharmacological bioassays is high, and rather than attributing this merely to a supposed imprecision of indigenous medicinal knowledge, we might find an explanation in the different working principles of this knowledge that we have tried to explore here. The herbal bath that we described in the first part of this chapter, and our subsequent ethnopharmacological research on the pharmacopoeia of Uhero underlines this point. Based on the consensus of Uhero mothers, we identified several plants for bioassay-guided identification of 'active compounds' (Geissler et al. 2002, see Geissler and Prince 2009 for a further ethnographic analysis). That this aim was not reached is maybe unsurprising if one compares the notions of cause, effect and capacity, which underlie such 'bioguided purification': dried plants were extracted and extracts tested for their ability to kill pathogens; from those able to kill at low concentrations, the molecules likely to have the deadly effect were identified. In this work, disease is caused by external enemies of the body, effective medicine kills these, and the capacity to kill rests, objectively, within elementary particles. Throughout, the emphasis is on distinct, whole entities – be it bodies, pathogens, or atoms – linked by an oppositional logic of either-or: the body or the pathogen, the medicine or the germ. This procedure proved successful in identifying antibiotic pharmaceuticals, but it is obviously not an ideal model of herbal bathing and its procedures, aims and meanings. Plants are dried, extracted in solvent rather than boiled, and applied to the isolated pathogens rather than the whole human body; and the medicine is treated like a selective poison, a notion, which is absent from *JoUhero's* explanations of healing.

Such differences need not prevent us from continuing to study plant remedies like those described here, in order to find medicines that 'work' within a scientific logic of cause and effect and chemical properties. One could search for other models of efficacy than crude bioassays, and explore different mechanisms of absorption and exposure, such as those involved in herbal baths; new modes of assessment should be designed that are more sensitive to the local preparations and applications of medicines.[20] In this way, maybe more 'effective' medicines will be found in the global phytopharmacopoeia. The purpose of this chapter was not to discourage or discredit such innovative research, but to propose that, irrespective of sensitive and sensible adaptations, the outcomes of such research will remain fundamentally different from the Uhero women's quest for their children's life.

Their particular construction of medicinal capacity – and body, illness and treatment – as *in-between* entities has a further implication: herbal medicinal knowledge and healing are not only *contingent* in the original sense of the word – relying upon physical nearness and relation – but also in the sense of being unpredictable, surprising, driven by hope and not by certainty. This logic of 'trying', illustrated in the last part of our chapter, needs to be acknowledged as constitutive of herbal medicinal knowledge, instead of being attributed to a deficiency of knowing, an incomplete, pre-scientific grasp of nature. Too often, dialogues like the one we cited are interpreted as communicative weaknesses or a messiness of everyday life, which the scientific ethnobotanist can remedy by carefully systematizing the causal pathways of medicine use and treatment, for example by asking informants rather than listening to their conversations, thereby eliciting 'clearer' answers and condensing these into botanical tables (see Geissler et al. 2002). We think that such systematization does more than extracting the underlying truth of medicinal practices that is hidden in the confusions of real life; by applying unquestioned assumptions of causality and capacity, another 'ethnomedical' knowledge is created. One overlooks in this way the fact that imprecision is an essential part of this epistemology of healing. Momentary relations, material encounters always engender transformation, something new springs from them, which is never entirely predictable. It is this surprising potential of the relation, upon which the healing practices we described here rely.

Acknowledgements

We are grateful to the women of 'Okoth's' homestead and their families for their hospitality and patience, which we hope they will extend to the shortcomings of this account. We also wish to thank Philister Adhiambo Madiega, friend and colleague for many years. Susan Benson and Susan Reynolds Whyte, Jens Aagaard-Hansen and Todd Sanders for their advice during fieldwork and writing, and Stephen Harris for the identification of medicinal plants. This work was carried out in association with the Kenyan Danish Health Research Project, and received support from the Danish Council for Development Research, the Institute of Anthropology, University of Copenhagen, the Danish Bilharziasis Laboratory, the Wenner-Gren Foundation and the Smuts and the Rivers Funds, Department of Social Anthropology, University of Cambridge.

Notes

1. Names of places and persons (except larger areas and clans) have been changed.
2. *Riwo* means to mix, merge, join, unite, be together and collaborate. *Riwo* can also mean 'cross' or 'step over', possibly suggesting an association between merging and transitions. It designates a range of forms of material contact: bodily intercourse (*riwruok*); sharing food (*riwo chiemo* [food] or *riwo lwedo* [one's hands, by eating from one plate]); sharing conversation (*riwo weche* [words] or *riwo ji* [people]); joining a dance (*riwore e miel*); sharing beer (*riwo kong'o*) or liquor (*riwo chang'aa*); sharing a common grandfather (*riwo kwaru*) or a kinship bond (*riwo wat*); reuniting, through shared food and medicine in the context of healing (*riwo gi manyasi*); or planting and harvesting together (*riwore waguru* [work-group] or *riwo tich* [work] or *riwo lowo* [earth]). All these activities can also be designated by other terms, but the shared reference to *riwo* underlines the aspect of substantial merging that they all imply.
3. Between 2000 and 2003, thirty *JoUhero* died (above three per cent, a likely underestimation due to our census procedures) per year and about half of these deaths affected young adults, possibly related to HIV/AIDS. Likewise,

the age-distribution showed the mark of AIDS, with the middle age groups being reduced by deaths among younger adults. Accordingly, *JoUhero* recognized 'the death (*tho*) of today', which many saw as the end of a long-term loss and decline captured in the expression: 'the land [*piny*, also 'earth' and 'community'] is dying'.

4. Accordingly, the term for medicines, *yath* (pl. *yiende*) also means 'plant'.

5. Only one of over 200 adult women in Uhero stated that she would not use these herbal medicines.

6. While home-based plant remedies are usually prepared and administered by women, injections of antibiotics and anti-malarials are exclusively administered by men, who usually have had some exposure to biomedical practices.

7. This generational gap also allows for a homogenization and some degree of stability of 'Luo' medicinal knowledge in this exogamous, virilocal society. If a woman learns about medicines from her grandmother as a child, and from her mother as a women, she has acquired knowledge from two different clans and areas in addition to those of the villagers among which she grows up in her father's village, and to the people of her marital home. According to the rules of exogamy, these four areas must be different; in this way, women's movements are critical to the maintenance of a coherent 'ethnic' knowledge, such as that of medicines.

8. Within the same logic, the work of cooking sticks in the pot, notably the shaping of the staple stiff porridge (*kuon*) is likened to sexual intercourse, and the cooking stick is considered a wife's lethal weapon in marital strife.

9. On one occasion only did an old man suggest that an aluminium pot would 'offend' the ancestors if medicine were prepared in it. Usually, such associations would be made in more subtle ways – in statements that 'this is the right pot for medicines', 'this is how Luo people do' or 'this is how our mothers have done' – without direct reference to the ancestors (many younger people boiled medicines in modern pots).

10. We place these translations in inverted commas, because both measles and chicken pox have many unspecific symptoms and the straight translation of local illness terms into biomedical diseases does not seem appropriate. This impression is supported by the fact that, in Uhero, individual children often have numerous episodes of these childhood illnesses.

11. A similar, gradual transition between different places and different (botanical and social) environments can be observed in the fact that young mothers, who only recently came to live in their husband's patrilineal home, tend to rely on their mother's medicinal plants and advice, especially for their first children. Later, they and their children grow into the new place, and old women usually rely entirely on local plants for their treatment of grandchildren.

217

12. This does not apply to certain Pentecostal churches' struggle against 'demons', or to born-again Christians' rejection of all temporal or social contiguity. Indeed, different *JoUhero* take different stances to the porosity of persons and bodies, but even those who strive towards tighter boundaries of body and self acknowledge that the person is potentially porous, and that boundaries must thus be made.

13. For example, after the death of a parent, the remaining parent must be re-united with his children through food and medicine, after his or her re-engagement in sexual relations with a new husband or wife.

14. In recent times, an alternative treatment – *tako*, incising the skin on the child's belly and 'sucking out' the clotted food or similar objects – has become common, possibly reflecting a biomedical influence and changing medicinal paradigms. The assumption is that the belly is opened and objects extracted from its cavity, but our repeated close observation of one particularly popular *jatako* near Uhero suggests that only a superficial cut is made, and that the objects that the patient or his mother are presented with after the operation have been hidden in the healer's mouth. Nevertheless, this by now very popular treatment poses great risks of infection for healer and patient in this area with a high prevalence of HIV, which mothers try to reduce by bringing their own razor blade for the intervention.

15. All pre-industrial things of daily use in Luo society, such as pots (Dietler and Herbich 2001: 97), musical instruments (Anyumba 1970), hoes (Dietler and Herbich 2001: 249), boats (Odhiambo 1970) or houses (Prince and Geissler 2010), are beings, 'others' that people have relations with, and who one confronts with respect (some of them may carry [ancestral] names, they may be talked to or receive libations, be given in marriage and even receive funerary rites).

16. The trajectories of medicinal knowledge follow those of women, who in this patrilineal, virilocal society move from elsewhere to their husband's home, and who due to strict rules of exogamy often come from far away. Young women are often confronted with different practices, plant names or preparations in their marital home, and it is common for them to seek their mothers' advice for the nurture of their first children (as well as to quarrel with their mothers-in-law). Only gradually do they merge their knowledge with that of the other women of the husband's home, notably the more senior ones. This is described by older women as an adjustment to the new, the husband's place, its particular illnesses, ecology and medicines. However, as this knowledge is entirely controlled by women, who all have moved at some point, a more complex process of negotiation is at play here, which (re)produces medicinal knowledge in the everyday life of the co-resident women, and creates as well as changes locally specific medicinal traditions.

17. In a very similar vein, 'knowing' another person (be it in the sense of knowing how to address him, or in the sense of being able to harm him with sorcery or heal him from it) means to know his relations and ancestry; hence, the extended searches, between strangers, for shared relations that eventually allow one to address the another.

18. *Ober* (*Albizia coriaria*) is one of the most common medicinal trees. Its bark and root are used in preparations for young children, such as the steambath or *fundo*. It is usually combined with other bark and root parts, such as *roko* (*Zanthoxylum chalybeum*), *akado* (*Euclea racemosa* ssp. *schimperi*), or *ochuoga* (*Carissa edulis*) (see Geissler et al. 2002).

19. 'False teeth' are a widespread concern among those who care for infants (see also Maj?????). Mothers in Uhero sometimes pointed at a whitish cover of their infant's gums, when we asked what 'false teeth' were. More often the treatment for 'false teeth' was commenced not because these had emerged, but because of the suspicion that they might be on their way, usually triggered by abdominal symptoms, such as diarrhoea. The most common preventive treatment of false teeth consists of massaging the gums with *atipa* (*Asystasia schimperi* T. Anderson) (see Prince et al. 2002). A recently introduced and very intrusive and risky operation 'extracts' false teeth from the infant's gums, using a razor blade or sharpened bicycle spokes, presenting a maggot-like structure as the origin of the illness. A possible explanation of the recent popularity of this intervention might lay in the influence of biomedical models of surgery and the ideas of illness-agents and causation associated with it: here the illness-agent is, unlike in the worm models above, an enemy that must be taken out of the body for good. Just before this conversation, Mary had argued with another daughter in-law, who had brought different plants from her home area, about the use of another plant *nyunyudhi* (*Leonotis nepetifolia*) for that purpose – hence the debate about the choice of the plant.

20. Together with chemical pharmacological effects, the 'placebo effects' of medicines could also be studied, with a more careful look at the particular meanings that work on the body (but noting that the 'effect' of the placebo effect is based on the same assumptions as the pharmacological effect: altering a diseased body, an individual entity by strengthening its 'defence'; taking placebos into account does not imply getting closer to local understandings and practices!).

References

Abe, T. 1981. 'The Concepts of Chira and Dhoch among the Luo of Kenya. Transition, Deviation and Misfortune', in N. Nagashima (ed.), *Themes in Socio-Cultural Ideas and Behaviour among the Six Ethnic Groups of Kenya*. Kinutachi/Tokio: Hitotsubashi University, pp. 127–39.

Amuyunzu, M. 1998. 'Willing the Spirits to Reveal Themselves: Rural Kenyan Mothers' Responsibility to Restore their Children's Health', *Medical Anthropology Quarterly* 12: 490–502.

Anonymous. 2004. 'Bank to Help Kenya on Herbs', *Daily Nation* (18 June 2004), p. 3.

Anyumba, H.A. 1970. 'The Making of a Lyre Musician', *Mila. A Biannual Newsletter of Cultural Research (Institute of African Studies, University of Nairobi)* 1: 28–33.

Atieno Odhiambo, E.S. 1974. 'The Movement of Ideas: A Case Study of Intellectual Responses to Colonialism Among the Liganua Peasants', in B.A. Ogot (ed.), *History and Social Change in East Africa*. Nairobi: East Africa Literature Bureau, pp. 165–85.

Cohen, D.W. 1985. 'Doing Social History from Pim's Doorway', in O. Zunz (ed.), *Reliving the Past: The Worlds of Social History*. Chapel Hill and London: University of North Carolina Press, pp. 191–228.

———— and E.S. Atieno Odhiambo. 1989. *Siaya. The Historical Anthropology of an African Landscape*. Nairobi: Heineman Kenya.

———— and E.S. Atieno Odhiambo. 1992. *Burying SM. The Politics of Knowledge and the Sociology of Power in Africa*. London: James Currey.

Dietler, M. and I. Herbich. 2001. 'Theorising the Feast. Rituals of Consumption, Commensal Politics and Power in African Contexts', in M. Dietler and B. Hayden (eds), *Feasts. Archaeological and Ethnographic Perspectives on Food, Politics and Power*. Washington and London: Smithsonian Institution, pp. 65–114.

Evans-Pritchard, E.E. 1950. 'Ghostly Vengeance Among the Luo of Kenya', *Man* 50: 86–87.

———— 1965. 'Marriage Customs of the Luo of Kenya', in E.E. Evans-Pritchard (ed.), *The Position of Women in Primitive Societies and Other Essays in Social Anthropology*. London: Faber and Faber, pp. 228–44.

Geissler, P.W. 1998. '"Worms are our life". Understandings of Worms and the Body Among the Luo of Western Kenya (Parts 1 + 2)', *Anthropology and Medicine* 5: 63–81 and 133–44.

———— 1999. 'Learning to Heal: Women, Children and Medicines Among the Luo of Western Kenya'. M.Phil. Dissertation. Cambridge: University of Cambridge.

———— 2000. 'The Significance of Earth-eating. Social and Cultural Aspects of Geophagy Among Luo children', *Africa* 70: 653–82.

———— and R.J. Prince. 2004b. 'Shared Lives: Exploring Practices of Amity Between Grandmothers and Grandchildren in Western Kenya', *Africa* 74: 95–120.

———— and R.J. Prince. 2007. Life Seen: Touch and Vision in the Making of Sex in Western Kenya. *Journal of Eastern African Studies*, 2007, 1(1), 123 – 149.

———— and R.J. Prince. 2009. Active Compounds and Atoms of Society: Plants, Bodies, Minds and Cultures in the Work of Kenyan Ethnobotanical Knowledge. *Social Studies of Science*, 39 (4): 599–634.

———— et al. 1998. 'Geophagy as a Risk Factor for Geohelminth Infections: A Longitudinal Study Among Kenyan School Children. *Transactions of the Royal Society of Tropical Medicine and Hygiene* 92: 7–11.

———— et al. 2002. 'Medicinal Plants Used by Luo Mothers in Bondo District, Kenya', *Journal of Ethnopharmacology* 83: 39–54.

Hauge, E.H. 1981. 'The Spirit World of the Luo People in Kenya, East Africa', *Temenos* 17: 27–34.

Hauge, H.-E. 1974. *The Luo Religion and Folklore*. Oslo: Universitetsforlaget.

Hay, M.J. 1982. 'Women as Owners, Occupants and Managers of Property in Colonial Western Kenya', in M.J. Hay and M. Wright (eds), *African Women and the Law: Historical Perspectives*. Boston: African Studies Centre, Boston, pp. 110–23.

Johns, T., J.O. Kokwaro and E.K. Kimanani. 1990. 'Herbal Remedies of the Luo of Siaya District, Kenya: Establishing Quantitative Criteria for Consensus', *Economic Botany* 44: 369–81.

Kawango, E.A. 1995. 'Ethnomedical Remedies and Therapies in Maternal and Child Health Among the Rural Luo', in I. Sindiga, C. Nyaigotti-Chacha and M.P. Kanunah (eds), *Traditional Medicine in Kenya*. Nairobi: East African Educational Publishers Ltd., pp. 80–93.

Lonsdale, J. 1977. 'The Politics of Conquest: the British in Western Kenya 1894–1908', *The Historical Journal* 20: 841–70.

Luoba, A.I. 2003. 'Geophagy and Other Risk Factors for Helminthiasis Among Pregnant and Lactating Women in Bondo District'. Ph.D. Dissertation. Nairobi: University of Nairobi.

Mwenesi, H.A., T. Harpham, K. Marsh and R.W. Snow. 1995. 'Perceptions About Symptoms of Severe Childhood Malaria Among Mijikenda and Luo Residents of Coastal Kenya', *Journal of the Biosocial Sciences* 27: 235–44.

Obado E.A.O. and J.A. Odera. 1995. 'Management of Medicinal Plant Resources in Nyanza', in I. Sindiga, C. Nyaigotti-Chacha and M.P. Kanunah (eds), *Traditional Medicine in Africa*. Nairobi: East African Educational Publishers Ltd., pp. 153–67.

Ocholla-Ayayo, A.B.C. 1976. *Traditional Ideology and Ethics among the Southern Luo*. Uppsala: Scandinavian Institute of African Studies.

———— 1980. *The Luo Culture*. Wiesbaden: Franz Steiner Verlag.

Odhalo, J. 1962. 'A Report on the Luo Culture and Health', *East African Medical Journal* 39: 694–701.

Odhiambo, E.S.A. 1970. 'Some Aspects of Religious Activity Among the Uyoma Fishermen: the Rites Connected With the Launching of a Fishing Vessel', *Mila. A Biannual Newsletter of Cultural Research (Institute of African Studies, University of Nairobi)* 1: 14–21.

Ogot, B.A. 1963. 'British Administration in Central Nyanza District, 1900-1960', *Journal of African History* 4: 249–73.

Olenja, J.M. 1991. 'Women and Health Care in Siaya District', in G.S. Were, C.A. Suda and J.M. Olenja (eds), *Women and Development in Kenya. Siaya District*. Nairobi: Institute of African Studies, pp. 44–70.

Olsen, A. et al. 2003. 'Effects of Multi-micronutrient Supplementation on Helminth Reinfection: a Randomised, Controlled Trial in Kenyan Schoolchildren', *Transactions of the Royal Society of Tropical Medicine and Hygiene* 97: 109–14.

Ominde, S.H. 1952. *The Luo Girl from Infancy to Marriage*. Nairobi: East African Literature Bureau.

Pala, A.O. 1980. 'Daughters of the Lakes and Rivers: Colonization and the Land Rights of Women', in M. Etienne and E. Leacock (eds), *Women and Colonisation. Anthropological Perspectives*. New York: Praeger, pp. 186–213.

Parkin, D. 1978. *The Cultural Definition of Political Response. Lineal Destiny among the Luo*. London and New York: Academic Press.

Pool, R. and P.W. Geissler. 2005. *Medical Anthropology in Public Health*. Milton Keynes: Open University Press.

Prince, R.J. 2006. 'Popular Music and Luo Youth in Western Kenya: Ambiguities of Mobility, Morality and Gender in the Era of AIDS', in C. Christiansen, H. Vigh and M. Utas (eds.), *Navigating Youth, Generating Adulthoods: Social Becoming in an African Context*. Uppsala: Nordic Africa Institute, pp. 47–98.

_____ and P.W. Geissler. 2001. 'Becoming "One Who Treats": A Case Study of a Luo Healer and Her Grandson in Western Kenya', *Anthropology and Education Quarterly* 32: 447–71.

_____ and P.W. Geissler. 2009. *'The Land is Dying'. Contingency, Creativity and Conflict in Western Kenya*. Oxford: Berghahn Books.

_____ et al. 1999. 'Geophagy is Common Among Luo Women in Western Kenya', *Transactions of the Royal Society of Tropical Medicine and Hygiene* 93: 515–16.

_____ et al. 2001. 'Knowledge of Herbal and Pharmaceutical Medicines Among Luo Children in Western Kenya', *Anthropology and Medicine* 8: 211–35.

_____ et al. 2002. 'Adhiambo-born in the Evening. Two Months in the Life of a Kenyan Mother and her Newborn Daughter'. Hamburg, Copenhagen and Cambridge: Filmwerkstatt Dokumentarisch Arbeiten.

Reynolds, P. 1996. *Traditional Healers and Childhood in Zimbabwe*. Athens: Ohio University Press.

Shipton, P. 1989. *Bitter Money. Cultural Economy and Some African Meanings of Forbidden Commodities*. Washington: AAA.

Sindiga, I. 1995. 'Managing Illness Among the Luo', in I. Sindiga, C. Nyaigotti-Chacha and M.P. Kanunah (eds), *Traditional Medicine in Africa*. Nairobi: East African Educational Publishers Ltd., pp. 64–79.

Sternberg, R.J. et al. 2001. 'The Relationship Between Academic and Practical Intelligence: a Case Study in Kenya', *Intelligence* 29: 401–18.

Taylor, C.C. 1992. *Milk, Honey and Money. Changing Concepts in Rwandan Healing.* Washington and London: Smithsonian Institution Press.

Taylor, L., J. Seeley and E. Kajura. 1996. 'Informal Care for Illness in Rural Southwest Uganda: the Central Role that Women Play', *Health Transition Review* 6: 49–56.

Whisson, M.G. 1964. 'Some Aspects of Functional Disorders Among the Kenya Luo', in A. Kiev (ed.), *Magic, Faith and Healing.* New York: Free Press, pp. 283–304.

Whyte, S.R. 1997. *Questioning Misfortune. The Pragmatics of Uncertainty in Eastern Uganda.* Cambridge: Cambridge University Press.

Wilson, G.M. 1960. 'Homicide and Suicide Among the Joluo of Kenya', in P. Bohannan (ed.), *African Homicide and Suicide.* New York: Atheneum, pp. 179–213.

PLANT PORTRAITS
Editorial Introduction
Stephen Harris et al.

The use of plants in Western medicine has often been 'corrupted' by dogmatic statements, for example, that herbs cannot harm, only heal and that whole herbs are more effective than their purified active constituents. Two broad approaches to the medicinal exploitation of plants have been described: bioprospecting and ethnopharmacology. The overall goal of bioprospecting is to discover and purify natural products for use as drugs for international markets; in ethnopharmacology the goal is the development of complex plant extracts, as drugs for local use within cultural and social contexts.

Currently, the pharmaceutical industry has little interest in natural plant products, since rapid screening has yielded few important new products or leads to new commercial products and extensive controversies exist over intellectual property rights. A further drawback faced by the pharmaceutical sector is that potentially useful traditional knowledge about plants is patchy. A much greater market for plants as medicines is in the 'botanical medicine' market, where there is little emphasis on patents, since it does not have the same regulatory requirements to conduct research into safety or the efficacy of the preparations that are marketed.

The commercialization and patenting of plant-derived medicinal products has been the focus of much international debate and historical analysis, especially since the Convention on Biological Diversity explicitly recognized the rights of nation states to exploit their own resources and for indigenous and local communities to benefit from their traditional knowledge.

The passage of medicinal plant from indigenous use to acceptance in orthodox or heterodox medicine must therefore deal with the issues of traditional knowledge, the activity of biologically active compounds together with safety and efficacy. Furthermore, as the contexts in

225

which medicinal plants are used change, one must accept that future uses are unknown. Whilst past performance of a medicinal plant cannot guarantee its future performance, knowledge of how it was used remains invaluable for understanding its biological and cultural properties.

It is commonly assumed that anthropology is restricted to the study of 'primitive' tribes and has no relevance to the enlightened citizenry of economically advanced nations. Yet all cultures are constrained by their history and transmitted value systems and the communities of the West are no exception. Sir John Grimley Evans makes this once again evident in his article 'East goes West. *Ginkgo biloba* and dementia', which comments on opinions among the lay public, where the supposed medicinal virtues of ginkgo (*Ginkgo biloba*) stimulate responses ranging from instinctive acceptance of a pluripotential remedy provided by beneficent Nature to contemptuous dismissal as witchcraft or charlatanry. Grimley Evans notes that contemporary Western medical science is challenged by ginkgo being presented both as a traditional Chinese remedy and as a European manufactured and commercially successful extract. In particular, as he convincingly demonstrates, ginkgo offers a probing challenge to the epistemology of British medicine, an epistemology that has its own interest as a topic for anthropological reflection.

A similar transformation of local practices, involving caffeine-containing plants, is discussed by Caroline Weckerle, Verena Timbul and Philip Blumenshine in their article 'Medicinal, stimulant and ritual plant use: an ethnobotany of caffeine-containing plants'. They highlight that of all the flowering plant genera known, caffeine synthesis has evolved in only six, *Camellia*, *Coffea*, *Cola*, *Ilex*, *Paullinia* and *Theobroma*. These genera have different places of origin and are scattered across the flowering plant tree of life. In every setting, local people discovered each caffeine-containing plant and domesticated or harvested it. The plants became integrated into the respective cultures first as stimulants in ritual contexts and as medicinal plants, and subsequently, as pleasant and stimulating drinks or food items. And in the case of coffee, tea and cacao, they have even become indispensable items of world consumption and trade. Whether used globally or locally, caffeine-containing plants, more so than most other types of plants, have played a critical social, cultural and economic role among the peoples who discovered them. The case of caffeine-containing plants fit into a bioculturalist framework if one argues that due to their psychotropic effects they were discovered independently of each other and integrated into cultural life. However, Weckerle and colleagues stress that caffeine became integrated into social life in culturally specific, different ways and thereby highlight the diverse forms of interaction between humans and their environment.

5. East goes West.
Ginkgo biloba and Dementia
Sir John Grimley Evans

Introduction

All cultures are constrained by their history and transmitted value
systems and the communities of the West are no exception. Among the
lay public, the supposed medicinal virtues of *Ginkgo biloba* stimulate
responses ranging from instinctive acceptance of a pluripotential
remedy provided by beneficent Nature, to a contemptuous dismissal
of witchcraft or charlatanry. Contemporary Western medical science
is challenged by *Ginkgo biloba* being presented both as a traditional
Chinese remedy and as a European manufactured and commercially
successful extract. In particular, ginkgo offers a probing challenge to
the epistemology of British medicine, an epistemology that has its
own interest as a topic for anthropological reflection.

Ginkgo biloba is a biologically unique tree. A 'living fossil' from the
time of the dinosaurs, it survived originally only in China, but is now
grown in many countries. Its fruit was used for centuries, for diet
and in traditional Chinese medicine, before an extract of its leaves
became a widely used medication in Europe and North America. As a
plant extract marketed as a pharmacological agent, ginkgo straddles
the boundary between conventional and alternative medicine.
Attitudes to its use provide revealing probes into the anthropology of
Western medicine.

Ginkgo biloba: the Tree Itself

In England, *Ginkgo biloba* is known as the maidenhair tree, not
because it resembles in any way the tresses of a young lady, but
because its leaves are vaguely similar in shape to those of the
maidenhair fern, which gained its name from its fine, shiny, hair-
like stems. In terms of evolutionary classification, *Ginkgo biloba*

lies between ferns and conifers. It is the only living member of the Ginkgoales, an order of plants whose fossils can be found in rocks from as long ago as 270 million years. Among the fossils from that earliest period, only two species have been found, but by the time of the heyday of the dinosaurs, the Cretaceous period, at least eleven species are identifiable in the fossil record. They seem to have been common and to have occurred in the land masses that now constitute Asia, Europe and North America. Then 65 million years ago (Alvarez et al. 1980) a large extraterrestrial object, probably a comet rather than an asteroid or meteorite (Hsu 1980), fell on what is now Yucatan in Mexico (Hildebrand et al. 1995). In addition to immediate widespread fires (Melosh et al. 1990), clouds of dust and smoke cut out the sunlight for many months, and the oceans were contaminated with toxins including cyanide and carbon dioxide. In the consequent worldwide biological catastrophe, all but one species of ginkgo (*Ginkgo adiantoides*) became extinct. Many other plant and animal species also disappeared, including, as is well known, the dinosaurs.

All this may be relevant to ginkgo's chemical peculiarities. The leaves of *Ginkgo biloba* contain several chemicals that are widespread in plants but also two, ginkgolides and bilobalide, which are found nowhere else. Plants evolve chemicals for a variety of reasons but a common one relates to interactions with animals (Harbourne and Turner 1984). A chemical may be of survival value to the plant's genes by attracting an animal involved in dispersing the plant's seeds, while an unpleasant or poisonous chemical may discourage a potential browser. Many plant extracts of medicinal value are poisons, acting on specific body systems of animals with which the plant has to contend. It is only in low doses that the potentially fatal effect may be of benefit to a human being whose bodily system is disturbed by illness. *Ginkgo* evolved in association with the dinosaurs, and its unique chemistry may be in part a relic of its relationships with them, although subsequent interactions with mammals must also have been significant (Del Tredici 1989).

About seven million years ago, *Ginkgo* species disappeared from the fossil record of North America and it was gone from Europe by about 2.5 million years ago. It is not clear why this should have happened – perhaps the reasons were climatic – but it survived in what was to become China. For at least a thousand years, it has been especially nurtured in temple gardens, but specimens are also to be found in natural conditions (Li 1956). It was introduced into Japan, probably for medicinal purposes, and was found there in 1691 by Engelbert Kaempfer, a German-born physician of the Dutch East Indies Company who brought seeds to Europe. Since then it has been widely planted in gardens and parks throughout Europe and North America, and is now being actively farmed in the U.S. and China.

Ginkgo biloba is a formidable tree which grows up to thirty metres tall and lives, it is said, up to 3000 years. (This does not make it the world's longest-lived tree species, a distinction held by the bristlecone pine tree of California at up to 4,767 years.) The tree is resistant to insect pests and fungi (Major et al. 1960, Major et al. 1967), urban pollution and heat. It is to be expected that long-lived and slowly changing species, such as *Ginkgo biloba*, will have highly efficient systems for detecting and repairing DNA damage due to cosmic and other forms of radiation. One specimen was within 1.4 kilometres of the hypocentre of the Hiroshima atomic bomb and survived (The Ginkgo Pages 2004).

Ginkgo biloba is dioecious (separate male and female trees) and has a system of sex chromosomes; females are XX and males XY, as in humans. Pollination is by wind, but when it lands on a female tree the male pollen develops cilia and actively swims to fertilize the ovum (Hirasé 1898; Coulter and Chamberlain 1917). The yellow fruits are the size of cherries, and develop even if the tree has not been fertilized. They produce butyric acid as they rot and give off an unpleasant odour that, in the past, may have attracted carnivorous, as well as herbivorous, animals, thereby facilitating dissemination. (The soft, unpleasantly smelling fruits are used as missiles by naughty Chinese and Japanese children – which also may facilitate dissemination.) Because of the litter of foul-smelling, messy fruit, it is usually male ginkgo trees that are planted for decorative purposes in roads and gardens.

Uses in China and Japan

Some enthusiasts would have us believe that ginkgo has been used in traditional Chinese medicine for 5000 years, but the earliest extant Chinese records mentioning the tree are from the eleventh-century

Sung dynasty (Li 1956). It seems to have been valued originally for its fruits rather than its leaves, and for food rather than medicine. It is not until the thirteenth century that ginkgo appears in Chinese herbals. Ginkgo nuts are mentioned in Japanese textbooks from the early sixteenth century as being used at tea ceremonies as sweets and dessert. Later they became a common feature in the Japanese diet. They can be boiled or grilled and, in the latter form, are frequently offered as a side dish to accompany sake. However, only a small number of cooked seeds – less than ten – should be eaten in a day (Foster and Chongxi 1992). Uncooked seeds are poisonous, especially for children in whom they induce diarrhoea, vomiting, and fits (Kajiyama et al. 2002, Wada et al. 1988).

Recent editions of the Chinese Pharmacopoeia (Elisabeth Hsu, personal communication 2004, based on the *Zhongguo renmin gongheguo yaodian*) contain an entry on *semen Ginkgo* under the name of *baiguo* ('white fruit') in the form of a powdered preparation of stir-fried nuts, with the seed coat removed. It is recommended for the treatment of asthma, leucorrhoea and urinary frequency. It is characterized as bittersweet in flavour, rough and, even in nature, potentially poisonous and active on the lung channel. The seeds have also been used for nocturnal seminal emissions, dental caries, fungal skin infections of the face, and for genital sores (Foster and Chongxi 1992). The leaves have been used in China, in combination with other herbs, as a treatment for angina pectoris (Foster and Chongxi 1992). Ginkgo bark ash has been used for benefiting the heart and brain and strengthening weak patients as well as for leucorrhoea and seminal emissions (Foster and Chongxi 1992).

Ginkgo Comes to Europe

Engelbert Kaempfer, who brought ginkgo seeds to Utrecht in 1691, seems to be responsible for the name 'Ginkgo', a word presumably of Japanese origin. According to legend, Kaempfer originally wrote 'Ginyo', but his handwriting was so poor that it was transcribed as 'Ginkgo'. Li (1956) doubts this story and thinks Kaempfer was transliterating a Japanese word derived from a Chinese original, *yinxing* ('silvery apricot') being the Chinese word for the living tree, whence the herbal drug is derived. Trees were then planted in many parts of Europe and were taken to the U.S. in the late eighteenth century. The tree was much prized for its decorative quality, and is valuable as a street tree as it is resistant to considerable levels of pollution (Handa 2000). The unusual biological nature of ginkgo was recognized long before it could be understood in scientific terms. Johann Wolfgang von Goethe wrote a famous poem about a ginkgo tree that he describes as growing in his garden in Heidelberg in 1815 (von Goethe 1999). His own fair copy of the poem with two ginkgo leaves pasted on the page can be seen in the Goethe Museum in Düsseldorf. He used the shape of the leaf to illustrate his sense of ambiguity between singleness and duality as a lover in relation to his beloved (Marianne von Willemer at the time) and, perhaps, as a poet in relation to his works (Unseld 1998).

It is only since the 1960s that ginkgo has come widely into medicinal and herbal use in the West, largely through the entrepreneurship of Dr Willmar Schwabe, who founded a company in Karlsruhe to manufacture leaf extracts. After several refinements of the now patented technique, Dr Schwabe's company produces a standardized extract (EGb761) which is marketed under a number of brand names including Kaveri, Tebonin, Tanakan, Rökan and Ginkgold. The extraction process is elaborate and involves eighteen stages and various solvents. Dr Schwabe registered EGb761 as a medication in Germany in 1965 (DeFreudis 1998).

Uses

Although prescribed as a medicine in Germany and France, ginkgo extract is not licensed as a medicine in the U.K., the U.S. and other countries but is sold over the counter as a 'food supplement'. Food supplements do not have to be subjected to the meticulous process of validation of effects, toxicity tests and quality control required of a licensed medicine. However, unlike many other herbal products, EGb761 has the virtue of being produced by controlled processes and with scrupulous care in a modern factory. There are many different preparations of ginkgo leaf extract on the market, and these vary in chemical content (Mantle et al. 2003).

In Germany and France, ginkgo is prescribed to treat a range of conditions including memory problems, confusion, depression, anxiety, dizziness, headache, tinnitus, leg pains and angina pectoris. EGb761 is under trial for the treatment of diabetes in France and

Russia, and cancer in Brazil and Germany (Anonymous 2003). One can only be sceptical about a medicine that seems to treat so many diseases, unless there is a single underlying mechanism for its actions. The original rationale for the use of ginkgo extract lay in the notion that it enhances blood flow, by dilating arteries and retarding blood clotting by inhibiting platelet activating factor (PAF). In the 1950s and 1960s it was widely thought in continental Europe that many of the non-specific problems associated with old age, such as the confusion and dizziness that figure in the preceding list, were due to impairment of blood supply to the brain. Such ideas have been modified in the advance of medical science. In the U.K. and U.S. the main claims advanced for ginkgo extract now are that it improves mental function and can retard deterioration in dementia by mechanisms such as antioxidant activity, or interruption of the pathogenesis of Alzheimer's disease (Colciaghi et al. 2004), in addition to its effects on blood supply (Ahlemeyer and Krieglstein 2003, Pietri 1997, Williams et al. 2004).

EGb761 has little in the way of adverse effects. While cases of allergy to the ginkgo tree have been recorded (Becker and Skipworth 1975), the chemicals responsible are removed during the preparation of EGb761. As with any medication, minor dyspeptic symptoms can occur with ginkgo extract. Serious adverse effects involving post-operative bleeding (Fessenden et al. 2001, Fong and Kinnear 2003), haemorrhage into the eye (Rosenblatt and Mindel 1997) or brain (Rowin and Lewis 1996, Vale 2003), but it is not definite that ginkgo extract was responsible in these cases. Researchers at Dr Willmar Schwabe Pharmaceuticals (Kohler et al. 2004) and others (Bal Dit Soller et al. 2003) have published data indicating that EGb761 has no effect on liability to haemorrhage (Kohler et al. 2004), despite the original claims for an antithrombotic action. Heart irregularities (Cianfrocca et al. 2002) and seizures (Granger 2001, Gregory 2001) affecting people taking ginkgo extract have also been reported. In view of possible interactions with prescribed medication (Izzo and Ernst 2001), doctors, and, indeed, dentists (Abebe 2003) need to be aware of any over-the-counter preparations their patients are taking. Possible interactions involving ginkgo have been described (Galluzzi et al. 2000, Meisel et al. 2003). At present, non-prescribed medications being taken by British patients seem to be poorly documented (Skinner and Rangasami 2002). This neglect probably reflects the assumption by doctors that herbal remedies are without pharmacological effects, desirable or otherwise.

Ginkgo biloba is now big business. There are 5 million prescriptions annually in Germany, generating $280 million. Sales in the U.S. amount to $100 million a year. A major supply of ginkgo leaves comes from a 400-hectare plantation in Carolina; at a reported density of 25,000 coppiced trees per hectare this is fairly intensive monoculture. *Ginkgo biloba* is pest-resistant (Major 1967) and contains a natural fungicide (Major et al. 1960) so it can be hoped that the pharmacology of ginkgo extract will not come to be complicated by pesticide residues. Herbicides are used sparingly to control weeds. Other plantations have been established in Korea and France, and China has established large plantations (Foster and Chongxi 1992).

Chemistry

Many chemicals are found in the leaves, bark or fruit of ginkgo; some, such as the ginkgolic acids, are potentially toxic or can generate allergies, and need to be removed during the production of standardized leaf extract. Preparations on sale for medical use vary in composition but the standardized extract EGb761 contains twenty-four per cent flavone glycosides (quercetin, kaempferol, isorhamnetin) and six per cent terpene lactones (ginkgolides, bilobalide), various organic acids and other constituents. Ginkgolide B accounts for about 0.8 per cent. Ginkgolides (Nakanishi 1967) and bilobalide (Nakanishi et al. 1971) are complex molecules composed on a framework of interlinked 5-carbon rings. Ginkgolide B was synthesized by the Nobel laureate Elias J. Corey and his colleagues in 1988 (Corey et al. 1988). As to be suspected from the similarities in their structures, several of the compounds in ginkgo extracts are metabolic derivatives of others.

Kleijnen and Knipschild (1992) have summarized what is known of the absorption and body disposition of standardized extract of ginkgo. Absorption of ginkgolides A and B is quite high but subsequent metabolic pathways are unclear. In rats, much of the absorbed chemicals are excreted unchanged in urine and faeces.

Ginkgo as a Scientific Anomaly

Although ginkgo in the form of EGb761 is marketed in the West as if it were a pharmacological agent, its vegetable origins make it readily acceptable to enthusiasts of herbal and complementary medicines. Conventional biomedicine often views such people and their practices with condescension. Some of the assumptions of alternative medicine are incompatible with modern scientific thought. A classic example is the rationale underlying the preparation of homeopathic medicines. To Western scientific thinking, some traditional ideas of Chinese medicine seem on a par with mediaeval models of the four humours in postulating physicochemical processes and anatomical connections that do not exist, if one reads the texts literally.

Of interest, anthropologically, are some more general Western notions – meta-ideas perhaps – relating to the place of man in the scheme of things, or indeed relating to the notion that there *is* a scheme of things. In one apologia for ginkgo we read: 'because it is non-synthetic, it works by supporting and enhancing the natural functions' (DeFeudis 1998). The notion that natural products are necessarily beneficent and harmless is cognate with ideas of the motherhood of Nature. To the post-Darwinian mind, Nature is no more Mother to us than she is to the smallpox virus, or the tapeworm. She provides even-handedly for the nurture of the cancer cell, as for the neuron. The whole history of human civilization has been a struggle against Nature's indifference to our species and to our sufferings. In so far as chemicals in plants have any biological relevance to us at all, they are at least as likely to have evolved because they kill us rather than because of a beneficial effect on our natural functions. Through natural selection, plants will acquire a range of different chemicals to meet the challenges or opportunities from a range of different predators or seed dispersers.

The apologists for ginkgo extract see its multiple components as a virtue, in that it can modify several different disease processes all at the same time (DeFeudis 1998). Linked with a superficial grasp of modern ideas of the multifactorial origins of disease states, this can be presented as a virtue. But there is no *a priori* reason why multiple compounds should occur naturally together in proportions appropriate to a multimodular amelioration of human disease. This is especially true when the original natural compound has been put through twenty stages of extraction in manufacture. Any active chemicals in the mixture may well have their beneficial effects nullified by other components.

Western medicine mistrusts mixtures. In addition to direct chemical interactions, drugs can interfere with each other by changing the body's metabolism and one drug may displace another from its target cell receptor or from binding to blood proteins. Furthermore, where multiple drugs have to be prescribed the dosage of each must be adjustable separately to the needs of the individual patient. The science of therapeutics is founded on single compounds, of known molecular structure and pharmacological properties. The last are divided into pharmacokinetic and pharmacodynamic properties. Pharmacokinetic properties are those of absorption, transport, metabolism and excretion in the body, and pharmacodynamic properties describe what the drug actually does in modifying bodily functions and how it does it in terms of which receptors of which cells it interacts with. Out of this knowledge emerge important parameters of a drug, its dose/response curve and specification of its therapeutic window, that is to say the range of dosages that produce useful benefits without unacceptable adverse effects. Where drugs have to be given in combination, the aim is usually to produce additive benefits by modifying different body mechanisms affected by disease, or so that one drug may counter the adverse effects of another. In practice, many interactions between Western drugs can lead to clinically undesirable effects, and doctors try to keep the number of different drugs being prescribed for a patient to a minimum.

Dr Schwabe's company markets its ginkgo extract not as a herbal in the traditional sense but as a pharmaceutical, a pharmacologically active compound analogous to any modern drug. Recently it has become apparent in the U.K. that some doctors have been recommending that patients with dementia should take ginkgo in the hope that it might benefit them. The drugs that have been shown to confer some benefit in dementia are expensive, and health service managers have been loath to fund them. Ginkgo is not a licensed drug in the U.K., and so is unavailable through the National Health Service; patients have to buy it with their own money. Many patients with dementia are poor, and recommending that they spend money on something that has not been shown to be effective raises an ethical problem. If a drug works, and is no more expensive than any alternative treatment, it should be provided on the National Health Service. But to satisfy principles of equity, all drugs so provided must have been through the same regulatory appraisal and shown to work by the same criteria as for any other candidate treatment. A crux, to which we return later, is what 'work' actually means.

But if the Germans and French think that ginkgo works, does that not suffice? The answer, bluntly is 'no', and this is not a matter of nationalism and Anglo-Saxon xenophobia. Ginkgo probes unexpectedly deeply into the epistemology of medical science, and the system of beliefs and values in which medical practice is embedded. Medicine in the English-reading world – the British Commonwealth, the U.S., Scandinavia and the Netherlands – to some extent diverged from that of continental Europe in the decades following the Second World War. Although this divergence is now becoming blurred in the imposed uniformities of the European Union, relics of the divergence are preserved in differences in the licensing of medications. The chief source of the divergence lay with changes in the social structure of the medical profession, and with the development and use of the randomized controlled trial.

Social Changes and Medicine

The status of the medical profession in traditional English society prior to the Second World War was ambiguous. As eighteenth- and nineteenth-century novels reveal, unless redeemed by particular birth or breeding, the ordinary local doctor was seen as not quite a gentleman, not part of the establishment and certainly socially inferior to the parson even though a successful doctor's income might be higher. The parson would have been to Oxford or Cambridge and would be versed in the ancient Latin and Greek authors. The doctor would probably have trained at a London hospital as the kind of raffish and unmoneyed medical student depicted in *The Pickwick Papers* of Charles Dickens. He might be unused to the manners of polite society, and his knowledge of ancient languages restricted to the Dog Latin necessary to write prescriptions. The successful London doctor was a rather different figure, and the contrast between the dedicated and the fashionable in the medical profession was portrayed in Bernard Shaw's play *The Doctor's Dilemma*. The distinguished medical scientist Almroth Wright (1861–1947) displayed open contempt for the popinjay physicians of Harley Street (Dunnill 2000). In its organization and in the frequency of a family tradition of doctoring as a trade, medicine was closer to a guild of artisans than to a profession.

British society was destabilized by the trauma of the First World War. The best of a whole generation of young men had been lost or scarred in the killing fields of Flanders. The unworthiness of the upper classes as national leaders had been exposed. Social revolution became inevitable, only to be delayed by the national unity imposed by the Second World War and the threat of German invasion in 1939. But even while the war was being fought, planning for a new social order went ahead. The National Health Service, instituted in 1948, was to lead the war on disease but was interdependent with the other divisions of a comprehensive Welfare State (Rivett 1998). The resulting social revolution changed British medicine forever and for the better. Clearer career structures for young doctors started to erode the informal system of patronage that had previously determined patterns of promotion and opportunity. Control of manpower limited the numbers of medical student places, so that young doctors could have a reasonable expectation of future employment that allowed them to spend time in their early careers broadening their interests and experience. In addition to some time in research, periods of experience in the U.S. and in the 'Third World' were commonplace for the medical graduates of the late 1950s. Most importantly, the availability of state scholarships and grants opened up medical training to all social classes. No longer could the profession be epitomized in a stereotype of a beer-swilling, boneheaded son of a doctor from a London teaching hospital. Within a decade medicine was recruiting from the top rank of scientifically minded school-leavers. The influx of bright young minds, uncluttered with the prejudices of medical parents, led to an intellectual liberation that was truly revolutionary. Although the hierarchical structure of the hospital medical team, for example, seemed unaltered, it was changed radically in function. Traditionally, senior doctors gave orders and junior doctors obeyed. With the junior doctors being more intelligent and better educated than many of their seniors, nominal hierarchies functioned as teams synthesizing the wisdom and experience of seniors with the

239

intellectual energy and wider knowledge of juniors. These changes were accelerated from the 1970s with the expanding recruitment of women to the profession, bringing new intellectual perspectives and more social sensitivity to a masculine world. It was to be many years before similar processes took place in parts of continental Europe, where rigid medical hierarchies have persisted longer, and over-recruitment of medical students has long sustained a debilitating system of patronage. In such settings, internationalization of medicine as established in the English-reading world is seen as a threat to local interests and status, and it is harder for a new idea to become adopted. The new idea that was to change Western medicine was the randomized controlled trial.

Medical Epistemology in the West

Before turning to the performance and appraisal of randomized controlled trials (RCTs) of *Ginkgo biloba* extract, it may be useful to explore the rationale of RCTs and their place in the epistemology of Western medicine. Much of the rationale of Western medicine is now founded in an understanding of physiological and molecular mechanisms, in an experimental tradition often seen as established in the seventeenth century by Harvey's demonstration of the circulation of the blood. But the epistemology of medical practice is essentially empirical. Medical practice is only partly based on modern science as a physicist or chemist would understand the term. Lord Rutherford is said to have summarized science as physics and stamp collecting. Physics works to precise formulae, medicine is largely based on collective observation and empiricism – stamp collecting.

All modern science aims at prediction. In this it differs fundamentally from some rival philosophical systems that can provide *post hoc* explanations of a sort, but fail at prediction. It begins with careful and systematic description of phenomena and what happens in particular circumstances (the necessary but unglamorous phase of 'stamp collecting'). It then goes on to establish the parameters of interactions and to elucidate the mechanisms whereby one thing leads to another. This is achieved through the setting up of testable hypotheses; current science is an assemblage of not disproved hypotheses, and only journalists and the ignorant talk of scientific 'proof'.

Originally, science worked to deterministic models in which if one knew all the relevant parameters of a situation one could predict precisely what was going to happen next. Deterministic models work well in the world of traditional physics. It is why people can make transistor radios, or land men on the moon. But there are two situations in which determinism breaks down. One is at the quantal level where uncertainty is unavoidable and where the act of observing seems to interfere with what happens. This uncertainty does not scale up into the realm of traditional physics because when, for example, two billiard balls collide, an effectively infinite number of atoms are involved and something analogous to the central limit theorem of statistics applies. What happens is the statistical mean with an infinitely small variance.

Deterministic models are also inadequate in the complex systems of biology. Biologists can create artificially simple situations where deterministic models work reasonably well. A frog's heart taken out of the frog and suspended in liquid of constant composition and constant temperature will beat in predictable ways. But in real life, for example, in trying to work out which way a particular frog on a particular lily pad is going to jump, we can only deal in probabilities. This is partly due to our ignorance about the many variables that may affect such complex situations. In theory we might be able to add in factors such as body temperature, whether the frog is hungry or sexually appetitive, to improve on our predictions, but there are some things that are unknowable. We do not know what it is like to be a frog, what its nervous system at any point of time has designated as the most important thing to react to in the external or internal environment. The internal environment of the human being, and his or her perception of the external environment are more complex than those of the frog because of consciousness and memory. Human behaviour is affected not only by culture but also by the cumulative baggage of individual experience – the half-remembered traumata of childhood, the only too vividly remembered embarrassments of adolescence, the half-understood article we read in the *Sunday Times* a decade ago, and the awful things that happened to Aunt Mildred in her last illness. All these will impact on a doctor-patient interaction, and in ways that neither the patient nor the doctor will be able fully to understand or predict. Treatment effects also vary between individuals and even within an individual over time. Many factors determine the rate at which a drug is absorbed, for example, and the rate at which it is destroyed in the body.

For all these reasons biology and medicine are probabilistic rather than deterministic. The problem is that although medical science can at best tell us what happens on average, the individual patient, and his or her doctor, will want to know what is going to happen in a particular case. Medical science is necessarily poor at such individual prediction, and can aim only at reducing, not abolishing, uncertainty. The art of medicine, doing the best thing for patients, has to include coping with uncertainty. Traditionally, doctors have tried to cope with uncertainty without transmitting it to add to the psychological burden of their patients; but it is usually better shared. For patients, coping can take various forms. Some become obsessional in following the best medical advice they can acquire from their doctors, the newspapers or the Internet. Some swoon into the arms of a fatalistic Infinite. Some, particularly people in medically desperate situations, will try an alternative and complementary remedy, reasoning that they might work and there is nothing to lose. But the reason that it can say that an alternative medicine might work is usually because it has never been adequately tested in scientific terms so that we do not know whether it works or not. In addition, without adequate testing the assumption that it can do no harm may also be unwarranted. This explains the anger felt by doctors at complementary practitioners who profit from raising hopes for which there is no empirical justification. (But it is not only alternative practitioners who may trade in false hopes. Some dubious claims can be heard from the private fringes of conventional medicine, notably in the anti-aging field.)

What Does it Mean to Say That a Treatment Works?

There are three related concepts involved in considering whether a medication 'works'. These are efficacy, effectiveness and efficiency. A drug has efficacy if it is shown to be able to produce physiological or psychological changes that might be of benefit to people with some state or risk of ill health. The drug is effective if it can be shown to produce actual benefit when tested in relevant samples of people. An efficacious drug might prove ineffective if the changes it produces are too small, or if it produces frequent severe adverse effects that outweigh any benefits. The efficiency, otherwise known as cost-effectiveness, of a drug is assessed by comparing the cost of the benefits it produces with the cost of equivalent benefits produced by alternatives. It is important to emphasize that a drug cannot be simply designated as 'cost-effective', as the question to be answered is 'compared with what?' The alternatives may be other treatments or may be no treatment at all, simply letting a disease take its course. Obviously the costs that go into a cost-effectiveness calculation are not just direct money costs. They may need to include patients' time lost from work, the cost of training specialist staff to administer the treatment, and, increasingly, ecological costs of producing a drug. Drug company factories may pollute rivers, and over-enthusiastic gatherers of herbs may threaten valuable species of plants with extinction.

A second dimension in considering whether a treatment works is the definition of what one is trying to achieve. Globally medicine is concerned with prolonging life, reducing distress from physical or mental symptoms, alleviating and preventing disability. At an individual patient level, goals may be much more specific, and related to quality of life rather than length of life; for most people there are fates worse than death. A growing function of modern medicine is to allow people to choose what to die of.

Alzheimer's Disease

The problem of deciding what is to be the primary therapeutic aim is particularly perturbing in the case of dementia. 'Dementia' is a clinical syndrome characterized by an acquired global deficit in cognitive abilities, usually progressive. One of the commonest brain diseases causing dementia is Alzheimer's disease which produces a microscopically recognisable pattern of brain cell destruction. The first sign of Alzheimer's disease is usually a characteristic defect in memory. It is often referred to as a defect in 'recent memory' but this can be misleading. Our brains support several types of memory, one of which is sometimes called 'scratchpad', 'notebook' or 'working' memory. This is short-lived, and presumably based on reverberating neuronal circuits. It is the memory we use to remember a telephone number while we write it down. By chance or conscious intention some of the material that passes through the scratchpad memory is stored in longer-term memory banks that presumably depend on changes in neuronal connections. What happens in Alzheimer's disease, and some other conditions, is that the two memories become separated. Material does not pass from scratchpad to long-term storage, or if it does it becomes irretrievable – almost as if it had been stored without a label or unindexed. The person with early Alzheimer's disease can remember a telephone number long enough to repeat it to you but within a few minutes has forgotten the number and often the fact that one had been presented. Memories of childhood remain vivid at first, although detailed testing shows that these also become impaired as the disease progresses.

There is more to dementia than memory problems. Reasoning power becomes impaired, especially with non-verbal tasks such as making patterns with wooden blocks. Speech and language skills are relatively well preserved until the later stages. Difficulties in memory may lead to inability to deal with 'activities of daily living' such as shopping or dressing. The sufferer may take to wandering aimlessly, getting lost in previously familiar surroundings. Personality may change; the sufferer may become agitated and physically or verbally aggressive. Many people with dementia become depressed, particularly in the early stages while they still have insight into their developing difficulties. Later, the world may come to appear unfamiliar and threatening to someone with deteriorating memory. An old lady who keeps forgetting where she has put her pension book may start thinking someone is stealing or hiding it and go on to develop paranoid ideas as a consequence. Behavioural problems are one reason why one outcome measure of interest in drug trials is burden on carers in terms of the intensity of care they have to provide to the patient and the consequence for their own mental health and quality of life. It seems probable that in an important proportion of people with dementia, agitation and aggressive behaviour are manifestations of underlying depression (McShane et al. 1998, Cohen-Mansfield and Werner 1998). Ideally we would also like to be able to measure directly the quality of life as experienced by the demented person by conventional questionnaires (Fitzpatrick et al. 1992). Unfortunately, once memory defects become so severe that patients cannot recall how they have been feeling over a period of days or weeks, experiential quality of life becomes impossible to assess.

Outcome measures in clinical trials to decide if a drug 'works' for Alzheimer's disease focus on these different aspects of the disturbance induced by a dementing illness. Tests of cognitive function deal with memory, perception and reasoning powers. Activities of daily living assess the various capabilities necessary for independent living. Behavioural measures record wandering, restlessness, sleep disturbance, and verbal or physical aggression. Mood scales are used to assess depression. Also of great importance, especially to the issue of cost-effectiveness, is the burden of care that falls to carers, or to the health and social services.

These various defects do not necessarily march in step, although at one time there was a tacit assumption that defects of cognition underlay all the other manifestations of dementia. Most drug trials are short in duration and focus on evidence of improvement in cognitive function. But a few points improvement in a cognitive function score may be of no relevance if they are not associated with improvement in the wandering, aggression or sleep disturbance that are ruining the life of the patient's husband or wife. With long-drawn out diseases like most forms of dementia there is an additional problem of offsetting short-term gains against longer-term disadvantages. For example, severe agitation can be controlled by major tranquillizing drugs, but these may cause complications in the form of various neurological disabilities.

To some enthusiasts of complementary and alternative medicine this catalogue of possible targets for drug action will seem banausic and deficient. There is no spiritual dimension except as viewed through the opaque glass of 'quality of life'. There is no direct assessment of autonomy or scope for meaningful choice, both considered important in contemporary secular culture. The outcomes are chosen on the basis of two qualities: first, they have to be measurable in valid and reliable ways; second, they must be relatable to costs of care, since the ultimate aim of trials is to facilitate comparison of cost-effectiveness – not just effectiveness – of different treatments; boring, but essential to any viable form of socialized medicine.

It is not just drugs and herbal remedies that are used in the care of people with dementia and need to be tested in clinical trials. Music therapy, aroma therapy, lighting levels, various types of 'talking therapy', subjective barriers to wandering, intermittent 'respite' admissions to institutions to relieve stress on carers are some of the interventions that have been used and need to be evaluated (Cochrane Dementia and Cognitive Improvement Group 2004).

The Randomized Controlled Trial (RCT)

There are no 'magic bullet' treatments in medicine, although the early antibiotics must have been seen as close. When streptomycin was discovered, its effectiveness in treating tuberculous meningitis was immediately apparent in that some patients treated for this previously uniformly fatal disease survived. Most treatments are for less dramatic diseases, have less dramatic effects, and may not benefit all patients. We are more often looking for small effects in prolonging life or improving its quality. These 'small' effects may, however, be important to patients or their carers.

The RCT represents the basic experimental paradigm for measuring the effects of varying only one variable at a time in a complex system. In the early days of scientific medicine it was thought sufficient simply to give a treatment and see what happened in a so-called 'before and after' study. The problem with this type of experiment is that the changes seen to occur might have happened whether the treatment had been given or not. The patient might have got better anyway. It is therefore necessary to look for differences between a group of patients given the treatment and a 'control' group of patients similar in everything except not being given the treatment. This is the basis of the RCT.

The RCT is all too commonly referred to as a 'gold standard' for truth in modern medicine. This can mislead the unwary. But other information is needed; a single RCT cannot tell us everything a doctor needs to know when deciding whether to recommend a treatment to a particular patient. When scrupulously designed and performed – and through error or misfortune many trials fall short of these ideals (Thornley and Adams 1998) – the RCT is a good way of showing that a treatment can work in some circumstances. It will not necessarily tell us that it is going to work in all circumstances or in a particular case. It may also alert us to the fact that a treatment can be harmful. It is less good at proving that a treatment does not work. To be useful an RCT has to be: randomized; double-blind; placebo-controlled; epidemiologically relevant; powerful.

Randomization and 'Blinding'

If one is aiming to find if a treatment is efficacious, and there is no already established treatment, patients who meet the requirements for entry to a trial are allocated to a treatment group or placebo group by the use of random numbers. The placebo, in the case of a drug trial, is a harmless substance, such as lactose, made up into a pill indistinguishable from that of the drug under investigation. For this process to be ethical, the doctor carrying out the trial must be genuinely uncertain as to whether the treatment is better or worse than the placebo. Also for ethical reasons, patients must be told that they might be allocated to the placebo group, but neither patient nor investigator assessing the effects must know to which group the patient has been allocated. This is the process of 'double blinding'. 'Single blinding', in which only the assessing investigator is ignorant of what treatment the patient has received has to be used for trials where blinding of the patient would be impossible or unethical. An example would be comparison of surgical and medical treatment for some disease.

Confounding

Randomization and blinding seek to fend off the two terrors that haunt the medical scientist investigating a treatment, *confounding* and the *placebo effect*. Confounding is the phenomenon whereby two things seem to be linked but this is only because both are linked to a third factor. Hormone replacement therapy (HRT) was thought for many years in the U.S. to cause all sorts of good health outcomes, including prevention of dementia (Zandi et al. 2002). Both feminists and doctors, for their different reasons, wanted this to be true. But when interventive trials were undertaken, the association was found to be non-causal (Writing Group 2002, Schumaker et al. 2003). The taking of HRT was linked to education and wealth, and with many associated forms of healthy lifestyle, all powerful predictors of health (Barrett-Connor 1991). A similar problem of confounding is relevant to Alzheimer's disease, which, as diagnosed clinically, is linked with low educational status (Ott et al. 1995), at least in women (Letenneur et al. 2000). Inevitably therefore anything that is strongly enough linked with educational status will seem to be linked with Alzheimer's disease in observational studies. The idea that one can 'adjust' reliably for such confounding by statistical means is an illusion. In an RCT it is hoped that randomization will distribute confounding variables, known and unknown, equally between the treatment and placebo groups. The larger the numbers of patients in the groups, the more likely this is to be achieved.

Placebo Effects and Control Groups

The placebo effect is a general term for the observation that if people believe that a treatment will work, they will feel better if they take it. It also seems that doctors who want a treatment to work can communicate their hopes and expectations to the patient. The strength of the placebo effect is increased by the drama of the treatment; whirring machines and dancing witchdoctors have more effect than a simple pill. But even the colour of the pill can have an effect, as can the personality and charisma of the person who prescribes it. One powerful influence on the placebo effect is payment. Freud noted that patients valued their treatment according to how much they had paid for it and forbade his disciples to offer psychoanalysis for free. Many middle-class people feel that private treatment must be better than that provided by the National Health Service although the opposite is probably often true.

While the placebo effect undoubtedly exists in most situations, it varies in magnitude in unpredictable ways and opinions differ on its mechanisms. Some investigators believe that it works only through a patient's perception of the severity and significance of his or her symptoms. Others believe that the power of the mind over the body is such that beliefs can affect physiological mechanisms, such as the endocrine or immune systems, and change the course of a disease. Whatever the case, the possibility of a placebo effect has to be excluded in the scientific evaluation of a new treatment. Conversely, a good therapist will encourage the placebo effect to the benefit of a patient, but in these days of patient empowerment a doctor is more restricted than when a well-intentioned but pharmacologically ineffective bottle of coloured water could be prescribed.

Not everything that happens in the placebo group in an RCT is due to a true placebo effect (Ernst and Resch 1995). In particular, the response of participants to whatever investigations are taking place changes with familiarity and practice. In trials of anti-dementia drugs, performance on cognitive tests commonly improves initially in both treatment and placebo groups. Clearly, a placebo group is essential to isolate the effect of treatment from whatever other changes might be affecting the people enrolled in a trial. But because effects other than a true response to the placebo also occur, it is customary for the group being compared with the treatment group to be designated a 'control' rather than 'placebo' group.

It is not always easy to fit a complex complementary remedy into the Procrustean bed of a conventional RCT. With acupuncture, for example, there are two elements, sticking pins into a patient and the places, according to Chinese meridian lines, that it is thought appropriate to stick them. Using no pins at all, or sticking the pins in the 'wrong' place, are both possible control measures, but they will answer different questions. The first may mistake a placebo response for a true effect, while the second may fail to detect a therapeutic effect of pin-sticking in general. In the model of Western medicine it is easy to assume that any merit of homoeopathy lies in the preparations prescribed, but it might well lie in the nature of the consultation. The consultation process and the medications need to be tested separately against appropriate controls. This may be relevant to other types of complementary and alternative medicine.

Epidemiology and the Individual Patient
If the results of an RCT are to be generalized, it is necessary to know to what types of patient, and in what types of medical facility the results can be generalized. It cannot be assumed that a treatment found to be effective and safe in a modern metropolitan hospital will be equally effective and safe used in a Developing World polyclinic or in an overworked general practice. If the treatment has been tested on young and otherwise fit people with only one disease, will it work on frail, older people? We need therefore to know the epidemiological provenance of the patients participating in the trial. Apart from their age and sex, how were they selected, which patients with the target disease were not entered into the trial and why? All too often this vital information is not available. For this reason, RCTs alone are not an adequate basis for health policy. The deployment of a new treatment needs to be monitored by observational studies to see that the benefits predicted in the RCTs actually occur, and to generate hypotheses about the individual factors that determine which patients benefit and which do badly. Regrettably this is rarely done, despite evidence of its value (Soumerai et al. 1997, Thiemann et al. 2000).

Power and Precision

Finally, we need to consider how reliable, in a statistical sense, the results of the trial are. This is largely a matter of the size of the trial, that is, the numbers of patients enrolled in the treatment and control groups. Trials may be carried out with two different purposes. One is simply to find out if a treatment is significantly better than a placebo. 'Significantly' in this case will mean both statistically significant and of a difference large enough to be of medical significance. It is possible to calculate in advance how many patients in treatment and placebo group it would be necessary to enrol to ensure, say a ninety per cent chance of detecting a difference of a specified size at a probability level of 0.05. In this formulation the probability of 0.05 implies that there would only be a one in twenty chance of the observed difference occurring purely by chance and the power of the trial is ninety per cent. But the confidence limits on the size of difference estimable from such a trial may be very wide, and not good enough for working out cost-effectiveness. (Confidence limits are typically expressed as ninety-five per cent and interpreted − not strictly correctly − as implying that the true value of the difference being estimated has a ninety-five per cent chance of lying somewhere between those limits.) Another reason for wanting as large a trial as possible is the desire to detect any rare adverse effects that might not emerge if a trial is too small.

Systematic Reviews

A single trial can rarely settle an issue to everyone's satisfaction. While the designers of a high-quality trial will have taken care to make the results of the trial widely generalized, the fact remains that the results were produced by the particular way particular patients in particular places were treated by particular people. Furthermore, single trials are rarely big enough to provide results that are accurate enough for making fine comparative judgments of cost-effectiveness between alternative treatments for a disease.

To overcome these shortcomings, systematic reviews are undertaken in which all trials of a particular treatment are identified, and after inspection to make sure they are of adequate methodological quality, their results are combined using critical judgment supported by the statistical process of meta-analysis. If all is well this produces a 'super-trial', larger and more generalizable than any of its components. For various reasons all may not always be well, and it must not be assumed that the results of a systematic review will necessarily be more reliable than those of a single, large well-conducted trial. The statistical aspects, thanks to well-developed computer packages, are essentially trivial; the main problems that arise are at the earlier stage of identifying and appraising the trials.

A major problem is publication bias. Trials that have produced results in favour of a treatment are more likely to be published than trials that failed to produce statistically significant results. This is partly because early trials of a new drug are commonly funded by the pharmaceutical company that makes it. For obvious commercial reasons, the company is more motivated to publish results that favour its product rather than 'negative' trials. But there are other reasons. Editors want to publish exciting results in papers that will be quoted by others. Doctors disappointed to find that a new drug apparently does not work may not want to 'waste' time writing up the results. A reviewer who uses only published material, therefore, will disproportionately include trials with positive results. And even with a completely inactive compound there will, by chance, be some positive results. The authors of a review therefore need to search out the data from unpublished work and to incorporate them in the review. Pharmaceutical companies may prove less than entirely helpful in this, and researchers may not have kept data from their 'negative' trials, thinking them to be of no interest.

There are also anxieties about the actual way trials were carried out before modern ways of doing things were developed. In particular, the purpose of randomization was widely misunderstood, and assumed to be merely a way of achieving equal numbers in treatment and placebo groups. Randomization was carried out for many years by means of numbers in sealed envelopes, and there are anecdotal accounts of investigators holding envelopes to the light to decide whether to recruit a patient into a trial. The clinical motive for this might well have been unexceptionable but it would ruin the science of the trial in a way that would not be apparent in the report, and therefore not detectable by a subsequent systematic reviewer. Nowadays randomization is commonly carried out by computer, often on a remote site, after the decision to include a patient has been taken.

In recent years systematic reviews have undoubtedly been over-valued, especially by politicians and health service managers who are always in search of some device that can be substituted for thought and embodied in a guideline or protocol. The process of review is not foolproof. For example, a pervasive source of bias in a series of trials will be consolidated by systematic review and meta-analysis and may look like a treatment effect. Whether the results of a systematic review should be preferred to those a single large well-conducted trial depends on knowledge and judgment. Whether such results apply to a particular patient requires even more in the way of judgment. In clinical medicine there can be no substitute for thought.

Ginkgo Systematically Reviewed

An international organization, the Cochrane Collaboration, aims to set standards and develop methods for producing high-quality systematic reviews (The Cochrane Collaboration 2004). At the working end of the Collaboration are Review Groups, focused on particular diseases or health problems. One of these groups, the Cochrane Dementia and Cognitive Improvement Group is based in Oxford (Cochrane Dementia and Cognitive Improvement Group 2004), and has carried out a systematic review of *Ginkgo biloba* for the treatment of cognitive impairment and dementia (Birks and Grimley Evans 2009), as well as of conventional treatments (Grimley Evans et al. 2004).

As with many other systematic reviews the conclusion of the reviewers of ginkgo was that there are indications that the extract is worthy of further investigation as a possible treatment for ameliorating some manifestations of dementia, but that the evidence is at present insufficient to recommend its use. The preliminary search identified fifty-one trials. Of these thirty-three met basic methodological criteria for inclusion, thirty-two of them using EGb761. Only some five or six of these were originally published in peer-reviewed, English-language scientific journals. Despite help from the manufacturing company it was not possible reliably to exclude publication bias. Obviously, one cannot invoke the probable, but not proven, existence of unpublished negative trials as a reason for discarding the results of positive trials performed at the same time. A further pervasive problem was the use of outdated diagnostic criteria in selecting patients for the trials. How far the patients enrolled for early trials with diagnoses of 'cerebral sclerosis' or 'organic psychosyndrome' correspond with patients diagnosed according to the more modern concepts of 'Alzheimer's disease' or 'mild cognitive impairment' is uncertain. This makes generalization of results from the early trials difficult or impossible. Most trials were of fairly short duration, typically twelve weeks.

The review concluded that ginkgo extract appeared safe with no excess of adverse effects compared with the placebo. This observation is reassuring in one sense but not in another. A drug that has no adverse effects must be suspected of having no effects of any kind. Statistically significant results in favour of ginkgo extract were found in clinicians' global assessments, in some measures of cognitive function, and in improvements in activities of daily living. Measures of mood and emotional function also showed some benefit associated with ginkgo.

The reviewers commented on the significance of the mechanism whereby a treatment produces an apparently beneficial effect. The hope is to identify treatments that modify the causes or mechanisms of a disease rather than merely its manifestations. As an example, a common feature of dementia is depression of mood. A treatment that improves cognition and functional capabilities may well reduce depression as a secondary effect. However, a treatment with a simple anti-depressant action may also be expected to improve subjective well-being, capability in cognition and activities of daily living, as well as improving scores such as clinical global impression. In terms of clinical significance, however, a drug that helps people with dementia by lightening their depression is in a different category from one that prevents the condition or ameliorates its natural history, not least because there may be more effective and cheaper anti-depressant drugs available. The fact that drugs with anti-depressant actions may appear to be effective in the short-term treatment of dementia is a widely acknowledged problem in dementia research. It may be that an anti-depressant action is one of the mechanisms of the placebo effect in trials of treatments of dementia, particularly where participants and their carers have an underlying expectation of the drug's efficacy. It is therefore noteworthy that ginkgo extract appears to have an anti-depressant effect, and future trials should seek to separate an anti-depressant effect from other possible mechanisms of benefiting cognition.

Evidence-Based Medicine: Scepticism and Schism

At present, uncertainty remains about the future role, if any, of ginkgo extract in mainstream medicine as a treatment for Alzheimer's disease. New trials of ginkgo extract are in progress and may settle the issue as far as health service funders are concerned. On the other hand, the isolation and testing of separate chemical components of ginkgo extract might bring it more into the conventional scope of Western medicine by removing the uncertainties surrounding the evaluation of complex mixtures.

There is apparent inconsonance between the statistical findings of the meta-analysis and the prevailing scepticism in British medicine about the efficacy of ginkgo extract. This inconsonance is no doubt partly due to traditional patterns of prejudice, but it also marks a fault line between two distinctive traditions in English-reading medicine – 'individualism' and 'collectivism' (Grimley Evans 2007). Doctors of the former tradition are at least as sceptical of meta-analyses as they are of herbal remedies.

Within the last two decades the movement of 'evidence-based medicine' (EBM) has arisen as a new and to some extent imposed orthodoxy. The title is self-chosen and tendentious since medicine has always been evidence-based; the issue lies in what constitutes evidence. There are two main threads to EBM: one is the veneration of the randomized controlled trial and the systematic review with meta-analysis as ultimate criteria for truth; the other is an attempt to bring the logic of epidemiological reasoning to the bedside, for example in choosing and calculating the most efficient order of laboratory tests in making a diagnosis. The epistemological standing of EBM has its tireless advocates (Sackett et al. 2000) but it has been questioned (Shaher 1997); others have challenged its sufficiency for informing medical choices (Birch 1997, Maynard 1997, Charlton and Miles 1998).

The political stars smiled on the birth of EBM, because it offered the prospect of the total standardization of medical practice. EBM would define the one sequence of investigations that should be followed and the one treatment that should be provided for each disease. To each a price tag could be applied to control health service costs, and doctors deviating from the designated paths could be sued or sacked. At last, total managerial control of the health care system lay in the grasp of politicians and civil servants. Managers, with loyalties to their political masters, have now supplanted caring professions, dedicated to the well-being of patients, as the dominant caste in the NHS (Tallis 2004).

But medical scientists have ethical obligations deriving from their professional origins at the bedside and the uses to which their work will ultimately be put. The epistemology of medical science cannot be ethically neutral. There is a fundamental ethical tension in modern health services between collectivism and individualism. The collectivist view of a health service treats it as an activity of a State dedicated to producing a healthy population capable of serving the State through employment. The health service is in essence an instrument of public health alongside other activities such as vaccinations, screening and health education. The State is interested in providing the service at lowest possible cost and works to a commercial model in which output is measured in some unit such as Quality-Adjusted Life Years (QALYs). This measure of years of life gained by a treatment, multiplied by a quality factor ranging from 1.0 (perfect health) to 0.1 (almost dead) is widely beloved of economists (Williams 1988) but generally deplored by ethicists (Harris 1987) and geriatricians (Grimley Evans 1997). The individual disappears in the collectivist use of QALYs and human lives become commodities that can be heaped together like tonnes of coal. The individualist approach in contrast sees a health service literally as a service that should be designed to enable individuals to achieve individually chosen life goals. In so far as QALYs have any role in such a model they should be derived from an individual's personal value system (Mountain et al. 2004), and their use restricted to helping an individual to choose which of various treatment options best meet his or her needs and wishes. The individualist model is in fact simply an explicit statement of the ideals of traditional clinical medicine; it is significant that the prime movers of EBM are either not doctors, or they are public health specialists with no immersion in clinical practice.

Evidence-Based Medicine for the Individual

Individualized evidence-based medicine (IEBM) would be attainable from an extension of current research practice. A special instance of the RCT is the so-called 'n-of-1 trial' in which a single patient takes treatment and placebo, or two different treatments being compared, in a double-blind randomized sequence. This is potentially the most reliable way of finding if a treatment is suitable for an individual. It would have especial value for prescribing for older people (Price and Grimley Evans 2002) and could be particularly useful in the evaluation of alternative and complementary remedies (Canter and Ernst 2003) but is not yet in common use. One of the difficulties is that the number of observations in each trial is necessarily small and statistical testing consequently imprecise. Often one may be reduced to simply extracting a patient's preference or recognizing that the patient and doctor cannot tell the difference between the treatment and the placebo. There are also problems in ensuring sufficient time for 'washout' after each period of treatment or placebo. Collating the results from many such trials of a particular treatment could, however, synthesize the evidence on its average effectiveness provided by the standard RCT.

This approach could provide the common ground between conventional medical practice and alternative or complementary medicine. Both are, or should be, concerned with the empirical question of whether a treatment works, regardless of its supposed mechanisms of action. Both should be concerned with whether the treatment is working for each individual patient, both with the aim of avoiding harm and with the need to minimize costs. In an ideal world, no non-emergency treatment would be prescribed except as part of a preliminary n-of-1 trial and only continued if effectiveness becomes apparent. Unfortunately, the producers of medications, conventional or otherwise, have little interest in their treatments being stopped if ineffective (but also harmless). Treatment prescribers paid on a fee-for-service basis may have similar feelings. A systematic organization of n-of-1 trials could however be incorporated in at least a limited way in hospital practice in the NHS (Price and Grimley Evans 2002) if the need came to be recognized. Increasing pressure on NHS managers and politicians from middle-class voters more keen on alternative and complementary therapies than on paying for them might bring this about. Both conventional and non-conventional medicine would benefit from an extension of their knowledge bases, but most importantly more patients would receive demonstrably appropriate treatment. It might do the greatest good if ginkgo blazed such a trail for us rather than continuing down the signposted paths of evidence-based medicine.

References

Abebe, W. 2003. 'An Overview of Herbal Supplement Utilization with Particular Emphasis on Possible Interactions with Dental Drugs and Oral Manifestations', *Journal of Dental Hygiene* 77: 37–46.

Ahlemeyer, B. and J. Krieglstein. 2003. 'Pharmacological Studies Supporting the Therapeutic Use of *Ginkgo biloba* Extract for Alzheimer's Disease', *Pharmacopsychiatry* 36 (Supplement 1): S8–S14.

Alvarez, L.W. et al. 1980. 'Extraterrestrial Cause for the Cretaceous-Tertiary Extinction. Experimental Results and Theoretical Interpretation', *Science* 208: 1095–108.

Anonymous. 2003. 'EGb761: *Ginkgo biloba* Extract, Ginkor', *Drugs Research and Development* 4: 188–93.

Bal Dit Sollier, C., H. Caplain and L. Drouet. 2003. 'No Alteration in Platelet Function or Coagulation Induced by EGb761 in a Controlled Study', *Clinical and Laboratory Haematology* 25: 251–53.

Barrett-Connor, E. 1991. 'Postmenopausal Estrogen and Prevention Bias', *Annals of Internal Medicine* 115: 455–56.

Becker, L.E. and G.B. Skipworth. 1975. 'Ginkgo-Tree Dermatitis, Stomatitis, and Proctitis', *Journal of the American Medical Association* 231: 1162–63.

Birch, S. 1997. 'As a Matter of Fact: Evidence-based Decision-making Unplugged', *Health Economics* 6: 547–59.

Birks, J. and J. Grimley Evans. 2009. '*Ginkgo biloba* for Cognitive Impairment and Dementia', *Cochrane Database of Systematic Reviews* 2009;CD003120.7

Canter, P.H. and E. Ernst. 2003. 'Multiple n = 1 Trials in the Identification of Responders and Non-responders to the Cognitive Effects of *Ginkgo biloba*', *International Journal of Clinical Pharmacology and Therapeutics* 41: 354–57.

Charlton, B.G. and A. Miles. 1998. 'The Rise and Fall of EBM', *Quarterly Journal of Medicine* 91: 371–74.

Cianfrocca, C. et al. 2002. '*Ginkgo biloba*-Induced Frequent Ventricular Arrhythmia', *Italian Heart Journal* 3: 689–91.

Cochrane Dementia and Cognitive Improvement Group. 2004. http://www.jr2.ox.ac.uk/cdcig/WhatisCDCIG.htm

Cohen-Mansfield, J. and P. Werner. 1998. 'Predictors of Aggressive Behaviors: a Longitudinal Study in Senior Day Care Centers', *Journals of Gerontology Series B Psychological Sciences and Social Sciences* 53: 300–10.

Colciaghi, F. et al. 2004. 'Amyloid Precursor Protein Metabolism is Regulated Toward Alpha-Secretase Pathway by *Ginkgo biloba* Extracts', *Neurobiology of Disease* 16: 454–60.

Corey, E.J. et al. 1988. 'Total Synthesis of (+/-)-Ginkgolide B', *Journal of the American Chemical Society* 110: 649–51.

Coulter, J.M. and C.J. Chamberlain. 1917. *Morphology of Gymnosperms*. Chicago: University of Chicago Press.

DeFeudis, F.V. 1998. *Ginkgo biloba Extract (EGb 761). From Chemistry to the Clinic*. Wiesbaden: Ullstein Medical Verlagsgesellschaft mbH and Co.

Del Tredici, P. 1989. 'Gingkos and Multituberculates: Evolutionary Interactions in the Tertiary', *Biosystems* 22: 327–39.

Dunnill, M. 2000. *The Plato of Praed Street, the Life and Times of Almroth Wright*. London: The Royal Society of Medicine Press.

Ernst, E. and K.L. Resch. 1995. 'Concepts of True and Perceived Placebo Effects', *British Medical Journal* 311: 551–53.

Fessenden, J.M., W. Wittenborn, L. Clarke. 2001. '*Ginkgo biloba*: a Case Report of Herbal Medicine and Bleeding Postoperatively from a Laparoscopic Cholecystectomy', *American Journal of Surgery* 67: 33–35.

Fitzpatrick, R. et al. 1992. 'Quality of Life Measures in Health Care. I: Applications and Issues in Assessment', *British Medical Journal* 305: 1074–77.

Fong, K.C. and P.E. Kinnear. 2003. 'Retrobulbar Haemorrhage Associated with Chronic *Gingko biloba* Ingestion', *Postgraduate Medical Journal* 79: 531–32.

Foster, S. and Y. Chongxi. 1992. *Herbal Emissaries. Bringing Chinese herbs to the West*. Rochester, Vermont: Healing Arts Press.

Galluzzi, S. et al. 2000. 'Coma in a Patient with Alzheimer's Disease Taking Low Dose Trazodone and *Ginkgo biloba*', *Journal of Neurology Neurosurgery and Psychiatry* 68: 679–80.

Granger, A.S. 2001. '*Ginkgo biloba* Precipitating Epileptic Seizures', *Age and Ageing* 30: 523–25.

Gregory, P.J. 2001. 'Seizure Associated with *Ginkgo biloba*?', *Annals of Internal Medicine* 134: 344.

Grimley Evans, J. 1997. 'Rationing Health Care by Age. The Case Against', *British Medical Journal* 314: 11–12.

———— 2007. 'The Older Patient', in P.M. Rothwell (ed.), *Treating Individuals. From Randomised Trials to Personalised Medicine*. London: The Lancet, pp. 97–110.

————, G.M. Wilcock and J. Birks. 2004. 'Evidence-based Pharmacotherapy of Alzheimer's Disease', *International Journal of Neuropsychopharmacology* 7: 351–69.

Handa, M. 2000. '*Ginkgo biloba* in Japan', *Arnoldia* 60: 26–33.

Harbourne, J.B. and B.L. Turner. 1984. *Plant Chemosystematics*. London: Academic Press.

Harris, J. 1987. 'QALYfying the Value of Life', *Journal of Medical Ethics* 13: 117–23.

Hildebrand, A.R. et al. 1995. 'Size and Structure of the Chixculub Crater Revealed by Horizontal Growth Gradients and Cenotes', *Nature* 376: 415–17.

Hirasé, S. 1898. 'Etudes sur la Fecundation et l'Embryogénie du *Ginkgo biloba*', *Journal of the College of Science, Imperial University Tokyo* 12: 103–49.

Hsu, K.J. 1980. 'Terrestrial Catastrophe Caused by Cometary Impact at the End of Cretaceous', *Nature* 285: 201–203.

Izzo, A.A. and E. Ernst. 2001. 'Interactions Between Herbal Medicines and Prescribed Drugs: a Systematic Review', *Drugs* 61: 2163–75.

Kajiyama, Y. et al. 2002. '*Ginkgo* Seed Poisoning', *Pediatrics* 109: 325–27.

Kleijnen, J. and P. Knipschild. 1992. '*Ginkgo biloba*', *Lancet* 340: 1136–39.

Kohler, S., P. Funk and M. Kieser. 2004. 'Influence of a 7-day Treatment with *Ginkgo biloba* Special Extract EGb 761 on Bleeding Time and Coagulation: a Randomized, Placebo-controlled, Double-blind Study in Healthy Volunteers', *Blood Coagulation and Fibrinolysis* 15: 303–309.

Letenneur, L. et al. 2000. 'Education and the Risk for Alzheimer's Disease: Sex Makes a Difference. EURODEM Pooled Analyses. EURODEM Incidence Research Group', *American Journal of Epidemiology* 151: 1064–71.

Li, H.L. 1956. 'A Horticultural and Botanical History of *Ginkgo*', *Morris Arboretum Bulletin* 7: 3–12.

Major, R.T., P. Marchini and T. Sproston. 1960. 'Isolation from *Ginkgo biloba* L. of an Inhibitor of Fungus Growth', *Journal of Biological Chemistry* 235: 3298–99.

———— 1967. 'The Ginkgo, the Most Ancient Living Tree. The Resistance of *Ginkgo biloba* L. to Pests Accounts in Part for the Longevity of this Species', *Science* 157: 1270–73.

Mantle, D., R.M. Wilkins and M.A. Gok. 2003. 'Comparison of Antioxidant Activity in Commercial *Ginkgo biloba* Preparations', *Journal of Alternative and Complementary Medicine* (2003) 9: 625–29.

Maynard, A. 1997. 'Evidence-based Medicine: an Incomplete Method for Informing Choices', *Lancet* 349: 126–28.

McShane, R. et al. 1998. 'Psychiatric Symptoms in Patients with Dementia Predict the Later Development of Behavioural Abnormalities', *Psychological Medicine* 28: 1119–27.

Meisel, C., A. Johne and I. Roots. 2003. 'Fatal Intracerebral Mass Bleeding Associated with *Ginkgo biloba* and Ibuprofen', *Atherosclerosis* 167: 367.

Melosh, H.J. et al. 1990. 'Ignition of Global Wildfires at the Cretaceous-Tertiary Boundary', *Nature* 343: 251–54.

Mountain, L.A. et al. 2004. 'Assessment of Individual Quality of Life Using the SEIQoL-DW in Older Medical Patients', *Quarterly Journal of Medicine* 97: 519–24.

Nakanishi, K. 1967. 'The Ginkgolides', *Pure and Applied Chemistry* 14: 89–113.

———— et al. 1971. 'Structure of Bilobalide, a Rare Tert-Butyl Containing Sesquiterpenoid Related to the C-20-ginkgolides', *Journal of the American Chemical Society* 93: 3544–46.

Ott, A. et al. 1995. 'Prevalence of Alzheimer's Disease and Vascular Dementia: Association with Education. The Rotterdam Study', *British Medical Journal* 310: 970–73.

Pietri, S. et al. 1997. 'Cardioprotective and Antioxidant Effects of the Terpenoid Constituents of *Ginkgo biloba* Extract (EGb 761)', *Journal of Molecular and Cellular Cardiology* 29: 733–42.

Price, J.D. and J. Grimley Evans. 2002. 'N-of-1 Randomized Controlled Trials ('N-of-1'): Singularly Useful in Geriatric Medicine', *Age and Ageing* 31: 227–32.

Rivett, G. 1998. *From Cradle to Grave. Fifty Years of the NHS*. London: Kings Fund.

Rosenblatt, M. and J. Mindel. 1997. 'Spontaneous Hyphema Associated with Ingestion of *Ginkgo biloba* Extract', *New England Journal of Medicine* 336: 1108.

Rowin, J. and S.L. Lewis. 1996. 'Spontaneous Bilateral Subdural Hematomas Associated with Chronic *Ginkgo biloba* Ingestion', *Neurology* 46: 1775–76.

Sackett, D.L. et al. 2000. *Evidence-based Medicine: How to Practise and Teach EBM*. Edinburgh: Churchill Livingstone.

Schumaker, S.A. et al. 2003. 'Estrogen Plus Progestin and the Incidence of Dementia and Mild Cognitive Impairment in Postmenopausal Women. The Women's Health Initiative Memory Study: a Randomized Controlled Trial', *Journal of the American Medical Association* 289: 2651–62.

Shaher, E. 1997. 'A Popperian Perspective of the Term "Evidence-based Medicine"', *Journal of Evaluation in Clinical Practice* 3: 109–16.

Skinner, C.M. and J. Rangasami. 2002. 'Preoperative Use of Herbal Medicines: a Patient Survey', *British Journal of Anaesthesia* 89: 792–95.

Soumerai, S.B. et al. 1997. 'Adverse Outcomes of Underuse of Beta-Blockers in Elderly Survivors of Acute Myocardial Infarction', *Journal of the American Medical Association* 277: 115–21.

Tallis, R. 2004. *Hippocratic oaths. Medicine and its discontents*. London: Atlantic Books.

The Cochrane Collaboration. 2004. from http://www.cochrane.org/.

The Ginkgo pages. 2004. from http://www.xs4all.nl/~kwanten/.

Thiemann, D.R. et al. 2000. 'Lack of Benefit for Intravenous Thrombolysis in Patients with Myocardial Infarction who are Older Than 75 years', *Circulation* 101: 2239–46.

Thornley, B. and C. Adams. 1998. 'Content and Quality of 2000 Controlled Trials in Schizophrenia over 50 years', *British Medical Journal* 317: 1181–84.

Unseld, S. 1998. *Goethe und der Ginkgo. Ein Baum und ein Gedicht.* Leipzig: Insel Verlag.

Vale, S. 2003. 'Subarachnoid Haemorrhage Associated with *Ginkgo biloba*', *Lancet* 352: 36.

von Goethe, J.W. 1999. *Ginkgo biloba*, in D. Luke (ed.), *Selected Poetry*. London, Libris, p. 165.

Wada, K. et al. 1988. 'Studies on the Constitution of Edible and Medicinal Plants. I. Isolation and Identification of 4-O-Methylpyridoxine, Toxic Principle from the Seed of *Ginkgo biloba* L.', *Chemical and Pharmacological Bulletin (Tokyo)* 36: 1779–82.

Williams, A. 1988. 'Applications in Management', in G. Teeling-Smith (ed.), *Measuring health: a practical approach.* Chichester: John Wiley, pp. 225–43.

Williams, B. et al. 2004. 'Age-related Effects of *Ginkgo biloba* Extract on Synaptic Plasticity and Excitability', *Neurobiology of Aging* 25: 955–62.

Writing Group for the Women's Health Initiative Investigators. 2002. 'Risks and Benefits of Estrogen Plus Progestin in Healthy Postmenopausal Women. Principal Results from the Women's Health Initiative Randomized Controlled Trial', *Journal of the American Medical Association* 288: 321–33.

Zandi, P.P. et al. 2002. 'Hormone Replacement Therapy and Incidence of Alzheimer Disease in Older Women. The Cache County Study', *Journal of the American Medical Association* 288: 2123–29.

6. Medicinal, Stimulant and Ritual Plant Use: an Ethnobotany of Caffeine-Containing Plants

Caroline S. Weckerle, Verena Timbul and Philip Blumenshine

Of approximately 10,000 angiosperm genera, only six, *Camellia*, *Coffea*, *Cola*, *Ilex*, *Paullinia* and *Theobroma*, are known to have evolved caffeine synthesis (Figures 6.1–6.3). A seventh genus, *Citrus*, has been found to contain small amounts of caffeine (Kretschmar and Baumann 1999). Most of these six primary caffeine-containing genera are distributed in the tropics and sub-tropics; the Asian tea plant (*Camellia sinensis* [L.] Kuntze) is the only caffeine-containing species that extends into temperate regions. *Coffea* and *Cola* originated in Africa, whilst *Ilex*, *Paullinia* and *Theobroma* originated in the Americas. Not only do these plants have different places of origin, they are also placed in different taxonomic families. *Theobroma* and *Cola* both belong to the family Malvaceae, whilst the other four caffeine-containing genera are found in the families Aquifoliaceae (*Ilex*), Rubicaceae (*Coffea*), Sapindaceae (*Paullinia*) and Theaceae (*Camellia*). Furthermore, phylogenetic studies show that the ability to synthesize caffeine has evolved on several occasions on different continents (Soltis et al. 2000; Figure 6.4). Some of these plants have not been used widely outside of their native area. However, coffee, tea and cacao have become indispensable items of world consumption and trade, since they first became known during mediaeval times. Whether used globally or locally, caffeine-containing plants, more so than most other types of plants, have played a critical social, cultural and economic role among the peoples who discovered them. In every setting, local people discovered each caffeine-containing plant and domesticated or harvested it; the plants were used as stimulants, as well as medicinal and ritual plants. From these observations, two main questions arise: (i) how was it possible that all the caffeine-containing plants were discovered independently and used since ancient times?; and (ii) what are the underlying processes that led to the wide use of some of these species?

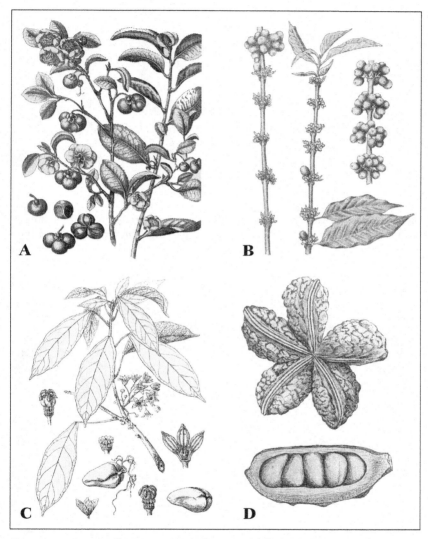

Figure 6.1: A, *Camellia sinensis* with flowers and fruits; B, *Coffea arabica* with floral buds and fruits; C, *Cola nitida* with flowers and germinating seeds; D, Indehisced fruit and dehisced mericarp of *C. nitida*. (Drawings from Sprecher Bernegg 1934, 1936; A from Engelbert Kaempfer 1712, Amoenitatum exoticarum politico-physico-medicarum fascicule V. Limgoviae: Typis and Impensis Henrici Wilhelmi Meyeri, Aulae Lippiacae Typographi.)

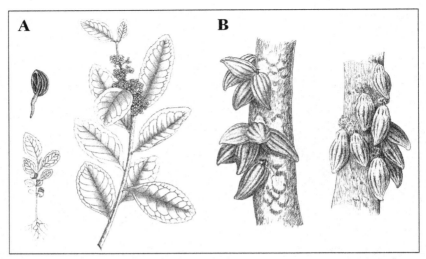

Figure 6.2: A, *Ilex paraguariensis* with flowers, germinating seed and seedling; B, *Theobroma cacao* with flowers and fruits; note the stem directly bearing the fruits. (Drawings from Sprecher von Bernegg 1934, 1936.)

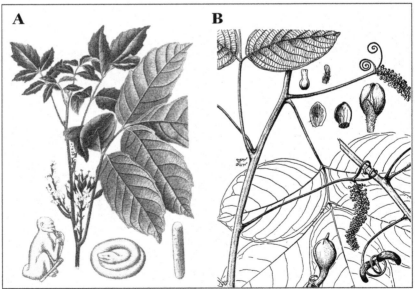

Figure 6.3: A, *Paullinia cupana* with flowers and young fruits; note the two animals and the so-called bastão at the bottom of the drawing, prepared from *guaraná* paste; B, *Paullinia yoco* with floral buds and fruit. (Drawings from Sprecher von Bernegg 1934 and Schultes 1942.)

264

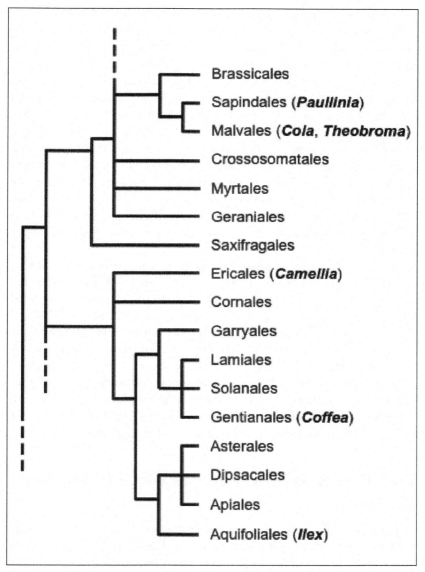

Figure 6.4: Phylogenetic tree showing that caffeine-containing plants are not closely related. These plants have evolved the ability to produce caffeine several times on different continents. (Modified after Soltis et al. 2000.)

The present chapter approaches these questions with arguments from historical, social and chemical ecological perspectives. First, we give an overview of the main caffeine-containing plant genera, with particular emphasis on their origin, botany, and traditional and recent uses. For coffee (*Coffea arabica* L.), tea (*Camellia sinensis*) and cacao (*Theobroma cacao* L.), we highlight historical and sociological aspects, whilst for cola (*Cola nitida* (Vent.) Schott and Endl.), maté (*Ilex paraguariensis* A.St.-Hil.) and guaraná (*Paullinia cupana* Kunth) we give attention to ritual use. For the genus *Paullinia*, which Caroline Weckerle has investigated extensively, we pay particular attention to phytochemical and ecological aspects. Secondly, we review caffeine and its related substances, their chemistry, primary activity and chemical ecology. Finally, we discuss potential reasons for the local usages and worldwide dispersion of caffeine-containing beverages.

Before embarking on the discussion of how caffeine of each of the six plant genera became integrated into social life, the following section will discuss the psychotropic effects of caffeine on humans. The case of caffeine is an example, *par excellence*, that lends itself to a bioculturalist argument, namely that due to their psychotropic effects the caffeine-containing plants were discovered independently of each other and integrated into cultural life, regardless of geographical region, and habit of the species. However, this chapter will also stress that caffeine became integrated into social life in culturally specific, different ways and thereby highlight the diverse forms in which humans nest themselves into their environment.

The Psychotropic Effects of Caffeine on Humans

In humans, caffeine is uniformly distributed within the body thirty minutes after drinking a cup of tea or coffee; it reaches the foetus through the placenta and is present in the mother's milk (Baumann and Seitz 1992, 1994). Chemically, caffeine is closely related to theobromine and theophylline, which are collectively known as purine alkaloids. In humans, purine alkaloid activity is characterized by stimulation of the central nervous system, relaxation of the smooth muscular system (vessels, bronchus), and a diuretic effect. Caffeine probably exerts most of its effects through antagonism of adenosine receptors, cellular structures sensitive to methylxanthines (Snyder 1984). Adenosine decreases the firing rate of neurones and inhibits synaptic release and transmission of most neurotransmitters, while caffeine increases the turnover of many neurotransmitters, including monoamines and acetylcholine (Nehlig 1999). However, there are differences in activities between caffeine, theobromine and theophylline. Caffeine is the strongest stimulant of the central nervous system; theobromine has the greatest diuretic effect; and theophylline causes pronounced bronchial dilatation (Hänsel et al. 1999: 1057).

The effects of caffeine on mood have been documented in many experimental studies, the most important of which have been reviewed by Smit and Rogers (2002). Smit and Rogers conclude that low doses of caffeine (80–100 mg, e.g. one cup of coffee), make people feel more relaxed and at ease. Higher caffeine concentrations, however, have a stimulating, energetic effect and can thus be used to combat fatigue and sleep deprivation. This effect is generally greatest approximately one hour after caffeine ingestion. Higher doses may also have negative effects, such as jitteriness, nervousness, stomach problems, headache and anxiety (Nehlig 1999).

Smit and Rogers (2002) show that the effects of caffeine vary both among individuals and according to time of day. The drug's effects on energy levels are much greater in the morning than in the evening, and the magnitude of caffeine's effect depends on an individual's physiology. While some individuals will feel effects from 10 milligrammes of caffeine, others may need as much as 178 milligrammes to feel a similar effect. Additionally, certain individuals experience the effects of caffeine within fifteen minutes of ingestion, yet others may not experience the effects until forty-five minutes after consumption. Caffeine's effects on mood are also highly related to the habitual consumption level of individuals and the related withdrawal symptoms. Withdrawal symptoms occur in individuals who consume from 129–2,548 milligrammes of caffeine per day (Strain et al. 1994). The most often reported withdrawal symptoms are headaches, feelings of weariness, weakness and drowsiness, impaired concentration, fatigue and work difficulty, depression and anxiety. Generally these symptoms begin twelve to twenty-four hours after cessation of caffeine consumption but may start after only three to six hours (Nehlig 1999). Thus, it is difficult to say if regular caffeine consumption has any overall beneficial effects on mood or if it just represents a repeated reversal of negative withdrawal effects (Smit and Rogers 2002).

Traditional and Recent Uses of the Most Important Caffeine-Containing Plant Species

Coffee

The wild progenitor of coffee has its natural distribution in the tropical mountain forests of southwestern Ethiopia, at elevations of 1000–1800 metres, where the plants grow abundantly in the forest understory. The seeds, which are roasted and pulverized for beverage preparation, contain up to 1.5 per cent caffeine, with little theobromine and only trace amounts of theophylline (Baumann and Seitz 1992). Whether Ethiopians consumed coffee naturally as berries or in a more processed beverage form is unclear (Hattox 1985: 16). The extensive use of coffee as a beverage, however, certainly originates in Yemen at the beginning of the sixteenth century CE, whence it spread throughout the Islamic world and reached Europe in the seventeenth century (Hattox 1985: 13, Albrecht 1988).

There are many publications about the early history of coffee use (e.g. Schröder 1991, Pendergrast 1999, Weinberg and Bealer 2001). The connection between coffee and mystical Sufi religious orders is consistent throughout early writings. In the fifteenth century CE, a Sufi priest probably brought the knowledge of coffee use from Ethiopia to Yemen. Coffee drinking quickly became important among Sufi groups, helping their members to stay awake during the devotional exercises, which were often held at night (Hattox 1985: 14). It is likely that coffee was first used for its physical effects; it may have complemented or replaced khat (*Catha edulis* [Vahl] Endl.).[1] Although it is not inconceivable that coffee may have been used for centuries in more isolated, mountainous regions of Yemen, the base for its spread to other areas of the Islamic world was its adoption by Sufi orders in larger cities of Yemen (Hattox 1985: 26). Sufi orders drew their members from a broad spectrum of social groups, and Sufis represented many professions and livelihoods. Thus, many different social groups became simultaneously aware of coffee as a beverage, and coffee rapidly achieved general popularity (Hattox 1985: 74).

Although the Sufi orders spread coffee as far as Egypt and Syria, it is most likely that merchants were responsible for its distribution and promotion in areas outside the Yemen (Hattox 1985: 79). The first coffeehouses were taverns without wine, and it was thus not shameful to be caught in one.[2] Coffeehouses therefore began to draw people from all strata of society, and coffee consumption became a secular pleasure rather than a religious ceremony. Around 1600 grand-style coffeehouses are mentioned for many cities in the Middle East. 'All the cafés of Damascus are beautiful – lots of fountains, nearby rivers, tree shaded spots, roses and other flowers; a cool, refreshing and pleasant spot' (de Thévenot in Hattox 1985). It was not until the middle of the seventeenth century, however, that Europeans began to drink coffee. A century later the beverage was as well known as the traditional European drinks wine and beer, and had become common and well-liked among all sections of society (Albrecht 1988). Coffee was introduced by a wide variety of publications, attracting attention among the educated members of the upper classes. It entered Europe via the large port cities and was consumed among overseas trading merchants. The first European coffeehouse was probably founded in Venice in 1647. Others followed in Oxford, London, Paris, Hamburg and Vienna.

Coffee and coffee drinking in Europe was interwoven with a series of social tensions. At the end of the Thirty Years' War (1648), many groups hoped to find a way back to the previous order of society, which was characterized by a strong hierarchy of class and political rights reserved for the few (Albrecht 1988). Between 1650 and 1750, social barriers between classes were upheld rigidly, although a growing number of people dismissed a strict class-oriented society. Against this background, coffeehouses, which brought together typically disparate parts of the society, for the first time, allowed the free exchange of ideas between educated men of different parentage and classes. These institutions soon became centres of social importance and may be seen as the first bourgeois-oriented public fora. Coffee and coffeehouses thus became a symbol of a new, more liberal and progressive attitude towards life and society (Bödecker 1987).

Early writings on coffee in both the Islamic world and Europe were concerned mainly with the effects of coffee intake on human health. The medical opinion on coffee in Muslim sources was mixed. When one group produced evidence that coffee was harmful and thus should be prohibited under Islam, another found evidence of its curative abilities (Hattox 1985: 64). Much of the debate about the health effects of coffee was based on the humoral system of medicine. While some Muslim scholars believed coffee to be cold and dry, others maintained that the beverage was hot and dry. However, most writers and physicians considered coffee's stimulating effects neither beneficial nor harmful but rather chose to view them as neutral (Hattox 1985: 65ff.).

Starting in the mid-seventeenth century, newsletters began to circulate in European towns announcing the various benefits derived from drinking coffee. As in the Arabian world, controversial pamphlets dealt with whether or not coffee was good for health, as well as the proper reaction to the new institution of the coffeehouse (Albrecht 1988). In England a 'Women's Petition Against Coffee' was filed, calling coffee a 'base, thick, nasty bitter stinking, nauseous puddle water', which turned men into impotent gossips (quoted in Adrian 1996). European medical practitioners, as their Arabian colleagues had one century earlier, debated the classification of coffee within the humoral system of medicine. They agreed that the beverage was dry because of the roasting process of the beans, and thus had a positive effect for people with an excess of phlegm (Zöllner and Giebelmann 2004).

Although coffee is now a familiar beverage across the globe, it is still used in some places as a ritual beverage. Sheikh-Dilthey (1985) describes recent ceremonial and medicinal use of coffee in its place of origin, East Africa, which is strongly influenced by Islamic religious practice. Locals use two different types of coffee for traditional medicinal applications: a hot preparation and a cold preparation. The preparation used depends on both the type of ailment and the type of energy needed by the patient. The cold preparation, which is used mainly against listlessness and unhappiness, is made by combining the powder of roasted coffee seeds with sweetened milk, quickly heating the mixture over a fire and cooling before use. The hot preparation, which is used as an analgesic and purgative, is made by heating the powder in water together with various spices. The hot preparation is also used for ceremonial purposes. Because of the different preparation methods, the hot preparation probably contains more caffeine than the cold, and the two are used accordingly. Furthermore, this difference in caffeine concentrations may be the reason why pregnant women are told to avoid hot coffee.

Coffee has become a widespread beverage in Europe during the last few centuries as, with the disciplining of time (Thompson 1967), patterns of labour changed to industrial capitalism, and today, it is one of the most widely used psychoactive beverages in the world. In mediaeval times Europe was virtually free of stimulating drugs. Instead, alcohol drinking started with breakfast and continued throughout the working day (Weinberg and Bealer 2001: 125–26). Hot, caffeine-rich drinks, like coffee and tea, possessed mood-altering properties different from those of the cold, alcoholic beverages (beer, wine and spirits; Selig-Biehusen 1995). Labourers, who used to arrive at work sleepy, having consumed beer for breakfast, became more alert after switching to coffee (Smith 1996). Thus, since industrialization, caffeine has helped large numbers of people to 'live by the clock' and to conform functionally to mechanical or electronic systems (Weinberg and Bealer 2001: 126). In late twentieth-century Europe, the highest consumption (more than 10 kg/person/year) of coffee occurred in the Scandinavian countries, Austria and the Netherlands, whilst the lowest consumption (less than 5 kg/person/year) was in Italy (Gilbert 1984).

The most notable behavioural effects of coffee occur after low to moderate doses (one to three cups); these are increased alertness, energy and ability to concentrate. Higher doses can induce negative effects such as anxiety, restlessness, insomnia and tachychardia; the latter are seen primarily in a small portion of caffeine-sensitive individuals. The discussion about the health effects of coffee is ongoing (Nehlig 1999).

Tea

The tea plant occurs in East Asia and has its centre of diversity in the forests of Southwest China (Sealy 1958: 20ff.). Two varieties are used to prepare tea: *Camellia sinensis* var. *sinensis* and *Camellia sinensis* var. *assamica* (J.Masters) Kitam. The *sinensis* variety tolerates cold temperatures and is cultivated in China, whereas the *assamica* variety needs high temperatures and is cultivated in Assam, Myanmar,

Vietnam and south China (Chang and Bartholomew 1984: 14). Cultivated plants are maintained as bushes, approximately 1.5 m high, although in nature tea plants can grow into small trees up to 10 m tall. For high-quality tea, only the bud and the first two leaves are used, which contain two to four per cent caffeine and ten times less theobromine (*c.* 0.2 per cent; Teuscher 1992) than mature leaves.

The four main types of tea, i.e. white tea, green tea, oolong tea[3] (sometimes also referred to as 'yellow' or 'red' tea) and black tea,[4] are made from the same species, and are differentiated based on the technique used to prepare the leaves for the infusion (Métailié 1997). The classification is based on the degree of enzymatic oxidation the leaves have undergone. For the production of white tea, the leaves and buds are simply steamed and dried. Since the buds are usually covered with fine silvery hairs, the tea has a light white/grey colour. For green tea the oxidation process is stopped after a very short time by application of heat, either with steam (Japan) or with roasting in hot pans (China). Oolong tea is produced by stopping the oxidation process somewhere between the standards for black tea and green tea. Black tea undergoes substantial enzymatic oxidation.

Tea is among the world's oldest beverages and its original discovery, which may date back to prehistoric times in China, is difficult to trace (Gutman and Ryu 1996). In the earliest Chinese writings, tea was considered exclusively a medicinal plant and was one of many medical plants at the disposal of Chinese healers (Evans 1992: 12). In practice, the plant was used for its stimulating as well as digestive properties (Sprecher von Bernegg 1936a). Already during the late Zhou dynasty (1100–221 BCE) tea was popular (Evans 1992: 13); however, it was not until the Tang dynasty (618–907 CE) that the art of tea in China was truly developed (Sprecher von Bernegg 1936a; Weinberg and Bealer 2001: 31). During this time, Lu Yu (733–c. 804 CE), a historically elusive figure, wrote the first great Chinese treatise on tea, the *Cha Ching* or 'Tea Classic' (Métailié 1997). For Lu Yu, who had been orphaned as a child and raised by scholarly Buddhist monks, drinking tea indicated harmony and mystical unity of the universe (Weinberg and Bealer 2001: 32). Included in the *Cha Ching* are descriptions of the different shapes of tea leaves, types of waters, and methods of preparing the beverage as well as the various methods of tea cultivation in ancient China. Toward the end of the Tang dynasty, Japanese Buddhist monks, who had observed tea's ability to enhance religious meditation in China, brought tea seeds back to Japan (Sen 1989).

The introduction of tea into Japanese life and culture coincides with a more general infusion of Chinese culture and technology into Japanese society (Pitelka 2003). Despite this relatively recent arrival, a rich cultural tradition has developed around the beverage. A number of tea rituals are currently practiced in Japan, but *Cha-no-yu*, which can be translated as 'hot water for tea', is the most common. It is inextricably linked with Zen Buddhism (Sen 1989). Hearn (1904: 358–59) gives the following description of this complex art form: '[The Tea ceremony] requires years of training and practice to graduate in art … Yet the whole of this art, as to detail, signifies no more than the making and serving of a cup of tea … The supremely important matter is that the act be performed in the most perfect, most polite, most graceful, most charming manner possible'.

While drinking tea was common in China by the tenth century and in Japan by the fourteenth century, information concerning tea only began to reach Europe during the beginning of the colonial era (Zöllner and Giebelmann 2004). The Portuguese were the first to develop a trade route that allowed them to ship their tea from the East to Lisbon. The Dutch followed closely and used a route that transported their tea to France, Holland and the Baltic countries (Gutman and Ryu 1996). As the consumption of tea increased dramatically in Dutch society, doctors and university authorities engaged in endless debates over the negative and/or positive benefits of tea. Yet 'tea heretics' in the public largely ignored the scholarly controversies and indulged in their new beverage (Sprecher von Bernegg 1936a).

Great Britain was the last of the three great sea-faring nations to break into the Chinese and East Indian trade routes. Coffee and tea both reached England in the middle of the seventeenth century, but coffee gained popularity more quickly than tea (Smith 1996). By the beginning of the eighteenth century, per capita coffee consumption was ten times higher than that of tea. Thereafter, the roles of the two beverages were reversed, and tea steadily became more popular than coffee. The preferential switch from coffee to tea in Britain resulted from a fiscal system that reversed the relative costs of the two beverages. Although the British later became strongly identified with tea, there is no evidence that the British abandoned coffee

273

because they differed from the rest of Europe culturally. Rather, the British seem to have switched to tea because of coffee's higher relative price.

The high demand for tea in Britain resulted in a huge trade deficit with China. From the beginning, the British paid for tea in silver, the only payment the Chinese would accept (Evans 1992: 109). The trade balance so favoured China that the British East Indian Company nearly went bankrupt. However, the British successfully balanced the trade deficit by selling the Chinese Indian opium, which soon because a popular drug. The opium trade produced hundreds of thousands of Chinese addicts and ultimately resulted in the Opium War of 1839–1842 (Evans 1992: 111ff.). The Chinese erroneously believed that the Europeans were absolutely dependent on their tea and that an embargo on the export would lead to an immediate British capitulation. However, in addition to tea stockpiles in London, which were large enough to supply tea for a few years, the British used Chinese tea plants to set up plantations in colonial India to provide their own tea supply. By the beginning of the twentieth century, India replaced China as the major tea exporter to Britain (Evans 1992: 129).

Today, Ireland and Britain still have the highest per capita consumption of tea in Europe (3 kg per person per year and 2.5 kg per person per year, respectively; Zöllner and Giebelmann 2004). Originally a traditional beverage associated with rituals, tea is now viewed in the West as a healthy beverage with important antioxidant properties. New tea-related products and uses are constantly emerging, and tea is being consumed in increasingly diverse manners. Iced tea is now a convenient alternative to soft drinks, and encapsulated green tea extracts appear on shelves of health stores (Dufresne and Farnworth 2001).

Tea's cultural popularity is fuelled by scientific findings supporting its health benefits. Recent studies confirm that the preventive effects of tea against heart disease and high blood pressure derive from catechins and related polyphenols (Stensvold et al. 1992; Leenen et al. 2000). Also their preventive effect against cancer has been confirmed (Tachibana et al. 2004). Thus, tea's status as a functional food lends credibility to what has been believed by tea drinkers about its health effects for centuries.

Cacao

The genus *Theobroma* occurs in the Neotropics, mainly between 18° N and 15° S and contains about forty species. Its greatest diversity is in north Colombia and Central America (Cuatrecasas 1964). The local people of these regions have used members of the genus, including *Theobroma grandiflorum* (Spreng.) K.Schum. and *Theobroma mammosum* Cuatr and J.León, as food or medicine since ancient times (Baumann 1996). Not only their seeds, but also the fleshy pulp is used to prepare refreshing beverages. The natural habitat of the species is the tropical rain forest, where the adult trees reach the low canopy region (Cuatrecasas 1964). The trees are cauliflorous, i.e., the stems directly bear the flowers and fruits.

Only one species, *Theobroma cacao*, has been cultivated on a larger scale. The seeds, enveloped within a white, fleshy pulp, are collected and fermented, a process that rids the seed of the pulp and develops its characteristic taste. In contrast to other caffeine-containing plants, the main compound of *Theobroma* seeds is theobromine (up to 3.5 per cent); caffeine occurs at *c.* 0.05 per cent (Baumann and Seitz 1994).

Just as with coffee and tea, the origins of cacao's use remain shrouded in mystery. Although historians often equate the emergence of cacao harvesting with the ancient Maya civilization (250–900 CE), recent archaeological findings suggest that the Olmecs (1500–400 BCE), a much earlier Mesoamerican ethnic group, gathered cacao pods to produce a chocolate drink (Weinberg and Bealer 2001: 41; Coe and Coe 2003). While the Olmecs were the first to cultivate the tree, the Maya were definitely the second to use cacao pods. After the decline of the Maya civilization in the 800s, the Toltecs (tenth to twelfth century CE) and the Aztecs (twelfth to fifteenth century CE) both used the cacao tree. In the beginning of the sixteenth century, the Aztecs transmitted knowledge of the cacao tree and chocolate to the Spanish (Weinberg and Bealer 2001: 41).

For the Maya, cacao was so valuable that the beans were used as currency throughout their empire (Weinberg and Bealer 2001: 42). Cacao and chocolate played a role in religion, as well as secular life. For example, the Maya of Chichen Itzá, before sacrificing a prisoner, offered him a cup of thick, cold chocolate. Once the cup was empty, they believed that the prisoner's heart, transformed into a cacao pod, and 'would be ripe for cutting from his chest and burning as an offering' (Weinberg and Bealer 2001: 43). The Aztecs continued many of the Mayan ceremonial and secular traditions, so *Theobroma cacao* became an important crop for the Aztecs as well (Sprecher von Bernegg 1934b). The Spanish observed the Aztecs's traditions when they first made contact with them, and multiple conquistadors found cacao beans were used as currency throughout Central America (Kihlman 1977: 38–40; Weinberg and Bealer 2001: 43). The ritual use of the plant that the Spanish observed is still reflected in its Latin name; *Theobroma* means 'food of the gods'.

The Aztecs prized cacao also because it provided a break from their traditional beverage, *octli*, fermented agave juice (Coe and Coe 2003: 78). The Aztecs did not approve of drunkenness, and the penalty for public inebriation was often death. Thus, the consumption of *octli* was limited to those of 'sufficiently mature' age, probably those old enough to have grandchildren. The Aztec aristocracy kept the drink largely to themselves but did permit merchants and warriors to drink it because of their importance to general Aztec society (Weinberg and Bealer 2001: 44).

Many Aztecs believed that chocolate provided strength and inspiration directly from Quetzalcoatl, one of their gods, further adding to the beverage's mystique and value (Weinberg and Bealer 2001: 43). Like the Maya, the Aztecs used chocolate in ritual sacrifices and drew similarities between the cacao pod and the heart, perhaps because both contained precious liquids – chocolate and blood (Coe and Coe 2003: 101).

Methods of preparing chocolate from cacao differed among Central American groups and show myriad ways of preparing cacao. As far as anyone can determine, the Maya served their chocolate drink both hot and cold and commonly added vanilla and 'ear flower' (*Cymbopetalum penduliflorum*) to their concoction (Coe and Coe 2003: 63–66). They also may have made other, more solid forms of chocolate, such as porridges, powders and even cakes. The Aztecs, on the other hand, probably consumed their chocolate as a liquid. The cacao beans were fermented, dried, crushed, and then ground into a paste. Chilli, vanilla, 'ear flower' and other spices were added, along with corn flour, to offset the drink's naturally bitter taste, and sometimes even colourings. The paste was then left outside to harden into cakes, which were subsequently crumbled, mixed with hot water and stirred rapidly with spoons (Coe and Coe 2003: 86–93).

Among the Cuna Indians of Panama, cacao seeds are also used for fumigation. They use the smoke of the cacao seeds to help with the diagnosis of disease. The smoke of the seeds, together with chillies, is applied as a remedy for fever. In their traditional folk medicine, the seeds are used as a tonic, diuretic and anti-diarrhoea agent (Baumann and Seitz 1994).

Theobroma was probably the first caffeine-containing plant to reach Europe. Columbus described it in 1503 and, according to Kihlman (1977: 39), the Spanish conquistador Cortez introduced the hot beverage together with vanilla and sugar into Spain around 1520. By 1580 it was already in common use, and by the late 1600s cacao was well known in most European countries. Chocolate has become popular around the world ever since the Spanish reached Mesoamerica, and cacao is cultivated on multiple continents, including Africa. Because of its wide international demand, it has remained economically important since the Olmecs and the Maya. Throughout Mesoamerican history, cacao-producing lands were often the object of military conflicts, due in large part to their economic value (Weinberg and Bealer 2001: 44, Coe and Coe 2003). Although little is written on the ritual use of cacao, the crop has been greatly discussed in economic and political anthropological contexts, with special emphasis placed on producer and consumer relations (Austin 1997; Danquah 1997; John 2002; Li 2002; Kondadu-Agyemang and Adanu 2003).

The medicinal and ritual use of cacao, and its history, is documented by Dillinger et al. (2000). The Florentine Codex, dated to 1590, which extensively describes Aztec culture, refers to cacao's medicinal use to treat stomach and intestinal complaints, childhood diarrhoea and infections when combined with bark from the panama rubber tree (*Castilla elastica* Cerv.). Mixed with ground dried maize kernels and 'tlacoxochitl' (*Calliandra houstoniana* [Miller] Standley var. *anomala* [Kunth] Barneby), cacao could also be used against fever and faintness. Due to its taste, it was also frequently used to make other medications more palatable. Literature on the topic from the sixteenth to nineteenth centuries in Europe and New Spain mentions more than 100 diverse medicinal uses and merits of cacao and chocolate. Analysis by Dillinger et al. (2000) identified the three main prescription areas as: i) treatment of emaciated patients to gain weight; ii) stimulation of the nervous systems of apathetic, exhausted or feeble patients; and iii) improvement in the digestion of patients with stagnant or weak stomachs. These roles reflect the classification of cacao as a 'hot' medicine, which could counter generally 'cold' ailments. This is consistent with the cosmic duality in Aztec culture and the hot/cold balance desirable in both Aztec and European healing systems at the time of contact and afterwards (Ortiz de Montellano 1990: 37 and 193). The effect of theobromine in the body is valued today as a diuretic, smooth muscle relaxant, cardiac stimulant and vasodilator (Weinberg and Bealer 2001: 280). The antioxidant effect of polyphenols also protects against heart disease, boosts the immune system and prevents cancer.

Cola

Cola nitida and *Cola acuminata* (P.Beauv.) Schott and Endl. are West African trees up to 25 m tall and are the only two species, of the approximately 100 African *Cola* species, that are cultivated. The fruits are star-like and contain seeds up to three centimetres in diameter. The seeds of *C. nitida* usually have two cotyledons, while those of *C. acuminata* have three to six (Baumann 1996). The fruits are harvested before dehiscence and the mericarps are opened manually to collect the seeds. The white seed coat is then removed either by soaking the seeds in water for one day or by piling them up for a few days and allowing fermentation and subsequent destruction of the testa. Then the cotyledons, the so-called cola 'nuts', are washed and can be stored for several months. They are eaten fresh or dried and contain 1.5–2.5 per cent caffeine and 0.05 per cent theobromine (Seitz et al. 1992). During the drying process, polymerization of the catechins takes place and the formerly white to reddish seeds turn dark brown and become hard (Seitz et al. 1992).

Cola nuts are widely used in traditional African folk medicines. They are often employed as a tonic and stimulant but are also used against diarrhoea, nausea, fever and headache. In the past, cola nuts were also used in Europe for the same medicinal purposes and were one of the traditional ingredients of Coca-Cola[5] (Kihlman 1977: 50).

The cola nut, a caffeine-containing seed, probably became popular for its stimulant properties, which allowed long travel and hard work without feeling hunger or exhaustion. Over the past decades and centuries, the nut has become such a prominent item in cultural and social life that these original benefits have lost their significance. In much of West Africa, the nut of the cola tree has great social significance in all aspects of life, including birth and death, marriage and divorce, hospitality and business, leadership and deference, and religion and magic. *Cola nitida*, in contrast to *Cola acuminata*, is grown as a commercial export and hence has high economic value. Nevertheless, both types of cola nut have important social and ceremonial value. Indeed, cola consumption occurs in both the individual and private sphere as well as the public and collective environment, the latter of which shall be discussed here (Russel 1955).

Amongst the Mamprusi of northern Ghana, the gift of cola symbolizes respect, gratitude and trust (Drucker-Brown 1995). It is also feared as a vehicle for poison; this second identity reinforces the metaphor of cola as a symbol for trust and love, as the person accepting the gift is placing himself in a position of vulnerability (Drucker-Brown 1995). To establish an honest relationship, the donor himself always consumes a portion of the cola gift first to demonstrate his good intentions. The breaking of cola nuts is necessary before any business commences and is therefore an important constituent of hospitality, business negotiations and development of future connections. The use of cola as a method of establishing trust is not unique to the Mamprusi. Among the Igbo of southern Nigeria, the presentation of cola nuts must precede personal discussions with a guest, private worship at home, village assembly and similar events. A prayer to God through the ancestors asks for the permission to consume the nut and thereby gain protection over host and guest, the assembly and all following business (Nwaezeigwe 1996).

Cola customs also serve a socio-political role. To the Igbo, the right to break the nut signifies leadership (Nwaezeigwe 1996). Traditionally the eldest male descendant of the group, the 'ok pala', who in pre-colonial times was the socio-political and religious head of the community, breaks the nut (or authorizes a younger man to do so) and says the prayer. Due to his age, the 'ok pala' is closest to the land of the dead and thus acts as a link between the ancestors and the community itself (Nwaezeigwe 1996). The social hierarchy therefore determines who is allowed to break cola as well as how the nut is distributed amongst the group. Notably, Igbo women are forbidden to break the nut. Among the Mamprusi, the seating positions and the different forms of greeting the chief during the cola nut's official presentation in the chiefly court reflect the established social hierarchy in terms of class and gender (Drucker-Brown 1995).

Certain ethnic groups of the Ivory Coast use the cola nut in customs pertaining to engagements, weddings, divorces, the birth of twins, different initiations, reconciliation, war, divination, sorcery, masks and certain secret societies (Hauenstein 1974). In these cultures, cola is valued as a symbol of wealth, prosperity and fecundity, as a prerequisite to success, and also as a delicacy. Particularly notable is its position in religious life and worship, where white cola nuts are the most important offerings to God, the manes and the genies (Hauenstein 1974). Cola in the Ivory Coast is often a sacrificial offering to spirits. For example, it is often offered before commencing long journeys, at key life stages, or when asking for protection from evil, poison and the bad will of others (Hauenstein 1974). Cola is employed in the magical-religious act of divination because of the nut's natural ability to split into convex and concave parts (Russel 1955). Many rites connected to the cola nut investigate the seeds' position after throwing them on the ground. If the surface faces up, it is a positive omen; a surface turned to the ground is a bad sign (Hauenstein 1974).

Maté

The maté plant occurs in South America, mainly in southern Brazil, Paraguay and Argentina, as an understory plant. It is related to the widely known holly (*Ilex aquifolium* L.), which is not only used for Christmas decorations but also as folk medicine against fever and constipation. However, in contrast to *Ilex paraguariensis*, *Ilex aquifolium* does not contain purine alkaloids (Hölzl and Ohem 1993). Beside *Ilex paraguariensis*, with its numerous hardly distinguishable subspecies and varieties, a number of other wild *Ilex* species are gathered to prepare caffeine-containing beverages and medicines, among them *Ilex brevicuspis* Reiss., *Ilex conocarpa* Reiss., *Ilex dumosa* Reiss., *Ilex guayusa* Loes., and *Ilex vomitoria* Aiton (Hölzl and Ohem 1993). As in *Camellia*, the leaves and the young stems of maté are used to prepare a stimulating beverage. Leaves are harvested every two or three years and contain up to 1.6 per cent caffeine and up to 0.5 per cent theobromine (Hölzl and Ohem 1993).

Maté is a tea-like beverage prepared almost exclusively from dried leaves of the species *Ilex paraguariensis*. Adopted from the native Guaraní Indians who fire-dried and crushed the leaves to prepare a stimulating drink, maté has been popular in Uruguay, Paraguay, Argentina and southern Brazil for centuries but has never been commercialized in Western countries (Vázquez and Moyna 1986). In the seventeenth century, Jesuit missionaries started cultivating the wild plant on plantations to make their missions in Paraguay, northeastern Argentina and Brazil financially self-sustainable (Sprecher von Bernegg 1936b, Caraman 1975: 126, Jamieson 2001). The Jesuits developed a regional commercial market for maté, extending its popularity throughout the Andes. The cultivation of maté on mission plantations ended when the Jesuits were removed from South America in 1767 (Giberti 1994). Nevertheless, maté has retained its popularity, and today most maté plant material originates from these plantations. In Brazil, however, huge amounts of *Ilex paraguariensis* are still collected in the wild (Hölzl and Ohem 1993).

In the traditional maté brewing process an empty gourd ('mate') is filled with the maté herb ('yerba maté') and hot water. The infusion is drunk through a wooden or metal straw with a filter at its end ('bombilla'; Kihlman 1977: 45; Figure 6.5). Drinking maté commonly takes place with several people, each of whom empties the contents of the gourd after which it gets refilled with water and passed on to the next person until the flavour diminishes. South American legends refer to maté as an important cultural and ritual plant (Sprecher von Bernegg 1936b). The Guaraní Indians who traditionally lived in south Brazil, Paraguay, Uruguay and northern Argentina look upon the plant as an avenue to the supernatural world, and Guaraní shamans drink it as a stimulant during long-lasting nocturnal rituals. In addition, most of their medicinal plants are taken together with maté. Pure maté is stomachic and used internally for fever and rheumatism and externally for abscesses (Hölzl and Ohem 1993). The tradition of preparing and drinking maté is still deeply rooted and has proven resistant to change over the centuries. Except for the substitution of silver bombillas for stainless steel ones, the consumption of and utensils for maté have remained unchanged (Vázquez and Moyna 1986).

Figure 6.5: A, maté and bombilla. 2005, photograph taken by Julien Bachelier;
B, Magistrate in an Argentinean village drinking maté. 1877, photograph taken
by Georges Claraz.

Ilex guayusa, which is native to the eastern highlands of Ecuador
and Peru, was valued as a tonic and stimulant beyond its native
area, as indicated by 1500-year-old plant material found in the tomb
of a Tiahuancacoid medicine man in the distant Bolivian Andes
(Schultes 1972). Traditionally, Ecuadorian Jivaro warriors drank
guayusa infusions to stay awake when they feared an enemy invasion
and to purify themselves before they shrank their enemies' heads
(Patiño 1968; Davis 1996: 187). Although Jesuit missionaries started
to commercialize guayusa on a local scale, growing it on a large

plantation in southern Colombia, *Ilex guayusa* was never grown or consumed to the same extent as *Ilex paraguariensis* (Schultes 1979). Indigenous people used guayusa after the Jesuit expulsion, but the plant never became a commercial product (Jamieson 2001). Today, it is still used by the Jivaros in the ritual cleansing of the mouth or, in concentrated form, as an emetic in ceremonial purifications and before important tribal conferences (Schultes 1995; Davis 1996: 187).

Ilex vomitoria is native to North America and forms the basis for a hot drink called 'yaupon' or 'black drink', which is consumed by Native Americans in the southeastern United States (Hu 1979). Traces believed to be from evaporated yaupon have been found in some shell drinking cups that were engraved with cult symbols (Milanich 1979). Such shell cups were found at burial sites dating from 1200 CE and are widespread in the southeastern U.S. The tea itself was made by boiling the roasted leaves. Apart from its practical stimulating effect, yaupon was valued for its property to cause sweating and vomiting and thereby aid physical and spiritual cleansing of body and soul before important meetings (Power and Chesnut 1919; Alikaridis 1987). The Indians might have named the beverage 'white drink' because it symbolized purity, happiness, hospitality and social harmony; Europeans called it 'black drink' probably in reference to its colour (Hudson 1976). Consumption of yaupon at council meetings mirrored leadership and social position. The chief ('miko') drank first, followed by important visitors, and then other members in order of status (Hudson 1976).

Paullinia

The neotropical genus *Paullinia* contains approximately 180 species, occurring in Central and South America (Radlkofer 1933). While in most caffeine-containing genera, purine alkaloids have been found among several species within each genus,[6] in *Paullinia* only three of approximately forty species tested were found to contain alkaloids. In addition to the two traditionally used species, guaraná and yoco (*P. yoco* R.Schultes and Killip), *P. pachycarpa* Benth. was found to contain purine alkaloids, namely theobromine (Weckerle et al. 2003).

Guaraná is the most widely known species in the genus, and is native to the central Amazon Basin. The most striking feature of the plant is the fruits, which look like human eyes: the shiny black seed is surrounded by a white fleshy layer (aril), the 'eye white', and embedded in orange capsule valves, the 'eye lids'. This morphological feature most probably influenced the origin myth of the plant by the Saterê-Maué Indians, which will be discussed below.

The traditional cultivation of the guaraná liana and the processing of the seeds into a caffeine-rich, stimulating beverage is carried out by the Saterê-Maué Indians in the Brazilian Central Amazon (e.g. Beck 1991: 178ff.). The seeds are harvested when fruits open and contain up to five per cent caffeine (Seitz 1994). For processing, the seeds of *Paullinia cupana* are stored until the aril ferments and can be removed. They are then roasted, ground and turned into a paste with water. Traditionally the guaraná is dried into sticks ('bastãos') over the fire and left to harden. Thereafter, these sticks can be stored for at least a whole year until they are grated into boiling water to prepare a guaraná infusion (Henman 1982). The Indians grate bastãos on the rough tongue of the Amazonian fish pirarucú (*Arapaima gigas* [Cuvier, 1829]). This form of preparation was the first method used and remains widespread (Lleras 1994).

Guaraná played an important role in the rituals and culture of the Saterê-Maué Indians long before European arrival (Erickson et al. 1984). A form of art has even evolved around the substance; jewellery and other decorative objects are created from guaraná paste. Indians continue to use the plant to stimulate the brain, keep the body active, cope with the extreme heat, carry them through long journeys, suppress appetite and relieve headaches, fevers and cramps. They also use the plant to treat diarrhoea, paralysis and neuralgia (Beck 1990). Finally, guaraná is often taken by shamans to conduct diagnoses. The Saterê-Maué Indians believe that it brings good luck in transactions, as well as joy and stimulus during work. Because of all these beneficial properties, guaraná is regarded as a gift from the gods and is surrounded by myths and rituals.

The very first written description of guaraná dates from 1669, when the Jesuit missionary João Felipe Betendorf penetrated the Saterê-Maué Indians' area of the Amazon. He noted the Indians' fondness for drinking guaraná as an everyday beverage, as well as its diuretic properties and its efficaciousness against headaches, fevers and cramp (Henman 1982). By the middle of the eighteenth century, local dignitaries used guaraná regularly, claiming that it provided relief from diarrhoea and the heat and oppressiveness of the climate. In recent years, however, claims have been made for guaraná's suitability as a tea and coffee substitute, particularly for those suffering from cardiovascular afflictions. This could be related to the counterbalance given to the stimulant alkaloids by the saponins, which are well represented in the plant (Hegnauer 1973). Pharmacological activities of saponins are manifold and include antiphlogistic and antiallergic, immunomodulating, antihepatotoxic, antiviral and hypoglycaemic activities. The cardiovascular and central nervous systems are affected as well (Lacaille Dubois and Wagner 1996). Since the twentieth century, guaraná has been used principally in the form of syrups, extracts and distillates, which are employed mainly as flavouring agents and caffeine sources by Brazil's soft-drinks industry (Henman 1982).

Yoco is used for the preparation of caffeine-containing beverages. Little is known about this plant. Richard Evans Schultes (1942: 301) wrote: 'During the course of ethnobotanical studies in the Putumayo, Colombia, in 1941 and 1942, I found that the most important non-alimentary plant in the economy of the natives of the tropical areas is yoco ... Infrequency of flowering is probably one of the reasons for the neglect by botanists of this important economic plant.' In the same publication, Schultes formally described *Paullinia yoco* (together with E. Killip) for the first time. Since this publication, little research has been done on the plant, and yoco is essentially 'neglected' by botanists, probably because of its restricted occurrence in politically unstable areas of southwest Colombia.

The ethnic groups that prepare a stimulating beverage of yoco are the Ingas, Sionas, Secoyas, Kofáns and Coreguajes. Interestingly, other ethnic groups in the region seem to ignore yoco's properties. It is the general custom of certain Indian groups to eat nothing until noon. Instead, yoco is taken each morning between five and six o'clock. This is sufficient to allay hunger for at least three hours and to enhance physical endurance (Schultes 1942).

Surprisingly, the stem of yoco is used by the Indians while the young leaves and seeds are largely ignored. This is unusual, as the leaves and seeds are typically the parts of the caffeine-containing plant consumed and not the stem or bark. To prepare the beverage, the cortex is rasped. The scraps of material obtained from this process are squeezed to procure a sap, which is then added to cold water (Schultes 1987). The sap has been reported to contain up to 2.5 per cent caffeine (Rouhier and Perrot 1926). Yoco is never prepared with hot water. In this respect, it differs markedly from other caffeine drugs, such as coffee, tea or maté, which require extraction with hot water to obtain sufficient stimulating properties.

Indians distinguish different types of yoco, including *yoco blanco*, *yoco colorado*, *yoco negro*, *tigre yoco*, *po-yoco* (Schultes 1986). Schultes (1942: 311) states that 'During my ethnobotanical studies in the Putumayo, I repeatedly questioned natives concerning the differences between *yoco blanco* and *yoco colorado* with conflicting replies. While it is true that the sap expressed from some stems make a light chocolate-brown mixture when added to cold water, that from other stems makes a whitish milky mixture. Both taste the same, and both are equally effective as a stimulant. The Indians do not prefer one to the other. I find that it is impossible to distinguish botanically the liana which gives *yoco blanco* from that which yields *yoco colorado*, but the natives can distinguish them immediately by slashing the bark with a machete.' Other researchers state that there are marked differences between the physiological activities of different yoco types (Bianchi 2003 pers. comm.).

The recognition of morphologically cryptic forms occurs in other species as well (Schultes 1986). This phenomenon is an enigma that botanists have not yet had much success in understanding. It is probable, especially with food, medicinal, narcotic or toxic species, that some of these 'varieties' represent chemovarieties,[7] yet it is still unclear how indigenous people can visually identify chemovarieties and name them correctly. Schultes (1986: 229) writes, 'I have tested the perspicacity of the Indians in this respect on many occasions and have rarely found them hesitant, doubtful or in error. And Indians of different ethnic groups and living at appreciable distances from one another will identify these variants with amazing consistency.'

Using herbarium specimens, Weckerle et al. (2003) examined possible correlations between the Indian designations for yoco and purine alkaloid patterns, together with the unusual allocation of caffeine to the periphery of stems. The results clearly showed that some of the indigenous yoco types are chemovarieties. For example, the highest median values for theobromine and caffeine in leaflets and cortices (0.263 per cent and 1.043 per cent; 0.110 per cent and 0.167 per cent dry weight, respectively) were found in *huarmy yoco*. This coincides with the note on the specimen *Klug* 1935 (NY), describing *huarmy yoco* as 'strongest' type, meaning that *huarmy yoco* has the strongest effect on the human body, most likely due to the high amount of caffeine. No purine alkaloids could be detected in the leaflets of *yagé yoco* and *canaguicho yoco*, and their cortices exhibited a low purine alkaloid content. Analyses of fresh plant material will be needed to fully explain the correlation between indigenous yoco types and chemovarieties.

Chemistry and Chemical Ecology of Purine Alkaloids

The above discussion highlighted the different ways in which caffeine plants became integrated into culture: as stimulants in a ritual context and as medicinal plants, and subsequently as pleasant and stimulating drinks or food items. It also highlights that humans recognized and used the specific plant organs of caffeine plants that contain the highest concentrations of physiologically active compounds, in order to get a tasty and stimulant beverage or snack, namely the roasted seeds for coffee and guaraná, fermented seeds for cacao, dried seeds for cola, but the young dried or fermented leaves for tea and maté and, exceptionally, the cortex for yoco. Finally, it highlighted different modes of preparation, all suitable for the extraction of physiologically active compounds from the plants: hot water extractions mainly in the case of tea, maté and coffee, the preparation of pastes and powders either to be mixed with water or for direct consumption in the case of cacao and guaraná, direct consumption of the seeds in the case of cola, and, in the case of yoco, a sap squeezed from the cortex and mixed with cold water. While we emphasize that most of the different cultural applications cannot be explained by the chemistry of the plants alone, there are aspects of the chemistry of purine alkaloids that may be explanatory.

In what follows, we discuss first the chemical properties of caffeine, as well as the other purine alkaloids and their distribution within the plant. Finally, we will discuss the extent to which the chemistry of the plant may explain its cultural application.

287

Purine Alkaloids and Their Chemical Properties

Caffeine (1,3,7-trimethylxanthine) was isolated for the first time in the 1820s from coffee and tea and is a product of purine metabolism (Kihlman 1977: 3). It is always accompanied by other methylxanthines, such as theobromine (3,7-dimethylxanthine) and theophylline (1,3-dimethylxanthine), which are collectively known as purine alkaloids (Suzuki et al. 1992). The purine alkaloids differ from each other by the number and arrangement of methyl groups on the phenol ring (Figure 6.6), and only recently have the biosynthetic and catabolic pathway of these compounds been fully elucidated (Ashihara and Crozier 2001).

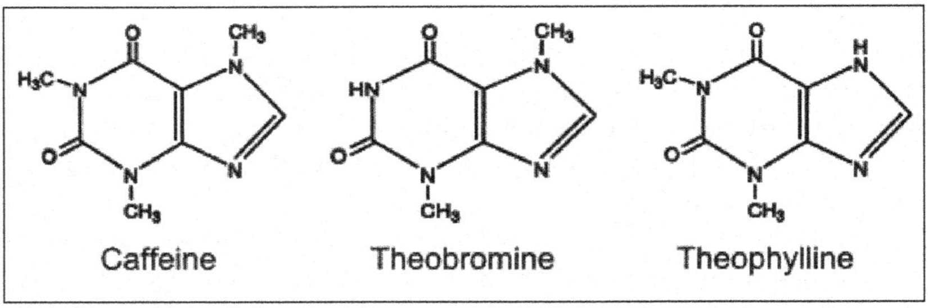

Caffeine   Theobromine   Theophylline

Figure 6.6: Chemical structure of caffeine, theobromine and theophylline.

Purine alkaloids have a dual lipophilic and hydrophilic character, which allows them to penetrate rapidly through many different biological barriers, and causes a rapid distribution in organisms. In the plants themselves, caffeine inhibits cell-plate formation and thus regular cell division (Verma and Gu 1996). To avoid autotoxicity, caffeine-containing plants produce high amounts of phenols, compounds that function to bind and neutralize purine alkaloids and thus allow the storage of caffeine in high concentrations in specific plant organs. Phenols include chlorogenic acids in coffee and maté, catechins in guaraná, cacao and cola, and gallocatechins in tea (Hänsel et al. 1992–1994). In general, phenols have diverse effects on biological systems and are characterized by protein binding and antioxidant activity. The traditional uses of caffeine-containing species as stomachic and anti-diarrhoea agents derive primarily from the former activity. Recent research has specifically focused on the

288

catechins and related polyphenols in tea and their beneficial health properties (e.g. Tachibana et al. 2004).

Primary Activity of Purine Alkaloids in Plants

Purine alkaloids inhibit insect feeding and act as pesticides at the concentrations found in plants (Harborne 1993: 197). The effects of caffeine on insects includes inhibited food consumption in the tobacco hornworm (*Manduca sexta* Linnaeus, 1763) and butterfly larvae (*Vanessa cardui* Linnaeus, 1758), sterility in the beetle (*Calosobruchus chinensis* Linnaeus, 1763), and inhibition of oviposition in the shot-hole borer beetle (*Xyleborus fornicatus* Eichhoff, 1868) of tea (Nathanson 1984; Hewavitharanage et al. 1999).

Recently, caffeine has been detected in the flowers of *Citrus* species, with the highest concentrations (up to 0.9 per cent) in the pollen (Kretschmar and Baumann 1999). Purine alkaloids are well-studied defence compounds (Harborne 1993), and might act as protection against pollen raiders. Honey-bees, the main pollinators of *Citrus* species, do not appear to be intoxicated by caffeine. In fact, feeding experiments show that after consumption of a sugar-caffeine solution there is a boost in oviposition by the queen, an enhanced activity of the bees outside the hive, and an improved defence against hornets (Ishay and Paniry 1979). Thus, caffeine in the pollen and nectar of *Citrus* flowers appears not to have a negative influence on bees, but probably act as protection against pollen raiders.

Distribution of Purine Alkaloids within the Plant

Researchers believe that the concerted action of both phenols and purine alkaloids is responsible for the plant's chemical defence against herbivores and pests (Sondahl and Baumann 2001). The exact amount of purine alkaloids found in a specific plant varies both between species and within a single plant. For example, some plant organs may have high concentrations of purine alkaloids whilst others may have almost none. Generally, the purine alkaloid percentage is

289

highest in young plant organs, such as young leaves or seeds. Young leaves have little mechanical protection from herbivorous attack and thus depend on chemical protection. Because of their higher caffeine content, it is these young plant parts that are typically used to prepare stimulating beverages.

The distribution of purine alkaloids within the coffee plant and the related levels of chemical defence have been well documented (Harborne 1993: 197). In coffee, caffeine is not restricted to the beans and occurs throughout the plant. During germination, the seedling leaves are covered by a solid, protective endocarp. As soon as this endocarp decays, the caffeine concentration in the seedling more than doubles, protecting the tender seedling leaves against herbivores (Baumann and Gabriel 1984). In juvenile leaves, which are most vulnerable to grazing, the caffeine percentage is generally high. During leaf maturation, however, the leaf's caffeine biosynthesis decreases exponentially as the leaf's mechanical protection increases (Frischknecht et al. 1985). At senescence, the leaves are virtually alkaloid-free and the caffeine is probably recycled within the plant for its valuable nitrogen (Harborne 1993: 197).

During fruit development, caffeine amounts increase in the seed and decrease in the pericarp. These biochemical changes in the pericarp are linked to animal dispersal, as the coffee seed's red exocarp attracts birds, which, like other organisms, are sensitive to caffeine (Baumann et al. 1995). The mesocarp, low in caffeine but high in sugars, acts as a reward, whilst the tough endocarp protects the seed from digestive enzymes and grinding in the bird's crop (Sondahl and Baumann 2001). Only the inner part of the endocarp, the coffee bean, is protected by high concentrations of caffeine (c. 1 per cent; Baumann and Seitz 1992). Not surprisingly then, the bean is the plant organ used by humans for their stimulating properties.

Similar distribution patterns of purine alkaloids are found in the conspicuous guaraná fruits. The deep red-orange pericarp, the white scentless aril and the glossy, almost black seed coat in the centre, also match the bird dispersal syndrome (van der Pijl 1982: 35). Indeed, large birds, such as toucans and guans, swallow guaraná seeds which they regurgitate after having digested the nutritious arils. For biochemical reasons, the extremely high caffeine levels do not intoxicate the birds. First of all, during fruit ripening the caffeine of the aril is completely degraded. The aril is the only caffeine-free tissue of the entire guaraná plant and contains mostly fructose and glucose. Moreover, the seed coat is furnished with a very effective caffeine barrier consisting of phenols of the catechin-type that efficiently bind the caffeine, so that only a few microgrammes of the seed caffeine are released during aril digestion (Baumann et al. 1995).

Yoco provides an exception to the above mentioned purine alkaloid distribution patterns. The highest concentrations do not occur in the young leaves and seeds, but in the cortex, which is traditionally used by the natives of Colombia and Ecuador to prepare a caffeine-rich beverage. One might therefore expect that purine alkaloids within the genus *Paullinia* are preferentially allocated to the older parts of the stem. Indeed, it was found that the axis of *P. cupana* exhibited a basipetal purine alkaloid gradient (0.005 per cent to 0.145 per cent). In addition, theobromine concentration in the stem cortex of *Paullinia pachycarpa* increased significantly towards the base of the plant. Moreover, analysis of young cortex samples and old stems (museum collection) revealed the same for *Paullinia yoco* (Weckerle et al. 2003). The characteristic allocation of caffeine in *Paullinia* stems further demonstrates the surprising strategies evolved by higher plants to establish optimal 'phytochemical architectures', i.e. allocate secondary compounds to various degrees in different plant organs such as the seeds, mericarp, young leaves or stem of the plant. As in the case of the other caffeine-rich genera, humans recognized and selectively used the specific plant organ in *Paullinia* that contains the highest concentrations of physiologically active compounds: the seeds of coffee, guaraná, cacao and cola, the leaves of tea and maté and the bark of yoco. Yet, why are coffee beans and guarana seeds roasted, coca seeds fermented, and cola nuts dried for consumption? Why are hot water extractions applied to tea and maté leaves, in dried or fermented states, and why is the sap of yoco bark mixed with cold water? Why is the consumption of dried cola nuts direct, while that of cacao, guaraná and coffee involves the preparation of pastes and powders? While the biochemistry of purine alkaloids can explain the selection of specific plant organs by the people, cultural considerations and the social aesthetics of taste appear to play an important role in the preparation and consumption of caffeine-containing plants.

Discovery of Caffeine Containing Plants

While it is obvious that the medicinal and stimulant properties of caffeine-containing plants were independently discovered in Asia, Africa and the Americas, their original discovery dates from prehistoric times and are difficult to trace (e.g. Gutman and Ryu 1996). Only myths about their origin and discovery remain. Nevertheless, how did early humans know to use particular plant parts for particular purposes? Johns (1990) gives a comprehensive overview of the origins of human diet and medicine. He combines findings from different disciplines and suggests four main approaches used by early humans to discover edible and medicinal plants: (i) humans learn much about the edibility of plants by watching animals; (ii) individuals acquire valuable knowledge through self-experiments, such as consuming a small portion of an unknown material; (iii) knowledge might be extended in dream-like states of consciousness; and (iv) plants are domesticated to allow chemical selection.

It can be assumed that knowledge of caffeine-containing plants has been acquired through empirical processes based on the interaction of perception, physiological processes and cultural contexts. Surprisingly, these main approaches are detected in the origin myths of caffeine-containing plants.

Coffee

Sprecher von Bernegg (1934a) tells the following legend of coffee's discovery. A shepherd told the monks of a nearby monastery that his sheep were jumping around all night without getting tired. The monks accredited this behaviour to the animal's fodder. While looking around the sheep's pasture, they found a plant with small red fruits, and suspected it to be the reason for the animals' strange behaviour. They brought some of the fruits to their monastery and prepared a decoction. After drinking this new beverage, they felt pleasantly stimulated and remained awake the whole night. From then on, the monks who had to celebrate during the night always drank coffee in the evening.

Tea

Goetz (1989: 27–28) recounts the following Japanese myth about the origin of the tea plant. Bodhidarma, a disciple of Buddha, often fell asleep during meditation. In order to stay awake, he decided to cut off his eyelids and throw them away. A plant grew out of them with leaves in the form of eyelids. The other monks prepared a beverage from these leaves and noticed that they no longer felt sleepy during meditation.

In another story, the legendary Emperor Shen Nong, known as the founder of agriculture and medicine in China, was on a journey, when a few leaves from a wild tea tree fell into his hot water. He tasted the mixture out of curiosity and liked its taste and its restorative properties. He then found that tea leaves eliminated numerous other poisons from the body and recommended it to his subjects. Because of this, tea is considered one of the earliest Chinese medicines (Unschuld 1977; Evans 1992: 1–2).

Guaraná

Particularly noteworthy is the origin myth of guaraná, which is related to the morphological properties of the fruits (Sprecher von Bernegg 1934c; Monteiro 1965 quoted in Erickson et al. 1984). A very wondrous young man lived among the Saterê-Maué Indians. He earned the adoration of the village because he was blessed with happiness and healing powers. Wherever he arrived delight and contentment came with him. Sick people were cured, and disputes were settled. However, the demon Juruparí got jealous and decided to take vengeance. He transformed himself into a poisonous snake and bit the young man while he was collecting fruits in the forest, killing him instantly. While everybody was still mourning, the young man's mother was instructed by Tupã, the great Indian god, to bury the beautiful eyes of her son in the earth. Out of the eyes, a sacred plant developed: the guaraná plant. It brought food and medicine to the Indians.

In these myths the psychoactivity of coffee is said to have been revealed to humans by animals. The same is known for other psychoactive plants, such as kava (*Piper methysticum* L.).[8] Together these myths suggest that the observation of animal behaviour was important for the recognition of physiologically active plants. The Chinese origin myth of Shen Nong's discovery of tea, however, stresses self-experimentation as being behind the driving force for the recognition of the medicinal properties of the plant. As with

293

tea, guaraná is said to have developed out of a human body part. The same idea is found in the origin myth of kava. Both kava and guaraná are domesticated and rarely found in the wild (Beck 1991: 202),[9] and the wild relatives of tea are found only in remote forests of southwest China (Baumann 1996). Hence, in all three species, wild relatives do not exist or are hardly known. The species depend on domestication by humans and have evolved through them. The tight connection between these physiologically active plants and humans seems to be reflected in the origin myths that use the metaphor of plants developing out of a human body part.

Conclusions

The processes which led to the independent discovery of caffeine-containing plants on different continents are as manifold as the ones which led to the wide use of some of these species hundreds of years later.

Scholars have proposed a number of empirical processes through which individuals and cultures might acquire plant knowledge, such as the observation of animals, self-experimentation, knowledge through dream-like states, and chemical selection through cultivation. Interestingly, these same processes are also described in the origin myths of caffeine-containing plants (e.g. the psychoactivity of coffee is said to have been revealed to humans by the strange behaviour of sheep, while the Chinese origin myth of Shen Nong's discovery of tea stresses self-experimentation). While this observation at first might seem astonishing or far-fetched, it may reflect a simple truth about the acquisition of plant knowledge. It is not only scholarly knowledge, but also traditional knowledge embodied within myths that is based on keen observations by humans of their environment; the myths may, in fact, represent a method of transmitting knowledge about important plants to other generations and possibly other cultures.

The basis for the wide spread of both coffee and tea within human societies was provided by their stimulating properties, which allowed people to use them to perform long-lasting nocturnal rituals. The use of coffee in Sufi orders and the use of tea in Buddhist and Taoist circles preceded the broad use of these beverages in eastern and western societies.

The processes that led to the wide use of caffeine-containing beverages in Europe were multiple, as physiological aspects intermingle with historical, social and economic ones. Similar processes were observed in the Arabic world one century earlier and in Asia preceding the wide use of coffee and tea in society.

Acknowledgements

For contributions, critical review and most valuable comments on the manuscript we would like to thank Jim Mant, Julien Bachelier, Stephen Harris, Elisabeth Hsu and Thomas Baumann. Franz Huber also reviewed drafts and helped greatly with his work on the tables.

Notes

1. Khat is a shrub that has been used for centuries in parts of Africa and the Arabian Peninsula. Its fresh leaves are chewed or, less frequently, dried and consumed as tea, in order to achieve a state of euphoria and stimulation. The leaves have a mild amphetamine-like effect (Adrian 1996), and they were used among Sufis (Hattox 1985: 24).

2. Although alcohol consumption was forbidden, there were taverns, or wine-houses, in late mediaeval Middle Eastern cities. However, they were invariably connected with low-life activities (Hattox 1985: 78).

3. The meaning of the Chinese name *wú lóng* is 'black dragon'. Various legends describe the origin of this curious tea name. In one legend, the owner of a tea plantation was scared away from his drying tea leaves by the appearance of a black snake; when he cautiously returned several days later, the leaves had been oxidized and gave a delightful brew.

4. The literal translation of the Chinese word for black tea *hóng chá* is 'red tea'.

5. Together with coca leaves (*Erythroxylum coca* Lam.). Today, caffeine obtained from the industrialized decaffeinating process of coffee is added to Coca-Cola, beside extracts of cola, which are mainly used for flavouring purposes (Kihlman 1977: 48).

6. *Coffea* (Sondahl and Baumann 2001); *Theobroma* (Hammerstone et al. 1994); *Citrus* (Kretschmar and Baumann 1999). In *Theobroma*, variations in purine alkaloids have been used for chemosystematic purposes.

7. Chemovarieties are groups of plants within a species, which differ in their chemistry but not their morphology. The distinction of chemovarieties is important for medicinal plants.

8. *Kava* has been cultivated for a long time in many regions of the Pacific, from Papua New Guinea eastward to Tahiti, and is completely domesticated. It never produces seeds and is entirely dependent on vegetative reproduction (Lebot 1991). It is the source of a drink consumed by the Polynesians during public ceremonies and private gatherings. Most of the origin myths mention that a human grave or a body part gave rise to the plant and the intoxication of a rat gnawing at the plant's roots revealed the psychoactivity of *kava* to humans.

9. In spite the fact that guaraná is considered to exist in cultivation only, evidence exists for Indians introducing wild material into their production (Lleras 1994).

References

Adrian, M. 1996. 'Substance Use and Multiculturalism', *Substance Use and Misuse* 31: 1459–501.

Albrecht, P. 1988. 'Coffee-drinking as a Symbol of Social Change in Continental Europe in the Seventeenth and Eighteenth Centuries', *Studies in Eighteenth-Century Culture* 18: 91–103.

Alikaridis, F. 1987. 'Natural Constituents of *Ilex* Species', *Journal of Ethnopharmacology* 20: 121–44.

Ashihara, H. and A. Crozier. 2001. 'Caffeine: a Well Known but Little Mentioned Compound in Plant Science', *Trends in Plant Science* 6: 407–13.

Austin, G. 1997. 'Cacao, Diseases, and Politics in Ghana', *International Journal of African Historical Studies* 30: 387–89.

Baumann, T.W. 1996. 'Coffein'. *Botanica Helvetica* 106: 127–58.

———— and H. Gabriel. 1984. 'Metabolism and Excretion of Caffeine during Germination of *Coffea arabica*', *Plant and Cell Physiology* 25: 1431–36.

————, B.H. Schulthess and K. Hänni. 1995. 'Guaraná (*Paullinia cupana*) Rewards Seed Dispersers without Intoxicating them by Caffeine', *Phytochemistry* 39: 1063–70.

———— and R. Seitz. 1992. '*Coffea*', in R. Hänsel et al. (eds), *Hagers Handbuch der Pharmazeutischen Praxis*, vol. 4. Berlin: Springer-Verlag, pp. 926–40.

———— and R. Seitz. 1994. '*Theobroma*', in R. Hänsel et al. (eds), *Hagers Handbuch der Pharmazeutischen Praxis*, vol. 6. Berlin: Springer-Verlag, pp. 941–55.

Beck, H.T. 1990. 'A Survey of the Useful Species of *Paullinia* L. (Sapindaceae)', *Advances in Economic Botany* 8: 41–56.

———— 1991. 'The Taxonomy and Economic Botany of the Cultivated Guaraná and its Wild Relatives and the Generic Limits within the Paullinieae (Sapindaceae)', Ph.D. dissertation. New York: City University of New York.

Bödecker, H.E. 1987. 'Das Kaffeehaus als Institution Aufklärerischer Kommunikativer Gesellingkeit', in F. Etienne (ed.), *Sociabilité et Société Bourgeoise en France, en Allemagne et en Suisse 1750–1850 Gesellingkeit, Vereinswesen und Bürgerliche Gesellschaft in Frankreich, Deutschland und in der Schweiz, 1750–1850.* Paris: ADPF, pp. 65–80.

Caraman, P. 1975. *The Last Paradise: The Jesuit Republic in South America.* New York: Seabury Press.

Chang, H.T. and B. Bartholomew. 1984. *Camellias.* London: B.T. Batsford.

Coe, S.D. and M.D. Coe. 2003. *The True History of Chocolate.* London: Thames and Hudson.

Cuatrecasas, J. 1964. 'Cacao and its Allies', *Contributions from the United States National Herbarium* 35: 379–614.

Danquah, F. 1997. 'Educating the Middleman: A Political and Economic History of Statutory Cacao Marketing in Nigeria, 1936–1947', *International Journal of African Historical Studies* 30: 470–71.

Davis, W. 1996. *One River: Science, Adventure and Hallucinogenics in the Amazon Basin.* London: Simon and Schuster.

de Thévenot, J. 1772. *Suite du Voyage de Levant,* 3rd edn, 2 vols. Amsterdam.

Dillinger, T.L. et al. 2000. 'Food of the Gods: Cure for Humanity? A Cultural History of the Medicinal and Ritual Use of Chocolate', *Journal of Nutrition* 130: 2057–72.

Drucker-Brown, S. 1995. 'The Court and the Kola Nut: Wooing and Witnessing in Northern Ghana', *Journal of the Royal Anthropological Institute* 1: 129–43.

Dufresne, C.J. and E.R. Farnworth. 2001. 'A Review of Latest Research Findings on the Health Promotion Properties of Tea', *Journal of Nutritional Biochemistry* 12: 404–21.

Erickson, H.T., M.P.F. Corréa and J.R. Escobar. 1984. 'Guaraná (*Paullinia cupana*) as a Commercial Crop in Brazilian Amazonia', *Economic Botany* 38: 273–86.

Evans, J.C. 1992. *Tea in China.* New York: Greenwood.

Frischknecht P.M., J. Ulmer-Dufek and T.W. Baumann. 1985. 'Purine Alkaloid Formation in Buds and Developing Leaflets of *Coffea arabica*: Expression of an Optimal Defence Strategy?', *Phytochemistry* 25: 613–16.

Giberti, G.C. 1994. 'Maté (*Ilex paraguariensis*)', in J.E. Hernández Bermejo and J. León (eds), *Neglected Crops: 1492 from a Different Perspective.* Rome: Food and Agriculture Organization of the United Nations, pp. 245–52.

Gilbert, R.M. 1984. 'Caffeine Consumption', in G.A. Spiller (ed.), *The Methylxanthine Beverages and Foods: Chemistry, Consumption, and Health Effects.* New York: Liss, pp. 185–213.

Goetz, A. 1989. *Teegebräuche in China, Japan, England, Russland und Deutschland.* Berlin: VWB.

Gutman, R.L. and B.-H. Ryu. 1996. 'Rediscovering Tea: An Exploration of the Scientific Literature', *HerbalGram* 37: 33–48.

Hammerstone, J.F., L.J. Romanczyk Jr. and W.M. Aitken. 1994. 'Purine Alkaloid Distribution within *Herrania* and *Theobroma*', *Phytochemistry* 35: 1237–40.

Hänsel, R. et al. (eds.). 1992–1994. *Hagers Handbuch der Pharmazeutischen Praxis*. Berlin: Springer-Verlag.

———, O. Sticher and E. Steinegger. 1999. *Pharmakognosie - Phytopharmazie*. Berlin: Springer-Verlag.

Harborne, J.B. 1993. *Introduction to Ecological Biochemistry*, 4th edn. London: Academic Press.

Hattox, R.S. 1985. *Coffee and Coffeehouses: The Origins of a Social Beverage in the Medieval Near East*. Seattle and London: University of Washington Press.

Hauenstein, A. 1974. 'La Noix de Cola: Coutumes et Rites de Quelques Ethnies de Côte d'Ivoire', *Anthropos* 69: 457–93.

Hearn, L. 1904. *Japan: An Attempt at Interpretation*. New York: Macmillan Company.

Hegnauer, R. 1973. 'Sapindaceae', in R. Hegnauer (ed.), *Chemotaxonomie der Pflanzen*. Basel: Birkhäuser, pp. 271–87.

Henman, A.R. 1982. 'Guaraná (*Paullinia cupana* var. *sorbilis*): Ecological and Social Perspectives on an Economic Plant of the Central Amazon Basin', *Journal of Ethnopharmacology* 6: 311–38.

Hewavitharanage, P., S. Karunaratne and N.S. Kumar. 1999. 'Effect of Caffeine on Shot-hole Borer Beetle (*Xyleborus fornicatus*) of Tea (*Camellia sinensis*)', *Phytochemistry* 51: 35–41.

Hölzl, J. and N. Ohem. 1993. '*Ilex*', in R. Hänsel et al. (eds), *Hagers Handbuch der Pharmazeutischen Praxis*, vol. 5. Berlin: Springer, pp. 506–12.

Hu, S.-Y. 1979. 'The Botany of Yaupon', in C.M. Hudson (ed.), *Black Drink: A Native American Tea*. Athens, GA: University of Georgia Press, pp. 10–39.

Hudson, C.M. 1976. *The Southeastern Indians*. Knoxville: University of Tennessee Press.

Ishay, J.S. and V.A. Paniry. 1979. 'Effects of Caffeine and Various Xanthines on Hornets and Bees', *Psychopharmacology* 65: 299–309.

Jamieson, R.W. 2001. 'The Essence of Commodification: Caffeine Dependencies in the Early Modern World', *Journal of Social History* 35: 269–94.

John, A.V. 2002. 'A New Slavery? The Uncomfortably Long and Close Links between Slavery and the Cacao Trade', *History Today* 52: 34–35.

Johns, T. 1990. *With Bitter Herbs They Shall Eat It: Chemical Ecology and the Origins of Human Diet and Medicine*. Tucson: University of Arizona Press.

Kihlman, B.A. 1977. *Caffeine and Chromosomes*. Amsterdam: Elsevier.

Kondadu-Agyemang, K. and S. Adanu. 2003. 'The Changing Geography of Export Trade in Ghana under Structural Adjustment Programs: Some Socioeconomic Implications', *Professional Geographer* 55: 513–27.

Kretschmar, J.A., and T.W. Baumann. 1999. 'Caffeine in *Citrus* flowers', *Phytochemistry* 52: 19–23.

Lacaille Dubois, M.A. and H. Wagner. 1996. 'A Review of the Biological and Pharmacological Activities of Saponins', *Phytomedicine* 2: 363–86.

Lebot, V. 1991. 'Kava (*Piper methysticum* Forst.f): The Polynesian Dispersal of an Oceanic Plant', in P.A. Cox and S.A. Banack (eds), *Islands, Plants and Polynesians: An Introduction to Polynesian Ethnobotany*. Portland, Oregon: Dioscorides Press, pp. 169–201.

Leenen, R. et al. 2000. 'A Single Dose of Tea with or without Milk Increases Plasma Antioxidant Activity in Humans', *European Journal of Clinical Nutrition* 54: 87–92.

Li, T.M. 2002. 'Local Histories, Global Markets: Cacao and Class in Upland Sulawesi', *Development and Change* 33: 415–37.

Lleras, E. 1994. 'Species of *Paullinia* with Economic Potential', in J.E. Hernández Bermejo and J. León (eds), *Neglected Crops: 1492 from a Different Perspective*. Rome: Food and Agriculture Organization of the United Nations, pp. 223–28.

Métailié, G. 1997. 'Der Tee in China: Allgemeiner Überblick', in R. Trauffer (ed.), *Manger en Chine – Essen in China*. Vevey: Alimentarium Vevey, pp. 316–33.

Milanich, J.T. 1979. 'Origins and Prehistoric Distributions of Black Drink and the Ceremonial Shell Drinking Cup', in C.M. Hudson (ed.), *Black Drink: A Native American Tea*. Athens, GA: University of Georgia Press, pp. 83–119.

Nathanson, J.A. 1984. 'Caffeine and Related Methylxanthines: Possible Naturally Occurring Pesticides', *Science* 226: 184–87.

Nehlig, A. 1999. 'Are We Dependent Upon Coffee and Caffeine? A Review on Human and Animal Data', *Neuroscience and Biobehavioral Reviews* 23: 563–76.

Nwaezeigwe, N.T. 1996. 'The Nri and Right of Breaking Kola-nuts: Resolving the Issue of Primogeniture among the Igbo of Nigeria', *Africana Marburgensia* 29: 56–66.

Ortiz de Montellano, B. 1990. *Aztec Medicine, Health, and Nutrition*. New Brunswick, NJ: Rutgers University Press.

Patiño, V.M. 1968. 'Guayusa: A Neglected Stimulant from the Eastern Andean Foothills', *Economic Botany* 22: 310–16.

Pendergrast, M. 1999. *Uncommon Grounds: The History of Coffee and How it Transformed our World*. New York: Basic Books.

Pitelka, M. 2003. 'Introduction to Japanese Tea Culture', in M. Pitelka (ed.), *Japanese Tea Culture: Art History and Practice*. London and New York: Routledge, pp. 1–17.

Power, F.B. and V.K. Chesnut. 1919. '*Ilex vomitoria* as a Nature Source of Caffeine', *Journal of the American Chemical Society* 41: 1307–12.

Radlkofer, L. 1933: *Sapindaceae*, Bd. 1. Leipzig: Engelmann.

Rouhier, A. and E. Perrot. 1926. 'Le "Yocco", Nouvelle Drogue Simple à Caféine', *Bulletin des Sciences Pharmacologiques* 33: 537–39.

Russel, T.A. 1955. 'The Kola of Nigeria and the Cameroons', *Tropical Agriculture* 32: 210–40.

Schröder, R. 1991. *Kaffee, Tee und Kardamom: Tropische Genussmittel und Gewürze; Geschichte, Verbreitung, Anbau, Ernte, Aufbereitung.* Stuttgart: Eugen Ulmer.

Schultes, R.E. 1942, 'Plantae Columbianae II, *Yoco*, a Stimulant of Southern Colombia', *Botanical Museum Leaflets (Harvard University)* 10: 301–24.

———— 1972. '*Ilex guayusa* from 500 AD to the Present', *Ethnologiska Studier* 32: 115–38.

———— 1979. 'Discovery of an Ancient Guayusa Plantation in Colombia', *Botanical Museum Leaflets (Harvard University)* 27: 143–53.

———— 1986. 'Recognition of Variability in Wild Plants by Indians of the Northwest Amazon: An Enigma', *Journal of Ethnobiology* 6: 229–38.

———— 1987. 'A Caffeine Drink Prepared from Bark', *Economic Botany* 41: 526–27.

———— 1995. 'Antiquity of the Use of New World Hallucinogens', *Integration* 5: 9–18.

Sealy, J.R. 1958. *A Revision of the Genus Camellia.* London: The Royal Horticultural Society.

Seitz, R. 1994. '*Paullinia*', in R. Hänsel et al. (eds), *Hagers Handbuch der Pharmazeutischen Praxis*, vol. 6. Berlin: Springer-Verlag, pp. 53–59.

————, B. Gehrman and L. Kraus. 1992. '*Cola*', in R. Hänsel et al. (eds), *Hagers Handbuch der Pharmazeutischen Praxis*, vol. 4. Berlin: Springer-Verlag, pp. 940–46.

Selig-Biehusen, P. 1995. 'Kaffee statt Schnaps: Die Bremer Werden ordentlicher', in C. Marzahn (ed.), *Genuss und Mässigkeit: Von Wein-Schlürfern, Coffee-Schwelgern und Toback-Schmauchern in Bremen.* Bremen: Ed. Temmen, pp. 142–62.

Sen, S. 1989. 'Reflections on Chanoyu and its History', trans. P. Varley, in P. Varley and K. Isao (eds), *Tea in Japan: Essays on the History of Chanoyu.* Honolulu: University of Hawaii Press, pp. 233–42.

Sheikh-Dilthey, H. 1985. 'Kaffee, Heil- und Zeremonialtrank der Swahiliküste', *Curare Sonderband* 85: 253–56.

Smit, H.J. and P.J. Rogers. 2002. 'Effects of Caffeine on Mood', *Pharmacopsychoecologia* 15: 231–57.

Smith, S.D. 1996. 'Accounting for Taste: British Coffee Consumption in Historical Pespective', *Journal of Interdisciplinary History* 7: 199–230.

Snyder, S.H. 1984. 'Adenosine as a Mediator of the Behavioral Effects of Xanthines', in P.B. Dews (ed.), *Caffeine.* Berlin: Springer-Verlag, pp. 129–41.

Soltis, D.E. et al. 2000. 'Angiosperm Phylogeny Inferred from 18S rDNA, *rbcL*, and *atpB* Sequences', *Botanical Journal of the Linnean Society* 133: 381–461.

Sondahl, M.R. and Baumann T.W. 2001. 'Agronomy II: Developmental and Cell Biology', in R.J. Clarke and O.G. Vitzthum (eds), *Coffee: Recent Developments.* Oxford: Blackwell Science, pp. 202–23.

Sprecher von Bernegg, A. 1934a. 'Der Kaffeestrauch', in A. Sprecher von Bernegg (ed.), *Kaffee und Guaraná*, vol. III/2. Stuttgart: F. Enke, pp. 1–264.

—— 1934b. 'Der Kakaobaum', in A. Sprecher von Bernegg (ed.), *Kakao und Kola*, vol. III/1. Stuttgart: F. Enke, pp. 1–213.

—— 1934c. 'Guaraná', in A. Sprecher von Bernegg (ed.), *Kaffee und Guaraná*, vol. III/2. Stuttgart: F. Enke, pp. 265–75.

—— 1936a. 'Der Teestrauch und der Tee', in A. Sprecher von Bernegg (ed.), *Tee und Maté*, vol. III/3. Stuttgart: F. Enke, pp. 1–297.

—— 1936b. 'Die Maté-oder Paraguayteepflanze', in A. Sprecher von Bernegg (ed.), *Tee und Maté*, vol. III/3. Stuttgart: F. Enke, pp. 298–417.

Stensvold, I. et al. 1992. 'Tea Consumption – Relationship to Cholesterol, Blood-pressure, and Coronary and Total Mortality', *Preventive Medicine* 21: 546–53.

Strain, E.C. et al. 1994. 'Caffeine Dependence Syndrome. Evidence from Case Histories and Experimental Evaluations', *JAMA* 272: 1043–48.

Suzuki, T., H. Ashihara and G.R. Waller. 1992. 'Purine and Purine Alkaloid Metabolism in *Camellia* and *Coffea* Plants', *Phytochemistry* 31: 2575–84.

Tachibana, H. et al. 2004. 'A Receptor for Green Tea Polyphenol EGCG', *Nature Structural and Molecular Biology* 11: 380–81.

Teuscher, E. 1992. '*Camellia*', in R. Hänsel et al. (eds), *Hagers Handbuch der Pharmazeutischen Praxis*, vol. 4. Berlin: Springer-Verlag, pp. 628–40.

Thompson, E.P. 1967. 'Time, Work-Discipline, and Industrial Capitalism'. *Past and Present* 38: 56–97.

Unschuld, P.U. 1977. 'The Development of Medical-pharmaceutical Thought in China', *Comparative Medicine East and West* 5: 109–15.

van der Pijl, L. 1982. *Principles of Dispersal in Higher Plants*, 3rd edn. Berlin: Springer-Verlag.

Vázquez, A. and P. Moyna. 1986. 'Studies on Maté Drinking', *Journal of Ethnopharmacology* 18: 267–72.

Verma, D.P.S. and X. Gu. 1996. 'Vesicle Dynamics during Cell-plate Formation in Plants', *Trends in Plant Science* 1: 145–49.

Weckerle, C.S., M.A. Stutz and T.W. Baumann. 2003. 'Purine Alkaloids in *Paullinia*', *Phytochemistry* 64: 735–42.

Weinberg, B.A. and B.K. Bealer. 2001. *The World of Caffeine: The Science and Culture of the World's Most Popular Drug*. London: Routledge.

Zöllner, H. and R. Giebelmann. 2004. 'Coffein, Kaffee und Tee – Eine Kleine Kulturgeschichte', *Deutsche Lebensmittel-Rundschau* 100: 255–62.

Notes on Contributors

Dr Françoise Barbira Freedman is an affiliated lecturer in social anthropology at the University of Cambridge, where she obtained her Ph.D. Following post-doctoral studies on local perceptions and patterns of use of shamanic plant medicine and modern health services in Peruvian Amazonia, she has developed a special interest in the anthropology of birth and women's health. Besides academic publications, applications of field research in Amazonia include a 'live pharmacy' project (1998 to date) and a plant knowledge base.

Philip Blumenshine is a third-year medical student at Weill Medical College of Cornell University. He is currently a Doris Duke Clinical Research Fellow at the University of California – San Francisco. His research interests include socio-economic and racial/ ethnic disparities in health and health care.

Dr P. Wenzel Geissler teaches social anthropology at the London School of Hygiene and Tropical Medicine and the University of Oslo. He studied biology in Hamburg and Copenhagen (Ph.D. 1998) and social anthropology in Copenhagen and Cambridge (Ph.D. 2003). Since 1993 he has worked in western Kenya, conducting first medical research and then several years of ethnographic fieldwork. He has published on kinship and ethics, religion and social change, and the anthropology of the body, healing and science, often in collaboration with his wife, Dr Ruth Prince.

Sir John Grimley Evans (MA MD FRCP FFPH FmedSci) is Professor Emeritus of Clinical Geratology at the University of Oxford and Emeritus Fellow of Green Templeton College Oxford. From 1985 to 2001 he was Consultant Physician to the Oxford Hospitals. Educated at the Universities of Cambridge and Oxford he pursued postgraduate training in clinical medicine and epidemiology in Oxford and at the University of Michigan. Membership of a New Zealand team studying the effects of migration on the health of Polynesian populations in the South West Pacific stimulated research interests in the prevention of disability in later life. Recent research work has focused on dementia.

Dr Stephen Harris is Druce Curator of Oxford University Herbaria and a Fellow of Green Templeton College. He completed a biology degree at the University of Leicester before taking a doctorate from the University of St. Andrews. He has a wide range of research interests in the evolutionary consequences of man's interactions with plants, and uses approaches as diverse as analyses of historical documents and DNA sequences. In addition, he has interests in the history of botany and plant exploration in seventeenth and eighteenth centuries.

Dr Elisabeth Hsu is Reader in Social Anthropology at Oxford University and Fellow of Green Templeton College. She completed a degree in biology at the ETH Zurich, has a doctorate in social anthropology from Cambridge University and a Habilitation in Chinese studies from Heidelberg University, Her research focuses on the practice of Chinese medicine, which she explores from different angles, in textual studies and ethnographic fieldwork.

Dr Frédéric Obringer is permanent researcher at the CNRS, Centre d'études sur la Chine moderne et contemporaine (CECMC), Paris. His fields of specialization include the history of Chinese medicine, the history of medical relations between China and Europe, and the cultural, social and technical history of natural substances. A pharmacist by training, he is writing now a book on the history of perfumes in China.

Dr Ruth J. Prince is presently Smuts Fellow at the Centre of African Studies at the University of Cambridge. She studied social anthropology in London and Copenhagen (Ph.D. 2004), after conducting ethnographic fieldwork in western Kenya since 1997. Her research focus initially was on medical anthropology and knowledge of plant medicines. Later she became interested in kinship, religion and ritual. She has published on kinship and ethics, religion and social change, and the anthropology of the body, healing and science, often in collaboration with her husband, Dr Wenzel Geissler.

Verena Timbul read Human Sciences at Somerville College, University of Oxford, where she was exposed to a variety of disciplines both from the natural and the social sciences. She subsequently completed an MSc in Medical Anthropology as a member of St Cross College at Oxford, developing a strong interest in the cross-cultural adaptation of medical practices. She now works as the International Marketing Director for a fundraising consultancy to educational charities worldwide.

Dr Caroline S. Weckerle is a post-doctoral research associate at the Institute of Systematic Botany, University of Zurich. She holds a Ph.D. in Botany from the University of Zurich and is currently convenor of the Certificate of Advanced Studies courses in Ethnobotany and Ethnomedicine at the Institute of Systematic Botany and the Institute of Complementary Medicine, University Hospital Zurich. Her research focuses on ethnobotany and ethnomedicine of ethnic groups in Southwest China.

Index

A
Acacia
  catechu, 55, 79
  senegal (Gum Acacia), 71n6,
    71n11, 79
Aconitum Nappelus (Monk's Hood),
  67, 79
active principles, 6, 60–62, 67–68,
  131–32, 157, 160, 162, 165
  compounds in medicine, 54, 61,
    68, 72n16, 74n36, 85, 157,
    159, 170, 225, 237
  extraction of, 56–57, 62, 72n16,
    83–124, 287
  in food, 271, 287, 291, 293
Aesculus Hippocastanum, 64, 70n4,
  71n6
Agave Americana (American Agave),
  63, 79, 276
Albizia coriaria, 184, 205, 219n18
Aleurites (Tung), 66, 79
Alexiades, M.N., 69
Allium
  cepa (Onion), 54, 79
  sativum (Garlic), 54, 79
Aloe, 55, 79, 194
Alzheimer's disease, 247–48
  characteristics and outcome,
    243–45, 253–54
  treatment with Gingko biloba, 7,
    234, 245, 253–54
Amazon and Upper Amazon
  cosmology, 131, 144, 174n5
  bodily connections in, 135, 173
  gendered plants in, 6, 132, 136,
    145, 148, 169
  inclusive levels of gender
    complementarity in, 151–53

  polarity and, 144–46, 149,
    154–55, 172–73
  shamans and illness in, 141–42,
    170–71
  urban shamans and, 139
anaconda, 148–49, 152–56, 158–59,
  172, 174n6
ancestral spirits (*juogi*), 23, 182, 191,
  195, 198
anti-malarials, 4, 14, 50, 54
  herbal, historical ones, 57–62,
    83–130, 121n36
  political economy of, 116–17
  synthetic, 68, 83, 85–86, 217n6
  See also Artemisinin, *qing hao*,
    quinine
Aquilaria, 55, 79
Arctostaphylos ura-ursi (Bearberry),
  71n11, 79
Aristotle, 53
Arnica montana, 54, 79
Artemether, 85
Artemisia annua (sweet wormwood),
  4, 83, 85, 104, 106, 111–17,
  123n55, 124n64
Artemisinin, 4, 50, 83, 85–86, 111,
  116–17, 118n2
Artesunate, 85
Aspidosperma excelsa, 166
Atran, S., 9, 11, 17–20, 33–35, 85
Atropa belladonna (deadly
  nightshade), 62, 79
Ayahuasca, 131, 138–39, 142, 144,
  151–52, 157–59, 163, 165, 168,
  170
Azadirachta indica (neem tree), 54,
  79

plants, transgendered shamanic relations
gendered plants, 6, 132, 135, 145, 149–54, 158–61, 164, 167–71, 173
gendered spirits, 6, 146–48, 153, 156–57, 160
See also Lamista Quechua, mother spirits, Amazon cosmology
Ginkgo adiantoides, 230
Ginkgo biloba, 7, 229–31, 235, 240, 252
biology and, 229–232
chemical extract of, 230, 234–35, 252
evolution of, 229–30
extract and economic value of, 229, 235–36
extract and uses of, 226, 252, 254
extract in western medicine, 229, 233–36, 252–53
fruit, 4, 7, 229, 231–32, 235
interaction with prescriptions, 234–35
marketing as pharmaceutical, 236–37
uses, 233–35, 252
Ginkgold, 233
See also EGb761 extract
ginkgolide, 230, 235
guaraná, 264, 266, 296n9
chemistry, 287–88, 290–91
discovery, 293–94
use and preparation, 283–85

H
Hamamelis, 71n11, 80
healers. *See* herbalists, Luo healers, shamans
health, bodily, 132, 138–43, 148, 152, 161, 166, 183–84, 189, 192–99, 203–4, 208, 210–19, 230, 293
herbal medicine
home-based, 181–84, 190–91, 195–96, 204–5, 217n6
herbal remedies, 132, 181, 211
biomedical understanding of, 235,

245, 254
children and, 183, 193, 202
clinical efficacy, 7
as cultural artefacts, 5, 51, 109
social relations and, 199–202
herbalists, 140–41, 150, 167
herbals, 55–56, 62, 71nn8–9, 232
Hevea, 66, 80
HIV/AIDS, 180, 216n3, 218n14
homeopathic medicines, 236
Honigsbaum, M., 57–58, 61, 72nn13–15, 72n21
horse chestnut, 70n4
See also Aesculus Hippocastanum
hunting, 131–32, 137, 139–40, 143, 146–47, 149, 152, 162–63, 165
hybrid ontologies, 23, 26–27, 35
Hypericum (St. John's Wort), 55, 81

I
Ilex, 226, 262, 264, 266, 280–83
illness, 5, 179, 181–83, 199–200, 218n16, 230, 241, 245
in Chinese texts, 88, 97, 100, 107
local conceptions of cause, 12, 141, 144–46, 162, 183, 190, 193–95, 211–14, 217n10, 219n19
medical anthropology and, 12–14, 18, 38n9
specialized expertise for treatment and, 156, 163, 181, 194–95, 199, 215
treatment of childhood illness by the Luo, 204–7, 209, 212–14, 219n19
See also disease, sickness, rainbow diseases
Incarvillea, 104, 111
Ingold, T., 5, 10, 22, 24–25, 27, 35
intergenerational knowledge, 49, 184, 188–91, 201
intuitive knowledge, 9

K
kava, 293–94, 296n8
Kaveri, 233
See also EGb761 extract

CPSIA information can be obtained
at www.ICGtesting.com
Printed in the USA
BVOW06s0500250817
493077BV00005B/50/P